Language
and
Ethnic Relations

Other Titles of Interest

CATALANO, R.
Health, Behavior and the Community

FURNHAM, A. & ARGYLE, M.
The Psychology of Social Situations

GARNICA, O. & KING, M.
Language, Children and Society

GILES, H., ROBINSON, W. & SMITH, P.
Social Psychology and Language

MAMAK, A.
Colour, Culture and Conflict: A Study of Pluralism in Fiji

POWER, J.
Migrant Workers in Western Europe and the United States

RICHARDS, T.
The Language of Reason

RICHMOND, A. H.
Readings in Race and Ethnic Relations

Language
and
Ethnic Relations

Edited by

HOWARD GILES
Reader in Social Psychology
University of Bristol, England

and

BERNARD SAINT-JACQUES
Professor in Linguistics
University of British Columbia, Vancouver, Canada

PERGAMON PRESS

OXFORD · NEW YORK · TORONTO · SYDNEY · PARIS · FRANKFURT

U.K.	Pergamon Press Ltd., Headington Hill Hall, Oxford OX3 OBW, England
U.S.A.	Pergamon Press Inc., Maxwell House, Fairview Park, Elmsford, New York 10523, U.S.A.
CANADA	Pergamon of Canada, Suite 104, 150 Consumers Road, Willowdale, Ontario M2J 1P9, Canada
AUSTRALIA	Pergamon Press (Aust.) Pty. Ltd., P.O. Box 544, Potts Point, N.S.W. 2011, Australia
FRANCE	Pergamon Press SARL, 24 rue des Ecoles, 75240 Paris, Cedex 05, France
FEDERAL REPUBLIC OF GERMANY	Pergamon Press GmbH, 6242 Kronberg-Taunus, Pferdstrasse 1, Federal Republic of Germany

First edition 1979

British Library Cataloguing in Publication Data

Language and ethnic relations.
1. Sociolinguistics - Congresses
2. Race relations - Congresses 3. Social interactions - Congresses 4. Intercultural communication - Congresses
I. Giles, Howard II. Saint-Jacques, Bernard
III. World Congress of Sociology, 9th, Uppsala, 1978
301.45'1042   P40   79-40709
ISBN 0-08-023720-7

In order to make this volume available as economically and as rapidly as possible the authors' typescripts have been reproduced in their original forms. This method unfortunately has its typographical limitations but it is hoped that they in no way distract the reader.

Printed and bound in Great Britain by
William Clowes (Beccles) Limited, Beccles and London

CONTENTS

CONTRIBUTORS   vii

PREFACE   ix

LANGUAGE AND THE MOBILIZATION OF ETHNIC IDENTITY
Jeffrey A. Ross   1

LINGUISTIC AND CULTURAL AFFILIATION AMONGST YOUNG ASIAN PEOPLE
IN LEICESTER
Neil Mercer, Elizabeth Mercer and Robert Mears   15

AN ECOLOGICAL AND BEHAVIOURAL ANALYSIS OF ETHNOLINGUISTIC CHANGE
IN WALES
Colin Haslehurst Williams   27

LANGUAGE GROUP ALLEGIANCE AND ETHNIC INTERACTION
Glyn Williams   57

THE SURVIVAL OF ETHNOLINGUISTIC MINORITIES: CANADIAN AND COMPARATIVE
RESEARCH
Alan B. Anderson   67

DEMOGRAPHIC APPROACHES TO THE STUDY OF LANGUAGE AND ETHNIC RELATIONS
John de Vries   87

LINGUISTIC VARIATION AND ETHNIC INTERACTION IN BELIZE: CREOLE/CARIB
Geneviève J. Escure   101

LANGUAGE IN ETHNIC INTERACTION: A SOCIAL PSYCHOLOGICAL APPROACH
Richard Yvon Bourhis   117

INTERETHNIC CONFLICT AND COMMUNICATIVE DISTANCE
Janet G. Lukens   143

INSIDERS, OUTSIDERS AND RENEGADES: TOWARDS A CLASSIFICATION OF
ETHNOLINGUISTIC LABELS
Bud B. Khleif   159

LANGUAGE AND ETHNIC INTERACTION IN *RABBIT BOSS*
Patricia A. Geuder   173

SOCIAL IDENTITY AND THE LANGUAGE OF RACE RELATIONS
Charles Husband   179

WHITE REACTION TO THE BLACK HANDSHAKE UNDER THREE EXPERIMENTAL
CONDITIONS
Walburga von Raffler-Engel, Joan Curl Elliott and Martha Stewart   197

LANGUAGE RESURRECTION: A LANGUAGE PLAN FOR ETHNIC INTERACTION
Carol M. Eastman   215

ETHNICITY, VALUES AND LANGUAGE POLICY IN THE UNITED STATES
Glendon F. Drake   223

AT THE CROSSROADS OF RESEARCH INTO LANGUAGE AND ETHNIC RELATIONS
Donald M. Taylor and Howard Giles   231

SUBJECT INDEX   243

AUTHOR INDEX   247

CONTRIBUTORS

ALAN B. ANDERSON

Department of Sociology, University of Saskatchewan, Saskatoon, Canada S7N OWO

RICHARD YVON BOURHIS

Department of Psychology, McMaster University, Hamilton, Ontario, Canada L8S 4KL

JOHN DE VRIES

Department of Sociology and Anthropology, Carleton University, Ottawa, Canada K15 5B6

GLENDON F. DRAKE

Department of Linguistics, San Diego State University, San Diego, California 92182, U.S.A.

CAROL M. EASTMAN

Department of Anthropology, University of Washington, Seattle, Washington 98185, U.S.A.

JOAN CURL ELLIOTT

Center for International Curriculum Development, Tennessee State University, Nashville, Tennessee 37203, U.S.A.

GENEVIÈVE J. ESCURE

Department of English, University of Minnesota Twin Cities, Minneapolis, Minnesota 55455, U.S.A.

PATRICIA A. GEUDER

Department of English, University of Nevada, Las Vegas, Nevada 89154, U.S.A.

HOWARD GILES

Department of Psychology, University of Bristol, 8-10 Berkeley Square, Bristol BS8 1HH, U.K.

CHARLES HUSBAND

School of Social Work, University of Leicester, Leicester LE1 7LA, U.K.

BUD B. KHLEIF

Department of Sociology and Anthropology, Social Science Center, University of New Hampshire, Durham, New Hampshire 03824, U.S.A.

JANET G. LUKENS

School of Social Welfare, University of Wisconsin-Milwaukee, Milwaukee, Wisconsin 53201, U.S.A.

Contributors

ROBERT MEARS — Department of Sociology, University of Leicester, Leicester LE1 7RH, U.K.

ELIZABETH MERCER — Department of Social Sciences, Loughborough University of Technology, Loughborough, Leicester-shire LE11 3TU, U.K.

NEIL MERCER — Department of Sociology, University of Leicester, Leicester LE1 7RH, U.K.

JEFFREY A. ROSS — Department of Government, Kirkland College, Clinton, New York 13323, U.S.A.

BERNARD SAINT-JACQUES — Department of Linguistics, University of British Columbia, 2075 Wesbrook Place, Vancouver, British Columbia, Canada V6T 1W5

MARTHA STEWART — Department of Linguistics, Vanderbilt University, Nashville, Tennessee 37203, U.S.A.

DONALD M. TAYLOR — Department of Psychology, McGill University, P.O. Box 6070, Station "A", Quèbec, Canada H3A 131

WALBURGA VON RAFFLER-ENGEL — Department of Linguistics, Vanderbilt University, Nashville, Tennessee 37203, U.S.A.

COLIN HASLEHURST WILLIAMS — Department of Geography and Sociology, North Staffordshire Polytechnic, Beaconside, Stafford ST18 OAD, U.K.

GLYN WILLIAMS — Department of Social Theory and Institutions, University College of North Wales, Bangor LL57 2DG, U.K.

PREFACE

Early philosophers used to define a human being as "animal loquens", an "animal who speaks". For them, the power of speech - language - was the most essential characteristic of humanity. Those deprived of this power could not be considered human beings and did not enjoy the same privileges: for instance, according to traditional ethics, animals could be killed. This ability to communicate through language was related to an inner spiritual principle - the soul of Christian philosophers - distinctive of Mankind.

Language has in fact a twofold significance. For the *individual*, it represents a constitutive element of his or her nature. In this respect, it is interesting to consider the renewed interest and the amount of recent research about the role of language in the cognitive development of monolingual and bilingual children. Whatever theory one favours, language plays a fundamental part in the learning and thinking processes. The *social* significance of language, however, is even more evident. Language is not merely a medium of communication - however important that medium is - but the unifying factor of a particular culture and often a prerequisite for its survival. No other factor is as powerful as language in maintaining *by itself* the genuine and lasting distinctiveness of an ethnic group. Indeed, all major works on nationalism have stressed the importance of language. The loss of a language or the acquisition of a new language might affect the identity of a social group; this is also true at the level of the individual. Social psychologists have shown that an individual successfully acquiring a second language gradually adopts various aspects of behaviour which characterize members of another linguistic-cultural group.

Ethnicity, like language, has a dual significance. It implies values and consequences for the individual and the group as well. Membership in an ethnic group is a matter of social definition, an interplay of the self-definition of members and the definition of other groups. Ethnicity usually corresponds to some linguistic unity but can exist without it. (In some cases, language is even used as a factor of national integration against ethnicity). Several other factors can contribute to the formation of an ethnic group: a common occupation, a territory, the persistence of loyalties and values towards a particular form of social organization. Ethnicity illustrates the more general function of intermediate groups intercalcated between the individual and the state. These groups can aid national integration or interfere with it.[1]

Language and ethnicity are basic elements of the identity and individuality of a human being. At the same time, they stand at the forefront of social interaction. The scope and variety of the papers in this volume, although not of course intended to be exhaustive of the field as a whole, reflect this importance. Versions of most of these papers were presented initially within the "Language and ethnic interaction" section (convened by the editors) of the Sociolinguistics Program of the IXth World Congress of Sociology, held at Uppsala, Sweden, in August 1978.[2] The multidisciplinary nature of the contributions is reflected in the geographical representation of the authors and in the different locales where research was conducted. Papers employing a wide variety of methodological approaches vary from the theoretical to the expository to the empirical. Let us examine these contributions in the chronological order in which they appear, with the proviso that much of the inherent richness of each of them will of necessity escape this briefest of overviews.

The volume commences with a theoretical paper by Jeffrey Ross which discusses different approaches to the study of ethnicity. Ross proposes that language plays different roles in ethnicity depending upon the nature of the identity patterns of the groups concerned; four such identity types are identified. The dynamic role of language in politicization is highlighted as is its contribution to ethnic mobilization. The next paper by Neil Mercer, et al. can be considered as underlining the fact that members of a particular group at any one identity stage cannot be viewed as ethnically homogeneous. These authors show that young, educated Asians in Britain can be categorized three ways according to group identity labels with members of each category having different attitudes towards their ethnic tongue (Gujarati). Colin Williams's paper provides data from Wales showing that members of a group having different attitudes towards language and their ethnicity can be *spatially* located within an ethnic territory. The analyses show how attitudes to language change over a ten-year period (1961-1971) and the manner in which particular macro-sociological factors may have facilitated the process. Glyn Williams's paper also contributes to the notion of ingroup heterogeneity by focusing upon social class as an important variable in the relationship between language and ethnicity. In his paper, which takes a political economic perspective, Williams argues that individuals' perceptions of their occupational and language group statuses can have important implications for language behaviour, particularly with regard to language maintenance and erosion. Alan Anderson's paper illustrates the complexity of the relationship between language attitudes and behaviour. Using Canadian data in the main, he shows that although some ethnic immigrant groups have very positive attitudes towards their mother tongues (whereas others do not), this does not necessarily mean that they all favour its usage to the same extent. Anderson also underlines the fact that language is sometimes important for ethnic survival while other times it is not; the loss of an ethnic tongue need not imply that a group will cease to survive as an identifiable entity. The first five papers in the volume then underline the different complex and dynamic relationships that operate between language and ethnicity and the manners in which members of an ethnic group are heterogeneous. These papers (excepting that of Mercer, et al.) pay par-

---

[1]Wallerstein in "Ethnicity and national integration in West Africa" has described the function of these groups (Cahiers d'Études Africaines, 3, 1960).

[2]We are extremely grateful to the International Sociological Association, the Research Committee on Sociolinguistics, and especially Jonathan Pool, for their administrative assistance and guidance, without which this volume would not have been possible. We are also extremely grateful to Mrs. Alma Foster for her diligence, patience and goodnaturedness in typing up the final manuscript.

ticular attention to the large-scale, socio-structural forces which can affect ethnic attitudes and behaviour towards language. The next paper by de Vries is concerned with methods for assessing the significance of many such variables, particularly the demographic ones. Adopting a so-called "quasi-population" model, he
outlines the advantages of various analytical tools for measuring birth and death
rates, immigration and emigration, nuptuality and intermarriage as they can be
seen to affect the language patterns of an ethnic group.

The next set of papers examine more closely the nature of intra- and inter-ethnic
interaction. In the first of these, Geneviève Escure provides a link with the
previous papers by discussing the relationship between interethnic attitudes and
actual language behaviour amongst Belizeans. She provides data on how Belize
Carib speakers differ at the syntactical and phonological levels in their use of
Creole (a second language) from native Belize Creole speakers. It is suggested
that the former's more decreolized varieties represent, at least in part, their
desire to dissociate linguistically (and socially) from the latter. Richard
Bourhis's paper examines the situational factors which affect how individuals talk
to members of their own ethnic ingroup, and also the factors which influence how
they speak to members of ethnic outgroups. Regarding the latter process, Bourhis
argues that group members' perceptions of the interethnic situation across many
dimensions affect the linguistic strategies they adopt in terms of speech convergence, maintenance and divergence. Janet Lukens's paper explores more specifically
the manners in which subordinate and dominant ethnic groups distance themselves
from each other linguistically. Her approach, labelled "proxemic linguistics",
outlines patterns of words and expressions group members use as they become progressively more ethnocentric in their reactions towards another group (termed
"distances of indifference, avoidance, and disparagement" respectively). The paper
by Bud Khleif focuses upon the labels of disparagement ethnic groups have for members of ethnic outgroups at varying levels of intensity, which operate, he suggests, as a means for maintaining valued group boundaries. Khleif also examines the
labels groups have for members of their own ranks they consider to be cultural
traitors, that is, those who are perceived as *diluting* the ethnic boundaries.
Patricia Geuder's paper takes on a literary perspective and illustrates the manner
in which ethnic groups disparage each other during the unfolding of a novel. Analyzing an ethnic relations situation, Geuder demonstrates how a novelist can echo
the linguistic sentiments of Redman and Whiteman in the United States towards each
other over four generations. The next paper by Charles Husband also attends to
the written word. Examining national press reports about race relations in the
United Kingdom in the 1960's, Husband shows how language can be used by the mass
media to maintain a positive British (White) identity, foster ethnic differentiation and denigrate Blacks as "immigration problems". He also discusses the ways in
which press language (often emotive) can be an important source of social influence
moulding or reinforcing public attitudes about ethnic relations because of its
supposed impartiality and expertness. Continuing the focus on the written word,
our emphasis moves away from the production processes (although this has not been
ignored thus far, particularly by Bourhis) to complexities of the *receptive* dimensions of ethnic language; in this instance, as they relate to *kinesic* behaviour.
Von Raffler-Engel, et al., in an experimental study, demonstrate how American
Whites' preconceptions about the social meanings of Blacks' nonverbal behaviour
affect their assessments of it. For example, they found that positive, relative
to neutral preconceptions about Black kinesic patterns (in the shape of the Black
handshake) made them more accurate in describing units of it, and also evoked more
emotive language in their written judgements.

Having discussed many of the factors which can affect the speech patterns of ethnic groups in interactions, and the rich linguistic repertoires available to them,
the next two papers shift towards more pragmatic issues of ethnic language policy.
In her paper, Carol Eastman proposes a plan for "language resurrection" in cases
where a minority language is not used anymore for communicative purposes yet none-

theless has strong links with group identity. Eastman describes strategies whereby
culture-loaded items found uniquely in the ethnic vocabulary - but not in the language of wider communication - can be introduced into the orthography and common
parlance as a means of facilitating cultural pride. The paper by Glen Drake suggests that we should consider carefully the ideological underpinnings of ethnic bilingual policies. He argues, on the basis of an historical perspective, that the
choice of either an assimilationist or (more currently) a pluralistic model of bilingualism in the United States and elsewhere is each fraught with insoluble problems. Drake argues in favour of programmes which bridge the gap *between* the two
perspectives and those which highlight bilingual education as an enrichment process.
The final paper by Donald Taylor and Howard Giles attempts to lay down priorities
for future work in language and ethnicity. They argue that language should be
studied not only as a barometer of ethnic relations but also, and more extensively,
as a creator and definer of them. In addition, a more social approach to ethnicity
and a more cognitive approach to language is advocated as well as the need for more
explanatory theoretical frameworks; an initial step in this latter direction is
outlined.

The different papers naturally enough reflect different perspectives on language
and ethnic relations (e.g., economic, political, demographic) owing to the various
background disciplines of their authors. This is obviously of value for the reader as it makes him or her more alert to the fact that no single discipline as currently defined is capable of capturing a *complete* understanding of all the dynamic
processes involved. However, the volume moves way beyond the usual static reflection of diverse insular approaches, to a state whereby the authors themselves are
not only cognizant of them but actively incorporate these within their conceptual
frameworks. Thus, for example, Khleif outlines an additional structural approach
to the study of ethnolinguistic labels as a complement to his own social psychological perspective. Glyn Williams attempts to incorporate a social psychological
viewpoint within his own socio-structural stance whereas Richard Bourhis includes
socio-structural concerns in his social psychological approach. Moreover, Colin
Williams collects data at both the macro- and the micro-sociolinguistic levels
while Jeffrey Ross attempts to bridge a gap between the objectivist and subjectivist schools of language and ethnicity. Perhaps for the very first time within the
confines of one book on language and ethnic relations, a healthy progression towards integrative *social* conceptualizations of the field can be documented. Although greater sophistication in this direction must, of course, be widely encouraged, we should also pursue the complementary goal of meshing it with more complex
linguistic analyses at a greater variety of levels. It is only when we "dirty our
hands" with other theoretical perspectives and other levels of empirical analysis
during the everyday routine of our research that a truly multi-disciplinary approach to language and ethnic relations can ever really emerge. It is our contention that the present volume is a significant step forward along this essential road.

Bernard Saint-Jacques
Howard Giles

January, 1979.

LANGUAGE AND THE MOBILIZATION OF ETHNIC IDENTITY

J. A. Ross

Hamilton College, Clinton, N.Y., U.S.A.

The question of the relationship between language and both ethnic identity and the politics of ethnicity is a matter of continuing controversy for both scholars and policy makers. This controversy is the result of a pervasive terminological confusion over the definition of ethnicity and an incomplete understanding of the changing meaning of ethnicity to those who maintain distinctive ethnic identities.

It is a truism in the social sciences, as in all fields of study, that the results of an inquiry are strongly influenced if not determined by the concepts that are used. Accordingly, conceptual refinement is probably more crucial to the advancement of social theory than is careful empirical scholarship. Clearly, without the former, the latter is most likely to remain either trivial or misleading. Therefore, before a comparative examination of the relationship between language and ethnic identity can be profitably undertaken, a compelling conceptual framework must be proposed and scrutinized. In constructing the beginnings of such a schema, I will briefly review the premises of the existing literatures and subsequently proceed to outline some alternate conceptualizations (Plotnicov and Tuden, 1970).

THEORETICAL AND METHODOLOGICAL ISSUES

Sociolinguists and others have been long concerned with a great many issues involving language and ethnic identity. It is obviously beyond the scope of this paper and the capabilities of this author to review them all here. Rather, I choose to concentrate upon two overriding concerns: one of which is theoretical and one of which is methodological. The theoretical issue revolves around the predicted impact of modernization upon the survival of distinct ethnic entities, and the methodological consideration refers to the way in which concepts of ethnic concern are formulated and to the rules of evidence that are to be followed in ethnic studies.

Modernization, Ethnicity, and Language

The dominant issues on the agenda of comparative studies in the 1960's consisted of the interrelated phenomena of development, modernization, and nation-building. Those theorists and empirical researchers who dealt with these topics usually portrayed ethnicity as a phenomenon that is most prevalent as a passing pathology in those states that are in the transition from a traditional, pre-developed to a modern, developed sociopolitical-economic nexus. As a pre-modern phenomenon, ethnicity must inevitably give way to more inclusive modes of identification with the

1

advent of mass industrial society. Geertz, for instance, in his famous essay, calls ethnic loyalties primordial givens (an image that suggests something that literally oozes out of some prehistoric condition) and suggests their transformation through an integrative revolution (Geertz, 1963). Parsons and those who have been influenced by him, such as Gabriel Almond, see modern politics as based on individual achievement, not ascription, and universal criteria, not particularistic ones (Parsons and Shils, 1962; Almond and Powell, Jr., 1966). Evidently, such a view implies that ethnic politics is something less than modern.

If ethnic groups are, in reality, societal fossils destined for little more than the dusty shelves of ethnographers, then it follows that the languages that they speak are similarly antique and disposable. Furthermore, if language lies at or close to the heart of ethnic distinctiveness, the transition of a group from what is viewed as a sub-national anomaly to an integrated part of a vital, modern, integrated nation involves a linguistic transformation, either voluntary or induced (Olorunsola, 1972; Cohen and Middleton, 1970). This line of reasoning is best expressed in the work of Deutsch and his disciples (Deutsch, 1966; Deutsch and Foltz, 1963; Pye, 1963). They view the process of development as one in which an integrated societal network of communications is established and elaborated. An increasing frequency of societal communications, a phenomenon that invariably requires a shared linguistic medium, brings in its wake an increased complementarity of values and a growing mutual predictability of behaviour. Ultimately, collective identity will be transformed along the lines of the emerging communications grid.

This mode of analysis has affected political decision makers as well as academics. A great many states have adopted plans for linguistic homogenization into their long-run development scenarios. Examples include the stress upon Hindi in India, Irish Gaelic in Eire, Russian in the U.S.S.R., Hebrew in Israel, and Spanish in the Andean republics of South America. In the United States, the school system was long viewed as a primary medium for the integration of immigrants into the majority culture by way of the teaching of the English language to immigrant children and even adults.[1]

I would argue that the concepts which characterize the literatures summarized above do not provide much of a basis for an understanding of ethnicity, ethnic politics, and the role of language in both. Indeed, they literally discourage any attempt to secure one. In rejecting this literature we should not fall into the trap of attributing its failings to the supposed ethnocentric myopia and ideological biases of its authors. Rather, the concepts that they use find their roots in the oldest extant tradition of Western political and social philosophy, the organic model of state and society. As I have argued elsewhere, the organic model with its holistic and teleological implications conditions us to judge the component parts solely in terms of their functional contribution to the harmony and progress of the whole body politic. Contemporary analytical schemes based upon systems and functions merely dress an old tradition in the new clothes of a special language (Ross, 1975).

Before we completely abandon the conceptual imagery of this theoretical approach, we can admit that much of it, although not all, has a saving grace in its dynamism. In the work of Deutsch, Riggs, Huntington, Holt and Turner, and others (not to mention the vital tradition associated with Marx) we see a view of political and social life that posits structural change over time as a basic unit of analysis (Deutsch, 1966; Riggs, 1973; Huntington, 1968; Holt and Turner, 1966).

---

[1]A recent and unresolved debate among U.S. education policy makers concerns the issue of bilingual education for non English-speaking children.

The late 1960's and 1970's have witnessed a new scholarly and popular look at the phenomenon of ethnicity. This revived interest has closely followed upon the heels of dramatic ethnic struggles in such relatively advanced industrialized countries as the United Kingdom, Canada, Lebanon, Belgium, France, and Spain. Walker Connor, for one, has shown the bankruptcy of prevailing conceptualizations of political development and Cynthia Enloe has gone as far as to suggest entirely new ones (Connor, 1972; Enloe, 1973). Such scholars have argued that ethnicity is a vital explanatory variable and that it does not automatically wither away with the advent of modernity.

Unfortunately, some of this literature has been read and misread to imply that ethnicity is an inevitable and unalterable facet of political life and that ethnic languages are a basically constant force in their structure and functions. It is one thing to state that ethnic language and politics need not decline in modern states and quite another to assert that they cannot. We have come close to accepting Geertz's categorization of ethnicity as a primordial given while only dissenting on the effectiveness of the so-called integrative revolution. A static view of ethnicity may be as analytically dangerous as a dynamic view which discounts it.

Methodology

Ethnicity has proven to be a very difficult concept to define with much precision. Indeed, those who have approached the task have not been able to achieve a consensus. Most usages are both vague and ambiguous in their applications to empirical research. What some scholars consider to be examples of ethnicity, others would consider to be cases of such other variables as regionalism, religious sectarianism, class conflict, and even sheer opportunism. When ethnicity is at best a fuzzy concept, it becomes rather difficult to convincingly establish its relationship to language.

This conceptual disarray is a product of a basic methodological gulf separating students of ethnicity. Most approaches to the analysis of ethnicity can be placed into one of two competing methodological stances. The nature of one's view of the language-ethnicity interface is essentially determined by the methodological stance that is chosen.

The first school of thought is composed of those theorists and researchers who subscribe to the objectivist approach to the analysis of ethnicity. Drawing upon ethnographic materials, they claim that ethnic boundaries can be drawn through the identification of discrete cultural institutions and processes. Chief among these tightly integrated cultural elements is the possession of a distinctive language that may serve as a daily language in use, or, alternately, serve only as a language of ritual. Such a language provides an interactive locus for an ethnic group and allows for the communication of unique emotive group symbols. It is the vehicle for a world view that makes the group different from all others. Objectivists, accordingly, view language as one of the primary defining characteristics of ethnic identity.

The second school subscribes to the alternate, subjectivist view. Subjectivists claim that ethnicity reflects a shared we-feeling among a collectivity that may be internally differentiated along several objective dimensions. Barth, for one, suggests that objective delimiters may be the result of subjective differences rather than their cause (Barth, 1969). Ethnic boundaries, therefore, are marked by lines of mutual recognition and reciprocity of exchange. Connor argues that language and other seemingly objective variables such as dress, ritual practice, etc., are really disposable symbols of an underlying sense of peoplehood. An individual can speak an alien tongue, change his clothes, and abandon or modify old

rituals without necessarily losing his sense of ethnic identification. In some
cases, as among American Indians, ethnicity may only emerge when individuals and
groups put aside their own language for a common lingua franca. The politics of
ethnicity may be fought around such objective issues as the language of instruction and administration, but the heart of the matter lies in the self-identification and political affirmation of a group of people who consider themselves to be
different (Connor, 1972).

The objective and subjective approaches have both strengths and weaknesses. The
objective approach is less likely than the subjective to fall prey to mysticism,
romanticism, and vagueness. In addition, it provides clear-cut empirical refer-
ents that simplify the task of comparative research. However, Connor is largely
correct in attacking this approach for its concentration on secondary rather than
primary factors. Unlike the subjective approach, the objective method never takes
the entirely reasonable phenomenological step of asking what ethnicity really means
to the ethnics themselves. While the subjective approach does not fall into the
trap of emphasizing what may actually be trivialities, it is seriously undermined
by its failure to posit a behavioural indicator of ethnicity. As such, the subjective approach seems very difficult to apply to cross-national research without
massive imprecision.

LANGUAGE AND COLLECTIVE IDENTITY

In analyzing the relationship between language and ethnicity, I must resolve the
theoretical and methodological issues that are raised above. I shall deal with
the theoretical issue by positing a conceptual scheme in which the relationship
between language and ethnicity is not static but subject to considerable alteration as the environment around them changes. I see ethnicity as only one particular form of collective identity. Different forms of collective identity have quite
different cognitive, evaluative, and affective meanings for those who hold them
(Almond and Verba, 1965). They are likely to emerge at different stages of societal development and intergroup relations. As ethnicity is only one form of
collective identity, the mobilization of ethnic consciousness is but one out of
several options that are available to the members and élites of various collectivities. Each different mode of collective identity carries with it a very different role for language. The role of language in the ethnic form of collective
identity is, therefore, very dissimilar from that of language in other identity
modes.

In methodological terms, I am suggesting that the objective and subjective approaches may have differential utility for the analysis of groups at different
stages of collective identity development. The subjective approach may be best
suited for the study of some forms of collective identity while the objective approach may be more suitable for the analysis of others. Accordingly, at one level
of development, language may be a primary defining characteristic of a collectivity while at another it may play only a modest, largely symbolic role.

Collectivities can be placed within a progression of identity modes that consists
of what I will call the *communal*, *minority*, *ethnic*, and *national* stages. Each
stage manifests a different combination of values of the following variables:
political power, reciprocity of exchange, technological development, and intergroup competition for scarce values and resources. Together, these variables
serve to predict the nature of collective identity.

Communal Groups and Language

Communal groups exist in primitive and some traditional societies. Such societies

are characterized by an absence of urbanization and by economic life styles including hunting and gathering; slash and burn agriculture; herding; and sometimes more
elaborate forms of farming. Such groups are largely isolated from the wider world,
having little or no sustained and penetrating contact with others. Intergroup
contact, where it exists, is likely to be rather infrequent, marginal in its
socio-economic impact, and highly formalized in tone. Indeed, such groups often
go to great lengths to reduce the incidence of polluting cross-cultural contact.
A communal society is quite self-sufficient and usually autarkic (a similar discussion is found in Furnivall, 1948).

Although I use the term communal identity, group identity is not really an issue
to an isolated or semi-isolated community. Since there is so little contact with
the outside world, although there is often a dim awareness of it, there is very
little incentive to subjectively differentiate a collective we from an external
they. Group and self identity is, rather, something that is taken pretty much
for granted. Characteristically, when communal groups devise a name for themselves, the name can usually be translated into something analogous to "the
people".

It would be entirely inappropriate for an outside observer to use a subjectivist
approach in trying to delimit the boundaries and specify the collective identity
of a communal group. Rather, an objective, ethnographic approach would seem to
offer the highest descriptive payoffs. Accordingly, it is fair to say that a distinctive language is basic to the collective life of a communal people. Such a
language is the vessel in which their entire cultural heritage is maintained and
transmitted. Such societies are pre-literate and rely on oral traditions for
their pattern maintenance. Oral literature, oral music, and oral history are
basic forms of intra-group interaction and entertainment (see Hyman in Pye (ed.),
1963). Communal languages are often quite complex and, in their vocabulary and
syntax, often reflect the environment in which the group lives and their mode of
adaptation to that environment. Great pride is taken in the language, as slight
nuances can carry great changes in meaning, and language changes very slowly over
time. In communal life, society, culture, politics, religion, and economics are
all tightly interwoven, and language is the thread that holds them in place.

Communal groups rarely survive the transition from primitive to traditional or
from traditional to modern society. As societal interdependencies grow, segment-
ation becomes more difficult if not impossible to maintain. Only those groups
that are small and isolated in particularly remote and inaccessible (as well as
undesirable) terrain are likely to remain untouched, and even they may eventually
succumb to the omnipresent reach of mass electronic media and modern means of
transportation. A case in point is the rapidly diminishing isolation of such
groups as the Eskimo and of the Bush Negroes of Surinam.

When communal groups come into sustained contact with other groups, especially if
these other groups are actively involved in state or empire building, their collective identification may be transformed, or, quite possibly, the group may be
absorbed entirely by another and, as a result, pass out of history. History is
replete with examples of lost peoples as larger groups have habitually expanded at
the expense of smaller and weaker peoples. Small, isolated, structurally simple
groups can be utterly devastated by cultural contact with stronger, more complex,
and technically advanced peoples.

Any asymmetric cross-cultural contact brings a degree of acculturation in its wake.
Language transfer is inevitably a major aspect of such acculturation as the language of the dominant group becomes the means through which the subordinate population can communicate with its new masters. However, as Connor has pointed out,
acculturation, especially linguistic acculturation, does not necessarily lead to
a changed self-identification in an individual or group of individuals (Connor,

1972). Full absorption only takes place when a group has been assimilated into another society. Assimilation is complete when the members of a collectivity see themselves as belonging to another group and when the members of that group fully accept their new members as equals and do not differentiate between them and themselves. A requisite for assimilation is the adoption of the language of the dominant group. While this is a necessary condition for assimilation, it is not a sufficient one. Peoples, such as the Magyars and Arabs, who view group membership in largely cultural terms, have been historically open to the large-scale assimilation of other groups who have adopted their language, and, in the case of Islam, their religion. Other peoples, like the Chinese and Afrikaners, who view group membership in terms of descent or physical characteristics, have not been open to large-scale assimilation regardless of the linguistic usage of subordinate populations (Verdery, 1978).

Minorities and Language

A communal group, regardless of its level of linguistic acculturation, may not wish to assimilate and/or may not be allowed to do so. In such instances the result may be the transformation of a communal into a minority group. I do not define a minority in numerical terms but in terms of relative power and structural inequality (Balandier, 1966). While a communal group can be described without reference to other collectivities, the existence of a minority implies that of a dominant majority. Such a majority dominates a society through its ability to impose unequal rates and terms of exchange upon minority groups rather than through its numerical strength. Indeed, as in white settler societies, the majority may comprise neither a majority nor a plurality of the total population.

A minority group, therefore, is a collectivity that is characterized by its powerlessness in deciding its own fate. This powerlessness even extends to its choice or lack of choice of language in administration, commerce, education, and religion. Unlike a communal group, a minority group enjoys sustained contact with others, yet this contact is inherently exploitative and lacking in reciprocity (see Rothchild, 1971). Since a minority cannot determine the nature of its relationship to the majority it cannot determine the nature of its own identity. A minority's identity is not endogenously defined by the group itself but is, rather, exogenously defined and coercively enforced by the majority upon the minority. This process often leads to the minority internalizing an image of itself as inherently inferior. Indeed, *Varna* and *Jati* in India have led large parts of the population to consider themselves to be not only inferior but ritually polluted. In such instances, manifest discrimination is not even required to maintain the subordinate status of the minority (see Blalock, 1967).

Minority groups may play a number of different socioeconomic roles depending on such factors as their relative technical skills, linguistic prowess, numbers, economic dispensability, and ritual status. Some minorities may be subject to an enforced marginality in which they serve as a non-functional, surplus population that is condemned to economically peripheral and often ritually unclean labour (see Ebuchi, 1971). Other minorities may have specialized roles in the industrial sector of an unevenly developing economy (see Armstrong, 1976). Still others may have a distinct, quasi-entrepreneurial, middleman role (Blalock, 1967). Nevertheless, whether the minority is a pariah, internal proletariat, or middleman, its basic role and identity have been largely chosen for it, not by it.[2]

Minorities are formed in transitional periods, especially in the early phases of modernization. The initial period of modernization represents a complex amalgamation of new and old elements. Communal isolation and boundaries are broken down as more and more groups are drawn into a centrally-oriented and linguistically homogenous network of socioeconomic-political transactions. Simultaneously, traditional bases of status and traditional power holders are left relatively intact. Mobility is still centered on ascription and not achievement. As a result, when new groups are drawn into a polity through the expansive actions of an assertive majority, they are given a fairly well-defined place in an expanding system of social stratification, and specific steps are taken to ensure their compliance. Through this process, the overt conflict that is often engendered by enforced intergroup contact is repressed by both normative and coercive means of social control. Thus, the creation of minority statuses is an important way in which a state-building élite can maintain and even extend its power in a period of social change.

Language, for the communal group, is an inseparable part of its society and culture. The minority condition, however, is one in which the integration of language into the adaptive genius of a people is weakened and often severed. The language that a minority uses or is permitted to use depends upon the needs of the majority, not the wishes of the minority. Language itself comes to reflect the subordinate condition in which a minority group lives. Sometimes, minority languages are retained, and even strengthened, so as to reinforce the social stigma of being different from the majority. A majority régime may maintain group languages so as to prevent contact and unity of action among minority peoples. The French, for example, worked to preserve linguistic differences between the Arabs and Berbers in North Africa, and between the Vietnamese and Montagnards in Indo-China. Even today, in formerly colonial countries, members of different groups can often only communicate with each other in a European language. In other situations, minority languages are ruthlessly stamped out and replaced by the dominant language or by a pidgin hybrid. Education in Wales, for instance, was long conducted exclusively in the English language and children were punished (often physically) for using Welsh in class. Slavery in the Caribbean and southern United States relied upon the destruction of the slaves' culture through the eradication of overt uses of African languages.

Where members of minority groups live in close physical proximity to members of the majority and where a patriarchal system of intergroup relations persists, the use of the dominant language and/or a modified pidgin is most likely. Whatever form is used, an elaborate special language of etiquette will usually develop. Such a special language will serve to demarcate the boundaries between permissible and non-permissible forms of behaviour. On the other hand, where physical segregation is practiced, and where group relations are manifestly or latently competitive, linguistic differences are maintained as mechanisms of boundary maintenance (van den Berghe, 1972). Even when the same language is spoken, different collectivities will evidence variations in vocabulary, intonation, and syntax - an ethnic division of labour, to use Hechter's term, will be complemented by an ethnic division of dialect (Hechter, 1977).

---

[2]In some cases, minority élites may find their own position enhanced by the enforcement of a minority identity. The Catholic clergy in Québec supported such a situation in the late eighteenth and nineteenth centuries. For an analysis see Dale Posgate and Kenneth McRoberts, <u>Québec: Social change and political crisis</u>. Toronto, McClelland and Stewart, 1976, pp.19-27.

Numerous ethnographers have described the fundamental ambivalence that minority group members feel for their derivative languages. These languages are simultaneously media of intra-group communication and cultural articulation, on the one hand, and are imposed symbols of inferiority, on the other. Language, in any event, reflects and reinforces the predicament of the minority group.

Ethnic Mobilization and Language

Needless to say, minority roles and identities may be highly stressful and frustrating to many of their holders. Accordingly, the more ambitious and able among them may be anxious to remove this stigma from themselves by assimilating into the majority. Methods of passing include alterations of dress, cuisine, religion and, most importantly, speech. An enlightened majority élite might find that a policy of co-opting such individuals could offer significant payoffs in increased social stability and more effective social control. However, in most cases, the majority will deny the opportunity of full assimilation to upwardly mobile minority group members. Reasons for doing so range from a desire to preserve the sanctity of the social order to an attempt to limit access to élite and sub-élite positions (Horowitz, 1971). As a result, acculturation may be widespread among aspiring minority élites but assimilation will be very rare. The latter find that assimilation cannot be a solution to an increasingly intolerable enforced status deprivation. Increasingly, an alternative is sought in minority group organization and political action. If individuals cannot escape minority status, they may seek to return to group life for the purpose of altering the group's inferior status through collective behaviour.

Once this process of organization and political action is undertaken, the generation and diffusion of a new collective identity becomes paramount. Such a change of collective identity involves the removal of much of the stigma associated with the previous minority identity because the new identity is to be defined by the collectivity itself, not imposed upon it. A number of alternatives present themselves in the form of a series of very different potential group identities and political strategies. The option chosen is dependent upon such disparate factors as the role of the minority group in the economy, the geographic concentration or dispersal of the group's membership, the availability of coalition partners, the reaction of the majority, the personality and ideological characteristics of the minority group leadership and the experience of referent models in the same or in other countries. The options include the redefinition of the minority in class terms, in regional terms, or even in terms of a religious community. One other option is the transformation of a minority group into an ethnic group.

Class, region and religion are objective characteristics around which a group may be mobilized. Ethnicity, however, results from a mobilization around an intersubjectively shared sense of peoplehood. It does not matter if this sense of peoplehood has any historic-genetic basis; what is important is that the members of an ethnic group differentiate themselves from others because they believe that they are unique. Ethnicity, in this sense, is a subjective reality rather than an objective characteristic.

Ethnic identity differs from communal identity in that it is explicit and not taken for granted, and it differs from a minority identity in that it is defined by the group rather than for it. In the process of self-definition, the group myths and cultural values, including language, that categorize the communal stage of collective development may be substantially revised, altered and reinterpreted so as to fit changed conditions. Clearly, ethnic identity is a distinctly modern phenomenon rather than a mere reiteration of primitive or traditional images. Ethnicity does not disappear in modern societies; it only emerges in modern societies.

Ethnicity, furthermore, is not only a question of revised collective identity. An ethnic group is also characterized by a degree of political action and organizat- ion. Indeed, I am defining an ethnic group as a politically mobilized collectiv- ity whose members share a perceived distinctive self-identity. Ethnicity is a group option in which resources are mobilized for the purpose of pressuring the political system to allocate values for the benefit of the members of a self-diff- erentiating collectivity. Ethnic groups are most likely to exist in situations in which there is a high level of intergroup competition and where multiple access points into the political system are available. Ethnic groups are a form of inter- est group, and, as such, are not quaint leftovers from a primordial past but a form of collective identity and organization that is well suited to a modern, structurally differentiated polity (Glazer and Moynihan, 1975).

Ethnicity, unlike communal and minority groups, is characteristic of relatively advanced levels of technical development. At relatively mature levels of societal elaboration, collectivities find that the state has become more complex and in- ternally differentiated. As a result, the number of politically-relevant access points increases as their sensitivity to disruption becomes more acute. Such a situation promises important payoffs to a well organized interest group. Similar- ly, the transition from a society based upon ascription to one in which achieve- ment criteria are dominant is one of the factors that allows ethnic mobilization to proceed and provides ethnic demands with a certain degree of ideological legit- imacy for the wider society.

The conceptual scheme outlined above emphasizes a developmental progression in which most groups progress from a communal stage to the ethnic stage by way of a minority situation. Indeed, most groups that are usually referred to as pre- or non-mobilized ethnic groups are, in reality, in either a communal or minority phase. Such groups might assimilate or take on such other collective identities as class, regional group, religious group, etc., rather than mobilize on an ethnic basis. Language, as we have seen, plays a different role and takes an alternate form depending on the strategy that is chosen. Some instances may exist in which the normal three-step progression is not experienced. In societies in which mod- ernization is very rapid and in which no clear-cut majority group exists communal groups can move directly into the mobilized ethnic stage and skip the indignities of minority status.

Majority groups, too, under certain circumstances, may travel the ethnic road. Such a phenomenon exists when a dominant group loses its predominance or comes to fear that it might lose it. Mobilizations of once dominant peoples along ethnic lines can be observed among Protestants in Ulster, Walloons in Belgium, Afrikaners in South Africa, and, to a degree, white Protestant males in the United States.

When communal and minority groups choose to eschew an ethnic identity for that of class, religion, etc., they do not forever give up the ethnic option. If these alternate collective identities prove to be unsatisfying or if social and politic- al conditions change, they can usually remobilize their resources in an ethnic manner. Glazer and Moynihan (1974), for example, argue that the resurgence of ethnicity in the United States in the 1970's is due, in part, to the decline in the importance of religious and occupational identities during the 1960's. Else- where, I have argued that ethnicity can be expected to replace class as a basis of political organization in post-industrial societies (Ross, 1976).

Even a cursory review of ethnic conflicts in such countries as Belgium, the United Kingdom, Canada, India, Finland, Yugoslavia, Malaysia, and the Soviet Union, to name but a few, reveals that language issues are quite salient. Language, as an issue, is important, not in itself, but as a symbol of an underlying image of group purpose and identity (see Connor, 1973). In this regard, language is probably the most powerful single symbol of ethnicity because it serves as a shorthand for all that makes a group special and unique. Many ethnic and nationalist movements trace their roots to literary and philological revivals. Ethnic movements often find their organizational precursors in language and literary societies (see Rawkins, 1978). It is around the issue of language that ethnic politicians and the ethnic intelligentsia may organize and interrelate. Language, given its affective potential, is a symbol that is very effective in fostering a mass mobilization on ethnic lines.

Depending on the circumstances, four major variants of language use may be observed in ethnic mobilizations. This is a suggestive enumeration of possibilities, rather than an exhaustive listing. Probably the best known use of language in ethnic mobilizations comes when a previously dead or little utilized tongue, usually from a group's communal past, is revived and purified. If previously used, it was spoken by the clergy for ritual purposes or used in isolated peasant backwaters. Now, however, a once acculturated intelligentsia takes up its ancestral language and makes it the mobilizing banner of its literature and politics. Bohemian intellectuals, for example, abandoned German in the nineteenth century and adopted the Czech language as the symbol of their ethnic rebirth. At the same time, the Irish intelligentsia called for the abandonment of English, the language of foreign oppression, for a revived Irish Gaelic. Zionists, too, abandoned one Jewish language, Yiddish, for another, Hebrew. Yiddish was seen as the symbol of exile and degradation while Hebrew would be the vehicle for a revived Jewish commonwealth. One final example is instructive. Beginning in the 1960's many Black Americans took up the study of Swahili in an attempt to foster a revised ethnic identity. It did not matter to them that most of their Black ancestors had been abducted from West Africa where Swahili has never been spoken to any great degree. As a symbol of ethnic consciousness, Swahili would do just as well as any West African language.

As a symbol of ethnic consciousness, a revived language need not be actually spoken by an ethnic population. After more than fifty years of Irish independence, English is still spoken by a large and growing majority of Eire's citizenry. Welsh and Basque nationalisms have prospered under the banners of languages that many of their adherents and activists cannot speak or speak with great difficulty.

A second role of language in ethnic mobilization arises when a native language comes under stress. Ethnic mobilization unites a population around the defence of its culture from a perceived linguistic threat. This is often a strategy used by dominant groups who feel their power threatened - such as the Afrikaners in South Africa. A common ethnic demand in such a situation is the restructuring of the state along linguistic lines. Such policies have been successfully advocated in Belgium, appear to be the essence of statecraft in Switzerland, and have increasing appeal in Québec. Mobilizing ethnic groups are also likely to act to purge their language of foreign vocabulary and syntax as a symbolic means of purging themselves from their minority stigma. Beginning in the nineteenth century, language purification became a salient theme in Norwegian politics.

A third, very common pattern involves an ethnic group that mobilizes by using the language of the dominant group. Indeed, as a type of interest group, an ethnic group finds that it must utilize the language of the prevailing political order so as to effectively communicate its demands. The Scottish nationalists, for instance, unlike their colleagues in Wales, have not emphasized the Scottish Gaelic language and operate, by and large, in English. To judge by the relative proportions of electoral support received, the S.N.P. has been much more successful than Plaid Cymru. Often, the dominant language serves as a lingua franca uniting various components of an emerging ethnic group that would otherwise be divided by their own divergent languages. As I have already suggested, Indians in the United States have found the English language to be a useful medium in their effort to become an effective ethnic force.

Finally, a fourth mode of ethnic language mobilization involves the creation of special usages from among the vocabulary and syntax of the dominant language in order to generate an ingroup ethnic patois. This ersatz language can then serve to maintain group boundaries and to further symbolic interaction and group consciousness. To a certain extent, Black English has played this role in the United States.

Nation and Language

The demands that an ethnic group makes upon the institutions of a state vary directly with the degree to which these institutions are willing and able to accommodate ethnic proposals. If the state is reasonably accommodating at a point well before polarization sets in, ethnic groups may not move beyond initial, minimal demands for a new, redefined role in the system. If the political system is not forthcoming, ethnic demands will inevitably escalate to calls for autonomy or separation in those cases in which the real or symbolic homeland of the ethnic group lies within the boundaries of the host society, and emigration in those cases in which the real or symbolic homeland is abroad. Once polarization sets in, an overdue accession to minimal demands will not satisfy the ethnic group but lead to an increased group efficacy in making maximal demands.

A nationalist solution is reached when an ethnic group acquires a state of its own. With nationhood, the question of an official state language becomes acute and may serve as the subsequent basis of internal cleavages over access to material and symbolic rewards and offices. When a revived or newly constructed language or linguistic code becomes the language of the state, those who do not speak it suffer a severe political liability. New states may successfully, like Israel, or unsuccessfully, like Eire, expend a great many scarce resources in trying to spread a national tongue. Linguistic differences that were not crucial to ethnic solidarity or were papered over in the national struggle may become politicized, thereby undermining national unity, and, paradoxically, leading to the creation of new ethnic groups (Horowitz, 1971).

CONCLUSION

This conceptual scheme represents only a tentative first step in an attempt to redress some of the conceptual confusion surrounding the use of the term ethnicity, and in the analysis of the relationship between language and ethnicity. I have argued that language has no single mode of relationship to collective identity. Rather, it plays a different role in different forms of collective identity and is, itself, a dynamic force in the unfolding progression of group interaction and identity formation.

Although much work needs to be done in filling in the gaps in this analysis, the proposed framework has a number of distinct analytical advantages: it provides a dynamic bridge between the objective and subjective approaches to the definition of ethnicity and the role of language in ethnicity; it accounts for differences in the bases of collective identity and in the role of language; it avoids the problem of how to account for the lack of mobilization in certain ethnic groups - indeed, it defines ethnicity in mobilized terms and sees language as a crucial vehicle of mobilization; it centres attention upon the political dynamic of ethnicity and the role of language in politicization; it accounts for the importance of ethnicity in modern and advanced countries without resort to assumptions of primordial longevity; it shows that languages can alter or even disappear without the simultaneous passing of collective identity and ingroup consciousness; and, finally, I believe that it provides a number of insights into the mobilization of

ethnic-like groups (i.e., the Women's Movement) that have also experienced the
deprivations of minority status.

REFERENCES

Almond, G. & Powell, Jr., G.B. (1966) Comparative politics: A developmental
approach, Little, Brown, Boston.

Almond, G. & Verba, S. (1965) The civic culture, Little, Brown, Boston, pp.20-22.

J.A. Armstrong, Mobilized and proletarian diasporas, American Political Science
Review, 70, 393-408 (1976).

Balandier, G. (1966) The colonial situation: A theoretical approach, in I.
Wallerstein (ed.): Social change: The colonial situation, Wiley, New York.

Barth, F. (1969) Introduction, in F. Barth (ed.): Ethnic groups and boundaries,
Little, Brown, Boston, pp.9-38.

van den Berghe, P. (1972) Distance mechanisms of stratification, in A.H. Richmond
(ed.): Readings in race and ethnic relations, Pergamon, New York, pp.210-219.

Blalock, Jr., H.M. (1967) Toward a theory of minority-group relations, Capricorn,
New York, pp.139-142.

Cohen, R. & Middleton, J. (1970) From tribe to nation in Africa, Chandler,
Scranton, Pa.

W. Connor, Nation-building or nation-destroying?, World Politics, 24, 319-350
(1972).

Deutsch, K.W. (1966) Nationalism and social communication, MIT Press, Cambridge,
Mass.

Deutsch, K.W. & Foltz, W.J. (eds.) (1963) Nation-building, Atherton, Chicago.

K. Ebuchi, The meaning of "ethnic" identity to Burakumin children: A case study
of an urban neighbourhood in Northern Kyushu, Japan. A paper presented at the
annual convention of the American Anthropological Association, New York (1971).

Enloe, C.H. (1973) Ethnic conflict and political development, Little, Brown, Boston.

Furnivall, J.S. (1948) Colonial policy and practice, Cambridge University Press,
London.

Geertz, C. (1963) The integrative revolution: Primordial sentiments and civil
politics in the new states, in C. Geertz (ed.): Old societies and new states,
Free Press, New York, pp.105-157.

Glazer, N. & Moynihan, D.P. (1974) A resurgence of ethnicity?, in R.J. Meister
(ed.): Race and ethnicity in modern America, D.C. Heath, Lexington, Mass.,
pp.115-123.

Glazer, N. & Moynihan, D.P. (1975) Ethnicity: Theory and experience, Harvard
University Press, Cambridge, Mass.

M. Hechter, Ethnicity and industrialization: On the proliferation of the cultural
division of labour, Ethnicity, 3, 214-224 (1977).

Holt, R.T. & Turner, J.E. (1966) The political basis of economic development,
    Van Nostrand, Princeton, N.J.

Horowitz, D.L. (1971) Multiracial politics in the new states: Toward a theory of
    conflict, in R.J. Jackson & M.B. Stein (eds.): Issues in comparative politics,
    St. Martin's Press, New York, pp.164-180.

Huntington, S.P. (1968) Political order in changing societies, Yale University
    Press, New Haven, Conn.

Hyman, H. (1963) Mass media and political socialization: The role of patterns of
    communication, in L.W. Pye (ed.): Communications and political development,
    Princeton University Press, Princeton.

Olorunsola, V.A. (1972) The politics of cultural sub-nationalism in Africa,
    Doubleday, Garden City, N.Y.

Parsons, T. & Shils, E.A. (eds.) (1962) Toward a general theory of action,
    Harper and Row, New York.

Plotnicov, L. & Tuden, A. (1970) Introduction, in L. Plotnicov & A. Tuden (eds.):
    Essays in comparative social stratification, University of Pittsburgh Press,
    Pittsburgh, pp.3-25.

Pye, L.E. (ed.) (1963) Communications and political development. Princeton
    University Press, Princeton.

P.M. Rawkins, Political action and the transformation of ethnic consciousness:
    A case study of Welsh language society activists. A paper presented at the
    annual convention of the International Studies Association, Washington, D.C.
    (1978).

Riggs, F.W. (1973) Prismatic society revisited, General Learning Press, Morristown,
    N.J.

J.A. Ross, Reflections on the philosophic and ideological assumptions of research
    on minorities: A re-examination of the literature on development. A paper
    presented at the annual convention of the International Studies Association,
    Washington, D.C. (1975).

J.A. Ross, The mobilization of ethnicity in post-industrial society: A test of the
    hypothesis, Working Paper no.53, University Center for International Studies,
    University of Pittsburgh (1976).

Rothchild, D. (1971) Ethnicity and conflict resolution, in R.J. Jackson & M.B.
    Stein (eds.): Issues in comparative politics, St. Martin's Press, New York,
    pp.181-194.

K. Verdery, Transylvania as a case of internal colonialism. A paper presented at
    the annual convention of the International Studies Association, Washington,
    D.C. (1978).

LINGUISTIC AND CULTURAL AFFILIATION AMONGST YOUNG ASIAN PEOPLE IN LEICESTER

N. Mercer, E. Mercer * and R. Mears * *

University of Leicester, Leicester
*Loughborough University of Technology, Loughborough
**University of Leicester, Leicester, U.K.

INTRODUCTION

This paper is concerned with the attitudes of a group of Asian students towards their traditional Indian language and culture, considered in the context of their lives in Leicester. The students in question were all bilinguals, speaking both Gujarati and English fluently, and were either themselves immigrants or the first generation offspring of immigrants from East Africa or the Indian subcontinent.

Asian immigrants began to arrive in Britain in large numbers in the mid-nineteen sixties, and many settled in Leicester. The most recent estimates by the Leicester Council for Community Relations suggest there are 41,000 people of Asian descent in a city population of approximately 300,000. Of these, there are an estimated 30,000 Gujarati speakers, most of whom came from East Africa although there are a few from the Gujarat state of India. Such numbers obviously created potential for a viable ethnic community, and most of the Gujaratis in Leicester now live in one area, Belgrave, where a large number of shops, travel agencies, insurance companies, banks, restaurants and a cinema are run by and for Gujaratis. In terms of their religion, family structure and culture orientation in general, most older Gujaratis maintain close ties with their Indian homeland. This applies even to those families who have come to England from East Africa, some of whom have not even visited India for many years. Communications are maintained with relatives in India to the extent that it is still fairly common for marriages to be arranged between partners from Britain and India who have had no previous personal contact. Likewise, the Indian caste system still exerts its influence on such matters as choice of friends, commercial patronage and membership of social organizations (e.g., ethnic schools and sporting clubs).

For the young people in this community, life has its own special problems. Most have now spent a good many years in Britain, being educated in the English language, mixing with British schoolchildren, watching British television, and so on. They have enjoyed some of the freedom which British children are allowed, yet the Indian community is highly integrated and places many social constraints on them. The differences between the immigrant and host community are many and striking. The older Asians in Leicester aim to continue their traditional way of life; adapting to circumstances but retaining the "core values" of their culture. Moreover, those Indian cultural moral values which are believed to be more at risk through the younger generation's contact with the indigenous British way of life are often accorded special emphasis by parents and elders. This includes moral rulings on such matters as the personal freedom of young people, their responsibilities to their family and other elders, and their relations with the opposite sex. With reference to a similar group (young Pakistanis) other researchers have noted:

> "There is general agreement that they should reform and mod-
> ify their present values rather than abandon them completely.
> The idea of "becoming English" in a cultural sense is almost
> universally rejected. Young people are, of course, thorough-
> ly conversant with the British cultural norms and are quite
> capable of presenting themselves as British whenever necess-
> ary. Nevertheless, they still feel that British self to be
> rather unreal." (Ballard and Ballard, 1977)

In considering matters of ethnic self-identity, it is important to realize that all
Leicester Gujaratis hold British passports; they are British citizens, and so may
perceive themselves as having a special relationship to British culture and a right
to a British self-identity in a way which other, alien, immigrants would not. We
were interested in the extent to which young Gujaratis were willing to identify
themselves with one or other of these cultural traditions.

Aspects of Ethnic and Cultural Identity

It has been pointed out by Joshua Fishman (1977) that there are many contrasting,
conflicting and contradictory conceptions of ethnicity. Fishman believes that the
consideration of ethnicity in the context of modern social theory has been hinder-
ed by certain conceptual "road blocks"; one of these is that which...

> "...fosters the view that ethnicity is pertinent to minority
> groups alone, and, therefore, leads to consideration of it
> in connection with issues of discrimination and intergroup
> relations, rather than as an aspect of all traditioned,
> large-scale, self-identifying behaviour". (p.44)

We would agree that an ethnic self-identity is something available to any socialized human individual, but would support the emphasis by other writers (Cohen,
1974; Watson, 1977) that only under certain social and psychological conditions
is ethnicity in any meaningful sense aroused, or, one might say, *constructed*.

> "The term ethnicity will be of little use if it is extended
> to denote cultural differences between isolated societies,
> autonomous regions, or independent stocks of populations such
> as nations with their own national boundaries. The differ-
> ences between the Chinese and the Indians, considered within
> their own respective countries, are national not ethnic diff-
> erences. But when groups of Chinese and Indian immigrants
> interact in a foreign land as Chinese and Indians they can
> be referred to as ethnic groups. Ethnicity is essentially a
> form of interaction between culture groups operating within
> common social contexts." (Cohen, 1974, p.XI)

An implication here, of course, is that the ethnic self-identity constructed by
members of a particular generation of a social group will be a function of the
cultural contacts of that group with other ethnic groups; different social circumstances will generate different "ethnicities". Young Gujaratis in Britain may
construct a rather different ethnic self-identity than did their forefathers in
Kenya, and this will require and be reflected in an emphasis on different aspects
of their cultural heritage. There is, moreover, no reason to believe that for
individuals, ethnic self-identity is stable across different social situations involving different participants – though this is not to say that central and per-
sistent characteristics could not be identified. For example, a Gujarati talking
to a Sikh may attend to very different ethnic contrasts than when dealing with an

Englishman, though the cultural resources from which his ethnic identity may be constructed are the same.

Language and Ethnicity

For these young people growing up in Leicester, bilingualism is a fact of social life. Many of the older generation, especially mothers and grandparents, speak poor English or none at all. On the other hand, all state schooling is in English and virtually no-one outside the immigrants' own linguistic community has even the slightest knowledge of Gujarati. Gujarati parents place a high premium on educational attainment and so encourage their sons, and to a lesser extent their daughters, to follow further education at least to "A" level. However, a better command of English and a more extended social and intellectual excursion outside the Asian community is inevitably required of these young people who do follow this path. Although parents expect competence in English from their children, concern seems to exist in the community about the future of the Gujarati language. In fact, a number of community-based ethnic schools have been established in the city, providing instruction in Gujarati.[1] We were therefore interested in the nature of the younger generation's attachment to this language.

Giles, Bourhis and Taylor (1977) have remarked on the surprising extent to which the part played by language in the dynamics of inter-ethnic relations has been ignored by researchers in the past and argue strongly for the importance of the linguistic dimension in the definition of a group's identity. It is clear that the cultural vitality of an ethnic group is often embodied in their distinctive language or ethnic speech style. However, in the present study, we felt we must initially treat the relation between ethnic identity and language loyalty as a problematic one. There are two important inter-related reasons for this. Firstly, the main identifying characteristic of this group in the social context of Leicester is *not* their language but their physical appearance, particularly their skin colour. Secondly, we have found from pilot studies and in more casual social encounters that a common expression of ethnic self-identity by Gujarati Asians in their interactions with white people is that they are *Indians*. Indian is an ethnic label, but not an ethnolinguistic one, as many Indian immigrants in Leicester speak languages other than Gujarati (e.g., Punjabi, Hindi, Bengali, Urdu[2]).

---

[1]The Leicester Council for Community Relations informally estimate that around 1,000 children from the Gujarati community in Leicester regularly attend ethnic schools in evenings and at weekends. These schools provide instruction in other aspects of Indian culture besides the Gujarati language; some also give teaching in academic subjects.

[2]These languages vary in the extent to which they are mutually intelligible. Hindi can be understood by both Gujarati and Punjabi speakers, who can also understand each other, although less well. Bengali and Urdu are not intelligible to Gujarati speakers.

This seemed to suggest that affiliation to a traditional Indian way of life might be symbolized in other ways than language loyalty. We were interested, then, in the extent to which choice of Indian identity is associated with loyalty to the Gujarati language.

To summarize: our aims in this study were to examine the extent to which our respondents identified with one or other of the two cultural traditions which they experience and whether language attitudes were systematically related to this self-orientation.

METHOD

Sample

Our sample was drawn from the population of young Gujaratis studying at two educational establishments within the City of Leicester, the first a College of Further Education, the second a boys' sixth form college. We obtained interviewees by various means - by asking for volunteers in classes, approaching people in the coffee bars and library. Although our sample was small, we have no reason to believe that it was in any important way unrepresentative of Gujarati-speaking students in these institutions. The sample consisted of 29 males and 9 females ranging in age from 16 to 22 with a mean of 18 years.

Some Comments on Ethnic Cueing

It seems appropriate here to reveal those aspects of our sociocultural background which seem relevant to this study. All three of us are white, and of British descent (two English and one Welsh) though not native to the City of Leicester. We all live in a part of the inner city in which many residents are Gujaratis, and they are represented amongst our neighbours, business contacts, friends and relatives.

We are aware that our non-membership of the ethnolinguistic group in question will undoubtedly influence our subjects' responses to questions about that group's culture and language. We would argue, however, that our special concern is with attitudes to language and culture which are generated out of ethnic interactions between white and Asian citizens of Leicester. The idea of an objective "truth" existing outside such social contexts is untenable. As Brah, Fuller, Loudon and Miles (1977) comment:

> "It seems much more helpful to regard such processes as the
> stuff of social science research which cannot be "controlled"
> out. The different presentations of self, the different re-
> sponses elicited by this *are* the social situation, or at
> least part of it." (p.3)

Interviews

Interviews were conducted in English by the researchers, and lasted on average 40 minutes. An attitude scale was then administered.

Questionnaire

The questionnaire was developed for use in an interview situation. Our aim was to encourage respondents to speak freely on a number of issues. We therefore kept the number of questions to a minimum, using non-leading prompts to encourage respondents to elaborate their opinions as fully as possible.

The questionnaire consisted of five sections, the first of which gathered information about the respondents' background, age, place of origin and so on.

In the second section, our aim was to investigate our respondents' ethnic identity. We asked them to say whether they regarded themselves primarily as Indian or as British, and whether they would qualify this in any way. We also asked if there were any occasions on which they felt particularly Indian or particularly British and if they ever wished to stress this in some way.

In the third section we wished to discover the nature of the respondents' affiliation to the two cultures, and they were here given the opportunity to discuss what they valued within each cultural tradition and what they would like to preserve or hand down to their children. Turning more specifically to Indian culture, we asked whether they thought it was *important* for Indians in Britain to preserve their culture and *how* they thought the culture should be preserved.

In the final two sections we focused on the role of language in the respondents' lives. Firstly, we wished to establish that respondents considered themselves fluent in their two languages. Secondly, we were concerned with the respondents' attitudes to Gujarati and English, and the perceived importance of each language in their everyday lives. We also asked whether they thought the use of Gujarati ought to be maintained and why.

The Attitude Scale

A Likert scale, consisting of 12 items, was used to examine the extent to which respondents were positively oriented towards the use of Gujarati in their present and future lives. The item pool has been made up from interviews and conversations with Gujaratis, and the scale piloted on a small sample of bilinguals.[3]

High scorers tended to *agree*, and low scorers to *disagree* with items like:

1. Speaking Gujarati is important because most of my friends speak it;

and 2. I am glad I know Gujarati because I like to listen to Indian songs.

Low scorers tended to *agree*, and high scorers to *disagree* with:

3. I prefer not to speak Gujarati if English people are around in case they disapprove.

RESULTS AND DISCUSSION

Recent writers (Ryan and Carranza, 1977; Giles, Bourhis and Taylor, 1977) have pointed out the danger of considering ethnic groups as homogenous with regard to attitudes and behaviour. Even within our group of respondents, who represent a very restricted sample of the Gujarati-speaking community, the diversity of attitudes to some aspects of language and culture was striking. In this section, we will first consider general findings which have relevance for understanding the particular social circumstances of the group as a whole, before examining the nature of this diversity.

---

[3]Using a split-half method, the stepped-up reliability coefficient $r_w = +0.86$. Comparisons of respondents' scores on this scale with their attitudes expressed in extended interviews support the scale's validity.

Attitudes to Traditional Indian Culture

The great majority of our respondents expressed an interest in supporting and maintaining Indian culture. In accord with the findings of other researchers (Ballard
and Ballard, 1977) we found that very few respondents wished to reject their Indian
cultural heritage altogether, but did consider some cultural elements more worthy
of support than others. Many (70%) hoped to preserve their religion, Hinduism.
Fifty per cent spontaneously expressed support for the Gujarati language, and 30%
said they wished to maintain cultural traditions and community festivals. One
recurring theme was the desire to retain aspects of the Indian extended family network because this represented a source of personal support and social contact
thought to be lacking elsewhere in British society. Our respondents often compared
the pattern of life in the British community unfavourably with that in the Indian
community. The stereotypical picture of the British family was one of nuclear isolation, with high divorce rates, neglect and lack of respect for the elderly,
disobedience and rebellion among the young. Their impression was of a fragmented,
highly individualistic and lonely society.

Despite their expressed support for some aspects of Indian culture, most respondents clearly felt some modifications to the traditional way of life upheld by the
older generation would be in order, and these were generally of the nature of
"liberalizations" towards British norms and values. For example:

> 1. "The parents must change a bit. I'm in the middle - you
>   don't know where you are."
>
> 2. "I would in some ways bring up children the same (tradit-
>   ional) way. But I would change some things. They could
>   go to certain places so long as they told us, maybe choose
>   a partner for themselves if we accepted them."
>
> 3. "I think Indians in Britain should preserve their culture,
>   but try to adapt to English ways."

Aspects of Indian life considered on the whole *unfavourably* were the system of
arranged marriages, and the caste system:

> 4. "I don't approve of the caste system - that's going out
>   now. My parents say in the old days when the caste system
>   worked, everyone was happy."

The system of arranged marriages is of crucial importance to young Asians who,
like our respondents, are coming up to a marriageable age. There has already been
some relaxation in the system, and it is now sometimes considered permissible for
two young people to make an informal arrangement which is then put forward for
parental approval. If the liaison is acceptable, the families involved then proceed in the traditional manner. However, the size of the community is such that
a suitable partner - of correct race, caste, family status, reputation, etc. -
cannot always be found. Many of our respondents commented unfavourably on the
practice, adopted by parents in such circumstances, of recruiting partners from
villages in India. As one girl said:

> 5. "There are very few suitable people here in Leicester so
>   my mother is always on about bringing someone over from
>   India. I couldn't stand that - marrying some village boy.
>   What would we talk about?"

Despite an obvious general reluctance to take part in arranged marriages, very few
respondents expressed an intention to defy their parents' rulings on this matter.
This probably reflects the fact that young people in the Indian community are
brought up to be obedient and to have an overwhelming respect for parental author-

ity. It is also worth noting that sanctions against those whose choice of partner
does not meet with approval may be severe and involve virtual isolation from the
community. Arranged marriages play an important part in maintaining the close-knit
community structure favoured by our respondents, creating and strengthening social
bonds between families to a much greater extent than is the case in the indigenous
British population.

Attitudes to the Use of Gujarati

Most of our respondents (85%) considered Gujarati to be important in their social
lives. They remarked on the absolute necessity of knowing Gujarati for communicating with "elders" in the community who spoke English poorly or not at all.

A large proportion (80%) also believed that younger Indians should learn Gujarati.
However, few were able to justify this in any explicit way, and the general feeling seemed to be simply that it would be unfortunate if use of the language died
out in Leicester. Of those who did justify this belief more precisely, most concentrated on the importance of oral use – at Divali[4] and other festivals, for example, and said that acceptance within the Indian community depended on knowing
the language. One further reason for maintaining Gujarati, suggested by a few
respondents, was that there was still some risk of Asians being expelled from
Britain, and so they might have to emigrate to India some time in the future.

A few respondents suggested that Gujarati was important for reading about Indian
history, or religion. However, only half our sample claimed literate ability in
Gujarati. Although a significant number of Indian children do attend ethnic
schools (see Introduction), it seems doubtful whether the next generation will
maintain even this standard of literacy.

Most (78%) respondents expressed the view that in their friendship groups the use
of both Gujarati and English seemed quite appropriate. They were aware that they
often "switched codes" (Gumperz, 1971) within conversations:

> 6. "We speak mixed; there is no occasion in which I would
>   feel it necessary just to speak Gujarati."

Some did say, however, that English seemed the most appropriate medium for discussing educational matters, with Gujarati being used in College for "chatting
and joking".

Many respondents commented on the fact that in many areas of social life the competence of other speakers denied them any real linguistic choice. However, remarks by two respondents on matters of appropriateness are interesting. The first
concerned conversations with older Asians:

> 7. "The only time I speak Gujarati is with older Asian people.
>   Even if they did speak English the old might think it was
>   impolite if I spoke English to them."

The second comment was by a respondent who said English was better for "getting
to know someone". She went on to say that she avoided speaking Gujarati to members of the opposite sex because this might reveal caste origins and so inhibit
the relationship (members of some castes tend to use rather different speech
styles).

---

[4]Divali is a major Hindu religious festival.

Identity Choice

In terms of their choice of ethnic identity, our respondents can be considered as three distinct groups: those who were prepared to identify themselves, without qualification, as *Indian* (15 respondents), those who similarly identified themselves as *British* (9 respondents), and those who described themselves as "both" or qualified their first choice of British (or Indian) by saying that they would also describe themselves as Indian (or British), (14 respondents).

Identity Choice and Attitudes to Culture

While the attitudes to Indian culture expressed by members of the three groups were not entirely distinct, there was some systematic variation. Those choosing Indian identity were, on the whole, less critical of traditional Indian moral and social norms than other respondents; this group included respondents who expressed unqualified support for arranged marriages and for the maintenance of strong parental discipline. They also tended to stress features which distinguish them from white Britons.

For example:

> 8. "I like the Indian way of life – the atmosphere, our rel-
>   igion. Being British means not caring whether your neigh-
>   bour is living or dying. Indians help each other and it
>   seems that the British don't."
>
> 9. "We are coloured Hindus – how can we be British?"
>
> 10. "We are different and in some ways we should stay diff-
>   erent. Who wants standardization? Why should everybody
>   be the same?"

Those choosing British identity tended, as one might expect, to emphasize their right to be British, while not ignoring the problems this involved:

> 11. "Parents try to keep us within their culture; this just
>   reflects their upbringing. But I feel I can behave in
>   certain ways because I am British."
>
> 12. "I am just like British people and I am faithful to this
>   country. I was in India but I always support this country
>   – even when I saw MCC play cricket in India. We have race
>   discrimination sometimes and then I want to say strongly
>   that I am British."

In this group were four of those five respondents who believed that there was nothing of Indian culture that they valued sufficiently to want to pass on to the next generation.

For example:

> 13. "I don't feel very proud of it (having an Indian back-
>   ground). I have a language problem because my parents
>   know no English at home."

Members of the "mixed" identity group represented in very general terms that body of opinion which favoured cultural development through the synthesis of British and Indian elements.

> 14. "At the moment I'm not fully in Indian culture or fully
>   westernized. On occasions I get the best from both sides."

Identity Choice and Attitudes to Language

In terms of their attitudes to the Gujarati language, members of the three identity
-choice groups were much more distinct. Those choosing Indian identity were much
more positively orientated towards the use and maintenance of Gujarati, being dis-
proportionately represented amongst the high scorers on the scale of attitudes.
Those in the "mixed" identity group generally obtained average scores, and those
choosing British identity tended to be amongst the lowest scorers. These findings,
and their statistical analysis, are summarized in Table 1 (below).

TABLE 1 Attitudes to Gujarati and Identity Choice

N	Identity Choice	Mean Attitude Score	H (Kruskal-Wallace one-way analysis of variance)
9	British	36.1	15.00
14	Indian/British	39.9	(significant at
15	Indian	47.3	χ = .001)

Identity choice was also related to views expressed on the importance of Gujarati
for social life. Those (18) respondents who believed either that it had no importance, or provided only "instrumental" reasons for its continued use (e.g.,
speaking to monolingual Indians or those whose standard of English was poor) were
drawn exclusively from British and "mixed" identity groups. Those choosing Indian
identity referred to the importance of the language in other cultural spheres,
including talking to friends, going to the temple, festivals, weddings. They also
laid most emphasis on the function of language for maintaining links with their
Indian homeland and cultural heritage, and so generally provided "integrative"
rather than "instrumental" reasons for knowing Gujarati (Gardner and Lambert,
1972).

15. "My mother teaches my little brother Indian fairy tales -
     we send him to a special Gujarat class for two hours twice
     a week. We encourage him to have some idea of the past."

16. "If everyone spoke English the (Indian) culture would die
     out."

Four of these respondents said they would always choose to speak Gujarati if this
were possible and all justified this in terms of stressing their ethnic relations
to other Indians.

For example:

17. "If I didn't speak Gujarati, I would feel drowned in a
     bucket of water. I would suffocate if I didn't speak
     Gujarati. If an Indian tries to speak to me in English
     I always ask 'Can't you speak Gujarati?' If he can't I
     feel distant from him."

In contrast, another four respondents said they would always prefer to use English,
and these were all drawn from the "mixed" and British identity choice groups.

For example:

18. "I was at a polytechnic in London and a year passed before
     I spoke any Gujarati. Even when I met a Gujarati from
     Leicester we got to know each other in English and wouldn't
     dream of speaking anything else."

Relation of Attitudes and Identity Choices to Demographic Data

Identity choice did not show any discernible relationship to demographic variables (years spent in Britain, country of origin, sex). Variation in attitudes to language and culture were also unrelated to these variables.

CONCLUSIONS

The range of attitudes to Gujarati and traditional Indian culture found within this narrow sample of Leicester's Gujarati-speaking population should warn against assuming that members of ethnolinguistic minority groups share, by virtue of their common background, a similar set of attitudes to their ethnic language and a similar conception of their place in wider society. Patterns of bilingual usage (rather than attitudes to language) studied by some researchers (e.g., Greenfield, 1972) do not draw attention to such variation. The assumption tends to be that the use of certain languages in certain situations has the same personal significance for all the members of a speech community. In many of their social interactions, the linguistic choice of young Gujaratis (and probably most other first and second generation immigrants) is determined by the competence of their interlocutors. They deal with monolingual, older Asian people at home and in community gatherings, and monolingual English people in school, in city stores and so on. Respondents' attitudes towards Gujarati, or about the significance of using a particular language for defining or stressing their cultural identity, will not necessarily be reflected in their patterns of bilingual usage.[5]

Earlier in this paper, it was suggested that ethnic self-identity could best be understood as an individual's constructive response to a particular set of social circumstances. It seems that the social circumstances of our respondents, as a group, are conducive to the development of different ethnic self-identities which reflect different degrees of attachment to one or other of the cultural traditions to which they are exposed.

It appears, moreover, that language has a significant role in this cultural self-orientation. For our respondents, the two languages, English and Gujarati, would seem to symbolize membership of the Indian ethnic community and of the wider British society respectively. The likelihood of encountering a student who proudly considers him or herself Indian (rather than British) but who has no special interest in the perpetuation of the Gujarati language is low. The development of a British identity, on the other hand, seems to be associated with a relative disinterest in Gujarati.

Thus, attitudes to language amongst our sample seem to be associated with, and are perhaps a function of, an individual's conception of the most desirable future for themselves and their ethnic group within British society. Those who opted for British identity seem to favour assimilation of their group into the mainstream, English-speaking society; those choosing Indian identity favour a more pluralistic

---

[5]Such attitudes may, of course, be reflected in aspects of *speech style* rather than language choice - for example, accent and the frequency of "interference" features from one language when speaking another (Giles, Bourhis and Taylor, 1977; Mercer, 1978).

cultural development, in which their group's ethnic (and ethnolinguistic) identity is maintained.

For our sample of Gujaratis, therefore, language does seem to be an important aspect of and focus for ethnic identity. Whether similar attitudes towards language and culture exist in the wider Gujarati-speaking population in Leicester we cannot yet say. It may be that the close association of language attitudes with ethnic identity is less pronounced amongst older members of the Gujarati community. Trudgill and Tzavaras (1977), in their study of Albanian Greeks (Arvanites), found that speaking their ethnic language (Arvanitika) was a less significant aspect of ethnic identity for older people who nevertheless spoke the language more than did younger Arvanites.

The attitudes of the more assimilationist Gujarati speakers (like those choosing "mixed" or British identity in our sample) may, of course, be affected in the future by the extent to which their expectations of becoming "truly British" are realized. As Giles, Bourhis and Taylor (1977) point out, frustration in that respect is likely to encourage a renewed interest in aspects of cultural heritage on the part of ethnic group members, and this may include enthusiastic language maintenance efforts. The developing situation in Leicester may prove a particularly interesting one for the study of the dynamic relationship between language and ethnicity.

Acknowledgements

We are grateful to the staff and students of Charles Keene College and Wyggeston College, Leicester, for their co-operation in this research. We also thank Howard Giles, Jennifer Hurstfield and Eta Schneiderman for their comments on the earlier version of this paper.

REFERENCES

Ballard R. & Ballard C. (1977) The Sikhs: The development of South Asian settlements in Britain, in A. Watson (ed.): Between two cultures, Blackwell, Oxford.

A. Brah, M. Fuller, D. Loudon & R. Miles, Experimenter effects and the ethnic cueing phenomenon, Working Papers on Ethnic Relations, No.3, S.S.R.C., Bristol (1977).

Cohen, A. (1974) Urban ethnicity, Tavistock, London.

Fishman, J.A. (1977) Language and ethnicity, in H. Giles (ed.): Language, ethnicity and intergroup relations, Academic Press, London.

Gardner, R.C. & Lambert, W.E. (1972) Attitudes and motivation in second language learning, Newbury House, Rowley, Mass.

Giles, H., Bourhis, R.Y. & Taylor, D.M. (1977) Towards a theory of language in ethnic group relations, in H. Giles (ed.): Language, ethnicity and intergroup relations, Academic Press, London.

Greenfield, L. (1977) Situational measures of normative language views in relation to person, place and topic among Puerto Rican bilinguals, in J.A. Fishman (ed.): Advances in the sociology of language, Mouton, The Hague.

Gumperz, J.J. (1971) Language in social groups, Stanford University Press, Stanford, California.

Mercer, N. (1978) Language and social experience, in N. Mercer & D. Edwards: Communication and context, (Block 4, P232 Language Development), Open University Press, Milton Keynes.

Ryan, E.B. & Carranza, M. (1977) Ingroup and outgroup reactions to Mexican American language varieties, in H. Giles (ed.): Language, ethnicity and intergroup relations, Academic Press, London.

Trudgill, P. & Tzavaras, G.A. (1977) Why Albanian Greeks are not Albanians: Language shift in Attica and Biotia, in H. Giles (ed.): Language, ethnicity and intergroup relations, Academic Press, London.

Watson, A. (1977) Between two cultures, Blackwell, Oxford.

AN ECOLOGICAL AND BEHAVIOURAL ANALYSIS OF ETHNOLINGUISTIC CHANGE IN WALES[1]

C. H. Williams

North Staffordshire Polytechnic, U.K.

In this paper I am concerned to examine some of the correlates of language change in contemporary Wales, and to focus specifically on the relationship between language decline and ethnic mobilization at the aggregate level. My aim is threefold: first, to identify the importance of a spatial perspective in the study of language change; second, to present the main results of a multi-variate analysis of culture regions for the period 1961-1971; and, finally, to present some general results of a behavioural level inquiry into attitudes towards language and nationalism, undertaken in Gwynedd, a region of North Wales (Williams, 1978).

LANGUAGE CHANGE: A SPATIAL PERSPECTIVE

Cultural geographers have traditionally adopted a structural approach to language analysis (Bowen and Carter, 1975a, 1975b). This involves the interpretation of cross-sectional distribution patterns as a pointer to the processes of ethnic change operative in the situation. Previous studies in Wales have concentrated on a core-periphery paradigm of intercultural relations, with a "domain" representing the social and spatial interface between the competing culture areas. It focuses on *areal patterns of change*. rather than the social initiators of change, and assumes a diffusion process of cultural encroachment whereby spatially contiguous zones of the minority culture area are gradually absorbed into the majority culture realm. This simple tripartite division into core, domain and periphery has been criticized not so much for its structure, but for its over-reliance on unidimensional language variables which are used to construct the distribution patterns of distinct culture areas in Wales (Williams, in press). Much can be learned about the regional variation in language density by mapping census derived language data. Figures 1 and 2 attempt to reveal the basic structure of spoken Welsh for 1971 and for the change in the period 1961-1971. It is apparent that by 1971 the pattern revealed a fragmented western core area of up to 70% plus Welsh speakers with deep indentations made along several major route-ways, e.g., the Conway Valley, Cardig-

---

[1]My thanks to Mr. Guy Lewis, University College, Swansea and Miss Jane Cartwright, North Staffordshire Polytechnic, for their assistance in the preparation of the maps, and to Margaret Boulton, North Staffordshire Polytechnic, for her assistance in typing.

anshire Bay coast, the Severn Valley-Aberystwyth corridor, Anglesey and North Pem-
brokshire. But even within the core we note that the actual percentage decline
(Figure 2) is quite strong especially around the urban areas of the north and west
and the industrial communities of the south west. These transitional areas (40 -
70% Welsh speech) where the decline is most acute form the domain zone, which, it
is suggested, is a critical feature of language change in Wales at the aggregate
level.

Previous studies have demonstrated the importance of the language issue in mobilizing Welsh national consciousness (Thomas and Williams, 1976, 1977; Butt Philip,
1975). It has been suggested that nationalism developed initially as a response
to cultural encroachment consequent to the increased incorporation of Wales into
the developing U.K. state system. The spread of Anglicization was identified as
the key process in the diminution of Welsh ethnolinguistic vitality. This has been
described as a complex process comprising seven main features, namely:

> 1. The large-scale immigration of unilingual English workers
>   into South Wales consequent to industrialization and the urban
>   development in the coalfield and port sectors.
>
> 2. The introduction of compulsory English education after the
>   1870 Education Act.
>
> 3. Closer economic and administrative association with the rest
>   of the U.K. following modernization and the standardization of
>   education.
>
> 4. The increasing rate of immigration into the Welsh core area
>   by unilingual English speakers, many of whom purchase second
>   homes at inflated prices causing a price spiral in the prop-
>   erty market which local prospective purchasers resent.
>
> 5. The rapid increase in rural depopulation and population
>   transfer which accompanies the emigration of young Welsh sp-
>   eakers and the immigration of predominantly aged English sp-
>   eakers. This age and economic imbalance is compounded by a
>   cultural imbalance operating through language shift, as the
>   local communities become increasingly acculturated to the
>   immigrant speech, a process which permeates the whole socio-
>   cultural structure of rural areas.
>
> 6. The fragmented nature of the internal communication system
>   (designed to facilitate through-traffic from London to Ire-
>   land) militates against the development of national cohesion,
>   which in the past has been partly predicted on cultural and
>   spatial isolation.
>
> 7. The final factor is the impact of the English dominated mass
>   media which consistently reinforces the dominance of English
>   as the appropriate medium of communication (Williams, 1976).

Ethnic Response

As a reaction to cultural encroachment the Welsh Nationalist Party (Plaid Cymru)
was founded in 1925. This was initially a cultural nationalist organization aiming
primarily to arrest the decline in the language and to safeguard the associated
Welsh ethnic identity rather than to promote political separatism. However, it
achieved very little support at this time. In the last decade, following the continued decline in the use of Welsh, from 26% of the population in 1961 to 20.8%
(542,425) in 1971, the future of the language and the resurgence of nationalism
have emerged as major social issues. In this situation the language has re-emerged
as the main symbol of ethnic identity and again provided the initial impetus for the

resurgence of political separatist feeling. A variety of organizations have been
formed to reverse the linguistic decline, most notably the Welsh Language Society
in 1962 (Williams, 1977). This organization aimed to obtain "official status for
the Welsh language equal to that of English in Wales". With a subsequent programme
of demonstrations and campaigns, the Society constantly publicized the inequalities
of the language. This and similar activity by other Welsh organizations resulted
in the establishment of the Hughes-Parry Committee in 1963 to inquire into the legal status of Welsh. This culminated in the Welsh Language Act (1967) designed to
allow movement towards the "Principle of Equal Validity of Welsh and English" in
such spheres as the courts and public administration in Wales. Support for Welsh
nationalism has been spatially uneven, as has involvement in the cultural pressure
groups. Plaid Cymru success has been greatest in the core area, but even here
ethnic mobilization has not been channelled exclusively into nationalist support;
key spatial variations in political affiliation remain, which language-related data
alone cannot explain. In an attempt to provide a more comprehensive description of
the correlates of language change a multi-variate analysis was undertaken for the
period 1961-1971.

AN ECOLOGICAL APPROACH TO LANGUAGE CHANGE 1961-1971

The study adopted a form of factor analysis, a generic method of areal classification which permits the construction of grouped data units into regions which display certain similarities (Johnston, 1976; Olsen, 1976). The justification for
using a regionalization procedure rests on two convictions. First, it is of interest in its own right, as a traditional concern of spatial analysis. Second, it
can describe spatial patterns of association and provide ecological contexts within which more detailed behavioural studies of the processes of ethnic change can
be undertaken. In addition, the resulting regions can be used as preliminary
frameworks for the implementation of functionally and culturally related language
planning zones (Cox, 1970).

Data on 48 variables were calculated for the 168 Local Authority Units existent in
Wales prior to the 1974 Local Government Reorganization. The variables (Table 1)
related to age structure, social class, residential mobility, linguistic characteristics, socio-economic attributes, household tenure and amenities, variations in
the levels of educational experience, voting behaviour and religiosity. Thirty-
four of the variables used in the 1961 analysis were derived from the national census returns for that year, and inevitably reflect the limitations of that source.
The eight voting behaviour variables were taken from the published results of the
elections of 1959 and 1964, the two primary indicators of partisan choice either
side of the 1961 census data source. The other political variable selected was
the incidence of Plaid Cymru branches per 1,000 population. As with the electoral
behaviour, the branch organization data was transformed from constituency data units to local authority data units. The final group of variables reflects the basic dimension of organized religion in Wales. Past research has shown the critical
role played by religion in the maintenance of a distinct Welsh culture, whilst significant spatial variations in the distribution and strength of major religious
systems have been evident throughout modern Welsh history. Data on the four major
types of religious adherence were collected from denominational handbooks and converted into appropriate indices of denominational strength per Local Authority Unit.
It was anticipated that the additional data on voting and religion would supplement the valuable information derived from the census, and provide a more meaningful differentiation of culture regions than had hitherto been accomplished.

The Analysis

Sixty-two per cent of the estimated variance in the set of 48 variables was acc-

ounted for by 8 components with eigen values greater than 1.5. The primary solution of the Principal Components Analysis produced distinct components relating to
the following dimensions: ethnic composition, housing amenities with a rural-urban
divide, employment, housing tenure, Conservative voting, migration balance, out-
migration and low social status, female unemployment and nursery school provision
(Busteed, 1975)[2].

Now, although the primary solution is able to summarize the greatest proportion of
the variance, for purposes of precise interpretation, the components may be too
generally structured. Consequently, a varimax rotation procedure was adopted with
interesting results. The main effect of the rotation has been to reconstitute component one as a more precise dimension of Welsh ethnicity with component seven re-
organized as a component of social class and education. In addition, component
five now emerges as a separate Labour-Liberal voting component (Table 1). This
paper will deal with only the principal component (ethnicity) for 1961 and 1971[3].

Component 1 may be interpreted as a Welsh ethnic dimension which is comprised of
three elements, namely Welsh speaking, religious non-conformity and radical political support for the once firmly established Liberal Party and its more modern com-
petitor in the form of Plaid Cymru. At the negative end of the scale we have a
strong loading showing the stability of the Conservative vote at both the 1959 and
the 1964 election. Historically, the Conservative Party has been perceived mainly
as a political organization reflecting both class interests alien to the mass of
the rural Welsh electorate, and as an agent for constitutional consolidation related to the Anglicization process. The persistence of this politico-cultural antipathy supports the distinctiveness of "Y Fro Gymraeg" in terms of its electoral
history (Carter, 1976). The analysis also demonstrates the organizational structure of Welsh Nationalism as being closely associated with the proportionate density of Welsh speakers in 1961. Thus, at the aggregate level these three elements,
Welsh speaking, non-conformity and radical voting behaviour, can be suggested to
constitute the core of Welsh ethnicity during this period.

----

[2]The religious data was compiled from denominational handbooks and the official
records of the Church in Wales and the Catholic Directories. The data units were
then matched as closely as possible to the Local Authority units used in the analysis; some matching problems were encountered in the transformation procedure, but
they were resolved satisfactorily by aggregating parish units upward to the Local
Authority boundaries. The need for including religion as a variable is clear as
evidenced by this call from Busteed in 1975, "There has been no enumeration of
religious affiliation in Great Britain since 1851, yet it is undeniable that Protestant non-conformity was a powerful element in Welsh politics in the late nineteenth and early twentieth century serving to reinforce the anti-Conservative and
radical tendencies in the Welsh electorate and still surviving in some areas today".

[3]Less conservative but generally accepted cut-off points (eigen values equal to or
greater than 1.0) resulted in thirteen components accounting for 75.45% of the data
variance.

The Core

The scores for each Local Authority unit indicate a distinct spatial pattern of
variation. Figure 3 shows that the Local Authorities with high Welsh ethnicity
rates (+0.5 S.D.) are concentrated in a single culture region running north-south
from Anglesey to Carmarthenshire. The rates are highest in Merionethshire centred
on the two culture nodes of Bala and Dolgellau together with their adjoining rural
districts. Other prominent high order culture areas include the Llyn Peninsula
and a number of rural market centres, viz., Llangefni, Tywyn, Newcastle Emlyn and
Llandeilo. A further category of tourist centres may also be delimited, e.g.,
Pwllheli and Barmouth. Interestingly enough, the only settlement in this core area
characterized by a traditional industrial-economic base is Ammanford on the west-
ward fringe of the South Wales coalfield, which stands in marked contrast to the
remainder of the coalfield area.

A substantial part of Cardiganshire and Carmarthenshire is included in the categories falling between +1 S.D. and +1.5 S.D. displaying a strong internal homogeneity for these counties in terms of the variables enumerated by this component.
It is evident that rural areas are far more "Welsh" than are urban areas, a finding which tends to support the interpretation that urban locales tend to act as
Anglicizing agents in this process of culture change. The same rural-urban divide
is repeated in Gwynedd, with Caernarfon, Gwyrfai, Porthmadoc and Criccieth all substantially differentiated from their rural hinterlands. In addition, Caernarfonshire exhibits a clear divide between the western and eastern part of the county
in terms of its cultural composition. Below this level at the +0.5 S.D. cut-off
point are the outlying fringe areas of the core complex. They are characteristic
of the industrial and urban parts of "Y Fro Gymraeg" and include such locations as
Carmarthen, Burry Port, Llanelli and Cwmaman in the south, Aberystwyth and New
Quay in the west and Llanidloes, Machynlleth R.D. and Llanrwst further north. If
the tripartite division elaborated earlier is valid it can be suggested that these
are the towns most subject to the influences which dominate the domain and are thus
most likely to be removed from the culture core if the Anglicization process continues unabated.

Thus far we have suggested a close social and spatial relationship between these
contributory factors of language, religion and radicalism. However, not all the
core area, as traditionally defined, has been described by component one; the most
striking exception is Anglesey. This county has always been prominent in Welsh
affairs, so much so that historically it is referred to as "Môn the mother of
Wales", which epitomized Welsh rural life. The evidence of 1961 suggests that most
of the county is marginal to the core region in terms of the variables of our analysis. Although the ability to speak Welsh is as high as that recorded elsewhere
ethnic identity has not been mobilized to the same extent, in that Anglesey continues to have a political structure quite distinct from the core. Its party allegiance is more typical of the U.K. norm, with a bi-polar contest between Labour
and Conservative dominating the 1959 and 1964 elections. (Labour's share of the
votes rose from 47.0% in 1959 to 48.2% in 1964, whilst the Tory share remained
steady at 24.9%. Plaid Cymru's share dropped considerably from 14.6% in 1959 to
only 6.4% in 1964. The Liberals, meanwhile, appeared to have gained most from the
Nationalist decline, their vote climbing from 13.5% to 20.4% in 1964).

Religious affiliation in Anglesey also showed a more even distribution than was
true of the core, both in inter-denominational and inter-areal terms. Although
Welsh non-conformism was the leading religious system it was not nearly as dominant as it was in the core, e.g., Bala or Dolgellau, whilst both Anglican and Catholic adherence remained relatively strong. Consequently, although the percentage
of Welsh speakers was the second highest per county in 1961 at 75.5% (cf., Merionethshire at 75.9%), it would appear that Anglesey's cultural composition is more

similar to the Welsh average than to the mobilized core region. This being so, it
will prove interesting to see whether her socio-cultural environments will prove as
capable of reinforcing the maintenance of Welsh in the succeeding decade.

The Domain

The Local Authority units which cluster either side of the mean form two distinct
regions. The first is a girdle stretching inland from the north Caernarfonshire
coast skirting the core area as far as Builth in Mid-Wales. The second is a region
corresponding to the Glamorganshire and Monmouthshire coalfield district with out-
lyers along the coast from the Gower to Cowbridge. In general terms, this fringe
may be related to Meinig's domain concept (Meinig, 1967), that is, an area which
was until recently still dominated by the indigenous culture, but with less intensity and less homogeneity than in the core. However, this description would seem
to be too gross as extensive tracts of Dyffryn Conwy, Myndd Hiraethog, Aled R.D.,
Nant Ffrancon, Amlwch and Beaumaris would thereby be divorced from the core.
Nevertheless, we may be witnessing differential rates of absorption within the
domain, with the northern sector more able to withstand cultural encroachment
than the southern sector. It is suggested that within this domain more micro-
level research should be undertaken to measure whether it does represent an intercultural interface at anything but an aggregate level.

The Periphery

The cultural periphery, where Welsh culture traits are weakest and ethnic mobilization slight, is comprised of four distinct areas, namely: 1. the North Wales
coastline where tourism and retirement functions have become dominant since the
early 'fifties; 2. the border counties of Brecon and Radnor which have long since
been completely Anglicized since Tudor times; 3. South Pembrokeshire, "Little England beyond Wales", an English enclave since the late sixteenth century, and; 4.
the Severn coastal plain comprising the major urban-industrial corridor in the
Welsh economy and including the conurbations of Newport, Cardiff, Penarth and
Barry. These are the areas where proportionately the language and nationalist voting is weakest and where the largest religious system is the Anglican Church followed by English non-conformist and Catholic adherents, a feature not untypical of
urban areas throughout the nation. Despite their position at the polar extreme of
the core, these areas have recently become significant in terms of Welsh cultural
revival as they represent the locales of Local Authorities who have attempted to
promote the use of Welsh at all levels of education with some creditable success.
This is in large measure due to the Welsh-speaking middle classes resident in the
south east, but it also reflects the development of an indigenous urban Welsh-
speaking generation for whom the appeals of nationalists to return to the core in
order to consolidate the existing order holds little sway. They have sought to
argue that it is only by concentrating efforts in the Anglicized areas that Wales
will eventually become a fully bilingual nation. This forms a major policy schism
within the ranks of cultural nationalists who appear not to accept that both core
and periphery can be mobilized in defence of the culture.

Thus we have demonstrated a principal component which covers a spectrum of linguistic, religious and political correlates of Welsh culture. The ecological pattern
points to clear, spatially defined culture regions, within which a number of processes affecting the position of the Welsh language in 1961 may be identified
prior to a more detailed analysis.

Welsh Culture Change 1961-1971

A second Principal Component Analysis was undertaken for the 1971 census period.
It was hoped that as several new sources of information were available, the 1971
analysis would be an improvement in terms of the range and sensitivity of the measures used to define culture regions. Comparison of Tables 1 and 2 will indicate
that the number of census-derived variables has declined; those that remain are
more specific, especially those related to language. It was possible to choose
from an increased range of language data, six variables being selected for the
final analysis: the extent of bilingualism (var.26), change in the past decade
(var.27), Welsh speech for two important age groups, 3-15 years old, and the aged
population 65+ (vars.24 and 25). It was also possible to include reading and writing proficiency (var.28) and the percentage aged 3 and over able to write in Welsh
(var.29). The final set of variables (38-43) does not have a 1961 counterpart.
It concerns the distribution of cultural societies, namely the Urdd (a school-based
organization promoting the language and culture), the Aelwyd centres (adult Urdd
centres) and cells of the Welsh Language Society, together with Nursery School and
Plaid Cymru branches. More attention has thus been paid to specific manifestations
of cultural activity as well as the more traditional, yet static, indices derived
from census sources.

A varimax rotation was adopted for the seven components identified by the primary
solution with the result that the first component summarized 19.06% of the data
variance to form a Welsh "ethnic" component similar to 1961. Two variables correlate over 0.9, namely the percentage able to speak English and Welsh (var.26),
the percentage aged over 3 able to read Welsh (var.28). These language functions
are strongly associated with support for Plaid Cymru at the 1970 election, its
branch organization and with non-conformist adherence, a repeat of the 1961 findings. However, the addition of new variables in 1971 has served to enrich the
character of this dimension. Thus, the Welsh medium junior schools variable, Urdd
centres and Aelwyd centres are all strongly associated on the component. Three
modifications to the 1961 component structure are evident and indicate, in part,
how the culture complex has changed in the decade. The first is the stronger loading of non-conformity in general and of Welsh non-conformity in particular by 1971,
indicating a strengthening of the tie between religion and culture maintenance in
the core. The second change is the relative decline in the strength of the negative Conservative loading from -0.8165 for 1959 to -0.487 in 1970. This suggests
a weakening of the party polarization evident in the 1961 analysis. Given this,
an even more significant modification is the virtual eclipse of Liberal support by
1970. (In 1959 the Liberal variable loaded at 0.5431, by 1970 it had failed to
register above the minimum threshold of 0.4). Conversely, Plaid Cymru's level of
association has risen consistently from 0.7574 in 1959 to 0.831 by the 1970 election. The analysis suggests that the Nationalist Party is replacing the Liberal
Party as the dominant political organization in much of rural Welsh-speaking Wales.

The spatial pattern of culture regions confirms the 1961 division of Wales into
core, domain and periphery, but at a reduced level and with some major changes.
The core may be defined by those areas scoring over +1.0 S.D., the domain by those
areas scoring between ±1.0 S.D. either side of the mean, and the periphery by those
areas falling below the mean on Figure 4. To the leading nodes of Bala and Penllyn
has been added Gwyrfai R.D. at 2.0 S.D. This addition reflects an increase in the
activity of Plaid Cymru, the Welsh Language Society and Welsh medium junior schools
in these areas during the intervening decade. However, the solid western core of
1961 has become fragmented by 1971 such that a bifurcated pattern is now evident
with two complementary culture regions centered respectively on Llŷn and Merioneth
in the north and Cardigan and Carmarthenshire in the south. Elsewhere the core
area has experienced decline, especially around urban centres. Because of this
decline, especially the Liberal vote, Anglesey and the middle core are now more
similar than they were in 1961. In view of this, Anglesey in 1961 might be des-

cribed as in an advanced stage of decline, which other parts of the core have reached subsequently by 1971.

The domain has also experienced a complex pattern of change. Signs of an increase in cultural organization are apparent in the Ogwen, Aled, Ruthin and Hiraethog districts which reflect the establishment of more Urdd and Aelwyd branches, together with moderate increases in Nationalistic support and an extension of Plaid Cymru branches. Other areas in the domain have experienced a decline in the maintenance of the language and culture, especially around the urban centres of Wrexham, Newtown and Llanllwchaiarn emphasizing the apparent difficulty of halting language erosion. The southern portion of the domain is a paradox. It has suffered acute losses in terms of actual numbers of Welsh-speakers (cf., Figure 1) and yet has also witnessed increases in all the cultural activities included in the component, together with the election of a Nationalist M.P. and the expansion of Plaid Cymru's branch network. Consequently, the southern domain appears to have been relatively stable during the decade, able to maintain its position vis à vis the core which it fringes. This stability, as recorded on Figure 3, obviously hides quite marked changes in the cultural composition of the area, and reveals one of the main deficiencies of the ecological approach. A significant decline is also evident in the coalfield district of the south. The 1961 pattern showed a broad band of "Welshness" extending from Pontardawe to Abercarn. By 1971 only pockets of distinctiveness remain, as at Aberdare and Caerffili where there are strong Welsh junior schools, above average concentrations of Welsh-speakers and where Nationalist support is well above average for industrial South Wales.

For the rest of Wales, the periphery is in the process of becoming more uniform; witness the absence of the distinctiveness which separated the coalfield from the coast in 1961. In part, this is attributable to the less extreme negative Tory correlation but it also relates to the general decline of a predominantly aged Welsh-speaking population which have previously inhabited the coal-rich valleys of the south. A similar uniformity characterizes most of Pembrokeshire, Brecon and Radnor. However, the cultural interface of the Camarthenshire/Brecon and Cardiganshire/Radnor border area is still a well-established feature of Welsh geography and continues to be a distinctive zone where core and periphery adjoin.

Comparison of the leading components for 1961 and 1971 suggests that the fragmentation identified by the structural analysis (Figure 1) is providing a more complex pattern within the core area. Cultural regeneration and the nationalist resurgence in predominantly Welsh-speaking environments and in selected Anglicized areas has served to offset, in part, an increased polarization between the two speech communities at the aggregate level, and is suggesting an overall diminution in regional variation which is likely to continue apace.

Interim Conclusion

It is apparent that the Welsh culture has undergone substantial structural change recently (a feature examined in the remaining components of the original analysis). Some of the more significant changes have been identified, e.g., the stronger identification of religion and nationalism in certain areas, i.e., Gwyrfai, Bala and Dolgellau; the comparative failure of nationalist appeals in other areas, e.g., Cardiganshire and the Machynlleth area; the increased penetration of the core by the Conservatives and the eclipse of Liberal support throughout most of the Welsh heartland, and finally a significant cultural decline in the domain and in the southern coalfield district in particular. When these findings are supplemented by the results of the other component structures in the P.C.A. we find that unemployment, an aged population structure, sub-standard housing and increased rates of depopulation offer a depressing forecast for the core's ethnolinguistic vitality in the future. Some redress of grievances has been used as the main justification

for continued nationalist growth, especially those economic grievances which can
be attributed as emanating from "English misrule". Rhetoric apart, it does seem
that Plaid Cymru's development is primarily based on its ability to mobilize
"ethnic" consciousness amongst the population of the core. We have demonstrated
how traditionally Liberal areas have swung towards the Nationalist camp and suggest that future Nationalist gains will be in the areas of continued Liberal decline (e.g., Cardiganshire). However, because of their tenuous hold on existing
constituencies (Carmarthen, Merioneth and Caernarfon) there is no guarantee that
they will remain the dominant party of the core. If the national trend towards
uniformity continues it is likely that other parties, especially the Labour Party,
will be able to mobilize support on the Welsh issue. This is particularly appos-
ite if the current devolution proposals under discussion in Westminster serve to
appease much of the hitherto Nationalist channelled regional discontent in rural
Wales.

THE NORTH WALES CASE STUDY: A BEHAVIOURAL APPROACH

The methodology adopted in this second case study was adopted as a result of the
need for more discriminating indices of language decline and nationalist affiliation than previously discussed. The ecological approach, whilst improving on the
structural approach of earlier studies, does nevertheless produce a pattern of
broadly homogeneous culture areas reflective of their dominant socio-cultural
traits. A behavioural study, adopted in conjunction with the ecological approach,
allows a more specific investigation of behaviour traits and attitudes at the individual level.

We have seen that the two issues of the decline of the Welsh language and the resurgence of Welsh nationalism have been examined by geographers via the spatial
analysis of published data at an essentially macro-ecological scale only. From
the findings of such studies the processes of change operating have been inferred.
It was the intention of this study to test whether the inferred processes could
be demonstrated to occur at the micro-behavioural scale of analysis. The hypotheses to be tested which were suggested by the ecological investigations were:

> 1. The continued significance of a diffusional spatial patt-
> ern of linguistic decline suggested that this resulted from
> the development of "attitudes which acknowledge the supremacy
> of English" in areas which sequentially become characterized
> by "moderate percentages of Welsh-speakers".

> 2. That, with regard to nationalist resurgence, support was
> strongest in the predominantly Welsh-speaking "cultural" core
> areas – suggesting to 1974 an "ethnic" rather than widespread
> "political" basis of support for Plaid Cymru and national sep-
> aratism.

It was clear from the work of Bowen and Carter (1974) and Thomas and Williams
(1976) that the language decline had been greatest in the areas characterized by
moderate levels of Welsh-speaking (40%-70%) mainly located in a broad north-south
belt extending along the eastern margin of the core area from Flint to Pembroke.
Bowen and Carter considered this feature particularly significant, because in the
most recent inter-censal period they had expected that the influence of the English
language dominated mass media would have reduced the relationship between the pattern of decline and spatial contiguity to Anglicizing forces. Consequently, they
hypothesized that the continued importance of a spatial pattern of decline was related to the fact that it is in areas where the Welsh language is only spoken by
a moderate proportion of the population that it begins to be rejected as the accepted medium of communication, and that once this process is initiated there quickly follows "a slow and tacit acceptance of attitudes which acknowledge the suprem-

acy of English" – which in turn accelerates the process of linguistic decline.
Their study has identified some of the processes operative at the aggregate scale
but they conclude:

> "No study such as this can successfully identify the mechan-
> isms of change. Decrease in the proportion speaking Welsh
> can come about by differential emigration of Welsh-speakers
> from an area, the immigration of English monoglots, or by
> the death of Welsh-speakers, presumably the elderly, where
> the young have not been brought up to speak the language.
> But beyond the mechanism and at the disaggregated scale of
> inquiry lies the whole field of motivation and attitudes.
> Both mechanism and attitude can, of course, be inferred from
> changes in pattern, but such a procedure, when unrelated to
> direct investigation, is most dangerous. Nevertheless, these
> changes in pattern can be used to identify distribution pro-
> cesses and the inferences drawn provide the hypotheses which
> need to be tested in a behavioural context." (Bowen and Carter,
> 1975).

The survey was conducted in the spring of 1975, and the sample population (n=605)
was divided into three categories relative to the socio-cultural environments in
which they lived:

    A – areas of predominant Welsh speech (+70%)

    B – areas of moderate Welsh speech (40%-70%)

    C – areas of predominant English speech (-40%)

The location of the survey sites are identified on Figure 5. If the character of
the local socio-cultural environment is a major determinant of linguistic decline
and nationalist resurgence, it is hypothesized that attitudes to the Welsh language and nationalism are likely to be most favourable amongst respondents residing
in Category A areas and to become less favourable progressively towards Category
C areas. The details of the sample population and their socio-cultural characteristics are discussed in detail elsewhere (Williams, 1978, chapters 6 and 7). In
general, the socio-cultural backgrounds of the three categories of respondents varied in accordance with the requirements of the analysis.

The Attitude Profiles

The respondents were presented with fourteen stimulus statements to which they
could respond on a five-point attitude scale ranging from strong agreement to strong
disagreement (Table 3). The attitude profiles constructed from the mean responses
of the three categories are presented later as a useful summary of a more comprehensive analysis undertaken in the original work.

Attitudes to the Welsh Language

The attitude profiles for the seven statements relating to the evaluation of Welsh
are illustrated by Figure 6. Only one statement (no.3) failed to produce the hypothesized progression from A to C. The first statement produced broadly similar
mean responses from each of the three categories which suggested an aggregate
agreement that Welsh is a difficult language to learn. The Anglicized Category C,
as anticipated, recorded the highest agreement with a mean response of 3.35, falling to 3.26 in the intermediate Category B, and to 3.21 in the Welsh core area A.
The strongest disagreement came from within the core group (11.5%), whilst 19.0%
recorded in the neutral position for Category C reflects an ambivalence towards the

language in this group. The second statement is more emotional in that it suggests that "Welsh people should not speak Welsh in the company of English people". It reflects a sentiment heard often in bilingual states whose languages differ in the relative status accorded to their members and to the often unbalanced nature of bilingualism as a societal feature. This statement reflects the status different-ial of Welsh and English and implies deference as a means of avoiding interpersonal tension and confrontation. Two main reactions were anticipated, either (a) disag-reement, indicating a degree of language loyalty and a conviction that it is app-ropriate to continue to use Welsh in the presence of unilingual Anglophones, or (b) agreement, based upon an individual's assessment of notions of politeness and correct behaviour involving language switching to accommodate the outsider. The responses to this statement may be taken as a partial indicator of the future strength of Welsh in an increasingly mixed linguistic situation. The process of language switching is recognized as an important mechanism by which minority lang-uages decline in general use. Overall, each category of respondents agreed with the suggestion of language switching, categories A and B recording identical mean responses (Table 4). In detail, there is a slight tendency for category A to ex-hibit a more positive response than category B which runs counter to the hypothes-ized progression. Two interpretations may be advanced to explain the unanticipated similarity of A and B. Core area deference could be interpreted as an expression of strength, allowing language switching because Anglophones in the core do not, as yet, pose a significant threat to the supremacy of Welsh. Consistent with this interpretation is the suggestion that there exists a far greater degree of inter-personal language tension within the intermediate category B, producing a more polarized set of attitudes and providing more conscious expressions of language loyalty among supporters of Welsh than was initially expressed.

The third statement suggested that "an increase in the use of Welsh would be a bad thing for life in Wales". The mean responses of the categories, although similar, did not vary in the hypothesized fashion from A to C. Category C's response at 71.4% disagreement surpasses B at 69% and comes close to Category A's response of 72.3% disagreement. These results indicate a clear majority in each category who do not think that attempts to increase the use of Welsh are necessarily detrimental to social well-being, an indication of the general sympathy towards the language in Wales, especially in the Anglicized areas. As anticipated, it is within the core that the strongest expression of disagreement with the statement is recorded at 30.9% (strongly disagree) compared with 18.5% in B and 16.7% in C (Table 2).

The fourth statement suggested a positive way in which the use of Welsh might be increased by stating that "the compulsory teaching of Welsh in schools should be increased considerably". This statement reflects the long term aim of Welsh lang-uage activists who have recently increased their pressure on central and local government to promote formal Welsh education. This is seen as the most effective method of introducing the language in areas where it is not habitually spoken by the majority. However, the element of compulsion is likely to add an emotional component to this statement. Thus it is possible that it could provoke an anti-pathetic response because of the limitation on language choice in educational mat-ters. The mean response for each category (Table 2) indicated that Category A respondents were the strongest advocates of increased Welsh education. Categories B and C recorded almost identical mean responses (3.10 and 3.11). The intermediate category is interesting as it recorded the lowest level of support, 44.5%, and the highest level of opposition, 42.0%, a very small margin indeed of 2.5% in favour of increased Welsh teaching. Opinion on Welsh-language education in intermediate areas is thus more polarized than in the other categories, as well as being more antagonistic to the increased use of Welsh than was initially anticipated.

The fifth statement also reflects a live issue in Welsh culture promotion, the provision of an expanded network of Welsh-medium radio and television programmes. The statement suggested that "more Welsh language programmes are needed on tele-

vision and radio". Unlike the previous profiles, which revealed an overall sympathy
to various facets of the promotion of the language, the present profile reveals a
more marked division of opinion between the Welsh influenced socio-cultural environments of A and B and the Anglicized environment of C. However, the internal pattern of response of B is more akin to C, because these latter categories have a
more even distribution of responses than A. Overall, the difference between supporters and opponents of Welsh broadcasting developments in Category A was some
25.4%, whilst respondents in B and C were less polarized, the difference in favour
of Welsh broadcasting being 7.5% and 6.1% respectively. It suggests that the generally tolerant sympathies towards the language can be replaced by opposition when
decisions to promote Welsh can be interpreted as a diminution of English services.
In such instances, choices are often perceived as zero-sum situations.

Statement six attempted to measure the utility of learning Welsh compared with
learning another European language, thus introducing a comparative, functional element into the assessment of Welsh. The profiles indicate a clear opinion divide
between A and C, with Category B's mean response taking up a medium position of
3.00. As with all measures of the mean, this position hides a delicate internal
balance in the distribution pattern of core area and intermediate area responses,
whilst the Anglicized area's aggregate response is clearly in favour of substitut-
ing another European language for Welsh in the sphere of education. The core area
pattern of response reveals that 43.7% are agreed with the statement, whilst only
42.9% disagree, with a further 13.0% recorded as being unsure of their opinion.
This is a remarkable finding, when one considers that 81% of core area respondents
are fluent Welsh-speakers. If such attitudes become implemented it has obvious
implications for future language maintenance in terms of the limited scope afforded
to Welsh even amongst those living in the heartland. It appears as though there is
some element of discrepancy between this response and previous patterns described
above. It reveals an inherent ambiguity towards Welsh which is common amongst many
minority language speakers. Members of such cultures readily admit the limitations
and idiosyncracies of their language (c.f., Basques, Frisians and Catalans), in an
international context, but defend their right to use and promote the language precisely because it is their own. However, it is clear that a substantial portion of
Category A respondents (43.7%) are, in principle, convinced that it is more useful
for children in Wales to learn another European language rather than Welsh. The
intermediate category revealed a near even division of opinion (43% in favour and
43.5% against the replacement of Welsh) indicating the polarized nature of attitudes in this intercultural milieux. These findings do not bode well for the future
utility of Welsh in an increasingly interdependent European community.

The final statement referred to the self-assessed ability of the respondent to bring
about a change in the Welsh language. It suggested that "there is nothing I can do
to change the present status of the Welsh language". The core area respondents
expressed the strongest disagreement with the suggestion of individual ineffectiveness, their mean response being 3.00. The intermediate category tended to support
the statement, with the highest percentage agreement of all categories at 61.0%,
accepting their lack of ability to influence the language situation. This tendency
was more pronounced for Category B than C where 56.4% agreed with the statement.
A substantial proportion of Category C (22.9%) were neutral on this issue indicating
their lack of will and/or capability to change the socio-political status of Welsh.

In general, it appears that all categories have a sympathetic attitude towards the
maintenance of Welsh. Clearer differences in response occur when questions of utility or compulsion are introduced (e.g., learning an alternative European language
or increasing Welsh media output). In such circumstances the sympathetic response
gives way to a more polarized set of attitudes both within and between categories.

Category Response Variance

A more detailed statistical examination of the distribution of responses was undertaken via a series of chi-square tests of the variation in the pattern of response
between adjacent categories for each statement. In general, the difference between Categories A and B was greater than that between B and C. In three cases
the difference was significant at the 0.01 level (statements 6 and 7) and in one
other (no.3) it was significant at the 0.05 level. By contrast, in only one case
was there a significant difference recorded between B and C (statement no.7 at
the 0.001 level). This suggests that Category B respondents were more inclined
to express attitudes similar to Category C, often unfavourable towards the maintenance of the language, although the difference was not marked in every case. A
more decisive break occurred between Categories A and C. In all seven cases the
difference was significant at at least the 0.05 level. In two of these cases (nos.
5 and 6) it was significant at the 0.01 level, and in one other case (no.7) it was
significant at the 0.001 level. Thus, the respective position of the three socio-
cultural environments had been confirmed at this aggregate level, with evidence
that the intermediate area expresses ambivalence towards Welsh and a pattern more
akin to the Anglicized periphery rather than the culture core area. A number of
features have been identified in this simple, preliminary analysis, which, if representative of more general processes, indicate that the use of Welsh will decline
further in the study area. Important mechanisms within this process are language
switching and the moderate levels of language loyalty recorded even within the
core. Also, much ambivalence was demonstrated re their own position as Welsh-
speakers in an increasingly interdependent modernizing state. The minority position is often more difficult to reconcile with the realization that little functional value is attached to the acquisition of the minority tongue by members of
the majority. The question then becomes one of retaining fluency and motivation
to use Welsh amongst members of the minority group even within the culture core
area.

Attitudes Towards Welsh Political Statements

The discussion on voting behaviour suggested that as Plaid Cymru was traditionally
a cultural nationalist party its strongest electoral base would be within the core
area. This association was confirmed by both the February and October elections
of 1974. Thus, it is anticipated that attitudes favourable towards Welsh independence would be strongest within Category A, and as with the language issue, become progressively weaker through the intermediate area (B) to reach its nadir in
Category C.

Only one of the statements (no.10) failed to produce the hypothesized decline in
the mean response score for each category. Consequently, support for the relationship between language intensity and political separation was found. The first
statement suggested that "Welsh people should be self-governing if they wish".
The strongest support for the issue came from the core, where 54.8% agreed on the
right of the majority to be granted self-government if that was the dominant popular will (Table 5). A similar level of support was recorded in Category B at
53.5%. Even though the statement deals with self-government in principle, only
47.9% of Category C were able to support such a move. These levels are in general lower than were anticipated, a feature influenced no doubt by the respondent's
perception of the desirability of self-government. Interestingly, the strongest
disagreement on this question came from within the core area, 10.6% of whom were
very strongly opposed to the statement.

The ninth statement built on the general notion of the previous issue and probed
for the effect of scale on attitudes towards self-government. It suggested that
"Wales is too small to have self-government". The attitudes profile indicates a

different mean response pattern for this statement (Figure 6). Category A is separated from the other categories by the neutrality line, the only occasion on which
this happens amongst this set of respondents. Whilst Category A respondents are
inclined to disagree with the statement (mean of 2.89), both B and C endorse the
suggestion of territorial and institutional deficiency hindering the operation of
a separate government structure. The initial conception of the language struggle
was closely related to the ideal of independence. Early nationalists such as
Saunders Lewis had suggested that the "language struggle...would bring self-government in its wake"; and hinted that the position of the language should be strengthened regardless of whether self-government was a realistic alternative. Currently,
nationalists maintain that self-government is the most feasible political solution
to guarantee the functional continuance of Welsh, as it would then become incorporated into the institutional machinery of government. In order to test this hypothesized dependency of Welsh on future self-government the tenth statement suggested that "the preservation of the Welsh language can only be achieved if there
is a separate Welsh government". The mean response of the categories indicates
highest agreement within the intermediate area B (2.70) although, in general, the
response of the majority in each category was negative. Category C respondents
recorded the strongest disagreement (64.2%), followed by A (60.5%) and then B
(57.5%). The intermediate category's position is interesting in that 29.5% supported the contention, as against 27.4% of the core area, indicating a stronger
conviction of the value of self-government in areas where the language is under
most pressure.

Opponents of autonomy within the United Kingdom often point to the status quo arrangements of guaranteeing economic and social well-being. They argue that an integrated, centralist state is more effective in distributing the goods and services
citizens in peripheral regions have come to expect. Advocates of devolution suggest that the existing political and financial relationship between state core and
dependent periphery inevitably favours the accumulation of capital and power at
the centre. This in turn acts as a barrier to the full realization of economic
potential within peripheral areas, because lack of capital investment and poor
political initiative within the regions militate against dynamic economic performance. What nationalist propaganda has to produce is a firm understanding by the
electorate that the framework within which decisions are currently taken is one
based on exploiting core-periphery disparity. A transference of decision-making
from state core to national capital thus becomes a necessary condition for tackl-
ing the regional economic problem. Indeed, the distance of government from the
relatively backward region is often interpreted as the root cause of the problem.
In such circumstances, much nationalist rhetoric contrasts the ailing, underdeveloped present with an attractive, dynamic, and, above all, prosperous future should
the separatists' dream become a reality. The touchstone of such debates, in Québec, no less than Wales, is the basic effect that independence will have on the
individual and corporate standard of living. In order to test how effective separatist arguments have been, the respondents were asked whether they thought "The
people of Wales are better off as part of the United Kingdom rather than as a
separate state". If the hypothesis concerning grievance and structural strain
being directly related to the mobilization of ethnic identity is valid then it is
anticipated that this "status quo" would elicit greatest dissatisfaction within
the core area of Welsh ethnicity. The mean responses of both Category A and B
were very similar (Table 5) whilst all three categories produced majorities in
favour of the existing state on economic grounds. However, the level of support
for the British option differs appreciably. Category C recorded 67% in favour of
a continued integration within the U.K., a level which drops to 51.0% in category
B and 51.3% in A. Conversely, opposition to this statement from A and B (34.9%
and 33.0% respectively) was more than double that recorded for C (14.3%) indicating a distinct minority favouring separatism. Thus, general support for separatism
on economic grounds was lower than that expressed for self-government in principle,
though still greater than that recorded for the preceding statements nine and ten.

A common element of many nationalist movements is the emphasis placed on cultural uniqueness as a distinctive group marker for national identity development. Leaders of renewal nationalist movements often consider themselves to be the "true guardians" of national culture. National ideology elevates the ill-defined nation as the sole historical reality; other social divisions such as class, occupation or territorial identification become subservient to the wider appeal of the "Nation". One of the effects of such transformations is that nationalists tend to eclipse other political activists in terms of their legitimacy to speak on behalf of the nation. The twelfth statement attempted to measure whether this relationship between nationalist concern for the Welsh future had penetrated the electorate's conception by asking "if you care about the future of Wales you should be a Welsh nationalist". Both Category A and B respondents recorded a similar mean score (2.47 and 2.45) indicating an overall disagreement with the relationship implied in the statement. An even clearer level of opposition was recorded for C (2.18). The balance of opinion in all three categories rejected the nationalists' monopoly of concern for the future. Yet, it is evident that a minority of around 27% in A and 23% in B do equate the two features, supposedly rationalizing their own position and convictions. It suggests that nationalism has enlisted no more than minority support in the region and highlights the gap between élite pronouncements and mass support.

The final specifically political statement repeats the index of self-involvement introduced in statement seven by suggesting that "there is nothing much I can do to change the political relationship between Wales and the U.K.". The attitude profiles reveal that Category A produced the lowest level of agreement with the individual's ineffectiveness implied in the statement. Their mean response of 3.18 indicates an overall support for the contention which received more support than the comparable question asked concerning language change (3.0, Table 4). The intermediate category's mean of 3.28 is, however, less than that recorded for statement seven (3.39). Similarly, Category C's mean of 3.39 is also less than for statement seven (3.89). Two factors help explain the difference. Firstly, more of B's respondents are undecided as to their political effectiveness, and secondly, it reveals more agreement between the categories at the aggregate level on their political effectiveness than on their language effectiveness. This relates to the nature of the two issues discussed. The language issue is both individual and national, and is amenable to situational improvement, where the respondent has a direct influence on the choice of language spoken and used socially, especially in Categories A and B, somewhat less so in C. The political relationship is much less situational, less open to individual manipulation, being primarily a power-related question at the macro-level and therefore the respondent may feel that his own activity has very little impact on the total situation. It is evident that such stimulus statements are measuring the respondents' desires for change as much as their perception of their own ability to bring about a change in the status of the language or the political relationship of Wales with the rest of the U.K.

Statement fourteen relates to a third element identified by the ecological analysis as being an important, if declining, component of the traditional Welsh culture complex, Sabbatarianism. Carter and Thomas have demonstrated the utility of using the vote on Sunday opening of public houses as a criterion for delimiting culture regions and a recent updating study has confirmed that relationship between language intensity, political radicalism and support for Sabbatarianism. The present study aimed to add a behavioural dimension to this issue with a statement which suggested that "public houses in Wales should be closed on Sundays". The greatest support for this statement came from the core with a mean of 2.90 declining to 2.77 for B and 2.35 for C. Twice as many respondents in the core agreed with Sunday closing (41.0%) compared with the Anglicized peripheral category (20.6%), which came out strongly against such a move (65.3%). Characteristically, category B maintained its intermediate position on this question also, with 52.5% opposing Sunday closing and 33.5% favouring such a policy. Commentators have suggested that the demise

of the "Welsh dry Sunday" is reflective of the continued decline of Welsh culture.
However, such contentions tend not to interpret culture as a dynamic, ongoing process. Often appeals to revitalize specific characteristics, such as the dry Sabbath, relate to a situation of past conformity and ignore the changing aspirations
and behaviour patterns of succeeding generations. The significance of the response
pattern is that the core and transitional area display different conceptions of the
value of the dry Sabbath. It is a conception which has not been totally eroded by
modernization, the mass media or by the increased immigration into these areas of
non-Welsh speakers. Spatial contiguity still seems to feature as an important element in culture maintenance and attitude formation, especially in the intermediate
area.

Category Response Variance

An additional measure of the variance in attitudes expressed by the categories is
revealed by a chi-square analysis of the patterns of response of the three socio-
cultural environments (Table 7). Whilst the language section indicated that Category B respondents were more likely to demonstrate attitudes similar to C rather
than A, the political section indicated a broad similarity of pattern for Categories A and B. A more significant difference occurs between Categories B and C
with two statements (no.10 and no.13) significant at beyond the 0.05 level, and a
further statement significant at beyond the 0.01 level (no.11).

The clearest pattern of dissimilar responses was the one recorded for the core and
the Anglicized categories. For all but one statement the differences were significant beyond the 0.05 level. Of these statements, no.13 was significant beyond the
0.01 level, whilst a further four (nos.10, 11, 12 and 14) were significant at the
0.001 level (Table 7).

The section on political identification has revealed that there is little overall
support for national separation within the Gwynedd sample, most of the broad nationalist claims having been rejected. However, a firm minority, committed to the
ideal of independence, was recorded, especially within the core area. This analysis and the more extensive cross-tabulations of the original study confirm the
close relationship between language density and the support of separatist ideas,
providing further evidence for the interpretation of separatism as a function of
group maintenance and ethnic demands. In addition, the category response differences illustrate the relevance of taking due account of socio-spatial contexts when
undertaking behavioural studies of ethno-political phenomena.

                    CONCLUSION

Both of these studies reported on here suggest that it is highly likely that Welsh
will continue to decline, especially within the domain, and amongst category type
B respondents. Evidence was also presented in both studies that the situation in
the core area itself was far from stable. In the past practical policies designed
to arrest further decline have been suggested for areas characterized by "moderate"
levels of Welsh speech where the decline in attitudes favourable to the language
were most critical. Such suggestions have usually stressed the importance of education through Welsh as a means of complementing the effect of a "moderately"
Welsh home background on future generations of children. Future sociolinguistic
research in Wales might concentrate more on the influence of economics and population mobility on ethnolinguistic vitality, as the root of language decline is primarily economic, status differentials and unfavourable attitudes being in large
part a reflection of the lack of strong instrumental motivation to maintain proficiency even among first language Welsh-speakers. Thus, the discourse has to focus
on the political and socio-structural factors which retard the economic develop-

ment of the core. This necessitates consistent and clear policy proposals regarding regional economic planning to offset depopulation and economic stagnation. Specific attention to the implications of adopting language-related measures as part of this wider planning brief would be an innovation, as currently there is little government recognition that language and culture are also amenable to planning. My contention is that a more comprehensive interpretation of socio-economic planning in Wales is required if substantial attempts to redress the fortunes of the language are to be successful. Essentially, it is a matter of political priorities, and in this respect the growth of Welsh nationalism has been functional in focusing government attention on peripheral regions. However, concern, as we know, is no guarantee of remedial action, and can never be substituted for the popular will which ultimately determines ethnolinguistic vitality. What this paper hopes to have demonstrated is that there is a spatial variability to this pattern of vitality, which sociolinguistics in the past has not fully explored. Further, it has highlighted the relevance of location in the process of attitude formation by concentrating on aggregate differences between distinct sociocultural environments, just one of the many mechanisms by which language groups interact and determine each other's vitality within specific contexts.

REFERENCES

E.G. Bowen & H. Carter, Preliminary observations on the distribution of the Welsh
    language at the 1971 census, The Geographical Journal, 140, 432-444 (1975a).

E.G. Bowen & H. Carter, The distribution of the Welsh language in 1971: An analy-
    sis, Geography, 60, 1-15 (1975b).

Busteed, M. (1975) Geography and voting behaviour, Oxford University Press, Oxford.

H. Carter, Y Fro Gymraeg and the 1975 referendum on Sunday closing in Wales,
    Cambria, 3, 89-101 (1976).

Cox, K. (1970) Geography, social contexts and voting behaviour in Wales, 1861-1951,
    in S. Rokkan & E. Allardt, Mass politics: Studies in political sociology, The
    Free Press, New York.

Johnston, R.J. (1976) Residential area characteristics: Research methods for id-
    entifying urban sub-areas - Social area analysis and factorial ecology, in
    D.T. Herbert and R.J. Johnston, Social areas in cities, Vol.I, Wiley, New York
    and London.

D.W. Meinig, Cultural geography, introductory geography: Viewpoints and themes,
    Association of American Geographers, no.5, Washington (1967).

Meinig, D.W. (1969) Imperial Texas, University of Texas Press, Texas.

Olsen, S.M. (1976) Regional social systems: Linking quantitative analysis and
    field work, in C. Smith (ed.): Regional analysis, Vol.2, Academic Press,
    New York.

Philip, A.B. (1975) The Welsh question, University of Wales Press, Cardiff.

C.J. Thomas & C.H. Williams, A behavioural approach to the study of linguistic
    decline and nationalist resurgence: A case study of the attitudes of sixth-
    formers in Wales, Cambria, 3, 102-124 (1976).

C.J. Thomas & C.H. Williams, A behavioural approach to the study of linguistic
    decline and nationalist resurgence: A case study of the attitudes of sixth-
    formers in Wales, Cambria, 4, 152-173 (1977).

C.H. Williams, Cultural nationalism in Wales, Canadian Review of Studies in
    Nationalism, 4, 15-37 (1976).

C.H. Williams, Non-violence and the development of the Welsh Language Society,
    The Welsh History Review, 8, 426-455 (1977).

C.H. Williams, Linguistic decline and nationalist resurgence in Wales, Unpub-
    lished Ph.D. Thesis, University of Wales (1978).

C.H. Williams, Some spatial considerations in Welsh language planning, Cambria,
    A Welsh Geographical Review, 5 (in press).

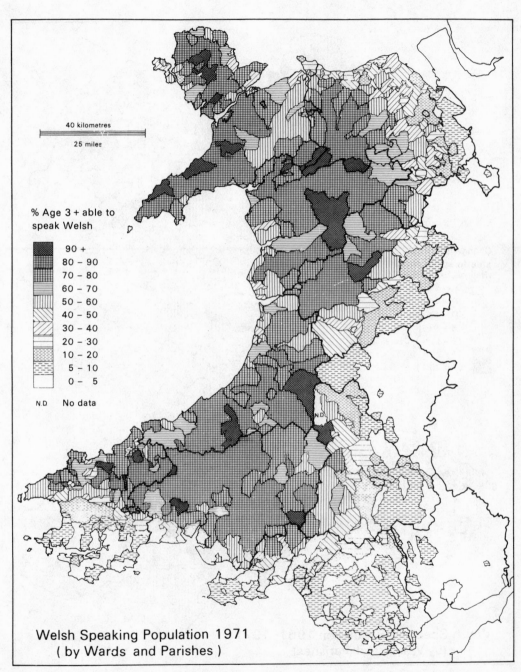

% Age 3 + able to
speak Welsh

90 +
80 – 90
70 – 80
60 – 70
50 – 60
40 – 50
30 – 40
20 – 30
10 – 20
5 – 10
0 – 5

N.D.   No data

Welsh Speaking Population 1971
(by Wards and Parishes)

Fig 1

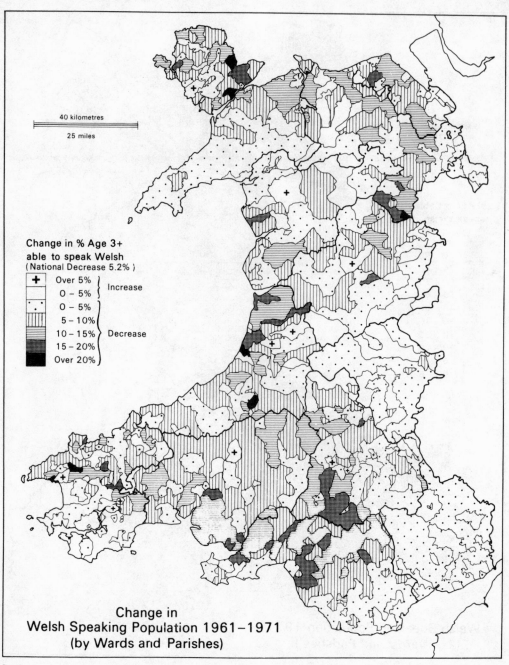

Change in % Age 3+
able to speak Welsh
(National Decrease 5.2%)

+	Over 5%	⎫ Increase
	0 – 5%	⎭
	0 – 5%	⎫
	5 – 10%	
	10 – 15%	⎬ Decrease
	15 – 20%	
	Over 20%	⎭

40 kilometres

25 miles

Change in
Welsh Speaking Population 1961–1971
(by Wards and Parishes)

Fig 2

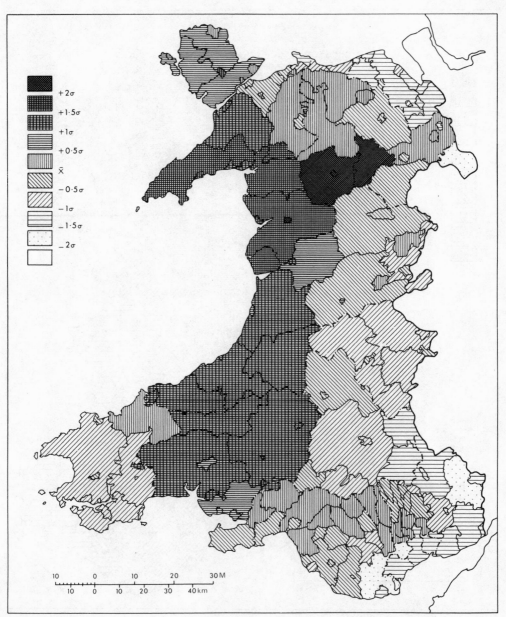

Fig 3   PCA 1961 Component 1

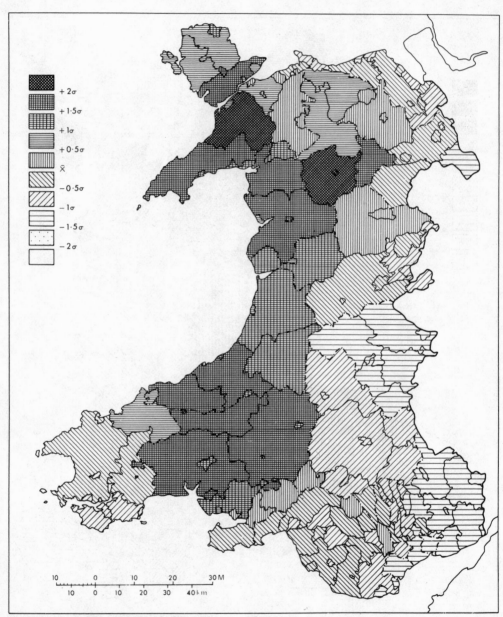

Fig 4   PCA 1971 Component 1

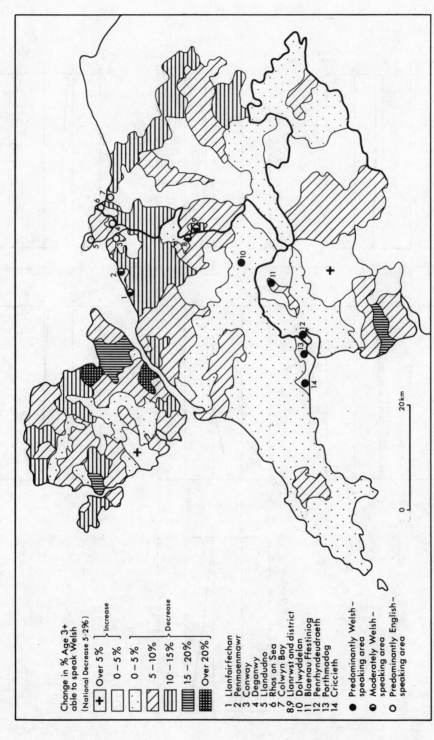

Change in % Age 3+
able to speak Welsh
(National Decrease 5·2%)

+	Over 5%
	0 – 5%	} Increase
	0 – 5%
	5 – 10%
	10 – 15%
	15 – 20%	} Decrease
	Over 20%

1 Llanfairfechan
2 Penmaenmawr
3 Conway
4 Deganwy
5 Llandudno
6 Rhos on Sea
7 Colwyn Bay
8,9 Llanrwst and district
10 Dolwyddelan
11 Blaenau Ffestiniog
12 Penrhyndeudraeth
13 Porthmadog
14 Criccieth

● Predominantly Welsh –
  speaking area
◐ Moderately Welsh –
  speaking area
○ Predominantly English –
  speaking area

20 km

Fig 5

Fig 6 Attitudes to the Welsh Language

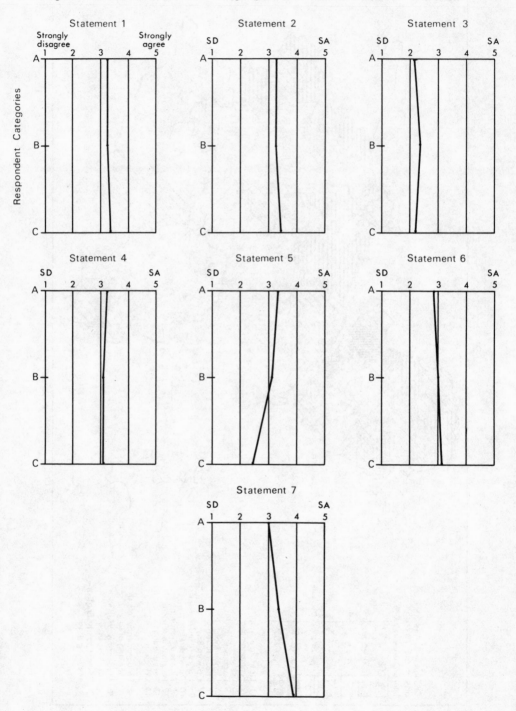

Fig 7   Attitudes to Welsh Political Identification

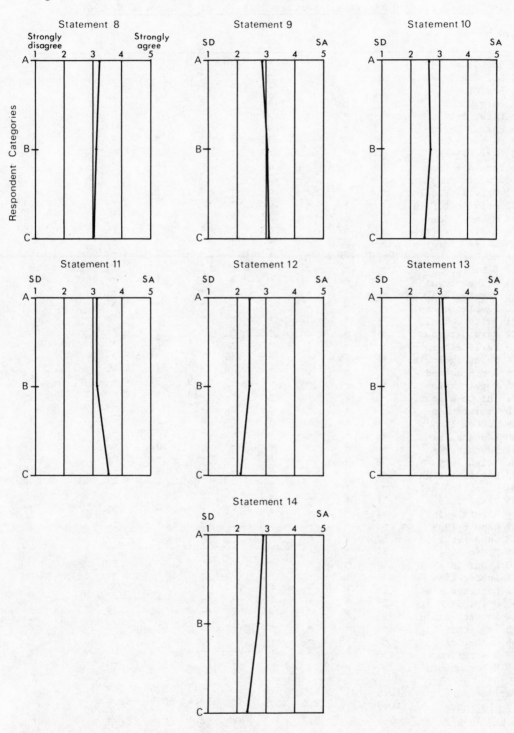

TABLE 1

Principal Components Analysis.   Varimax Rotation of 8 Components, 1961

No.Variable

	1	2	3	4	5	6	7	8
1 Soc.Class 1+2	−	+	+	+	−.38	−	−.40	−
2 Soc.Class 4+5	−	−	−	−	+	−	.72	−
3 Soc.Class 5	−	.37	−	−	−	−	.59	−
4 Pers.Under 4	−	−	+	−.68	+	+	+	+
5 Pers. 5-14	−	+	−	−.39	−	−	+	−
6 Pers. 15-24	−	−	−	−.31	+	−	−	.36
7 Pers. 25-44	−	+	+	−.33	+	+	+	+
8 Pers. 45-64	+	−	+	.70	−	−	−	−
9 Pers 65+	+	−	−	.61	−	+	−.40	−
10 Owner Occup.	−	−	−	.53	+	.35	−	+
11 Priv.Rent.Unfn.	+	−	+	.44	+	−	+	−
12 Priv.Rent.Furn.	+	+	−	.41	−	−	−.41	+
13 Council House	−	.68	−	−.52	+	−	+	−
14 Basic Amenities	−	.87	+	−.68	−	+	−	−
15 Water Closet	−	.87	−	+	+	−	−	+
16 No Bath	+	−.86	−	+	+	−	+	+
17 % Employed	−	−	.91	−	−	+	−	+
18 % Unemployed	+	+	−.91	+	+	−	+	−
19 Females empl.	−	.55	+	+	−	−	+	+
20 Females unempl.	−	−	−	+	−	−	−	−.53
21 Males unempl.	+	+	−.92	+	−	−	+	+
22 Pers.per room	−	−	−.45	−	+	+	+	+
23 Pers.per H:H	−	−	+	−	−	−	.32	+
24 Males agricult.	+	−.79	+	−	.33	+	−	−
25 % H:H shared	−	+	+	+	.52	+	+	.40
26 Outmigration	−	+	−	−	−	−.59	−.57	+
27 Int.Cens.Char.	−	.39	+	−	+	.32	+	−
28 Immigration	−	+	+	+	+	.56	−.53	−
29 School 15	−	−	+	−	+	+	.72	+
30 Educate 18+	+	+	+	+	−	−	.57	−
31 Educate 20+	+	−	+	+	−	−	−.57	+
32 Welsh Only	.58	−.42	−	−	−	+	−	−
33 English+Welsh	.78	−	−	+	−	+	−	−
34 Migration Bal.	−	−	+	+	+	.92	+	−
35 Plaid 1959	.76	+	−	+	−	+	−	−
36 Liberals 1959	.54	−	+	+	−.62	+	−	.31
37 Labour 1959	−	−	−	−	.92	−	+	+
38 Conservs.1959	−.82	+	−	−	−	+	−	−.38
39 Plaid 1964	.77	−	−	+	−	−	−	+
40 Liberals 1964	.47	−	+	+	−.70	+	−	+
41 Labour 1964	−	+	−	−	.93	−	+	+
42 Conservs.1964	−.73	+	−	+	−.40	+	−	−.32
43 Units of Plaid	.53	+	+	+	−	−	+	−
44 Nursery Schools	−	+	−	+	+	−	+	.48
45 Anglicans	−	−.43	+	+	−.41	−	−	−
46 Catholics	−	.59	−	+	−	−	+	+
47 Nonconformist	.50	−	+	+	−	−	−	−
48 W.Nonconformist	.64	−	+	+	−	−	−	−
						−		
Variance	10.9	10.7	7.0	7.8	9.4	4.5	8.5	3.9
Cum.Variance	10.9	21.7	28.6	36.5	45.9	50.4	58.9	62.8
Eigen Values	5.2	5.1	3.3	3.7	4.5	2.1	4.1	1.9

TABLE 2

Principal Components Analysis.   Varimax Rotation of 7 Components, 1971

Variable

	1	2	3	4	5	6	7
1 Soc. Class 1	+	.58	−	−	−	−	−
2 Soc. Class 5	−	−	+	+	+	+	+
3 Employed Total	−	−	+	+	−	+	+
4 Pers. > 4	−	+	+	.82	+	−	+
5 Pers. 5-14	−	−	−	.76	+	+	−
6 Pers. 16-24	−	+	+	+	+	−	.65
7 Pers. 17-44	−	+	+	.80	−	−	−
8 Pers. 45-64	+	−	+	−.56	−	+	−
9 Pers. > 65	+	+	−	−.74	−	+	−
10 Owner Occup.	+	+	+	−	−	−	−.76
11 Priv.Rent.Unfn.	+	−.47	−.60	−	+	−	−
12 Priv.Rent.Furn.	+	+	−	−	.51	−	+
13 Local Auth.Hous.	−	+	+	.44	−	+	.62
14 Basic Amenities	−	.77	−	+	+	+	+
15 Water Closet	−	.86	−	+	+	+	+
16 No Bath	+	−.64	−	+	−	+	−
17 Car Owner	+	+	−.53	+	+	−	−
18 Pers.per room	−	−	+	.74	−	−	+
19 Pop.Change	−	.70	−	.45	+	−	−
20 Anglican	+	−	−.57	−	+	−	−
21 Catholic	−	.44	+	+	−	+	−
22 Nonconformist	.62	−	−	−	−	+	−
23 W. Nonconform.	.76	−	−	−	−	+	−
24 Welsh 3-15	.81	+	−	−	+	+	+
25 Welsh 65	.83	+	−	−	+	−	+
26 Welsh+English	.91	−	−	−	+	+	−
27 Int.Cens.Lang.	−	+	−	+	−	+	−
28 Pop.Read.Welsh	.92	−	−	−	+	+	−
29 Pop.Writ.Welsh	.90	−	−	−	+	+	−
30 Plaid 1966	.74	−	−	−	+	+	+
31 Liberals 1966	.44	−	−.51	−	−	+	+
32 Labour 1966	−	−	.77	+	−	−	−
33 Conservs. 1966	−.49	.40	−.49	−	+	+	−
34 Plaid 1970	.83	−	+	−	+	−	+
35 Liberals 1970	+	−	−.64	−	−	+	+
36 Labour 1970	−	−	.80	+	−	−	−
37 Conservs. 1970	−.44	.44	−.52	+	+	+	−
38 Urdd Centres	.60	−	−	−	−	+	−
39 Plaid Branches	.56	−	−	−	−	+	−
40 Nursery Schools	+	+	−	−	+	.60	−
41 Welsh Schools	.70	−	−	+	+	−	−
42 W.L.S. Cells	+	+	−	−	−	.59	+
43 Aelwyd Branches	.65	−	−	+	−	+	−
44 Unemployed	+	−	−	+	−	+	−
45 Female employed	−	+	+	−	−	+	+
46 Males agricult.	+	−.42	−.68	+	−	−	−
47 Males Unskilled	+	−	+	+	.91	+	−
48 Males Professional	+	−	+	+	.92	+	−
Variance	19.0	8.8	10.5	10.0	4.9	4.6	4.4
Cumulative Variance	19.0	27.8	38.4	48.5	53.5	58.1	62.5
Eigen Values	9.1	4.2	5.0	4.8	2.4	2.2	2.1

TABLE 3

Stimulus Statements, The Welsh Language and Political Identification

1.   Welsh is difficult to learn

2.   Welsh people should not speak Welsh in the company of English people.

3.   An increase in the use of Welsh would be a bad thing for life in Wales.

4.   The compulsory teaching of Welsh in school should be increased considerably.

5.   More Welsh language programmes are needed on television and radio.

6.   It is more useful for children in Wales to learn another European language rather than Welsh.

7.   There is nothing I can do to change the present status of the Welsh language.

8.   The Welsh people should be self-governing if they wish.

9.   Wales is too small to have a separate government.

10.   The preservation of the Welsh language can only be achieved if there is a separate Welsh government.

11.   The people of Wales are better off as part of the U.K. rather than as a separate state.

12.   If you care about the future of Wales you should be a Welsh nationalist.

13.   There is nothing much I can do to change the political relationship between Wales and the U.K.

14.   Public houses in Wales should be closed on Sundays.

TABLE 4

Attitudes to the Welsh Language: Mean Responses

	1	2	3	4	5	6	7
A N = 226	3.21	3.29	2.15	3.25	3.32	2.88	3.00
B N = 200	3.26	3.29	2.37	3.10	3.12	3.00	3.39
C N = 179	3.35	3.42	2.26	3.11	2.46	3.15	3.89

TABLE 5

Attitudes to Political Identification: Mean Responses

	8	9	10	11	12	13	14
A	3.23	2.89	2.65	3.18	2.47	3.18	2.90
B	3.15	3.06	2.70	3.19	2.45	3.28	2.77
C	3.02	3.11	2.50	3.58	2.13	3.39	2.35

TABLE 6

Chi-square values for the contingency tables of pairs of categories of respondents against the five point attitude scales.

Attitudes to the Welsh Language

Statement	1	2	3	4	5	6	7
Categories A-B	6.5	1.2	9.9	3.7	8.9	13.5*	14.1*
Categories B-C	5.1	4.3	5.0	4.7	5.0	4.2	20.8**
Categories A-C	10.6		13.0	10.7	14.9*	14.7*	23.0**

Chi-square   18.46 significant at 0.001 level with 4 degrees of freedom**
             13.28 significant at 0.01 level with 4 degrees of freedom*
              9.49 significant at 0.05 level with 4 degrees of freedom

TABLE 7

Chi-square values for the contingency tables of pairs of categories of respondents against the five point attitude scales.

Attitudes to Welsh Political Identification

Statement	8	9	10	11	12	13	14
Categories A-B	6.4	9.0	2.8	3.3	4.6	1.0	7.4
Categories B-C	6.2	3.3	12.0*	13.5*	8.8	12.6*	9.1
Categories A-C	12.1*	9.3	19.6**	18.4**	19.8**	16.8*	22.6*

Chi-square   18.46 significant at 0.001 level with 4 degrees of freedom**
             13.28 significant at 0.01 level with 4 degrees of freedom*
              9.49 significant at 0.05 level with 4 degrees of freedom

LANGUAGE GROUP ALLEGIANCE AND
ETHNIC INTERACTION

G. Williams

University College of North Wales, Bangor, Wales, U.K.

Almost all complex societies contain ethnic or minority enclaves which evidence a long-standing adaptive relationship with the larger society and its socio-political and economic institutions.[1] When such groups consist of people who speak a minority language, the changing condition of that language can be seen as part of this adaptive relationship. Thus, language erosion can be seen as an integrative adaptation and language maintenance as a rejection, in part at least, of the integrative pattern, a rejection which may involve the generation of an alternative structure. The existence of a language which is not spoken by one of the two ethnic groups generates the possibility of a restriction upon interaction between members of the two ethnic groups. If the monolingual community consists of members of the majority ethnic group, it is conceivable that the existence of a second language will be perceived as a threat by the majority group with the result that cultural assimilation will be of advantage to it.[2] Thus an analysis of patterns of minority language erosion and maintenance should throw light upon the role of language in structuring interaction within the ethnic niche and across the ethnic boundary.

In this paper I intend to consider this problem by focusing attention upon the structural forces which influence people's language identity. Although this objective will inevitably lead to a discussion of the socio-psychological aspects of language use, it is not my intention to dwell upon them. Since I take the view that it is the influence of the political, economic forces upon the relevant structural variables which determines how language and ethnic organization is produced, reproduced, controlled and legitimated, the relevance of the paper to the theme of language and ethnic interaction should be evident. I begin from the viewpoint that it is the competition for control of the infrastructure by the relevant ethnic groups

---

[1]Minority and majority refer to the power dimension and not the demographic dimension throughout the paper.

[2]Sociologists tend to discuss ethnic change by referring to cultural and structural assimilation (Gordon, 1975). The former applies to the process whereby the cultural features of different ethnic groups become similar whereas structural assimilation involves the tendency for the integration of the social structure of the two ethnic groups. In discussing language and ethnic interaction it would appear that the focus is upon cultural assimilation. However, sharing a language does not guarantee interaction and it is also clear that cultural assimilation cannot be considered without reference to social structure.

which determine the vitality of the respective languages in any bilingual setting.
Language allegiance is firmly rooted in the economic order rather than in any independent cultural order.

This perspective has not been too evident in studies of language erosion where there
has been an unfortunate tendency to view language as a primordial quality, as a
given rather than as a variable. A neo-evolutionary, diffusionist perspective was
assumed in which minority language was viewed as backward, often rural, survivals,
characteristic of a population uninterested in change and unarticulated to mass
society and the state. The converse was the modern mass society of the majority
language group and culture. The relationship between the ideal types at either end
of this continuum was rarely considered except in the context of the exchange of
traits. The argument was made that once the traits of the modern-urban end of the
spectrum were diffused to the minority society the population would assume the
"rational" frame of reference necessary to assimilate into the superior modern society. The result of such a perspective is the tendency to view the minority population as defective in a life-style characterized by the minority language with
the result that perjorative, moralistic attitudes towards the minority group are
adopted. It also fails to comprehend the role of the social structures of minority
language groups in adaptations to the structural inequalities implicit in minority-
majority relationships.[3]

By no means all of the students of bilingualism have assumed this position. Several
students have adopted a perspective which focuses attention upon the economic basis
of the relationship between the majority and minority society which are respectively represented by the majority and minority languages. Thus Angle (1976) argues
that the control of Puerto Rican commercial activities by mainland companies generates a push in favour of the English language among Puerto Ricans. Similarly, the
studies undertaken in Canada (e.g., Morrison, 1970; Canada, 1969) indicate that the
dominance of the English language among large industrial companies in Québec pene-
trates to administrative functions and becomes a status language which influences
patterns of occupational mobility. Mackinnon (1977) in his study of Scottish Gaelic makes a similar point in his consideration of the societal process linking the
articulation of language as an institution within the value system to the macro-
societal processes. Hughes (1972), also referring to Canada, claims that the economic structure results in the majority language assuming some functions which the
minority language could well assume. Discussing Belgium, Tabouret-Keller (1962)
indicates that the association of certain occupations with the French language results in a tendency to emphasize this language at the expense of Flemish.

Investigations such as these bring two issues into focus in the study of language
erosion and maintenance: language prestige and occupational mobility.[4] Rubin (1968)
drawing upon Weinreich (1953) refers to language prestige as the relative value of
one language over another in social advancement. She maintains that:

> "...the more difficult it is to move from one social class
> to another, the more significant the association between

---

[3]These limitations are by no means unique to studies of the sociology of language
but derive from structural, functionalist, and modernization perspectives.

[4]It is unfortunate that a conceptual confusion appears to be developing as a result
of the lack of clarity in the use of concepts in the sociology of language. Some
social psychologists refer to social mobility as the movement from one social group
to another although it is not clear whether this is an identity or a structural
change, whereas sociologists tend to refer to social mobility as change in social
class position. In this paper I tend to use the concept in its sociological sense.

language and social class will be and the greater the prestige of one of the languages".

Fishman has made a similar point:

> "...the repertoire of those who gain most in economic,
> political or other socio-cultural statuses are most likely
> to be adopted or copied by others who see opportunities for
> desirable changes in their status by so doing". (1972).

The tendency to interchange the concepts "prestige" and "status" that is so common
in sociological studies of inequality appears to have crept into the sociology of
language and it might therefore be useful to distinguish between them. The above
conceptualization of language prestige by Weinreich and Rubin has become widely
accepted. Language status should therefore refer to the status rank of one language relative to another, often deriving from a historically based system of evaluation. Clearly, language prestige influences language status and an improvement
in the former can in some contexts result in an improvement in the latter. However, the two are not synonomous. Neither is language status coterminous with
ethnic status since if we recognize that ethnic status is a multidimensional phenomenon it is possible that those who do not speak the minority language may still
perceive of themselves as members of the relevant ethnic group – while others may
well identify the ethnic group as being represented by those who speak the minority
language. This issue pertains to the relationship between cultural and structural
assimilation.

It should also be clear that we need to distinguish between language group and
ethnic group as distinct but overlapping status groups with the former often being
a sub-category of the latter. Weber (Gerth and Mills, 1970-72) refers to a language group as a status group albeit a status group where closure is never absolute
in that individuals can learn a language or can refuse to acknowledge their ability
to speak a language. However, the existence of a status group does not preclude
the possibility of action based upon class affiliation. Indeed, the two can be
conceived of as complementary bases of group formation carrying different identities. In some contexts they can be viewed as competing types of identification
while in others they may well be complementary. Membership of the status group
cuts across class lines and permits the possibility of collective action. Class
activity on the other hand is seen as individual action within the market place;
it does not constitute action based upon community. It is maintained that an understanding of the relationship between the two types of identification within the
context of social mobility is crucial to an understanding of language erosion and
maintenance. The vitality of a minority language is seen as varying in time in
accordance with the relationship between ethnic stratification and social stratification which in turn depends upon a number of intervening variables.

In discussing the concept of identification we have introduced a micro-perspective
which must be integrated with the structural or macro-level of analysis if we are
to understand the relationship between identity and the societal forces which help
to structure identity. This is assisted by viewing man as a rational being capable
of making choices between alternatives rather than as a being manipulated by his
cultural background. However, the range of choices from which the individual can
select is restricted by the constraints imposed by his social structural position.
This does not imply that man is always rational nor that his status group allegiance is always a matter of rational choice.[5] What is suggested is that language

---

[5]Giles, Bourhis and Taylor (1977) claim that an identity shift must be preceded by
an awareness of cognitive alternatives.

allegiance gives the individual the possibility of exploiting his ethnic identity
within the context of rational choice by transforming a status group into an interest group.

It is maintained that people will align with different groups as a result of rational choice with, for example, language being seen as facilitating or blocking
access to particular wants, goals, values, or utility functions. Viewing language
groups as status groups in terms of rational choice means that such groups are not
of a permanent character but change because individuals are constantly calculating
the advantages and costs likely to result from different courses of action. The
subjective utility of different alignments and associations is not constant and
power relatives will affect the values people will place upon different outcomes.
Furthermore, the subjective utility will vary for different sociological categories. The principle of reconciliation of interests proposes that the individual
with several allegiances will, whenever possible, seek to reconcile the varying
interests implicit in their separate allegiances. On the other hand, the principle
of optimization posits that, in all those instances where interests can not be re-
conciled, that is, where there is inevitable conflict of interests implied in the
individual's varying allegiances, there will be a tendency to choose the set of
allegiances which maximize material and social gains in the society at large, while
also minimizing security risks. Thus alignment or non-alignment with the language
group must be seen from two perspectives, that of utility maximization on the one
hand, and risk minimization on the other.

We can now conceive of a simple matrix of subjective language group status and
subjective occupational status. There are subjective evaluations on the part of
the actors which may well differ from any objective evaluation. However, it is
reasonable to assume that where divisions are broad there will be a fairly high
degree of congruence between subjective and objective evaluations. We can now
begin to come to terms with the relationships between language, status acquisition,
and social mobility. Status can accrue to the individual from his occupational
position or from his ethnic affiliation. Conversely, if we conceive of status in
terms of social credit it can detract from a person according to class or ethnic
allegiance.

Occupational Status

	High	Low
High	1	2
Language group status		
Low	3	4

Consider cell 1, representing those who perceive their occupational and language group status as high. This congruence of status offers the possibility of enhancing the status that derives from one's occupation by using the language as a means of emphasizing one's allegiance with the language group and thereby gaining status. Among this group will be professionals who will use the language in order to find clients from among the language group. They are also able to derive a greater degree of deference from other members of the language group than would be the case in the wider society. This emphasis does not preclude the possibility of attempting to improve their occupational status and the minority language may well be a means to achieve such an objective. Language loyalists who play a leading role in the struggle to improve the status of the minority language group are usually found within this category.

In cell 2, we have the person of low occupational status who perceives the minority language group status as high. In terms of status maximization there is every reason for this person to emphasize his allegiance with the language group. It allows him the opportunity to draw upon the linguistic allegiance in order to interact with fellow speakers of a high occupational position, or at least those in cell 1. From this association patronage relationships may develop which can be invaluable in facilitating social mobility. As in cell 1, there is no incompatibility between class and language group status.

Cell 3 represents a situation where the two sets of allegiances are in conflict. Here we find those who seek recognition exclusively within the prestige structure of the dominant group and draw upon the patronage of members of the dominant group in attempting to achieve this end. They view the minority language as stigmatic and attempt to remove it from their own status composition. The identity which it would carry is felt to detract from their social credit, and the tendency is to place almost the entire status emphasis upon one's occupational standing. This, of course, is what is termed passing in which one's status group identity is denied and an attempt is made to elaborate the markers of majority group identity. Passing can involve far more than language behaviour one of which is the tendency to seek allegiances with important members of the majority group. This can be of advantage to the ruling class of the dominant group who can refer to them as token members of the minority group who share their political perspective.

Perhaps there is a greater tendency to pass among those associated with cell 4. Unlike those in cell 3, they do not have a high occupational status to fall back on. The tendency is to try to avoid the stigma which the language is associated with and to draw off the identity of the wider society. This does not necessarily mean assuming the ethnic identity of the majority ethnic group but merely the denial of minority ethnicity and the simultaneous emphasizing of one's class identity.[6] This means that the working class affiliation of the wider society is held to be preferable to the ethnic identity of the minority group. It can also mean that the individual perceives his ethnic identity as hampering any potential upward social mobility. This situation tends to arise when there is a tendency in the wider society for the ethnic status to be equated with a low class status so that there is a tendency to equate the two identities and even to account for the

---

[6]Giles, Bourhis and Taylor (1977) maintain that when the individual does not perceive a cognitive alternative to the existing intergroup relationship he/she will resort to individual action in order to generate a positive identity. Since I conceive of class-based action as individual action it is assumed that their statement is akin to opting for class-based action and the rejection of status group action although this is by no means clear in their discussion.

low socio-economic status by reference to self-blame via ethnic or language factors. This is typical of a situation where the cultural division of labour pertains.

It would appear from the preceding discussion that when class and language group
interests reinforce each other there is a tendency for members of the language
group to draw upon common reference points which serve as the basis for strata
awareness in ethnic terms in order to maximize status credit. Given that there
exists an acceptable degree of institutional support for the minority language
there will be a tendency for the group to be centrifocal in tendency with the associated restriction in inter-ethnic interaction. On the other hand, when class
and language group interests are in conflict the tendency is to reject the ethnic
identity associated with the minority language and to emphasize their occupational
status. This will tend to reduce intra-ethnic interaction and there may well be a
series of avoidance practices associated with this reaction.

Sociologists interested in social inequality have tended to ignore the inter-rel-
ationship between class and status group. Nowhere is this more evident than in the
consideration of the relationship between social behaviour and social context. Indeed, many sociologists go as far as to imply that action based upon status group
is irrelevant and that we should expect only to understand action in class terms.
If we reject this position the most relevant question that we can ask pertains to
the context of class and status group action: in what context does the individual
behave as a member of his or her social class and in what situation does he or she
behave as a member of a status group? It is also, of course, possible that both
actions can operate simultaneously. In terms of the above model we need to know
who and under what conditions operates as a member of his language group rather
than as a member of his social class or even ethnic group. This exercise has yet
to be undertaken, perhaps because most of the relevant work has been of an experimental psychological nature, a methodology which is not relevant to answering
such a question.

Thus far we have discussed action as it were based upon status maximization. However, such action does not always conform with a rational choice based upon an attempt to minimize risk. It should be clear that the language group can and does
serve this function especially when regional and language association are strong,
mutual assistance is prevalent, and trust is retained among members of the language group. This implies that social organization based upon language or ethnic
group serves as adaptive responses to conditions of structural marginality wherein
institutions are of value in counteracting relative deprivation and minimizing
risk. It is suggested that this function can serve to generate orientations to
the language group which are quite distinct from the status acquisition perspective. That minority languages in industrial states tend to survive in rural areas
of the periphery where the service and welfare functions of the State find most
difficulty in penetrating can be explained in this context. The functions which
elsewhere are assumed by the State are taken over by ethnic institutions which function through the minority language. Such peripheral areas invariably also have
the lowest standard of living and the higher incidence of indicators of social deprivation.

Such relative deprivation will apply to those in cells 2 and 4 of our schematic
model. However, we would expect those in cell 2 to be among the language loyalists
on the basis of their subjective evaluation of the minority language status. The
crucial category consists of those in cell 4. It is conceivable that although
these actors will view the minority language status as low and even as stigmatic
they will recognize the value of the ethnic institutions and community in providing support mechanisms which are of advantage to them in counteracting their relative deprivation. The net result is a situation of ambivalence in which the individual actively supports the minority language while also feeling that it detra-

cts from his overall social credit in the wider society. It is from the same support function of these institutions that those in cell 1 derive their roles as
ethnic leaders and the associated status and esteem. Within a community it might
even be possible for a person of low occupational status to assume a leadership
position which would not normally be available to him or her in the wider society.
This lack of congruence between class, status, and power may well be a major fact-
or in the development of the high subjective evaluation of minority language status among those in cell 2. This situation might even pertain under a situation of
cultural division of labour if the language serves as a basis for excluding members of the majority culture, who, within such a situation, will have exclusive
access to the high occupational positions, from assuming relevant local leadership
positions. Thus, for those in cell 2 there may well be the compulsion to align
with the minority language group that derives from risk minimization, status enhancement and potential social mobility. However, we should not lose sight of the
fact that the salience of these ethnic institutions will depend largely upon the
demographic vitality of the ethnic group locally.

It would appear clear from the above discussion that the crucial variable is language group status. If we accept that this is largely determined by the language
prestige then what must be considered is the extent to which the majority ethnic
group dominates the infrastructure. Where the class system is dominated by the
majority ethnic group the opting for class-based action on the part of the members
of the minority ethnic group is synonymous with opting for majority ethnic status,
this being accompanied by a rejection of the markers of minority ethnicity in favour of the markers of the dominant ethnic group. This, of course, is synonymous
with Gordon's (1975) cultural assimilation. It highlights the question of hegemony which has tended to have been discussed almost exclusively with reference to
class relationships (Williams, G.A., 1960). However, when we discuss multi-ethnic
societies it is equally clear that there is an important ethnic ingredient which is
of relevance in any discussion of inequality and hegemony. The ethnic group which
controls the infrastructure will also dominate the ideological forces through
which language status and the institutionalized use of language are legitimized.
It is solidified by the influence which the controllers of the means of production
have over the subordinate classes or language group, especially as it relates to
social mobility as a reward system. A major ingredient of the legitimization process is the expression of an ideology wherein the minority language is viewed as
an irrational allegiance of traditionally orientated population unarticulated to
mass society and the State. Indeed, it is often conceived of as a threat to the
State. The tendency for members of the minority language groups to reject the
minority language is largely a result of this process.[7] Another weakness in the
hegemony argument is the tendency to think of the infrastructure as uniform when
in ethnic terms the hegemony might not be complete. Thus, the dominant ethnic
group might completely dominate the infrastructure and generate a cultural division

---

[7]Referring to situations wherein members of a subordinate group perceive no cognitive alternatives to their subordinate position Giles, Bourhis and Taylor (1977)
claim that the actors will consider the position of their own group vis à vis the
dominant group as stable and legitimate. It is possible that the question of this
perception relates, in part at least, to the condition of economic growth or stagnation. During a period of growth the benefit accrues to all sectors of the society and the trickle effect makes it appear as if upward mobility is almost universal. Under such conditions there will be a tendency to emphasize class action
and to limit the ethnic context by regarding the ethnic stratification as legitimate. On the other hand, under conditions of stagnation there is a tendency to view
economic relationships in terms of a zero-sum game and to envisage competition for
scarce resources between regions, ethnic groups, etc.

of labour (Hechter, in press). On the other hand, the minority ethnic group might
well retain control over some economic sectors and thereby offer a variety of occupational opportunities to members of the ethnic group. In the former situation
social mobility is blocked to the minority ethnic group or is possible only within
the context of the majority ethnic group. In the second situation occupational
mobility might well be possible within the context of the minority language albeit
in only a few occupational sectors. If closure in this respect is ethnically complete there will be a tendency for members of the majority ethnic group to claim
that a discriminative process against their interests or hegemony is in operation.

While also recognizing that language prestige may be limited to certain occupational categories we should also recognize that it is also likely to be restricted
spatially since occupations are not evenly distributed geographically. Where there
exists a spatial limitation we can expect to witness contrasting mobility patterns
involving burghers, who are most likely to be minority language supporters, and
spiralists who are less likely to recognize the relevance of the minority language
in terms of social mobility.[8]

When a minority ethnic group's access to power is high it is probable that the language groups will become a reference group which in certain contexts also serves as
an interest group. What we must recognize is that for every language status system
every structure of association and power is itself an embodiment and expression of
public policy towards constituent language groups whether these groups are new-
comers or hosts, minority and majority. The power relatives, in part at least,
involve a competition for scarce resources by members of different language groups.
The freedom of physical and social mobility and of role options represent a major
set of variables in overt or covert language policy.

CONCLUSION

In this paper I have argued that language behaviour in a multi-lingual situation
can be seen as a reflection of the actors' perception of the relationship between
occupational and language group status. The forces which influence this relationship emanate from the control over the economic and ideological structures, which
are inherently interrelated.

In some respects the argument is not too far removed from that of Giles, Bourhis
and Taylor (1977). They argue that people's orientations derive from their social
identity and that orientations in terms of language derive from the relationship
between social identity and comparison with the group represented by the alternative language. It is claimed that linguistic behaviour is an indication of in-
group/outgroup orientations and identity. However, this work tends to have a limited structural input focusing as it does on a social psychological perspective.
The emphasis upon the structural aspects of language behaviour and their relationship to power relatives places language in the same context as is discussed in
more conventional sociological discussions of inequality and behaviour. It should
generate a discussion of speech style within the context of relationships of power
and conflict involving deference, domination, manipulation, etc., rather than the
consensus orientations involving values, attitudes, etc.

---

[8]This does not mean that they will reject the minority language unless there is a
congruence with a low subjective language status.

REFERENCES

J. Angle, Mainland control of manufacturing and reward for bilingualism in Puerto Rico, American Sociological Review, 41, 2, 289-307 (1976).

Canada (1969) Royal commission on bilingualism and biculturalism, The Queen's Printers for Canada, Ottawa.

Fishman, J. (1972) The sociology of language, Newbury House, Rowley, Mass.

Gerth, H.H. & Mills, C.W. (eds.) (1960-72) From Max Weber: Essays in sociology, Oxford University Press, Oxford.

Giles, H., Bourhis, R.Y. & Taylor, D.M. (1977) Towards a theory of language in ethnic group relations, in H. Giles (ed.): Language, ethnicity and intergroup relations, Academic Press, London, 307-348.

Gordon, M. (1975) Towards a general theory of racial and ethnic group relations, in N. Glazer & P. Moynihan (eds.): Ethnicity, Harvard University Press, Harvard.

M. Hechter, The cultural division of labour, American Sociological Review (in press).

Hughes, E. (1972) The linguistic division of labour in industrial and urban societies, in J. Fishman (ed.): Advances in the sociology of language, II, Mouton, The Hague, 296-310.

Mackinnon, K. (1977) Language, education and social processes in a Gaelic community, Routledge and Kegan Paul, London.

Morrison, R. (1970) Corporate adaptability to bilingualism and biculturalism, The Queen's Printers for Canada, Ottawa.

Rubin, J. (1968) National bilingualism in Paraguay, Mouton, The Hague.

A. Tabouret-Keller, Observations succinctes sur le caractère sociologique de certains faits de bilinguisme, Journal d'Études, 25, 95-109 (1962).

Weinreich, V. (1953) Languages in contact: Findings and problems, Publication of the Linguistic Circle at New York, No.1.

THE SURVIVAL OF ETHNOLINGUISTIC MINORITIES: CANADIAN AND COMPARATIVE RESEARCH

A. B. Anderson

University of Saskatchewan, Saskatoon, Canada

1. LANGUAGE AND ETHNIC IDENTITY

Sociolinguists, sociologists and other social scientists have devoted much attention to the relationship between languages and ethnic consciousness (e.g., Lewis,
1947; Fishman, 1965; Giles et al., 1977); in fact many have stressed that language
is the most important component of ethnic identity. For example, Freeman (1958)
has referred to language as "the rough practical test of nationality"; Shibutani
and Kwan (1965) as "an essential part of culture and at the same time the instrument
through which other aspects of culture are organized", as well as - with Bram (1955)
- "a symbol of group identity" through socialization; Park (1950) as the keynote to
a "common community of purpose"; and Handlin (1951) as the main focus of immigrant
group identity in North America rather than place of origin. However, Fishman
(1965) and others (e.g., Bram, 1955; Potter, 1960; Trudgill, 1974) have pointed out
the difficulty which sociologists have had in defining ethnicity (as distinct from
nationality, race, religion, etc.), while linguists have found it no simple task to
precisely delimit languages (as distinct from dialects, patois, argots, etc.).

Moreover, if the linguistic factor is *usually* important for most ethnic groups, it
is not *always* an important, much less the *only* component of ethnic identity. The
variable significance of language, religion and diverse customs as components of
ethnicity can be very complex. Numerous sociological studies have stressed that
among ethnic minorities religion has frequently been used to bolster ethnic consciousness and perhaps language maintenance (e.g., Fishman, 1966b; Bram, 1955;
Shibutani and Kwan, 1965; Gordon, 1964; Yinger, 1963; Park, 1950; Allport, 1954).
Among ethnic minorities in Canada, the Hutterites, essentially an ethno-religious
group, have completely maintained use of their unique Austro-German dialect as well
as distinctive dress, food, values and socialization practices, and communal organization. Whereas certain other ethno-religious groups, such as progressive Mennonites (another Anabaptist group) or Reform Jews, have chosen to identify primarily
in religious rather than ethno-linguistic terms.

Some ethnic minorities may be internally divided by religious affiliation, and may
place little emphasis on maintenance of a traditional mother tongue, while retaining a considerable degree of ethnic consciousness. For example, two of the numer-
ically most significant ethnic categories in Canada, the Canadians of Scottish and
Irish origin (together comprising at least one fifth of the total Canadian population), have little familiarity with Celtic languages (except, perhaps, Scots in
north Nova Scotia) yet exhibit many folk traditions. Of course, this particular

situation does not represent linguistic assimilation in Canada as much as it reflects the fact that only a small minority of Scots in Scotland (except in several remote areas in the Highlands and the Hebrides) or a larger minority of Irish in Ireland (except in the "Gaeltacht") are fluent in Scottish or Irish Gaelic (despite attempts at Celtic linguistic revival in both of these countries and more successfully in Wales).

As a final case in point, the Ukrainian minority in Canada merits mention; this minority is particularly significant in the western prairie provinces and is also prevalent in the larger central Canadian cities. The Ukrainian Orthodox Church of Canada, in contrast to the Russian Orthodox Church but largely similar to the eastern-rite Ukrainian Catholic Church, has steadfastly refused to adopt English as the principal language of the liturgy. Yet it could be pointed out that little more than half of the people claiming Ukrainian origin in Canada are still Orthodox or (eastern-rite) Catholic in religious affiliation, and little more than half can still speak Ukrainian. At the same time, a fairly high degree of ethnic consciousness prevails among Ukrainian Canadians, who exhibit a rich tradition of folk music, dancing and arts.

In sum, different criteria may be stressed by various ethnic or ethno-religious groups as the primary basis or focal-point for group identity.

2. ETHNIC IDENTITY CHANGE AND LINGUISTIC CHANGE

It is quite possible, then, for an ethnic group to lose its traditional mother tongue eventually without losing its sense of identity, as Borrie (1959) and others have cautioned. Ethnic consciousness is not necessarily dependent on maintenance of a unique traditional language, although linguistic change in an ethnic group may be to some extent an indication of acculturation and assimilation. The degree to which an ethnic group feels that its identity is being eroded is related to the emphasis which the group traditionally places on language, religion and/or customs as the keynote to group identity. In other words, if an ethnic group has tended to emphasize maintenance of its own traditional language, loss of that language will be equated largely with loss of group identity. While many ethnic groups could well be defined as ethno-linguistic groups, others could be called ethno-religious groups; but both language and religion tend to be important components of ethnic identity for most ethnic groups. Which aspects of ethnic identity are dispensable in situations of change is not so easy to determine, however.

To cite a Canadian example again, French Canadians (the largest single ethnic group in Canada, comprising about 28% of the total population) have traditionally stressed the survival ("la survivance") of both their Roman Catholic religion and French language, as represented in their slogan "notre foi, notre langue". Yet the Roman Catholic Church has recently lost much of its once-strong influence in French-speaking Québec. Church attendance has declined dramatically during the past couple of decades, from an estimated 70% in 1957 down to only 30% in 1975 of Montréal's 1.5 million Catholics (Associated Press: Dec.8. 1977). Clearly, then, it seems possible to identify as a French Canadian without being a practicing or even a nominal Catholic. But separatists in Québec have tended to conveniently dismiss "les assimilés", the more than half a million French Canadians who cannot speak French out of 1.4 million French Canadians outside Québec, as no longer being truly French.

3. CANADIAN AND COMPARATIVE RESEARCH ON LINGUISTIC ASSIMILATION

There is a considerable and increasing literature on language maintenance or loss among ethnic minorities in many countries, particularly in Canada and the United

States; yet there is relatively little evidence of an attempt to compare these studies in formulating theoretical generalizations about sociological processes. Even within Canada, where ample sociological research on ethnic minorities has been produced, few studies have systematically sought to compare linguistic trends among a variety of ethnic groups: e.g., the Report of the Royal Commission on Bilingualism and Biculturalism (1969), vol.4, chapter 5 on language transfer patterns; Kelly (1975) on research problems concerning language maintenance in Canada; A.B. Anderson (1978a) on linguistic trends among ethnic groups in Saskatchewan; Priestley's (1978) symposium on language loyalty; and de Vries's several papers on language maintenance and shift among Canadian ethnic groups (1974, 1977, 1978). Particular attention has been devoted to linguistic problems related to education, exemplified in the Report of the Royal Commission on Bilingualism and Biculturalism (1969), vol.4, chapter 6 on education; Kovacs's collection of papers on "Ethnic Canadians: Culture and education" (1978); recent articles in a volume of Canadian Ethnic Studies (1976, vol.8, no.1) on "Education and ethnicity"; and a recent paper on "Ethnicity and language in Saskatchewan schools" (1978c) by the present author. Most Canadian research on language maintenance or loss has concentrated on specific minorities rather than on cross-cultural comparison of trends: for example, apart from a proliferation of studies on French Canadians, on Central and East Europeans (A.B. Anderson, 1978b), Ukrainians (Young, 1931; Lysenko, 1947; Marunchak, 1970; A.B. Anderson, 1976; Kostash, 1977, etc.), Poles (Grabowski, 1975; Radecki and Heydenkorn, 1976: chapter 5), Mennonites (A.B. Anderson and Driedger, 1978), Italians (Boissevain, 1970:chapter 4; Jansen, 1941), Portuguese (G.M. Anderson, 1974, 1976), Scots (A.B. Anderson, 1973; Campbell and MacLean, 1974:chapter 5; Emmerson, 1976), and so forth.

While European scholars have extensively studied linguistic accommodation or patterns of language use (multi-lingualism, bilingualism, dialects, etc.) among ethnolinguistic minorities (see below), perhaps relatively few studies have focused more specifically on the actual survival of those minorities in Europe. One recent example of research on language retention in longitudinal perspective would be a paper by Vanneste (1974) referring to the steady retreat of the Franco-Flemish linguistic frontier, i.e., the contraction of the area occupied by Flemish speakers within France.

4. FACTORS AFFECTING THE SURVIVAL POTENTIAL OF ETHNOLINGUISTIC MINORITIES

Sociolinguists have devoted ample attention to the complexity of language maintenance and change among ethnolinguistic minorities. One might note, for example, Fishman's many papers on language maintenance in the United States (1965, 1966a, 1966b, 1966c, 1968a, etc.) and Bram's succinct yet pertinent description of the social forces which could relate to linguistic change (1955), contrasting with a recent issue of the International Journal of the Sociology of Language on "language death" (vol.12, 1977, edited by Dressler and Wodak-Leodolter).

In a recent paper (A.B. Anderson, 1975) the present author has outlined the complexity in analyzing the survival potential of ethnic minorities in Canada. The survival potential of ethnic groups is inevitably closely related to definitions of ethnicity, to the organizational capacity of ethnic groups, and to interaction between ethnic groups. A single model of ethnic survival for Canada is possible, if improbable, to formulate. The difficulty lies in the fact that while every ethnic group within Canadian society is a minority, at least at the national level (however this is not necessarily the case at a local, regional or even provincial level), there are at least fifty clearly defined ethnic categories in Canada (not to mention further sub-group distinctions), ranging in size from several thousands to several millions, many exclusively urban yet others completely or primarily rural, and most embracing a wide range of opinions among their members as to what

exactly constitutes ethnic identity and to what extent this identity should be
stressed. While it would indeed seem pretentious to attempt a summary of the fifty
propositions or working hypotheses concerning the survival potential of ethnicity
in Canada stated in that (1975) paper, one could generalize that the survival potential of Canadian ethnic groups tends to be enhanced: *first*, where ethnic group
members reveal a strong "conscience collective" (to borrow from Durkheim) as a unique ethnic group (e.g., emphasis of ethnic identity, culture and history - real or
romanticized - and possibly already a long history of survival as a minority), also
where certain basic criteria defending ethnicity are clearly defined and stressed
(language, religion, customs, etc.); *second*, where a pan-national identity seems
weaker than *intra*-national identifications (ethnic, regional); *third*, where demographic characteristics (possibly age, generation, or length of residence in Canada, sex, occupation, education, class position and social mobility, etc.), serving
as intervening controls related to ethnic persistence, enhance rather than decrease
an emphasis on ethnicity; *fourth*, where various demographic/ecological situations
or trends are evident (such as relative concentration of ethnic groups, particularly
in urban neighbourhoods and rural "bloc" settlements, and of course maintenance of
these concentrations through continued immigration); *fifth*, where the "institutional completeness" of an ethnic community (as defined by Breton, 1964) ensures a
fairly high degree of ethnic enclosure; *sixth*, where the relationships between
ethnic groups are such that the preservation of ethnic identity is mutually accepted, tolerated, or encouraged (it is important to note that *negative* aspects of ethnic relations, e.g., ethnic conflict, could serve to encourage awareness of ethnicity). In short, the survival of ethnolinguistic minorities in Canada, if not in
any society, cannot be studied effectively without taking into consideration the
often significant differences between these minorities in their identifying criteria, history, geographical concentration, institutionalization, social relationships, etc.

5. LINGUISTIC ASSIMILATION IN WESTERN CANADA

Ability Compared to Desire to Speak a Traditional Language

Recent research on linguistic trends among ethnic groups in Saskatchewan (A.B.
Anderson, 1978a) has provided much interesting data on linguistic assimilation.
To summarize some of the more pertinent findings, according to census data there
has been in recent decades a fairly steady and rapid decrease in the proportion of
ethnic group members in this western Canadian province still conversant in their
traditional mother tongues. Using census data to compare language trends between
1961 and 1971 for a wide variety of ethnic groups in Saskatchewan, out of 29 ethnic
categories studied, only two had more than three-quarters of their members able to
speak the traditional mother tongue by 1971 - Greeks (82.8%) and Chinese (78.1%).
In another three ethnic groups approximately two-thirds could speak the mother
tongue in 1971 - Italians (71.2%), native Indians (64.3%), and Ukrainians (62.1%).
A majority of French Canadians in the province, as well as of the far less numerous Indo-Pakistanis and Slovaks, could speak their relevant traditional languages.
In most of the other ethnic groups only a minority, between a quarter and half, of
the members still retained the mother tongue; among people of Norwegian, Danish,
Swedish, Dutch, and Jewish descent the proportion fell below one quarter. Between
1961 and 1971, in four ethnic groups - Greeks, Italians, Yugoslavs (i.e., mostly
Croatians in Saskatchewan), and the few Estonians - actual increases in the proportion of members able to speak their traditional language could be noted. In several other groups the trend seemed to be fairly static. But most ethnic groups
showed significant declines within this one decade. Moreover, the fact that they
could speak their traditional mother tongues does not necessarily indicate that
they were *actually* speaking those languages. Thus, according to 1971 census data
only 28.4% of the French were actually using French more often than English at
home, compared to 28.9% of the Ukrainians, 14% of the Russians, 8.2% of the Poles,

9.4% of the Germans and Dutch combined, and only 1.0% of the Scandinavians.

In order more fully to comprehend language trends within the western Canadian prairie region, particularly within the context of ethnic or ethno-religious rural bloc settlements, an extensive field survey (N=1000) was conducted in eighteen settlements (seven French Catholic, one German Catholic, two Mennonite, two Hutterite, three Ukrainian Orthodox, Ukrainian Catholic, and Polish Catholic, one Russian Doukhobor, and two Scandinavian Lutheran) located in the north-central region of Saskatchewan. This field survey, in contrast to the more general census data for the province as a whole (i.e., including urban areas), revealed that an extremely high proportion of all respondents could still speak a traditional mother tongue other than English, regardless of group. Virtually all (100%) of the Hutterite, Ukrainian Orthodox, and Polish Catholic respondents could still speak such a mother tongue as well as almost all French (99.0%), Ukrainian Catholics (98.7%), and Mennonites (97.2%), and a high proportion of Doukhobors (95.0%), German Catholics (93.2%), and Scandinavians (89.5%). However, considerable variety was noted in the respondents' actual preference for using their traditional mother tongues. All (100%) of the Hutterites were using their language at least "fairly often", compared to most of the Polish Catholics (86.7%), French (78.2%), Doukhobors (70.0%), Mennonites (68.9%), and Ukrainian Catholics (68.8%) and Orthodox (62.7%), but only a small minority of Scandinavians (37.2%) and German Catholics (29.0%) interviewed still preferred to use their languages fairly often. Thus *ability* to speak these traditional languages was consistently high compared to *desire* to speak them, and very significant group differences were apparent in language preference and in response to linguistic assimilation.

The brevity of this paper does not permit repetition of the extensive discussion accounting for the maintenance or loss of traditional languages in Saskatchewan; yet a few brief comments would be appropriate. Despite census data revealing considerable linguistic assimilation for French-origin minorities outside Québec, particularly in most urban areas, French Canadians in certain largely rural settlements outside Québec have revealed a devotion to their traditional language; a sizeable proportion of children may reach the teen-age before learning English well because the latter is spoken seldom at home or perhaps even in the separate schools. There have been many forces serving to preserve French identity in general and the French language in particular - the French parishes of the Roman Catholic Church, various organizations (such as l'Association Culturelle Franco-Canadiènne in Saskatchewan), a close connection maintained between the minorities and Québec, the availability of mass media in the French language, "écoles designées" (French schools), etc. French Catholicism and the French language have traditionally been considered inseparable in Québec as well as among the minorities; this view was long supported by clergy who have maintained that the language is the guardian of the faith and vice-versa. On the other hand, urbanization, rural depopulation, and secularization have tended to weaken the survival potential of French-speaking minorities outside Québec (A.B. Anderson, 1974a; Joy, 1972; Sealy, 1978).

Linguistic assimilation of some German groups has been a long but inevitable process. Gone was much of the German (particularly Catholic) admiration for German cultural superiority after the world wars. The Mennonites, being pacifists, had a long tradition of intense opposition to militarism, so during the early years of settlement in Canada they chose to stress their unique Mennonite identity (rather than German). Younger Mennonites, especially in the more liberal sects, were expressing disdain for so much use of the German language (Driedger, 1955:82-85). The churches of the liberal sects adopted English, and use of German in public schools was outlawed even earlier. The Russlander Mennonite immigrants who arrived during the 1920's expressed their eagerness to learn English, unlike the Old Colony Mennonites who had emigrated from Russia several decades previously (Epp, 1962: 207-208). Among the Hutterites, the possibility that English would replace German due to schooling in the former language was effectively countered when the Hutterites also set up their own schools using the latter. Thus, while the Hutterites interviewed still used German most of the time, almost a third of the Mennonites and three-quarters of the German Catholics preferred English, despite a high proportion being able to speak some German, as we have already noted.

Similarly, the respondents of Scandinavian origin preferred to speak English much of the time; while almost 90% of them could speak a Scandinavian language, little more than a third of them did fairly often. The Norwegian language was used quite extensively, if not exclusively, in Norwegian Lutheran churches in Saskatchewan during the first couple of decades in this century. But in 1921 only 1.4% of foreign-born Norwegians in Canada were illiterate in English (Young, 1931:179).

Frequent use of the Ukrainian language - and a corresponding failure to prefer English - was long enhanced in Saskatchewan by the illiteracy of Ukrainian immigrants, by what other non-Ukrainian settlers considered to be their backwardness, by a lack of familiarity with English, reinforcing seclusion from the outside world, by a deep-rooted, nationalistic pride in Ukrainian identity and a love for the mother tongue, and by traditional institutions resisting all attempts to tamper with the mother tongue (Young, 1931:179, 186-190; England, 1929:55-56, 76-77). When the first Ukrainians immigrated "en masse" to the Canadian Prairies, an estimated half of them were illiterate; by 1921 40% of the immigrants were still illiterate; by 1931 almost a third of them in Saskatchewan were probably still unable to speak any English (Milnor, 1968; Young, 1931:179). It has already been noted that in the field survey almost all of the respondents in the Ukrainian-Polish group could still speak their mother tongue, while about two-thirds of the Ukrainians and a higher proportion of the Poles were using their mother tongue fairly often.

Another research paper by the same author (A.B. Anderson, 1978b) revealed that the ability of Eastern European ethnic groups in Canada to preserve their traditional mother tongues has varied considerably, not only from group to group but also from time to time. A high proportion (over 75%) of Canadians of Estonian, Latvian, Yugoslavian and Greek descent retained their languages by 1971, compared to a lower proportion (50-75%) of Canadians of Hungarian and Lithuanian descent, and only a minority among those of Czech and Slovak, Russian, Ukrainian, Polish and Rumanian descent. But again it must be stressed that a far lower proportion actually were using these languages at home than those claiming an ability to speak their mother tongue. For example, while 48.9% of Canadians declaring Ukrainian origin claimed an ability to speak Ukrainain, only 22.8% actually spoke that language at home (more than English); among Poles, 38.4% cf. 19.9%; Russians 37.0% cf. 16.0%; Hungarians 53.7% cf. 30.2%; Czechs and Slovaks 48.4% cf. 26.0%.

Rural-urban Differences in Traditional Language Maintenance

Comparatively little sociological research in Canada has been concerned with linguistic trends among ethnic minorities in rural areas or with specific contrasts between trends in rural and urban areas, whereas innumerable studies have described the assimilation, including linguistic, of urban ethnic minorities. The research in Saskatchewan has indicated that ethnic group members resident on farms have been more retentive of traditional languages than members in small towns and villages, who in turn have not been as linguistically assimilated as the members in larger urban centres, although some exceptions to this pattern could be noted. However, while this seems to be quite a safe generalization in Saskatchewan, it does not necessarily hold true for all of Canada, because the vast majority of members of many ethnic groups are urban residents and/or relatively recent immigrants to Canada.

Language Maintenance and Population Characteristics

Much research needs to be done on the relationship between language maintenance and population characteristics such as age and generation differences, sex and the effect of intermarriage, occupation and education, local community size and ethnic heterogeneity or homogeneity of the local community, etc. In exemplifying the utility of examining such factors as possible controls on language maintenance, let us again refer to the survey on linguistic trends among ethnic groups in Saskatchewan (A.B. Anderson, 1978a).

Among the five major ethnic groups in Saskatchewan (French, Germans, Ukrainians, Poles and Scandinavians), clearly there is an increase in the proportion of ethnic group members able to speak the relevant traditional mother tongue concomitant with an increase in age level. The sample data tended to support the hypothesis that the younger the respondents, the more likely they will be to prefer speaking English rather than their traditional mother tongue. However, the trend is not a steady continuum in certain ethno-religious groups or subgroups, and marked differences could be noted between groups.

Many sociologists have suggested that among immigrant groups the longer the period since immigration (during the first generation, that is), the less will be the emphasis on ethnic identity and on speaking a traditional mother tongue (e.g., Shibutani and Kwan, 1965; Park, 1950; Borrie, 1959; Gordon, 1964; Herberg, 1960). This generalization was clearly supported by the data from the Saskatchewan survey, excepting the Hutterites and to some extent the Doukhobors.

In cross-tabulating language with sex for each ethno-religious group studied in the Saskatchewan survey, the working hypothesis that more males would prefer the English language in most situations than females was somewhat acceptable for some groups (German Catholics, Mennonites, Ukrainian Orthodox, Scandinavian) but not for others; thus, these data were quite inconclusive. Moreover, in 1917 it was reported that in Ukrainian settlements in Saskatchewan the women were consistently less literate and less able to speak English than the men (Archives of Saskatchewan, Martin Papers, No.168).

Intermarriage is a vital yet frequently neglected consideration in language maintenance. Canadian research has indicated that some ethnic groups reveal an increasing and already high degree of ethnic exogamy (e.g., Royal Commission on Bilingualism and Biculturalism, 1969; Kalbach, 1975; Heer and Hubay, 1975). While there has been relatively little intermarriage across ethnic lines within rural ethnic settlements in Saskatchewan, recent research has indicated that attitudes towards ethnic intermarriage, and to a lesser extent religious intermarriage have been changing rapidly even in these homogeneous settlements (A.B. Anderson, 1974b). It goes without saying that ethnic intermarriage could have a profound effect on both the ability and desire to retain traditional languages.

Occupation, education and physical and social mobility may be intimately related to language preference (e.g., Simon, 1975b). Finally, the size and ethnic homogeneity or heterogeneity of the local rural community or urban neighbourhood could be considered as possible important factors bearing on the survival potential of ethnolinguistic minorities; still less research has been done to date on such demographic factors, although these factors were taken into consideration in the Saskatchewan survey.

Five basic processes have affected the survival potential of ethnolinguistic minorities in western Canada (A.B. Anderson, 1978a): *first*, widespread intermarriage between people of different ethnic origins; *second*, several decades of discriminatory provincial legislation against use of "foreign" languages in school instruction, a conscious policy of using schools as assimilatory agents to ensure conformity to the dominant Anglo-Canadian mode; *third,* the breakdown of the institutional completeness and segregation of ethnic communities, largely through the consolidation of formerly highly localized and ethnically homogeneous schools and other focal points of local community activity into more heterogeneous units; *fourth,* a steady process of secularization together with a progressive de-emphasis of the one-time close link between ethnicity, language and religion; and *fifth,* very large-scale rural depopulation and the decline of smaller communities, concurrent with rapid urbanization.

6. LINGUISTIC CHANGE: ASSIMILATION OR ACCOMMODATION?

The increasingly voluminous literature on linguistic change among ethnic minorities has largely failed to distinguish clearly between linguistic change as *assimilation* and as *accommodation.* The former term implies loss of a traditional minority mother tongue in favour of adopting the language of the majority or the general society. The latter term implies linguistic change but not necessarily loss. In describing linguistic assimilation in this paper we have taken into account the distinction between ethnolinguistic minorities in their ability to speak a traditional mother tongue compared to their *desire* to speak it; rural-urban differences in language maintenance; and how language maintenance may relate to age, generation, and other characteristics of ethnic populations. In describing linguistic accommodation, we will briefly consider patterns, forms, and conditions of bilingualism and multi-lingualism; partial linguistic change as represented in neoligisms and dialectical innovations or survivals; and finally name-changing. While our concern in this paper is with the survival potential of ethnolinguistic minorities, hence primarily with linguistic assimilation (actual or potential), the alternative of linguistic accommodation must be considered.

7. BILINGUALISM AND MULTI-LINGUALISM

If linguistic assimilation (implying loss of a traditional mother tongue and adoption of the prevailing dominant national language) is increasingly apparent among many ethnolinguistic minorities such as among most ethnic groups in Saskatchewan, other alternative responses to ethnic contact are also apparent, notably bilingualism (whereby an ethnolinguistic minority adopts the language of the dominant society yet also retains its own traditional language) and multi-lingualism (whereby more complex patterns of language use emerge, involving three or more languages).

Sociologists and sociolinguists have produced an extensive literature on bilingualism and multi-lingualism. Apart from numerous case studies of bilingualism and multi-lingualism in particular societies, this literature includes many general comparative studies of multi-lingualism furnishing useful theoretical insights, (e.g., Fishman, 1971c; N. Anderson, 1969; Simon, 1969, 1975a, 1975b; Herman, 1972; Stewart, 1972; Lieberson, 1972; Giles, et al., 1977, etc.); as well as many discussions of the relationship between multi-lingualism and multi-culturalism in political perspective (e.g., a variety of papers in Savard and Vigneault (1975), published by the Centre International de Récherche sur le Bilinguisme at Université Laval, Québec; and papers by Fishman, 1971b; Kloss, 1975; De Meyer, 1975; Jakobson, 1968; Deutsch, 1968; Petersen, 1976; Connor, 1976, etc. on multi-lingualism and multi-culturalism in Europe).

Extensive research has been done by sociologists and sociolinguists on the conditions for, and resulting varieties of, bilingualism (see, for example: Shibutani and Kwan, 1965; Borrie, 1959; Lieberson, 1963; Mackey, 1967, 1972; Edwards, 1976; and a wide variety of papers by Fishman). Bilingualism may be regarded as a transitional stage between alteration of the mother tongue and complete loss, although it is not necessarily subsequent to, but would usually be concomitant with,

alteration. The bilingual members of an ethnic group are not easy to classify.
They may favour cultural pluralism to the extent that they could speak the dominant
national language easily but prefer to use their mother tongue as much as possible.
Or they could speak both languages poorly, being in a marginal, transitional phase.
Or they could prefer to use the national language much of the time because they are
concerned about improving the ability of their group to speak that language well.
The residents of a rural ethnic settlement or urban neighbourhood may see little
reason to learn or use the national language. And adoption of the national language may also be regarded by linguistic revival as an important feature of ethnic
subnationalism. Fishman (1968b, 1968c, 1968d, 1971a, 1972c) has distinguished
between stable, unstable and transitional bilingualism in the United States; Rydnyckyj (1975) between official, semi-official, unofficial and extended or multiple
bilingualism, also between perfect, basic and passive bilingualism in Canada.

In Canada, as in other officially bilingual states (Belgium, South Africa, Finland,
etc.), research on bilingualism has been restricted largely to the two official
languages. Recent writing, for example, has described political-economic aspects
of English/French language use (e.g., Morris and Lanphier, 1977; Lieberson, 1970;
and papers in Savard and Vigneault, 1975); psycholinguistic aspects of bilingualism (e.g., Lambert's papers on "A social psychology of bilingualism" (1967) and
"The roles of attitudes and motivation in second language learning" (1972), as
well as Hubbell's current research on "The bilingual child's acquisition of code-
switching rules"). Some recent work has been done on bilingualism or multi-lingualism among immigrants of non-British, non-French origins in Québec (e.g., Henripin, 1974; Dion, 1975; Smith et al., 1977). However, in Canada relatively little
systematic, detailed research specifically focusing on bilingualism in an official
or dominant national language (generally English outside Québec) and in a traditional ethnic minority language, or on more complex patterns of language use, has
been done (apart from the profusion of studies which refer, at least tangentially,
to linguistic assimilation in particular ethnic groups).

One such analysis of patterns, forms and conditions of language use is the survey
of linguistic trends in rural ethnic settlements in Saskatchewan (A.B. Anderson,
1978a). Comparing a thousand respondents in nine ethno-religious groups, it was
learned that the total sample was almost equally divided between respondents who
were bilingual (in English and their ethnic language) and preferred to use their
ethnic language more frequently than English both in the home and out in the local
community (38.5%), on the one hand, and those who were bilingual yet preferred to
use English both in the home and community (36.2%). Most of the remaining respondents (18.3%) preferred their mother tongue in the home but English in the community; only a small proportion were unilingual in an ethnic language (3.6%) or in
English (3.4%). However, significant differences between these ethno-religious
groups were revealed.

8. PARTIAL LINGUISTIC CHANGE: NEOLOGISMS AND DIALECTS

Ample discussion of neologisms, dialects and argots is found in sociological and
sociolinguistic literature; again, apart from numerous studies of particular ethnolinguistic minorities, some chapters and papers have synthesized research into
broader comparative perspectives conducive to theoretical generalization (e.g.,
Fishman, 1971b; Haugen, 1966; Hall, 1972; Edwards, 1976; Trudgill, 1974; Ray, 1972;
Hymes, 1977, etc.).

The development of neologisms and dialects may be indicative of linguistic accommodation in essentially two respects: first, contact between ethnic groups may
stimulate acculturation in the sense of cultural exchange, exemplified in the alteration of the traditional language of the ethnolinguistic group, so that an immigrant ethnic minority in Canada, for example, may after some time be speaking a

version of the mother tongue somewhat different from that now spoken in the mother
country. Neologisms may be introduced through adoption of slang by the younger
generation, or perhaps through some degree of Anglicization, especially with reference to modern appliances. Or the language of the immigrants may differ from
that of members of the same ethnic group back in the "old country" through lack of
contact between the former and the latter; the immigrants continue to speak regional dialects, which have become anachronistic (at least in part) in the countries
where they originated. Levelling influences break down such distinctions, though,
such as the ethnic-oriented media, the importation of reading material from the
mother country, education in an updated, standardized non-English language, interaction in urban as opposed to isolated rural areas, continuing immigration, etc.
(Shibutani and Kwan, 1965:285; Bram, 1955: 19, 23).

Second, members of ethnolinguistic minorities often tend to have become functionally multi-lingual in a standard form of their ethnic language, in a localized
dialect of that language, and in a dominant national language of the society in
which they are a minority. Such functional multi-lingualism has become very complex among certain ethnolinguistic minorities in Europe as well as North America.
In Europe, for example, in Alsace the bulk of the population may in effect be trilingual, speaking the Alsatian dialect of German as well as being conversant and
literate in "standard" German and French (Sautter, Simon and N. Anderson, 1969).
In Luxembourg Letzeburgesch, a German dialect, is widely spoken, while standard
German and French are recognized as official language (Humblet, 1974). French
minorities in north-western Italy speak Savoyard or Waldensian dialects of French,
tend to be familiar with the Piemontese Italian dialect, yet are taught to be literate in standardized French and Italian (Humblet, 1974; Massucco-Costa and N.
Anderson, 1969). Moreover, multi-lingualism in dialects and standardized national
languages, as a form of linguistic accommodation resulting from ethnic contacts,
may be even more complicated when one encounters the situation of ethnolinguistic
minorities existing within larger minorities. To cite a couple of examples in the
Italian Alps, first, in the Val Gressoney within the Valle d'Aosta region, a German
dialect is spoken, but the Valle d'Aosta is an autonomous political region where
Savoyard French is an official language; thus, the people in this valley might
speak their German dialect locally yet be expected to be familiar with Savoyard
French as the prevalent language of the general region, while being educated in
Italian as the national language, not to mention being literate in standard German
or French and being familiar with the Piemontese Italian dialect which is also
spoken widely in the region. Second, in the Val Gardena within the Alto-Adige
(Süd-Tirol) region, Ladin, a Rhaeto-Romansch language, is found, but this general
region enjoys limited political autonomy and German is recognized as an official
regional language; so the people in this valley may be trilingual in Ladin, German
and Italian. (For a summary of research on these and other ethnolinguistic minorities in Western Europe, see A.B. Anderson, 1978d).

In western Canada the French settlers came from a wide variety of origins reflecting divergent dialects. Probably most came directly from France and Belgium, but
these immigrants included Walloons and Flemings from Hainaut and French Flanders,
Bretons (many speaking the Breton language, a Celtic language, besides French), as
well as immigrants from a diversity of other regions in France. Many French Canadians in western Canada came directly from Québec due to colonization schemes;
but these included some Acadians from Québec, while others were Québecois from
American mid-western states. The first Francophone settlers were Métis of mixed
French-Indian extraction. However, these various sub-group distinctions and dialect differences have tended to become fused into a common French Canadian identity
during several decades of settlement in western Canada (A.B. Anderson, 1974a).
Undoubtedly, the traditionally German-speaking groups generally failed to unite to
preserve the German language, not only due to religious differences but also due
to the fact that they actually speak distinct dialects so different as to hinder
easy communication in the mother tongue (see, for example, Leopold, 1972, on

German dialects). The Hutterites usually speak a Tyrolian dialect, little influenced by Slavic languages, while the language of their own "German school" is Hochdeutsch, High German (Gross, 1965; Hostetler, 1974). The Mennonites, on the other
hand, use a variety of dialects. The language of the first Mennonites in the
Netherlands of course had been Dutch. By the mid-eighteenth century their Dutch
had been gradually transformed into the Frankische, Niedersachsische and Friesis-
che dialects of Niederdeutsch or Plattdeutsch (i.e., Low German). In West Prussia
the dialect spoken by most Mennonites was Westpreussische Plattdeutsch. With migration to South Russia, a Schwarzmeer-Deutsch (Black Sea German) dialect of Low
German with limited Russian admixture was adopted. In western Canada the Old
Colony Mennonites used a Low German dialect not only as their daily speech but
also in their churches. Other Mennonites, however, tended to look upon this dialect as crude German used only by the uneducated; for their part, they used standard Low German in everyday speech and Schriftsprache, Bibeldeutsch or Hochdeutsch
("literary language", Bible German or High German) in their churches and schools
(Driedger, 1955; Epp, 1962, 1974; Will, 1978). Until very recently many of the
older Mennonites, especially those of the Old Colony sect, spoke English very
little and very poorly. The German language was considered a focal point in the
avoidance of contact with the larger society, such avoidance being positively
valued and backed by xenophobia, and it was considered the only proper language
for Mennonite church services (Driedger, 1955; Smith, 1957). In western Canada a
wide variety of Ukrainian dialects (Volynian, Lemko, Sianian, Hutzul, Boyko, Pod-
olian, Dnister, Transcarpathian, etc.) are spoken by people of Ukrainian, and to
some extent also of Polish and Russian origin, depending on the precise area from
which they or their predecessors emigrated (Royick, 1968; Royick and Pohorecky,
1968). The Ukrainian language bears a fairly close similarity to Russian; in
fact, to emphasize the distinctiveness of Ukrainian, Ukrainian nationalists in
Canada replaced letters of the Russian alphabet with new "Ukrainian" ones (Young,
1931:32). Evidently, considerable Anglicization of the Ukrainian dialects began
to occur at a fairly early date in the bloc settlements of western Canada. Numerous Ukrainian-Canadian words were derived from English, though others acutally
from the Ukraine were similar to English. English combined with Ukrainian was increasingly adopted, although English verbs were conjugated by the settlers as if
they were Ukrainian and Ukrainian sentence structure was imposed when speaking
English (this practice became typical of the second generation, whereas the third
generation often tended to reverse the process, imposing English structure on
Ukrainian) (A.B. Anderson, 1976; J.T.M. Anderson, 1918; Lysenko, 1947; Sherbinin,
1906).

9. NAME CHANGE

Finally, the changing of given names or surnames may be closely related to language change as a part of ethnic identity change. As linguistic assimilation or
accommodation occur, some names undergo change and therefore become progressively
less reliable indicators of ethnic identity. Name changing is not necessarily a
deliberate attempt to obscure one's ethnic origin; rather, it may be a practical
attempt to alleviate the embarrassment over people of other ethnic origins not
being able to pronounce a name typical of a particular ethnic group. Given names
tend to change before surnames. Not infrequently in North America the changing
of given names was the result of the arbitrary action of immigration officials at
the time of first immigration. Yet either given names or surnames may be altered
without being converted entirely into – or exchanged for – an English name; the
name may be shortened for convenience, or the spelling may be changed for easy
phonetic pronunciation by English-speakers.

10. <u>SUMMARY</u>

To summarize the foregoing discussion, several conclusions may be drawn from this
paper.

First, we have stressed that language can be an important criterion of ethnic identity. But, while retention of a traditional ethnic language is usually the most
significant identifying criterion for ethnic groups (i.e., most ethnic groups could
be defined as ethnolinguistic groups), it is not the only criterion, nor is it
necessarily the most significant for all ethnic groups (e.g., some ethnic groups
could more readily be defined as ethno-religious groups than as ethnolinguistic
groups).

Second, if an ethnic group largely or completely loses its traditional mother tongue, it does not necessarily cease to exist as an identifiable entity. Criteria
other than language may become emphasized as keys to ethnic consciousness.

Third, a wide variety of factors may serve to determine the survival potential of
ethnolinguistic minorities (including subjective awareness of ethnicity by ethnic
group members, the greater strength of trans-ethnic nationalism than of minority
intra- or sub-nationalism, demographic/ecological considerations, institutionalization of ethnic communities, and ethnic relations).

Fourth, ethnolinguistic minorities (with some notable exceptions), particularly
immigrant groups, tend to eventually lose their traditional languages, for a
variety of reasons. But these minorities differ in their tendency and capability
to resist linguistic assimilation.

Fifth, the ability of minority group members to speak a traditional ethnic language
may differ significantly from their desire (or possibly even freedom) to speak that
language.

Sixth, linguistic change among ethnolinguistic minorities may assume the form of
linguistic assimilation (implying loss of a traditional mother tongue) and/or of
linguistic accommodation (implying change or compromise but not necessarily loss).
Perhaps the former is more typical of immigrant groups in North America, the latter
of ethnolinguistic minorities in Europe (where many examples of remarkable longevity of minority languages can be noted, such as among Basques, Bretons, Sorbs
or Wends, etc.).

REFERENCES

Allport, G.W. (1954) The nature of prejudice, Doubleday/Anchor, Garden City, N.Y.

Anderson, A.B. (1973) The Scottish tradition in Candada: Its rise and fall, in
    A.H. Brodie (ed.): Scottish colloquium proceedings, vol.617, University of
    Guelph, Guelph, Ontario.

A.B. Anderson, Ethnic identity retention in French Canadian communities in Sas-
    katchewan. Research paper presented in a session on "Social organization of
    Francophone communities outside Québec", at the annual meetings of the Canad-
    ian Sociology and Anthropology Association, University of Toronto (August,
    1974a).

A.B. Anderson, Intermarriage in ethnic bloc settlements in Saskatchewan: A cross-
    cultural survey of trends and attitudes. Research paper presented at the annual
    meetings of the Western Association of Sociology and Anthropology, Banff,
    Alberta (December, 1974b).

A.B. Anderson, Ethnic groups: Implications of criteria for the examination of
    survival. A paradigm presented in the workshop in "Ethnicity and ethnic groups
    in Canada", at the annual meetings of the Canadian Sociology and Anthropology
    Association, University of Alberta, Edmonton (May, 1975).

Anderson, A.B. (1976) Ukrainian identity change in rural Saskatchewan, in W.W.
    Isajiw (ed.): Ukrainians in American and Canadian society: Contributions to
    the sociology of ethnic groups, The Ukrainian Center for Social Research,
    New York City, and the Harvard University Ukrainian Research Institute,
    M.P. Kots Publishing, Jersey City, N.J.

Anderson, A.B. (1977) Ethnic identity in Saskatchewan bloc settlements: A socio-
    logical appraisal, in H. Palmer (ed.): The settlement of the West, University
    of Calgary/Comprint Publishing, Calgary.

Anderson, A.B. (1978a) Linguistic trends among Saskatchewan ethnic groups, in
    M.L. Kovacs (ed.): Ethnic Canadians: Culture and education, Canadian Plains
    Research Center, Regina.

A.B. Anderson, East European ethnicity in Canadian society: Recent trends and
    future implications. Proceedings of the Second Annual Banff Conference on
    Central and East European Studies, Banff, Alberta (March, 1978b).

A.B. Anderson, Ethnicity and language in Saskatchewan schools. Research paper
    presented at a session on "Language and ethnicity" at a symposium on "Ethnic-
    ity on the Great Plains", sponsored by the Center for Great Plains Studies,
    University of Nebraska at Lincoln (April, 1978c).

A.B. Anderson, Language minorities and international frontiers: The contemporary
    situation in Western Europe. Paper presented in a session on "Language minor-
    ities and international relations", I.S.A. Research Committee on Sociolinguist-
    ics, Ninth World Congress of Sociology, Uppsala University, Sweden (August,
    1978d).

Anderson, A.B. & Driedger, L. (1978) The Mennonite family: Culture and kin in
    rural Saskatchewan, in K. Ishwaran (ed.): Canadian families: Ethnic variations,
    McGraw-Hill/Ryerson, Toronto.

Anderson, G.M. (1974) Networks of contact: The Portuguese and Toronto, Wilfred Laurier University, Waterloo, Ontario.

Anderson, G.M. & Higgs, D. (1976) A future to inherit: The Portuguese communities of Canada, McClelland and Stewart, Toronto.

Anderson, J.T.M. (1918) The education of the New Canadian, J.M. Dent, Toronto.

Anderson, N. (1969) Studies in multi-lingualism, E.J. Brill, Leiden, Netherlands.

Boissevain, J. (1970) The Italians of Montréal: Social adjustment in a plural society, The Queen's Printer, Ottawa.

Borrie, W.D. (1959) The cultural integration of immigrants, UNESCO, Paris.

Bram, J. (1955) Language and society, Random House, New York.

R. Breton, Institutional completeness of ethnic communities and personal relations of immigrants, American Journal of Sociology, 70, 193-205 (1964).

Campbell, D. & MacLean, R.R. (1974) Beyond the Atlantic roar: A study of the Nova Scotia Scots, McClelland and Stewart/Carlton Library, Toronto.

Connor, W. (1976) The political significance of ethno-nationalism within Western Europe, in A. Said & L.R. Simmons (eds.): Ethnicity in an international context, Transaction Books, New Brunswick, N.J.

De Meyer, J. (1975) La situation juridique des Societés Polyethniques en Europe, in P. Migus (ed.): op.cit.

Deutsch, K.W. (1968) The trend of European nationalism - the language aspect, in J.A. Fishman (ed.): op.cit., 1972b.

J. de Vries, Language maintenance and shift among Canadian ethnic groups. Unpublished ms., Department of the Secretary of State, Ottawa (1974).

de Vries, J. (1977) Languages in contact: A review of Canadian research, in The individual, language and society in Canada, The Canada Council, Ottawa.

J. de Vries, Demographic approaches to the study of language and ethnic relations, Paper presented in a session on "Language and ethnic interaction: Political, ecological and demographic issues", I.S.A. Research Committee on Sociolinguistics, Ninth World Congress of Sociology, Uppsala University, Sweden (August, 1978).

Dion, L. (1975) French as an adopted language in Québec, in P. Migus (ed.): Sounds Canadian: Languages and cultures in multi-ethnic society, Peter Martin, Toronto.

W. Dressler & R. Wodak-Leodolter, Issue on "Language death", International Journal of the Sociology of Language, 12 (1977).

L. Driedger, A sect in modern society: A case study of the Old Colony Mennonites of Saskatchewan, M.A. Thesis in Sociology, University of Chicago (1955).

Edwards, A.D. (1976) Language in culture and class, Heinemann, London.

Emmerson, G.S. (1976) The Gaelic tradition in Canadian culture, in W.S. Reid (ed.): The Scottish tradition in Canada, McClelland and Stewart, Toronto.

England, R. (1929) The Central European immigrant in Canada, MacMillan, Toronto.

Epp, F.H. (1962) Mennonite Exodus, D.W. Friesen, Altona, Manitoba.

Epp, F.H. (1974) Mennonites in Canada: 1786-1920, MacMillan, Toronto.

Fishman, J.A. (1965) Varieties of ethnicity and varieties of language conscious-
    ness, in J.A. Fishman, op.cit., chapter 8, 1972a.

Fishman, J.A. (1966a) Planned reinforcement of language maintenance in the United
    States: Suggestions for the conservation of a neglected national resource, in
    J.A. Fishman, op.cit., chapter 2, 1972a.

Fishman, J.A. (1966b) Language maintenance in a supra-ethnic age, in J.A. Fishman,
    op.cit., chapter 3, 1972a.

Fishman, J.A. (1966c) Language loyalty in the United States: The maintenance and
    perpetuation of non-English mother tongues by American ethnic and religious
    groups, Mouton, The Hague.

Fishman, J.A. (1968a) Language maintenance and language shift as a field of
    inquiry: Revisited, in J.A. Fishman, op.cit., chapter 4, 1972a.

Fishman, J.A. (1968b) Societal bilingualism: Stable and transitional, in J.A.
    Fishman, op.cit., chapter 5, 1972a.

Fishman, J.A. (1968c) The description of societal bilingualism, in J.A. Fishman,
    op.cit., chapter 6, 1972a.

Fishman J.A. (1968d) The multiple prediction of phonological variables in a bi-
    lingual speech community, in J.A. Fishman, op.cit., chapter 7, 1972a.

Fishman, J.A. (1971a) The sociology of language, in J.A. Fishman, op.cit., chapter
    1, 1972a.

Fishman, J.A. (1971b) The impact of nationalism on language planning, in J.A.
    Fishman, op.cit., chapter 10, 1972a.

Fishman, J.A. (1971c) The relationship between micro- and macro-sociolinguistics
    in the study of who speaks what language to whom and when, in J.B. Pride &
    J. Holmes (eds.): op.cit., 1972.

Fishman, J.A. (1972a) Language in sociocultural change: Essays by Joshua A.
    Fishman, Stanford University Press, Stanford, Calif.

Fishman, J.A. (1972b) Readings in the sociology of language, Mouton, Paris/The
    Hague.

Fishman, J.A. (1972c) Bilingual and bidialectal education: An attempt at a joint
    model for policy description, in J.A. Fishman, op.cit., chapter 15, 1972a.

Freeman, E.A. (1958) Language as a basis of racial classification, in E.T. Thompson
    & E.C. Hughes (eds.): Race: Individual and collective behaviour, Free Press,
    Glencoe, III.

Giles, H., Bourhis, R.Y. & Taylor, D.M. (1977) Towards a theory of language in
    ethnic group relations, in H. Giles (ed.): Language, ethnicity and intergroup
    relations, European Monographs in Social Psychology, no.13, Academic Press,
    London.

Gordon, M.M. (1964) <u>Assimilation in American life: The role of race, religion and national origins</u>, Oxford, New York.

Grabowski, Y. (1975) Languages in contact: Polish and English, in P. Migus (ed.): op.cit.

Gross, P.S. (1965) <u>The Hutterite way</u>, Freeman, Saskatoon.

Hall, R.A. (1972) Pidgins and Creoles as standard languages, in J.B. Pride & J. Holmes (eds.): op.cit.

Handlin, O. (1951) <u>The uprooted</u>, Grosset & Dunlap, New York.

Haugen, E. (1966) Dialect, language, nation, in J.B. Pride & J. Holmes (eds.): op.cit., 1972.

Heer, D.M. & Hubay, C.A. (1975) The trend of interfaith marriages in Canada: 1922 to 1972, in S.P. Wakil (ed.): <u>Marriage, family and society: Canadian perspectives</u>, Butterworth, Toronto.

Henripin, J. (1974) <u>Immigration and language imbalance</u>, Manpower and Immigration, Ottawa.

Herberg, W. (1960) <u>Protestant, Catholic, Jew</u>, Doubleday/Anchor, Garden City, N.Y.

Herman, S.R. (1972) Explorations in the social psychology of language choice, in J.A. Fishman (ed.): op.cit., 1972b.

Hostetler, J.A. (1974) <u>Hutterite society</u>, Johns Hopkins University Press, Baltimore and London.

L.J. Hubbell, The bilingual child's acquisition of code-switching rules (French/English in Canada). Research project in progress (1978).

J.E. Humblet, Réflexions sur la place du dialecte dans la vie sociale: Comparaison entre le Luxembourg, le Val d'Aoste et la Wallonie. Research paper presented at a session on "Language and national identity" at the sessions of the I.S.A. Research Committee on Sociolinguistics, Eighth World Congress of Sociology, University of Toronto (August, 1974).

Hymes, D. (1977) <u>Pidginization and Creolization of languages</u>, Cambridge University Press, London.

Jakobson, R. (1968) The beginning of national self-determination in Europe, in J.A. Fishman (ed.): op.cit., 1972b.

Jansen, C.J. (1971) The Italian community in Toronto, in J.L. Elliott (ed.): <u>Minority Canadians</u>, vol.2: <u>Immigrant groups</u>, Prentice-Hall, Scarborough, Ontario.

Joy, R.J. (1972) <u>Languages in conflict</u>, McClelland and Stewart/Carlton Library.

Kalbach, W.E. (1975) The demography of marriage, in S.P. Wakil (ed): op.cit.

Kelly, L.G. (1975) Language maintenance in Canada: Research problems, in P. Migus (ed.): op.cit.

Kloss, H. (1975) Pygmies among giants - small minority groups in the multinational state, in P. Migus (ed.): op.cit.

Kostash, M. (1977) <u>All of Baba's children</u>, Hurtig, Edmonton.

Kovacs, M.L. (ed.) (1978) <u>Ethnic Canadians: Culture and education</u>, Canadian Plains Research Center, Regina.

Lambert, W.E. (1967) A social psychology of bilingualism, in J.B. Pride & J. Holmes (eds.): op.cit., 1972.

Lambert, W.E. et al. (1972) A study of the roles of attitudes and motivation in second-language learning, in J.A. Fishman (ed.): op.cit., 1972b.

Leopold, W.F. (1972) The decline of German dialects, in J.A. Fishman (ed.): op.cit., 1972b.

Lewis, M.M. (1947) <u>Language in society</u>, Thomas Nelson, London.

Lieberson, S. (1963) <u>Ethnic patterns in American cities</u>, Free Press, Glencoe, Ill.

Lieberson, S. (1970) <u>Language and ethnic relations in Canada</u>, John Wiley, Toronto.

Lieberson, S. (1972) An extension of Greenberg's linguistic diversity measures, in J.A. Fishman (ed.): op.cit., 1972b.

Lysenko, V. (1947) <u>Men in sheepskin coats: A study in assimilation</u>, Ryerson, Toronto.

Mackey, W.F. (1967) <u>Bilingualism as a world problem</u>, Harvest House, Montréal.

Mackey, W.F. (1972) The description of bilingualism, in J.A. Fishman (ed.): op.cit., 1972b.

Marunchak, M.H. (1970) <u>The Ukrainian Canadians: A history</u>, Ukrainian Academy of Free Sciences, Winnipeg.

Massucco-Costa, A. (1969) Torre Pellice and its people, in N. Anderson (ed.): op.cit.

Migus, P. (1975) <u>Sounds Canadian: Languages and cultures in multi-ethnic society</u>, Peter Martin, Toronto.

Milnor, A. (1968) The new politics and ethnic revolt: 1928-1938, in N. Ward & D. Spafford (eds.): <u>Politics in Saskatchewan</u>, Longmans and John Dyell, Lindsay, Ontario.

Morris, R.N. & Lanphier, C.M. (1972) <u>Three scales of inequality: Perspectives on French-English relations</u>, Longman Canada, Don Mills, Ontario.

Park, R.E. (1950) <u>Race and culture</u>, Free Press, Glencoe, Ill.

Peterson, W. (1976) On the subnations of Western Europe, in N. Glazer & D.P. Moynihan (eds.): <u>Ethnicity: Theory and experience</u>, Harvard University Press, Cambridge, Mass. and London.

Potter, S. (1960) <u>Language in the modern world</u>, Penguin, Harmondsworth, U.K.

Pride, J.B. & Holmes, J. (1972) <u>Sociolinguistics</u>, Penguin, Harmondsworth, U.K.

T. Priestley, Questionnaire on retention of Slovene in Canada and other papers presented in a session on "language loyalty". Proceedings of the Second Annual Banff Conference on Central and East European Studies, Banff, Alberta (March, 1978).

Radecki, H. & Heydenkorn, B. (1976) A member of a distinguished family: The Polish group in Canada, McClelland and Stewart, Toronto.

Ray, P.S. (1972) Language standardization, in J.A. Fishman (ed.): op.cit., 1972b.

Royal Commission on bilingualism and biculturalism, Report, Book IV: The cultural contributions of the other ethnic groups, The Queen's Printer, Ottawa (1969).

A. Royick, Ukrainian settlements in Alberta, Canadian Slavonic Papers, 10, 3 (1968).

A. Royick & Z.S. Pohorecky, Ethnolinguistic overview of Ukrainian-speaking communities in the province of Alberta, Canada, Napao: A Saskatchewan Anthropology Journal, 1, 2 (1968).

Rydnyckyj, J.B. (1975) The problems of unofficial languages in Canada, in P. Migus (ed.): op.cit.

Saint-Jacques, B. (1976) Aspects sociologiques du bilinguisme Canadien, Centre International de Récherche sur le Bilinguisme et les Presses de l'Université Laval, Québec.

Sautter, G. (1969) Alsatian and Vosgian relationships, in N. Anderson (ed.): op. cit.

Savard, J-G. & Vignealt, R. (1975) Multilingual political systems: Problems and solutions, Centre International de Récherche sur le Bilinguisme et les Presses de l'Université Laval, Québec.

Sealy, N. (1978) Language conflict and schools in New Brunswick, in M.L. Kovacs (ed.): op.cit.

Sherbinin, M.A. (1906) The Galicians dwelling in Canada and their origin, Manitoba Free Press, Winnipeg.

Shibutani, T. & Kwan, K.M. (1965) Ethnic stratification: A comparative approach, MacMillan, New York.

Simon, W.B. (1969) Multilingualism: A comparative study, in N. Anderson (ed.): op.cit.

Simon, W.B. (1975a) A sociological analysis of multilingualism, in P. Migus (ed.): op.cit., 1975.

Simon, W.B. (1975b) Occupational structure, multilingualism and social change, in J-G. Savard & R. Vignealt (eds.): op.cit., 1975.

Smith, C.H. (1957) The story of the Mennonites, Mennonite Publication Office, Newton, Kansas.

Smith, P.M., Tucker, G.R. & Taylor, D.M. (1977) Language, ethnic identity and intergroup relations: One immigrant group's reactions to language planning in Québec, in H. Giles (ed.): op.cit.

Stewart, W.A. (1972) A sociolinguistic typology for describing national multilingualism, in J.A. Fishman (ed.): op.cit., 1972b.

Trudgill, P. (1974) Sociolinguistics: An introduction, Penguin, Harmondsworth, U.K.

A.M.S. Vanneste, Aspects sociolinguistiques de la Flandre Française: Étude diachronique et synchronique. Paper presented in a session on "language and national identity", I.S.A. Research Committee on Sociolinguistics, Eighth World Congress of Sociology, University of Toronto (August, 1974).

W.H. Will, Linguistic isolation as a means of preserving cultural and religious identity: The Mennonites of the Great Plains. Paper presented in a session on "language and ethnicity" in a symposium on "Ethnicity on the Great Plains", sponsored by the Center for Great Plains Studies, University of Nebraska, Lincoln (April, 1978).

Yinger, J.M. (1963) Sociology looks at religion, MacMillan, New York.

Young, C.H. (1931) The Ukrainian Canadians: A study in assimilation, Thomas Nelson, Toronto.

DEMOGRAPHIC APPROACHES TO THE STUDY OF LANGUAGE AND ETHNIC RELATIONS

J. de Vries

Carleton University, Ottawa, Ontario, Canada

1. INTRODUCTION

The background for this overview is the admittedly ethnocentric observation that there appears to be an increasing amount of demographic research on language and ethnicity. Recent political developments in Canada have stimulated, among other things, fairly intense discussions about the past and future of Canada's Francophone population. These discussions are, to a large degree, based on demographic "facts" about language and ethnicity (mainly the information obtained from population censuses and immigration statistics) and on demographic assumptions about future developments.

It is, however, not the case that this type of research is a uniquely Canadian phenomenon. There is what I would call a fluctuating interest in the demographic aspects of the Swedish-speaking population of Finland. Current developments in the United Kingdom, as they relate to Scottish and Welsh nationalism, have clearly demographic concerns regarding language and ethnicity. In addition, there have been analyses of Eastern European populations with "demography" and "ethnicity" as main characteristics (see, for example, the series of papers by Mazur on the fertility of ethnic groups in the Soviet Union, 1967, 1976). There is, finally, the kind of work done by Lieberson and various co-authors, which is based on demographic information on language for a large number of societies, often covering a wide range over time as well (see Lieberson, Dalto and Johnston, 1975; Lieberson and Hansen, 1974; Lieberson and O'Connor, 1975).

It would appear that, generally speaking, three research activities are undertaken as separate enterprises, in the style of case studies. I am asserting, in this paper, that most of the existing work can fit into an analytical framework. Although the kind of framework I am developing is not unique to the demographic analysis of language and ethnicity, it is probably useful to spell out the specific application to language and ethnicity. Such an elaboration would facilitate the linkage of separate research findings, point to common problems and suggest the possibilities for analysis offered by existing techniques of data analysis and estimation.

The model, or framework, which I will discuss could be called a "quasi-population" model. It is a specific application of the general "population model" which underlies much of the work done in demography. In the general population model, we distinguish three components:

      (i)   the population: any aggregate of elements which conform to a given
            definition;

     (ii)   modes of entry: all mechanisms by which the population acquires
            new members;

   (iii)   modes of exit: all mechanisms by which the population loses exist-
            ing members.

For more detailed discussions of the general population model, readers may wish to
read Ryder (1964) or chapter 1 in Goldscheider (1971).

When the general population model is applied to a population of human beings residing in a particular territory, the modes of entry and exit are specified as fertility (= births), mortality (= deaths), immigration and emigration. Thus, we can
set up the familiar demographic "balancing equation":

$$P_t - P_o = (\text{Births} - \text{Deaths}) + (\text{Immigration} - \text{Emigration})$$

"Quasi-populations" are specifiable subsets of populations. If we can partition
a particular population into a set of mutually exclusive and exhaustive subsets,
where membership in a subset is determined by an unambiguous definition, and if
each subset has at least the same methods of entry and exit as the original population, then each subset may be called a "quasi-population". Obviously, the resulting quasi-populations have, in addition to the basic modes of entry and exit defined for the general population, at least one additional mode of entry and exit: the
mechanism by which elements "move" from one quasi-population to another. As is
the case with the general population model, we are generally interested in the
spatial distribution of quasi-population elements, and in their distribution in
time (for individual elements, this means that we are interested in their age).

It should be evident that language groups and ethnic groups, in linguistically or
ethnically plural societies, can be viewed as quasi-populations. In the following
sections of this paper I will attempt to outline how the quasi-population approach
can be used in the study of language and ethnic groups.

It may be useful to make one basic comment before I proceed with the proposed outline. It should be self-evident that the main concerns of any demographic analysis
are: the numerical size of a particular group, changes in that size in the past,
expected changes in size in the future, and, if possible, analysis of the processes
which produced the change. While I admit that size, and the change thereof, are
not the only aspects of ethnic and language contact worth studying, I am asserting
that these aspects are important ones in any study of ethnic or linguistic contact.
I agree with various critics that census data on language and ethnicity are far
from reliable in many cases. However, I think that such data, unreliable as they
may be, are still preferable to not having any data or to various alternative
measures of unknown reliability and validity.

2. THE NATURE OF DEFINITIONS

One of the basic requirements of the quasi-population model is that we can partition a population into a set of mutually exclusive and exhaustive subsets. In
principle, this should not be difficult to do when we are dealing with ethnic or
linguistic groups.

In the case of ethnic origin, for example, we are generally dealing with a classification based on descent. Analytically, it does not matter whether we use region, language, culture, religion, or some combination of these as criteria by which
we design our classification. It is even possible to devise specific categories to

accommodate individuals of mixed origins (consider, as an example, the classification employed in the New Zealand Census of 1961, illustrated in Shryock and Siegel, 1973:255). All one needs is a set of categories which are mutually exclusive and exhaustive, combined with unambiguous instructions to respondents regarding the way in which they should place themselves in one and only one category. Nevertheless, the Canadian censuses, which have combined a question on ethnic origin since 1871, provide a set of categories which is not mutually exclusive (see Ryder, 1955, and de Vries, forthcoming, for further details on Canada's ethnic origin).

With regard to language, census questions generally belong to one of the following three types:

> (i) *"mother tongue" questions*, which generally ask for the language usually spoken in the individual's home in early childhood;
>
> (ii) *"usual language" questions*, which ask for the language currently spoken, or most often spoken by the individual in his present home, and;
>
> (iii) *"designated language" questions*, which ask for the individual's ability to speak one or more designated languages (Shryock and Siegel, 1973; U.N., 1967:49-50).

For all these types of questions it should also be possible to construct proper classifications. Note that I am not concerned, at this stage, with the reliability or validity of any data obtained on the basis of these questions, but only with the logical adequacy of possible answers. As an example: even if we wish to accommodate those individuals who report having two "mother tongues", it is possible to designate that situation as a separate one, distinct from all single-language categories. The Canadian census questions on "designated languages" ask for the respondent's ability to speak English and/or French. One of the response categories is "both English and French", distinct from "English only" and "French only".

The first important aspect of any study of ethnic or linguistic quasi-populations is, thus, to ensure that there is a proper classification by which we can determine membership in a particular quasi-population. Each category in the classification becomes a separate quasi-population. For cases where no proper classification exists, we may sometimes be able to combine categories, in order to produce a classification which satisfies the elementary logical requirements.

The second aspect of definitions which demands some attention is that of consistency. Even for a simple analysis of change over time we require consistent classifications. In cases where we do not have totally identical classifications, we can sometimes achieve consistency through the collapsing of categories. A sometimes overlooked aspect of this need for consistency is the requirement that classifications should include a "no answer" category. There is currently a fair amount of debate between different groups of Canadian demographers regarding the census data on the population of French mother tongue for 1971 and 1976. The crucial element underlying this debate is the fact that in the 1976 census a "no answer" category was provided, while in the 1971 census, "no answer" cases were allocated to specified language categories through imputation. Aside from requiring classifications to be consistent over time for the same medium (e.g., population censuses), we will also need consistency in classifications between different media (for example, population census and vital statistics). Not only do we wish to compute rates of change over time, we normally also want to study the relative contributions of such processes as fertility or mortality to this overall growth rate. As a consequence, we must be able to combine data from vital statistics and censuses to compute such contributions.

A third aspect of definitions which needs to be noted is the degree to which membership in a given quasi-population is permanent ("inherited") or "achieved". In the case of ethnic origin, membership would be permanent when it is measured through criteria of descent or nativity; it would be "achieved" if we measured it through self-identification or affiliation. With regard to linguistic groupings: questions on "designated languages" and on "usual" or "main" language obviously produce categories in which membership is "achieved". Questions on "mother tongue" are producing groups in which membership is "inherited" if they follow the phrasing recommended by the United Nations (with the possible exception of very young individuals). The phrasing used in the Canadian censuses from 1941 to 1976, however, turns mother tongue into a potentially "achieved" characteristic by defining it as the language "first learned in childhood and still understood".

The last important aspect of definitions is formed by the rules by which "nonconforming" responses were handled. This, by the way, involves such things as instructions to interviewers and/or respondents, and the editing procedures followed in the processing of the data. Non-conforming responses include such things as "no answer"; multiple responses to questions which only demanded a single response; situations where respondents are not provided with a suitable response category; situations where respondents gave inconsistent answers to different questions in the same census; and so forth. Some examples: Canadian respondents who are no longer able to understand the language they spoke first in their childhood are instructed to respond with the next language they learned, provided that they are still able to understand that language. As another example, the 1971 census of Canada produced relatively large changes in some categories through some rather poorly publicized editing procedures. One such editing procedure "created" about 129,000 individuals able to speak both English and French. Another editing procedure assigned all individuals with Jewish as religion to the Jewish ethnic group; in this instance, it is not known how many individuals were affected.

I have devoted a lot of attention to the discussion of definitions for several reasons. Obviously, the fact that the quasi-population is a dynamic one implies that definitions must be consistent over time. If, moreover, we wish to conduct any kind of comparative research, then definitions must be comparable across societies, and across different ethnic or linguistic "groups". Finally, the nature of the definitions used has a rather important impact on the specific data requirements.

3. DATA REQUIREMENTS, DATA AVAILABILITY AND CONSTRAINTS ON ANALYSIS

As is the case for all demographic analyses based on a "population" model, the quasi-population approach to the analysis of linguistic and ethnic groups requires, ideally, that we have "stock" and "flow" data on our quasi-populations. I have outlined specific requirements in more detail in an earlier paper (de Vries, 1977, especially pp. 20-25). To summarize that discussion, let me just state that we need the following kinds of data:

a. *Census data*, giving the division of the total population into the set of quasi-populations we wish to study. Ideally, of course, we would wish to have a sequence of census data, at regular intervals (perferably five-year or ten-year intervals) with consistent definitions for all censuses involved.

b. *Data on entries and exits*. Since entries and exits fall into several distinct categories, we would like to have information on each mode which can be specified. Thus, we would need to have data on:

(i) *births*, by membership in a given quasi-population (e.g., by mother tongue or by ethnic origin). We often encounter problems at this stage already: babies are unable to speak *any* language at birth and thus do not really have a "mother tongue". Census statistics use a shortcut in this case by defining the mother tongue of infants as the language spoken most frequently in the home. The problem obviously does not arise when we deal with ethnic groups, in which membership is defined in terms of nativity or ancestry, or in the case of membership in "usual" language groups if such groups are defined at the level of families or households;

(ii) *deaths*, by membership in a given quasi-population. Although this presents fewer problems than would birth statistics by language or ethnicity, death statistics generally provide no relevant information;

(iii) *migration statistics* (both immigration and emigration) in which individuals are classified by membership in a given quasi-population;

(iv) *"transitions"* between quasi-populations. It is for this class of data that the definition of quasi-population membership becomes important. Obviously, such transitions form an empty set if the definitions refer to inherited and permanent characteristics. The Canadian census definition of ethnicity is of this kind; so is the definition of "mother tongue" recommended by the United Nations. Obviously, the higher the "achieved" (and thus potentially changeable) component of the definiendum, the higher is the probability that changes will occur.

These four classes of data have been ordered by descending likelihood of their being available. While a large number of nation-states has been collecting census information on ethnic or linguistic characteristics (see, for a summary, the United Nations' Demographic Yearbooks for 1956, 1963, 1964, 1971, and 1973), vital statistics (i.e., births and deaths) are only rarely classified by language or ethnicity. Migration statistics are much less common anyway (especially statistics on emigration), and the available statistics almost never provide information on language or ethnicity. The last data class, that of "interstitial moves" is, of course, entirely absent from all public data.

It is obviously not realistic to expect anyone to collect such "transition statistics". At best, such "events" could be studied through rather detailed surveys, preferably based on longitudinal panel designs. At present, we have only some surveys which contain part of the necessary statistics.

As a consequence of the difficulty in collecting the necessary data, the demographic analysis of ethnic and linguistic groups frequently encounters the problems of data deficiencies. This is not an argument that we abandon the demographic approach due to such substantial obstacles. By a similar argument, virtually no demographic analyses would be conducted in any area. There are, on the contrary, several topics in demography which suffer from comparable data deficiencies. The main ones which could serve as a model are:

(i) the study of populations for which *no* adequate statistics are available, e.g., underdeveloped societies without reliable vital registration systems, and often without a reliable census. The techniques developed for the demographic study of populations in tropical Africa (Brass et al., 1968; Caldwell, 1975) would appear to be highly relevant for our concerns;

(ii) the study of internal migration. The logical isomorphisms between the study of a population partitioned into a set of regional sub-populations and that of a population partitioned into a set of ethnic or linguistic quasi-populations should be self-evident. Here, too, there are methods of analysis and estimation which could be adapted to the study of ethnicity and language.

4. ESTIMATING LINGUISTIC OR ETHNIC FERTILITY

There are several peculiar problems one encounters in the demographic analysis of

ethnic or linguistic fertility. First of all, children do not speak any language
at birth and, consequently, can not be allocated to any language group (except if
it were done on the basis of language characteristics of the family of origin).
The customary census practice could be followed to reduce the impact of this problem.

A second problem is that births are associated with two parents, who themselves may
well belong to different quasi-populations. While the device of classifying births
by "home language" might give us a good estimate of the eventual mother tongue of
the child, it does not provide the link between the child's imputed characteristic
and those of its parents. Note that the problem is not unique - a comparable problem arises when we study age-specific fertility patterns. However, in that case a
convincing argument can be made for concentrating on female age-specific fertility
(given biological constraints on female reproductivity). I do not think one can
raise the corresponding argument (i.e., wishing to concentrate on the ethnic or
linguistic affiliation of the mother only) with equal tenability for the analysis
of ethnic or linguistic fertility.

A final confounding factor in the analysis of differential fertility by ethnic or
linguistic group is that, for some definitions, children can shift into categories
different from that of either the father, or the mother, or both (for example, when
we deal with the mother tongue of Canadian-born children of foreign parentage).

Quite obviously, the above problems are not terribly salient if our measure of fertility is based on the direct association between mothers (or fathers) and their
own children. Thus, estimates of fertility derived from the reponses to questions
regarding "number of children ever borne" would be the most reliable ones with
regard to differences between quasi-populations. (Note that I am not, at this
point, concerned with more general biases inherent in these methods). In contrast
to "direct" measures of fertility, some of the more commonly used "indirect" measures of fertility are affected by problems of definition and classification. As
an illustration, consider the "child-woman ratio", i.e., the ratio between the
number of children under five years of age and the number of women aged 20-24 (or
20-49). For example, Henripin (1978) provides child-woman ratios for various Canadian ethnic groups. Since Canadian ethnic origin is measured through one's pat-
ernal ancestry, children of ethnically mixed marriages will not be classified in
the same ethnic group as their *mothers*, but in the same group as their *fathers*.
Thus, some "child-man" ratios would be more appropriate for this situation. Such
effects of classification would be negligble if they cancelled out (e.g., if the
numbers of Ukrainian-English families equalled the number of English-Ukrainian
families, and so on). However, in the Canadian census data this is not the case.
For example, ethnic endogamy has been much higher for females of Italian ethnic
origin in Canada than it was for males of Italian ethnic origin (see Boissevain,
1970; de Vries and Vallée, forthcoming, chapter 7). In the 1971 census, there were
177,425 husband-wife families in which the husband was of Italian ethnic origin
(the children in *all* of these families would be of Italian ethnic origin), in contrast to only 162,565 husband-wife families in which the wife was of Italian ethnic
origin. Thus, the "ethnic" child-woman ratio overestimates, ceteris paribus, Italian ethnic fertility by about 9 per cent!

In summary: in the estimation of linguistic or ethnic fertility we have very little
chance of obtaining necessary registration data. Estimation through census data
will be relatively unbiased if we deal with data linking children with their mothers, but may contain biases if we are unable to establish this link (as in the case
of child-woman ratios). As such, several analyses of linguistic or ethnic fertility (e.g., Henripin, 1978; Mazur, 1967, 1976) contain potential biases of unknown
magnitude.

5. ESTIMATING LINGUISTIC OR ETHNIC MORTALITY

While the measurement of mortality is, generally, a simpler procedure than that of
fertility, it does require registration statistics on deaths, with sufficient details. As with the analysis of fertility for linguistic or ethnic groups, mortality analysis with "direct" measures is generally not possible, because countries
generally do not provide the relevant ethnic or linguistic information on death
statistics.

As a consequence, the estimation of ethnic or linguistic mortality has to rely on
the indirect techniques which have been developed for the analysis of populations
of statistically underdeveloped nations (see, for example, chapter 25 in Shryock
and Siegel, 1973). Unfortunately, these techniques almost invariably make at
least one of the following assumptions:

(i)   mortality is the only means of exit from the population, and fertility is
the only means of entry into the population (a "closed" population);

(ii)   other means of exit are insignificant in comparison with mortality, and
other means of entry are insignificant in comparison with fertility;

(iii)   the effects of other means of exit and entry can be estimated with sufficient accuracy.

In the estimation of linguistic or ethnic mortality, it may well be that none of
these three assumptions is tenable. Thus, the techniques outlined in Shryock and
Siegel, applied to the estimation of ethnic or linguistic mortality, will normally
have the effect of combining "mortality" and "net linguistic (or ethnic) shift"
under the rubric "mortality". Unless we have alternative means of estimating
ethnic or language shift, these techniques will inevitably produce estimates with
biases of unknown direction and magnitude.

6. ESTIMATING LANGUAGE SHIFT OR ETHNIC SHIFT

We obviously do not have the necessary equivalents of the vital statistics data
which were required in the analysis of fertility and mortality. Thus, all methods
of estimation of these modes of entry and exit are "indirect" ones. Techniques
for estimating "shift" have, so far, been based on two different types of situations:

a. *Multiple Observations on Respondents in a Single Census*

Many censuses contain multiple questions regarding the linguistic or ethnic affiliation of members of the population. It is often the case that, in such censuses,
data may be held to pertain to different stages in the respondent's life cycle.
For example, Canada's 1971 census contains a question on *mother tongue* (language
first learned in childhood and still understood) and one on *"home language"* (language most often spoken in the household). Analyses of language shift in Canada,
based on the 1971 census, have generally postulated that "mother tongue" information provided a valid and reliable measure of language behaviour during the respondents' childhood, while "home language" information has been taken as a measure
of current language behaviour. Differences between the two measures have been assumed to reflect language shift, to have occurred at some time during the intervening period.

These particular methods can be subdivided further into two categories:

(i) *"direct" measures*, in which the two (or, possibly, even more) relevant variables are cross-tabulated against each other. Such direct tabulations allow, of

course, the direct measurement of gross flows. For example, a cross-tabulation of
mother tongue with home language in the 1971 Canadian census gives us the number of
persons of English mother tongue and French home language, as well as the number of
persons of French mother tongue and English home language. As Kralt (1977) points
out, such direct tabulations are superior to the indirect measures (which I will
discuss below), especially when several language groups are involved. Unfortunately, specific tabulations of this nature are relatively uncommon. While several
statistical bureaux have shown increased willingness to provide analysis files and/
or special tabulations, this willingness tends to apply only to the most recent
census. Earlier censuses tend to be beyond this type of request.

(ii) *"indirect" measures*, obtained through the joint use of information in two or
more separate cross-tabulations. In the simplest version of this, two marginal
distributions are compared for the same population or sub-population (for example,
all inhabitants of a community, or all individuals in a certain age group). Differences in numerical size between corresponding categories (for example, French
mother tongue and French home language), then yield the size of the "net" flow.
As an example, there is a sequence of Canadian studies in which discrepancies between the number of persons of French mother tongue are taken as indicators of the
decline of the French language in Canada (e.g., Henripin, 1967; Maheu, 1970).

It should be obvious that such "indirect" estimates are potentially misleading, especially when more than two quasi-populations are involved. In the absence of
direct tabulations, however, researchers are often faced with the difficult choice
between using such deficient information, or having no information at all. Given
that choice, I would favour using admittedly deficient data, with the proviso that,
wherever possible, evaluations be done of the potential biases introduced by these
methods.

b. *Observations from two or more Censuses*

An alternative set of techniques for the estimation of shifts is based on the use
of two or more censuses, preferably adjacent in time (most commonly, five or ten
years apart). The most primitive approach consists of the simple comparison of
marginal distributions and an analysis of the differences in size for the quasi-
populations being studied. It is often possible to conduct more refined comparisons, for example through *cohort analyses*. This approach is based on the assumption that we can follow birth cohorts (usually in groups of five or ten years)
through successive censuses. For this approach, it is almost imperative that censuses are multiples of five years apart. The technique requires intercensal consistency in definitions of quasi-populations to be compared.

More complex than fairly simple comparisons are the "residual methods". In such
methods, we measure all means of entry and exit *other than shift* separately (or
estimate them with high reliability). We then calculate the effects of shift during the intercensal period with the customary demographic "balancing equation":
shift is then the residual quantity which is required to balance the equation.

It should be clear that such residual methods are afflicted with fairly substantial
problems. I have already referred to the importance of definitions, which must be
consistent. Moreover, data collection methods and editing procedures should be
identical, or only have minor variations. Despite these difficulties, residual
methods are often used simply because no alternatives are readily available. Examples of residual methods may be found for Finland (de Vries, 1974, 1977) and for
some ethnic and linguistic groups in Canada (see de Vries, 1974, forthcoming).

The reader with some exposure to general demographic methods will recognize that
the sequence of methods outlined for the study of language and ethnic shift is

closely related to the techniques used in the study of internal migration. The
logical status of the two problems is, in fact, almost identical: in both cases,
we are concerned with the estimation of "moves" across "boundaries".

As Lachapelle (1978) points out, this isomorphism can be extended to several other
domains. The most promising one appears to be that of social (occupational) mobility. Although most mobility research is based on direct tabulations obtained
through sample surveys, and may therefore be in a better situation to develop analytical techniques, there are several elements in the logic of mobility analyses
which could be adopted fruitfully in the study of language and ethnic shift.

7. ESTIMATING LINGUISTIC AND ETHNIC NUPTIALITY

Although nuptiality has, generally, no direct effect on the growth or structure
of ethnic or linguistic groups, it has rather pervasive "indirect" effects through
fertility. In most societies, the overwhelming majority of children is born to
legally married couples. Especially when we are dealing with ascribed characteristics such as ethnic origin, it is therefore important to have some knowledge of
the population exposed to the risk of producing new members for a particular
ethnic group.

Before I proceed, I should note that there are some instances where nuptiality has
a direct effect on the size and structure of an ethnic group. Canadian Indians
are, at the moment, faced with the somewhat peculiar situation that Indian women
lose their Indian status if they marry a non-Indian; the same is not the case when
an Indian man marries a non-Indian woman. The legislation regarding "status Indians" thus directly affects the size of the population of "status Indians" in Canada through nuptiality.

With regard to the study of nuptiality, we are interested in two classes of phenomena. The first, more general, class is that of the *quantity* and *timing* of nuptiality by quasi-population. By quantity we refer to the proportion of members of
a group ever marrying (or its complement, the proportion remaining celibate); by
timing we refer to "typical" (that is, mean or medium) ages at first marriage for
those who ever marry. These analyses require the information about quasi-population membership of those marrying (or those now married). Several analyses of ethnic nuptiality in Canada have appeared in recent years (Reddy and Krishnan, 1976;
De Ruyter, 1976).

Analytically more interesting is the second class of phenomena: ethnic or linguistic intermarriage. By this we refer to the tendency for those who marry to select
a mate from the same or from a different quasi-population. For those marrying
outside their own group, we might wish to know whether the selection is "random"
or systematic.

For a full study of intermarriage, we would require data from population censuses
as well as from marriage registrations. Generally, we are only able to use one
source of data: either data from vital registration on those marrying, or data
from censuses on husband-wife couples. As a consequence, I can mention studies on
linguistic intermarriage in Finland (de Vries, 1979) based on vital statistics,
and on ethnic and linguistic intermarriage in Canada based on census data (Norris,
1978).

An important analytical concern in the study of intermarriage is the linkage between the two styles of analysis. It is clear that census data on husband-wife
families are potentially biased, since they only deal with the "survivors" of
earlier marriages. At present, we have no knowledge about the extent of these
biases.

8. ASPECTS OF FAMILY STRUCTURE

Aside from the study of family formation through marriage, the analysis of ethnic or linguistic family structure is important. For example, ethnic or linguistic family size gives us clues about fertility and the prospects for growth or main-tenance of the quasi-population. Analyses of language use in linguistically mixed families could shed light on the process of inter-generational language shift.

Even more than for the preceding topics, data requirements for the study of family structure are poorly met. Census publications on families have only occasionally contained tables on the linguistic or ethnic structure of families. As an example, the Finnish census of 1970 contains a number of tables on families and households with *some* information on language, but there is no integrated set of tables which would facilitate analysis (see de Vries, 1979, for an attempt to co-ordinate the information from these separate tables). The 1971 Census of Canada does even worse: the only relevant table is one giving ethnic origins for husbands and wives in husband-wife families.

It is generally the case that the demography of families and households is rather poorly developed. This is even more the case for the study of ethnic or linguistic families. Virtually the only relevant work in this area is the analysis of the choice of language by children in Finnish-Swedish mixed marriages in Finland (Foug-stedt and Hartman, 1956).

9. BILINGUALISM

An important aspect in the study of linguistic quasi-populations is that of indiv-idual bilingualism. It is analytically important because bilingualism is a necess-ary (though not sufficient) condition for language shift. Census data normally give information on bilingualism through responses to questions regarding the ab-ility to speak *specific* languages. In some cases, these questions have, by them-selves, yielded information on the prevalence of bilingualism (e.g., Canada, 1901 to 1971; Belgium, to 1947). In other cases, the information is obtained by joint use of two questions, one of which is really supplementary to the other. For example, the Finnish census of 1950 contained a question regarding the respondent's main language, followed by a subsidiary question regarding the ability to speak the "other" official language. The strength of this approach is that one can id-entify the linguistic "origins" of bilinguals, while the former approach does not provide this information as straight-forwardly. As a consequence, there has been a development of estimation techniques, designed to estimate bilingualism by mother tongue in Canada. Illustrations may be found in Lieberson (1970), in Vallée and de Vries (1978), and Hurd (1937). External verifications have shown that such estimations have generally been quite accurate.

A different approach to the estimation of bilingualism in Canada was developed by de Vries and Vallée (forthcoming). The Canadian census gives fairly reliable information on what we have called "official" bilingualism (i.e., the ability to speak both English and French), but it does not give any direct information on what, by contrast, we have called "unofficial" bilingualism (that is, the ability to speak two languages, at most one of which is either English or French). In the absence of direct information, we combined the information contained in three language questions (mother tongue, home language, and "official languages spoken") to construct a typology of language ability. With the typology, we were able to locate individuals who were "unofficially bilingual". It might be interesting to know that, in 1971, there were almost as many "unofficial" bilinguals in Canada as there were "official" bilinguals.

As I already pointed out, bilingualism is an important analytical variable in the
analysis of language shift. Especially when we move into more complex analytical
modes of language shift, the analysis of bilingualism should be an integral part.

10. CONCLUSION

By way of summary, let me make the following comments. I have demonstrated that
it is possible to develop a "framework" for the demographic analysis of linguistic
and ethnic quasi-populations. Such a framework would give some coherence to the
now rather disjointed analysis of ethnic or linguistic fertility, language shift,
intermarriage, and so on. In addition, thorough utilization of the framework
appears to yield additional analytical techniques which can be applied by virtue
of the isomorphism between the study of linguistic or ethnic quasi-populations and
that of other kinds of quasi-populations.

REFERENCES

Blau, P.M. (1977) Inequality and heterogeneity: A primitive theory of social structure, The Free Press, New York.

Boissevain, J. (1970) Italians of Montréal: Social adjustment in a plural society, The Queen's Printer, Ottawa.

Brass, W. et al. (1968) The demography of tropical Africa, Princeton University Press, Princeton, N.J.

Caldwell, J.C.(ed.) (1975) Population growth and socio-economic change in West Africa, Columbia University Press, New York, N.Y.

B. De Ruyter, Ethnic differentials in age at first marriage, Canada 1971, Journal of Comparative Family Studies, 7, 2 (1976).

J. de Vries, Net effects of language shift in Finland, 1951-1960, Acta Sociologica, 17, 2, 140-149 (1974).

J. de Vries, Language maintenance and shift among Canadian ethnic groups, Unpublished ms., Department of the Secretary of State (1974).

J. de Vries, Explorations in the demography of language: Estimation of net language shift in Finland, 1961-1970, Acta Sociologica, 20, 2, 145-153 (1977).

de Vries, J. (1977) Languages in contact: A review of Canadian research, in The individual, language and society in Canada, The Canada Council, Ottawa.

J. de Vries, Local homogamy and linguistic endogamy in Finland, 1951-1972, Unpublished ms. (1978).

J. de Vries, Explorations in the demography of language: Estimation of the language composition of families and their children, Finland, 1970, Acta Sociologica (1979).

de Vries, J. (forthcoming) Explorations in the demography of language: The case of the Ukrainians in Canada, in Language patterns and language planning.

de Vries, J. & Vallée, F.G. (forthcoming) Determinants of language use in Canada.

G. Fougstedt & T. Hartman, Social factors affecting the choice of language by children of Finnish-Swedish mixed marriages in Finland, Transactions of the Westermarck Society, 3, 34-54 (1956).

Goldscheider, C. (1971) Population, modernization and social structure, Little, Brown and Co., Boston.

Henripin, J. (1967) Tendances et facteurs de la fécondité au Canada, The Queen's Printer, Ottawa.

J. Henripin, Évolution de la fécondité selon la langue maternelle, Unpublished ms. (1978).

Hurd, W.B. (1937) Racial origins and nativity of the Canadian people, 1931, The Queen's Printer, Ottawa.

Kralt, J. (1977) The case against net-language transfer: An alternate measure, in P. Lamy (ed.): Language maintenance and language shift in Canada, University of Ottawa Press, Ottawa.

R. Lachapelle, Quelques notes introductives en vue d'une étude de la mobilité linguistique au Canada, Unpublished ms. (1978).

Lieberson, S. (1970) Language and ethnic relations in Canada, Wiley, New York.

S. Lieberson, G. Dalto & M. Johnston, The course of mother-tongue diversity in nations, American Journal of Sociology, 81, 34-61 (1975).

S. Lieberson & L.K. Hansen, National development, mother tongue diversity and the comparative study of nations, American Sociological Review, 39, 523-541 (1974).

Lieberson, S. & O'Connor, J.F. (1975) Language diversity in a nation and its regions, in Proceedings of the roundtable on multilingual political systems, Laval University Press, Québec.

Maheu, R. (1970) Les francophones du Canada, 1941-1991, Éditions Parti Pris, Montréal.

D.P. Mazur, Fertility among ethnic groups in the U.S.S.R., Demography, 4, 172-195 (1967).

D.P. Mazur, Constructing fertility tables for Soviet populations, Demography, 13, 19-35 (1976).

M.J. Norris, The role of language and education in mate selection in Canada, Unpublished M.A. Thesis, Carleton University, Ottawa (1978).

I. Reddy & P. Krishnan, Ethnic differentials in age at first marriage, Canada 1961, Journal of Comparative Family Studies, 7, 1 (1976).

N.B. Ryder, The interpretation of origin statistics, Canadian Journal of Economics and Political Science, 21, 466-479 (1955).

N.B. Ryder, Notes on the concept of a population, American Journal of Sociology, 69, 447-463 (1964).

Shryock, H. & Siegel, J.S. (1973) The methods and materials of demography, U.S. Department of Commerce, Washington, U.S.

United Nations: Department of Economic and Social Affairs
    1956 Demographic Yearbook
    1963 Demographic Yearbook
    1964 Demographic Yearbook
    1971 Demographic Yearbook
    1973 Demographic Yearbook

United Nations, Principles and recommendations for the 1970 population censuses, Statistical Papers, Series M. No.44 (1967).

Vallée, F.G. & de Vries, J. (1978) Issues and trends in bilingualism in Canada, in J.A. Fishman (ed.): Advances in the study of multilingual societies, Mouton, The Hague.

LINGUISTIC VARIATION AND ETHNIC INTERACTION IN BELIZE: CREOLE/CARIB

G. J. Escure

University of Minnesota, U.S.A.

OVERVIEW OF THE LINGUISTIC SITUATION IN BELIZE[*]

This paper investigates some types of phonological and syntactic variables in the continuum ranging between Creole and English which functions as a *lingua franca* in Belize (previously called British Honduras). The ethnic factor is specifically examined as one of the determinants of language variability in different contact situations - namely, in intra- and inter-group communication.

Belize offers a particularly interesting sociolinguistic situation, due to its geographical position and its ethnic composition: located east of Guatemala, south of Mexico, and directly west of Jamaica, it is subject to both Latin American and Caribbean influences, with the latter being predominant. Five ethnic groups have preserved different racial and cultural features, and distinct native languages. *Creoles*, of mixed Afro-European descent, constitute the largest group, with Belizean Creole (henceforth BC), an English-based Creole, as their native language; *Black Caribs* are descendents of Arawak/Carib Indians and Africans[1], who speak Carib, an Afro-Indian Creole, or, as they prefer to call their language, "Garifuna"; *Mestizos* (Spanish/Indian) speak Spanish; *Amerindians* include the two subgroups of Maya and Kekchi Indians whose languages are not mutually intelligible; finally, *German Mennonites* speak a dialect of German. Not included in the present paper are the

---

[*]This research was supported by a University of Minnesota Graduate School grant No. 431-0350-4909-02, and a McMillan Travel grant. I want to express my thanks to all my Belizean friends and more particularly to the inhabitants of Placencia and Seine Bight who gracefully submitted to my relentless questioning. Special thanks to Errol Lopez who provided invaluable help in conducting interviews.

[1]Taylor, 1951, 1977.

Mennonites and Amerindians, since both groups rarely become fluent speakers of BC,
due to their almost total isolation[2], and Mestizos who are being studied elsewhere[3]. My observations will thus be based here on the two remaining groups,
Creoles and Black Caribs, with special emphasis on the variability of the language
they use in intercultural communication. Garifuna is reserved exclusively for
Carib intra-group exchanges. As it is never used as a *lingua franca*, it will
therefore not be discussed *per se*. BC, the native language of the Creole group is
widely stigmatized, even by its own native speakers, as is usually the case with
contact vernaculars, but it is learned as a second language and used to a certain
extent by the Caribs. Belize's official language is English, although it is no
one's native language in the country. Consequently, it functions solely as a
school-learned acrolect[4] in a wide spectrum of English-based varieties. Most situations involving contact vernaculars (e.g., the Jamaican situation as described
in DeCamp, 1971; Le Page, 1960, or the Guyanese situation as described in Bickerton, 1975) are characterized by a lack of homogeneity, due partly to the derogatory attitudes towards Creole languages which prevent standardization and lead to
a great deal of variability in the speech of native speakers of Creoles. The Belizean situation is made even more complicated by the fact that a large number of
individuals use in all cases of ethnic interaction a non-native language – some
form of Creole or English, the products of second or third-language learning.
Clearly, then, the linguistic situation in Belize cannot be described in terms of
discrete, separate varieties of Creole and English, but should rather be viewed
as a linguistic continuum of forms showing different degrees of creolization or
decreolization. The overall spectrum ranges between two poles: at the prestigious
end of the continuum there is a West Indian standard (henceforth WIS) – labelled
"English" by Belizeans – which is an unstable combination of American, British and
Creole (BC) features[5]. At the other end, there is BC, the basilect, locally referred to as "broad Creole" or "raw Creole", mostly spoken in remote rural or coastal areas. "Broken English" is a commonly used term to indicate mesolectal (i.e.,
intermediate, decreolized) varieties. The specific segments controlled by a
given speaker are determined by a network of social, environmental and psychologic-

---

[2]The Mennonites live in relatively well-organized and mechanized dairy-farming
villages; they are opposed to interracial marriage, keep their own schools and do
not participate in the country's social and political activities. Amerindians
also shun contacts with the rest of the population; they live in secluded villages
on scanty home-grown food. The two distinct groups of Indians, Mayas and Kekchis,
do not interact with each other. Separateness of identity for the Mennonites and
the Amerindians is characterized not only by distinct native languages and racial
physical features, religious and occupational patterns, but also by different dress
codes. Not surprisingly, they constitute the only two groups in Belize thus overtly displaying their separate ethnicity. For their limited but necessary contacts
with the rest of the population (markets, etc.) they resort to school-learned
English, or to Spanish.

[3]"Linguistic variation and ethnic interaction in Belize: Creole/Mestizo", in
preparation.

[4]The terms "acrolect", "mesolect" and "basilect" refer respectively to prestigious,
intermediate and stigmatized varieties.

[5]Belize is still a British colony, the question of independence being delayed by
borderline conflicts with Guatemala. On the other hand, the influence of American
English is fairly strong, since many Belizeans visit the U.S. for a more or less
extended period, bringing back a number of Americanisms, mostly lexical items
borrowed from Black English.

al factors, one of them being this speaker's ethnic membership, the variable under consideration here.

The intent of this paper is to identify the segments of this continuum which are used by native and non-native speakers of Creole - respectively Creoles and Caribs - in intra-group as well as in intergroup communication; then to compare the performance of the two groups in contact, in order to determine the range of variability in each case, and to understand the functioning of the code-switching process, as triggered by the ethnic factor.

METHODOLOGY

Previous attempts at analyzing the complex pattern of linguistic variation in a social context have usually been restricted to monolingual societies: the "inherent variability" approach (e.g., Labov, 1966, 1972; Wolfram, 1969, 1973) is based on the analysis of the frequency of variants in Black English, and its correlation to social factors. "Scalogram analysis" applied to Jamaican Creole and Black English (e.g., DeCamp, 1971; Fasold, 1970) reveals chains of implications by studying the co-occurrence of linguistic features within each idiolect.

Although I am deeply indebted to all of those previous works, my analysis has to be somewhat different, since in the Belizean multi-lingual situation, ethnicity as a social variable is of major significance and directly correlates with linguistic diversity. With the exception of Le Page (1972, 1974) who outlines a methodological approach to the problems of child language acquisition in a predominantly Spanish-speaking district of Belize, no special attention has yet been given to the problems of ethnic interaction in the Belizean society[6]. In this case, it is necessary to capture both the ingroup Creole-English variation and the intergroup variation in Carib-Creole interaction. I hypothesized that the continuum could be characterized by tabulating the frequency of occurrence of a combination of speech clues which would function as indicators of the social interactional situation. The following nine phonological and nine syntactic features were selected as speech clues:

Phonological Speech Clues:

(a) cluster simplification: i.e., *next* pronounced (nɛs), *first* (fɔs), *dust* (dɔs);
(b) unrounding of the lowback round vowel: *law* (la:), *small* (smal), *all* (al);
(c) rounding of the back unrounded stressed vowels /ʌ/ and /ɼ/: *duck* (dɔk), *bird* (bɔ:d), *first* (fɔs), *gun* (gɔn), *dust* (dɔs), *drum* (drɔ), *bunk* (bɔ̃k);
(d) colouring of vowels not bearing primary stress: *water* (wata), *pressure* (preša), *technical* (teknikal), *funeral* (fynueral), *recent* (risɛ̃t);
(e) lowering of the high front vowel before /r/. The liquid is rarely realized, or has a coronal glide reflex: *beer* (bɛ∂), *here, hear* (hɛ∂), *pier* (pɛ∂);
(f) monophthongization of /aw/ to (o): *now* (no), *town* (tõ), *house* (hos);
(g) occlusion of the voiced interdental fricative /ð/ to (d): *father* (fada), *weather* (weda), *other* (ada);
(h) occlusion of the voiceless interdental fricative /θ/ to (t): *thin* (tin), *think,* (tik), *thick* (tik), *north* (nat);
(i) unrounding of /ɔy/ to (ay): *oil* (ayl), *noise* (nayz), *enjoy* (injay), *boy* (bway), *choice* (čays).

---

[6]French, 1975; Hellinger, 1973; Young, 1973 deal exclusively with aspects of variation among native speakers of Creole, with little or no reference to other ethnic groups.

Syntactic Speech Clues:

(j) Ө 3.Sg.: absence of third person singular present marker: (he gets = *he get*);

(k) Ө Poss.: absence of possessive marker: (my mother's brother = *my mada breda*, the shark bites off my little brother's flesh = de shark bite aff *my li breda flesh*);

(l) Ө O.Pl.: absence of plural marker for nouns: (two boys = *two bway*, how many men? = *ho moǒ man?*);

(m) Ө Do Neg.: absence of the auxiliary DO in negative sentences: (he does not want it = *i no wǎ it*, he did not come back = *i no* come back any more);

(n) Ө Past: absence of past tense marking: (I never lived in Belize = I neva *live* a Belize, he went and found no one = i gǎ e i *fayn* nobady;

(o) Ө Cop.: absence of copula: (he is mad! = *i bex!* (vexed));

(p) DE: use of the particle DE as copula or continuous marker: (did you ever see that big blue hole that *is* there? = *yu eva see da big blue hole we DE deh?*, we *are* not paying attention to that = *we no DE stodi dat*);

(q) ME: use of ME particle as past marker; can be combined with DE: (where *were* you last year? = *we yu ME las ye?*, they *were* drilling there for oil = *dey ME de dril deh fu ayl*, who planted the tree there = *da ME who ME plant de tree deh?*);

(r) FI: use of FI as possessive marker: (*your* water is nicer than the one got in *my* house = *FI-yu wata naysa a Fi-we wan weh we gat da Fi-mi hos*).

The interviews were conducted by myself and by a native Creole fieldworker, and systematically designed so as to assess the effect of the ethnic membership of the interviewer on linguistic production[7]. Basic informant data are given in Table 1.

Tables 2-5 show the results of the analysis of 18 samples elicited from Creoles, and 13 samples elicited from Caribs[8]. For both groups, the whole spectrum is represented, ranging from BC, the basilect (at the top of the Tables), to WIS, the acrolect (shown at the bottom of the Tables). In some instances, two different samples produced by a single individual are included. For example, samples (1) and (15) in Tables 2 and 3 were produced by the same speaker (ER) in two distinct contextual situations thus illustrating individual variation.

---

[7]It was predicted that the presence of a white, non-native, female interviewer would trigger selection of a "higher" code tending towards English. This was borne out in most cases, but the topics discussed and the degree of familiarity attained were also determining factors in affecting repertoire selection. On the other hand, when the native assistant conducted interviews, the uncontrollable speaker's reaction to a stranger was eliminated, allowing elicitation of raw Creole data, especially from his peers or relatives when dealing with familiar topics such as fishing, girl-friends, jokes (what Creoles call "taakin raas"). However, even with the Creole interviewer, decreolized varieties were often produced by older people or members of different ethnic groups. Such matters were later openly discussed with some individuals, which led to interesting insights into the operation of the code-switching process.

[8]My observations are based on fieldwork conducted in 1977 and 1978. Most samples have been collected in Placencia and Seine Bight, two villages located in the southern coastal area, five miles apart on a narrow peninsula. Placencia is a Creole community (population about 400), whereas Seine Bight is exclusively Carib (population about 500). They constitute self-contained, homogeneous communities, but different in every respect, ethnically, economically, and of course linguistically.

All clues are analyzed in terms of their Creole realization or non-realization.
The figures show the ratio of the actual Creole occurrences of a feature to its
overall possible realizations. A 100% figure for all features identifies the basilect (see samples (1) and (2) for speakers ER and DU, for example) whereas an
overall 0% figure (see sample (13) for speaker RO in Tables, 4 and 5) indicates a
standard variety devoid of all West Indian characteristics - at least with respect
to the features under consideration. So, the higher the percentage, the closer to
a fully creolized model. Intermediate varieties involve different combinations of
the phonological and syntactic clues. They are increasingly decreolized until the
most formal variety is reached.

TABLE 1   Basic Informant Data

CREOLE SPEAKERS

	sex	age	origin	residence	occupation
ER (1,15)	M	26	Placencia	Placencia	accountant
DU (2)	M	23	Placencia	Placencia	fisherman
SO (3,8)	F	45	Placencia	Placencia	housewife, Village Council member
AN (4)	M	53	Belize City	Placencia	night watchman
BL (5)	M	28	Placencia	Placencia	fisherman, barman
EA (6)	M	20	Belize City	Belize City	sea-captain (tanker)
DO (7)	F	64	Placencia	Placencia	postmistress, Village Council member
LU (9)	F	39	Placencia	Placencia	housewife
PR (10)	M	62	Belize City	Belize City	waterfront worker, ex-sailor
DE (11)	F	60	Placencia	Placencia	housewife
KA (12)	M	23	Belize City	Belize City	unemployed
BU (13)	M	74	Belize City	Placencia	ex-fisherman
TE (14)	F	43	Placencia	Placencia	housewife
ED (16)	M	28	Boom	Placencia	teacher
PE (17)	M	40	Boom	Belize City	auditor
FL (18)	M	35	Belize City	Placencia	priest, school principal

CARIB SPEAKERS

ZU (1)	M	15	Punta Gorda	Punta Gorda	student
RO (2,13)	M	56	Seine Bight	Seine Bight	retired teacher, scholar of Carib
FR (3)	M	16	Seine Bight	Seine Bight	student-teacher
JO (4)	M	45	Seine Bight	Seine Bight	cuts bushes, does construction work in Placencia
SI (5)	M	35	Seine Bight	Seine Bight	cuts bushes, etc.; in Placencia and Seine Bight
AL (6)	M	14	Seine Bight	Seine Bight	student
LO (7)	F	78	Seine Bight	Seine Bight	housewife
MA (8)	F	56	Seine Bight	Seine Bight	housewife
GU (9)	F	32	Seine Bight	Seine Bight	housewife, washes laundry in Placencia
MZ (10)	M	48	Seine Bight	Seine Bight	school principal
PA (11)	M	55	Seine Bight	Seine Bight	teacher
DC (12)	M	32	Seine Bight	Seine Bight	teacher

INTERPRETATION OF RESULTS

I will briefly comment on each Table, then compare the results obtained for the two groups.

Variation in Creoles

Phonological Clues for Creoles (Table 2)

The frequency of creolized phonological clues for native speakers of Creole is generally high in all samples. This is shown not only when considering various speakers, but also when comparing two or three dialects as used by the same individual in different contextual situations (see ER, samples (1), (15)). For example, cluster simplification (a) achieves maximal or near-maximal figures

TABLE 2 Phonological Clues: Creole Speakers of BC-WIS

Speakers		(a) CC ǀ C	(b) ɔ ǀ a	(c) ʌ ǀ ɔ	(d) ə /ʌ o,a	(e) ir ǀ ɛ	(f) aw ǀ o	(g) ð ǀ d	(h) θ ǀ t	(i) ɔy ǀ ay
ERa	(1)	100%	100%	100%	100%	100%	100%	100%	100%	100%
DU	(2)	100%	100%	100%	100%	100%	100%	100%	100%	100%
SOa	(3)	100%	100%	100%	100%	100%	100%	90%	75%	100%
AN	(4)	100%	100%	100%	80%	100%	100%	92%	73%	100%
BL	(5)	100%	100%	100%	100%	100%	100%	89%	63%	100%
EA	(6)	100%	100%	100%	100%	100%	100%	71%	67%	100%
DO	(7)	100%	91%	100%	67%	83%	100%	90%	75%	100%
SOb	(8)	100%	100%	81%	83%	83%	100%	50%	38%	100%
LU	(9)	100%	100%	95%	75%	40%	80%	66%	40%	100%
PR	(10)	100%	100%	75%	100%	66%	100%	66%	50%	100%
DE	(11)	100%	99%	100%	85%	72%	100%	90%	60%	100%
KA	(12)	100%	69%	100%	50%	80%	80%	75%	71%	100%
BU	(13)	100%	95%	86%	60%	100%	58%	66%	50%	100%
TE	(14)	99%	90%	75%	45%	28%	72%	45%	33%	0%
ERb	(15)	100%	75%	50%	63%	50%	75%	50%	55%	90%
ED	(16)	100%	100%	33%	83%	50%	67%	44%	0%	50%
PE	(17)	85%	64%	52%	38%	86%	50%	62%	25%	0%
FL	(18)	90%	43%	33%	22%	0%	0%	0%	0%	0%

across the board; to a slightly lesser extent, the rounding of /ʌ,ɽ/ (c) and the unrounding of /ɔ/ (b) are also consistently high in all varieties ranging from BC to WIS, thus offering little clue to the code-switching process. Other features such as the monophthongization of /aw/ (f), the lowering of /ir/ (e), the colouring of schwa (d) are somewhat more stratified, sometimes dipping into low percentages among educated speakers to denote ambitious, success-oriented individuals. The degree of occlusion of interdentals (g,h) and the unrounding of /ɔy/ (i) constitute good measures of the variety that Creole speakers wish to achieve when shifting away from raw Creole. Notice that the percentage of stops as reflexes of interdentals decreases significantly - and generally the more so in the case of the voiceless member - as soon as any speaker is not using the broadest variety. On the other hand, only the most educated speakers show any unrounding of /ɔy/.

In conclusion, there is little phonological stratification across speakers and styles. The frequency of occurrence of typically Creole features remains high regardless of the variety used on the BC-WIS continuum[9]. It is interesting to relate the overall gradient phonological differentiation observed among Creoles to the subjective comments elicited on the matter of pronunciation. All Belizeans interviewed declared that there was no phonological difference between Creole and English. Local educators (teachers, priests) claimed that no problem was involved in teaching the correct "English" pronunciation to children. Even individuals who had been exposed to outside varieties are not aware of phonetic deviations of the WIS from an outside model - whether British or American. For example, Belizean teachers mention *hair*, *here* and *here* as homophonous English sets in the classroom, just like *sea* and *see* - there is thus a pervading creolization of the phonological component of the Belizean continuum, which is not stigmatized, since it is not associated with the basilect, but rather labelled "English".

Syntactic Clues for Creoles (Table 3)

The matter is different in the case of the syntactic component. Table 3 indicates that syntactic features are involved in a stratification more representative of the code-switching process. Certain syntactic forms or morphological elements are clearly associated with the Creole, and immediately removed if the speaker unconsciously intends to switch to a "higher" variety on the linguistic continuum. This is the case in particular for the Creole markers DE, ME, FI (p,q,r) whose absence (0%) constitutes a reliable indicator of the decreolization process which applies to mesolectal and acrolectal varieties alike, that is to "Broken English" and to the West Indian standard. Clearly, some of the grammatical markers usually associated with standard English have a very low incidence, even in relatively formal contexts, and thus are not significant clues to a subtle code-switching process from broad Creole to a decreolized "broken" English. For example, the 3rd. pers. Sg. marker, as well as the Poss. marker are virtually always absent in creolized and intermediate varieties - hence high percentages of zero-markers for features (j), (k) in samples (1-13) -, and appear regularly only in the most educated speakers when producing formal varieties (samples 15-18). Note that in the case of samples (16) and (17), the median percentages of 50% and 59% for θ 3.Sg. (j) are explained in terms of variations to Creole in the middle of an interview: PE (17) has 0% when he discusses the political situation in Belize, or makes

---

[9]Besides, there is the matter of intonation and word-stress which makes Belizean English unmistakably West Indian, regardless of the removal of the features selected as speech-clues. In fact, the strong secondary stress observable in WIS or Creole directly triggers the colouring of vowels bearing non-primary stress (i.e., feature (d) on Tables 2-5: i.e., *political* /pa'liti,kal/, *recent* /'ri,šet/).

Geneviève J. Escure

deprecatory statements about the Creole language which he defines as "nothing to be proud of", but he gradually switches to BC as the discussion turns to the touchy topic of - as he says - "the laziness and indifference of the Creole people" and the respective values of the different ethnic groups; then his figure of θ 3.Sg.

TABLE 3 Syntactic Clues: Creole Speakers of BC-WIS

Speakers		(j) θ 3.Sg	(k) θ Poss	(1) θ P1	(m) θ DoNeg	(n) θ Past	(o) θ Cop	(p) DE	(q) ME	(r) FI
ERa	(1)	100%	100%	77%	100%	100%	100%	100%	100%	100%
DU	(2)	100%	100%	63%	100%	100%	100%	100%	100%	100%
SOa	(3)	100%	100%	25%	100%	-	100%	100%	100%	100%
AN	(4)	100%	100%	60%	100%	100%	100%	100%	100%	100%
BL	(5)	100%	100%	62%	73%	60%	71%	80%	40%	75%
EA	(6)	100%	0%	60%	50%	100%	100%	0%	0%	0%
DO	(7)	100%	100%	33%	72%	73%	34%	34%	0%	-
SOb	(8)	100%	-	23%	46%	100%	36%	0%	0%	0%
LU	(9)	100%	100%	85%	75%	76%	54%	9%	0%	0%
PR	(10)	40%	-	70%	60%	62%	66%	0%	0%	0%
DE	(11)	100%	-	20%	16%	54%	50%	0%	0%	0%
KA	(12)	66%	-	21%	66%	75%	50%	0%	0%	0%
BU	(13)	90%	100%	27%	0%	75%	33%	0%	0%	0%
TE	(14)	87%	44%	43%	53%	22%	25%	8%	0%	0%
ERb	(15)	0%	0%	8%	9%	0%	0%	0%	0%	0%
ED	(16)	50%	0%	11%	0%	40%	0%	0%	0%	0%
PE	(17)	59%	50%	6%	11%	33%	33%	7%	0%	0%
FL	(18)	33%	0%	12%	0%	0%	0%	0%	0%	0%

reaches 100%[10]. On the contrary, feature (1) zero-plural marker decreases very gradually as the variety becomes more prestigious: plural is occasionally marked even in the basilect, as shown in frequencies of only 77% and 63% for the two Creole samples (1) and (2). As to features (m,n,o) - θ DoNeg., θ Past and θ Cop., - they are involved in a markedly different and sharper stratification: there is a clear increase in Do+Neg. forms, irregular preterites and copula occurrences whenever the speaker wishes to switch away from the broad Creole, thus producing decreolized varieties. Those three features function as markers of the distance that a speaker unconsciously attempts to keep from BC.

In conclusion, when a native speaker of Creole, in intra-group or in intergroup communication, shifts to WIS or to some intermediate variety closer to the standard, it is not through any drastic change of phonology, but rather by altering the syntactic structure of the sentence, often by removing or adding some morphological markers; then, syntactic features dip into much lower percentages than phonological features. These findings correspond to the claim made by Wolfram and Fasold (1972) that in social dialects syntactic features are more sharply stratified than phonological features. Besides, subjective comments reveal that the population is relatively aware of grammatical differences between English and Creole, due to the emphasis laid in the classroom on the use of the copula, of irregular preterites, etc. Obviously, the Creole production of a prestige variety is in fact determined by what has been taught in the classroom as a second language.

Variation in Caribs

It must be remembered here that Caribs who speak Garifuna as their native language learn Creole through daily interaction with other groups, and English in the classroom. The thirteen samples analyzed as Tables 4 and 5 have been elicited from Carib individuals in interaction with native Creoles (non-speakers of Garifuna).

Phonological Clues for Caribs (Table 4)

A brief comparison of Tables 2 and 4 shows that Carib speakers evidence a greater variability of certain Creole phonological features than native speakers of Creole when shifting between creolized varieties (1-3) and WIS (12-13). There are at least three Creole features, the lowering of /ir/ (e), the monophthongization of /aw/ (f) and the colouring of unstressed vowels (d) which are consistently minimized by Caribs. For example, the lowering or /ir/ feature (e) reaches low percentage figures of 50% and under in eleven out of the thirteen samples given for Carib speakers, against five out of eighteen for Creole speakers. On the other hand, the rounding of /ʌ,r̥/ (c), the unrounding of /ɔ/ (b) or cluster simplification (a) reach fairly high figures - although still somewhat lower than in the case of Creoles. They thus constitute relatively stable elements of WIS, associated with a prestige variety, for either Creoles or Caribs. The occlusion of interdentals decreases gradually in more prestigious varieties, not unlike what was found in Table 2. Note that Caribs using the most prestigious variety (12-13) show an al-

---

[10]This type of individual variation shows that measurements must be handled carefully: an overall percentage figure corresponding to the frequency of occurrence of a given feature in a given interview sometimes obscures the code-switching process instead of revealing its operation. In other words, a speaker not uncommonly switches from one variety to another within a single discourse situation, or even within a single sentence. Frequency figures could thus change dramatically from one section of an interview to another, and such drastic change should be given proper attention, as a significant indicator of the situation.

most null percentage of West Indian features, contrary to Creoles (12-15). On the whole, the phonological features evidenced in the continuum controlled by Caribs range closer to the mesolects and the acrolect than to the basilect. Even the most creolized samples (1,2,3) show significant deviations from the native Creole samples shown in Table 2.

TABLE 4   Phonological Clues: Carib Speakers of BC-WIS

Speakers	(a) CC ǀ C	(b) ɔ ǀ a	(c) ʌ ǀ ɔ	(d) ə ǀ o,a	(e) ir ǀ ɛ	(f) aw ǀ o	(g) ð ǀ d	(h) θ ǀ t	(i) ɔy ǀ ay
ZU (1)	100%	54%	88%	100%	100%	72%	66%	100%	100%
ROa (2)	100%	100%	50%	100%	16%	33%	50%	50%	100%
FR (3)	100%	100%	66%	100%	100%	60%	80%	90%	100%
JO (4)	100%	88%	81%	46%	50%	75%	87%	75%	100%
SI (5)	100%	66%	50%	25%	0%	0%	54%	57%	60%
AL (6)	100%	80%	50%	28%	40%	28%	100%	100%	100%
LO (7)	100%	100%	100%	50%	33%	50%	91%	71%	100%
MA (8)	90%	90%	75%	28%	25%	42%	64%	71%	100%
GU (9)	100%	71%	66%	0%	0%	0%	100%	85%	0%
MZ (10)	100%	66%	100%	100%	16%	28%	42%	20%	0%
PA (11)	60%	60%	89%	86%	50%	57%	40%	33%	0%
DC (12)	33%	0%	0%	0%	37%	0%	0%	0%	0%
ROb (13)	0%	0%	0%	0%	0%	0%	0%	0%	0%

Syntactic Clues for Caribs (Table 5)

Tables 3 and 5 show certain interesting similarities and discrepancies between creole and Carib usage of Creole syntactic features. Here again, there are two distinct sets of clues, the marked and the unmarked ones. Marked Creole features like DE, ME, FI are always eliminated (0%) when a speaker intends to switch to English or an approximate variety (4-13). Even for Caribs intending to use Creole - in interaction with Creoles in an atmosphere of comradeship and familiarity, and discussing the ever favourite topic of sex and women, the only case in which "raw Creole" could be elicited from Caribs - the DE, ME and FI features are subject to a very low incidence, contrary to the maximal figures occurring in the informal speech of native Creoles. Features (j) and (k) are stratified in a gradual manner which indicates a low incidence of 3.Sg. and Poss. English marked forms, even in formal varieties, not unlike what had been observed with Creoles (for example, there is an overall 69% of θ 3.Sg. for Caribs against 79% for Creoles). The marking of plural which had been found even in Creole basilectal speech is significantly increased, as evidenced in an overall 24% of zero plural for Caribs against 39% for Creoles. Other unmarked features like θ DoNeg. (m), θ Past (n) and θ Cop (o) are also more eliminated overall than for Creole speakers, which means that Caribs have somewhat more standard negative forms, irregular preterites and copula forms than Creoles in their intermediate dialects.

TABLE 5   Syntactic Clues: Carib Speakers of BC-WIS

Speakers		(j) θ 3.Sg	(k) θ Poss	(l) θ Pl	(m) θ DoNeg	(n) θ Past	(o) θ Cop	(p) DE	(q) ME	(r) FI
ZU	(1)	100%	100%	60%	60%	80%	40%	50%	20%	0%
ROa	(2)	100%	100%	20%	85%	66%	71%	50%	50%	15%
FR	(3)	100%	-	0%	50%	71%	50%	0%	0%	0%
JO	(4)	100%	100%	12%	8%	66%	11%	0%	0%	0%
SI	(5)	100%	100%	42%	53%	78%	14%	0%	0%	0%
AL	(6)	57%	-	50%	33%	57%	33%	0%	0%	0%
LO	(7)	71%	-	44%	0%	51%	66%	0%	0%	0%
MA	(8)	66%	100%	20%	11%	53%	66%	0%	0%	0%
GU	(9)	66%	-	42%	0%	40%	60%	0%	0%	0%
MZ	(10)	66%	66%	16%	0%	47%	0%	0%	0%	0%
PA	(11)	50%	100%	10%	0%	50%	16%	0%	0%	0%
DC	(12)	33%	0%	0%	0%	37%	0%	0%	0%	0%
ROb	(13)	0%	0%	0%	0%	0%	0%	0%	0%	0%

Comparison of Results

Table 6 illustrates the respective usage by Creoles and Caribs of the nine phonological and the nine syntactic clues selected to measure the continuum.

Geneviève J. Escure

TABLE 6   Comparison of Overall Percentages for Creoles and Caribs

Phonological Clues

Speakers	(a) CC | C	(b) ɔ | a	(c) ʌ | ɔ	(d) ə ∧ o,a	(e) ir | ε	(f) aw | o	(g) ð | d	(h) θ | t	(i) ɔy | ay
Creoles	98%	90%	82%	75%	74%	82%	69%	54%	80%
Caribs	83%	67%	63%	51%	36%	34%	60%	58%	58%

Syntactic Clues

Speakers	(j) θ 3.Sg	(k) θ Poss	(1) θ Pl	(m) θ DoNeg	(n) θ Past	(o) θ Cop	(p) DE	(q) ME	(r) FI
Creoles	79%	64%	39%	52%	63%	53%	30%	24%	28%
Caribs	70%	74%	24%	23%	54%	33%	8%	5%	1%

Decreolization

The segment·of the English-Creole continuum controlled by Carib speakers appears to be more restricted than the range of varieties available to Creole speakers. Native speakers of Creole claim that Caribs do not speak BC fluently. For example, certain Creole markers are used in the wrong environment, which is typical of imperfect second-language learning. Not uncommonly, the Carib rendition of a BC sentence is a literal translation of an English sentence, itself sometimes a direct translation of a Carib structure. For instance, FR (3), who intends to say "There was a boy...", first produces an English version, "They had a boy", then a Creole version "De me have a bway", whereas the correct Creole form would be: "e gã a bway"[11]. If Caribs rarely use marked syntactic Creole forms (DE, ME, FI), unmarked plurals and non-standard negative forms, even in basilectal varieties, in contrast they use more English marked forms than Creoles, even in intermediate varieties, and the phonological variants investigated cluster more towards the WIS end of the continuum. When comparing the overall performance of the two interacting ethnic groups in dealing with decreolization - or distance from the features identified with "broad Creole" - it is clear that the Carib group uses more prestige features and evidences a more advanced degree of "language decreolization" than the native Creoles. But the general process is the same regardless of ethnic

---

[11]There are other ways to identify a Carib speaking Creole, which are typical of second-language acquisitions in particular phonological interference. For instance, /š/ and /č/ occur in free variation, due to the phonological inventory of Carib which includes only one voiceless palatal phoneme: thus *fish* is often realized as /fič/, *bushes* as /bučiz/, *church* as /čoš/, /šoš/ or /šoč/, *teaching* as /tišin/, etc.

membership: decreolization is characterized for both groups by the sharp deletion of Creole markers, such as DE, ME, and the gradual addition of English markers such as copula or plural marking. Intermediate varieties can be ideally defined as unmarked – that is, lacking both Creole and English markers. However, the mesolects often include another type of decreolization which involves the co-occurrence of Creole, English markers *and* unmarked forms as illustrated in the following sentences, where marked Creole forms are circled, marked English forms framed, and unmarked forms underscored:

(1) I |forgot| who find 'im.
(2) Dat (de) we I |was| tryin to prove. (That's what I was trying to prove).
(3) I |don't| think dey could have (ME) do anytin about it. (I don't think they could have done anything about it).
(4) From then, I |didn't| see him any more; i (no) come back any more.
(5) The mother jus' (lef) 'im here and (gan) . She never even tell me i gwain. You know, if she |was| to tell me she was goin', I (ME) (DE) tell 'er I no care for de baby. (The mother just left him here and went. She never told me that "I am going". You know, if she had told me she was going I would have told her "I won't care for the baby".

Hypercorrection

There is, moreover, a peculiarity which has been observed only in Carib speakers and reflects an extension of the decreolization process as observed in the mixture of markers belonging to different codes: hypercorrected forms result from the incorrect combination of two prestige syntactic features like an irregular past and an auxiliary+negative structure, as illustrated in the following sentences:

(6) She *don't* hear*d* it.
(7) Her friend hear*ds* it.
(8) If you *doesn't* know the way the fish is travelling, you wouldn't know what kind of fish is that.
(9) Maybe you can sp*oke* to him.
(10) He *did*n't *came*.
(11) They belong*s* to me.

Such combination of marked English forms is highly representative of the negative social connotation associated with Creoles, so that socially-ambitious speakers strive towards achieving a variety as distant as possible from the stigmatized end, and as close as possible to the prestige model, through two main processes: elimination of marked Creole features, and saturation of marked English forms.

Creole Stigmatization and the Ethnic Factor

This type of hypercorrection results from the effect of imperfect second-and third-language learning (Creole-English) combined with the desire to avoid Creole. JO (Sample 4) is one of those individuals producing a decreolized variety heavily laced with English features distributed in hypercorrected fashion. He is proud of his ethnicity and of his native language and has clear-cut opinions on every topic. In particular, he openly criticizes Creole as a language. "There is no language of Creole...we (Caribs) try not to adopt it..." More educated speakers, like RO and DC (Samples 2, 13, 12) deliberately choose to use English in most situations when talking to Creoles, as well as occasionally to Caribs. RO, a retired teacher, says that he doesn't like to talk Creole "except when he is in the mood" – which means telling dirty jokes to his Creole friends. DC, an ambitious young teacher, says "I found out that I spoke too much Creole...I use English more; even when I talk to my friends, I avoid the Creole."

If the Caribs' speech reflects their reluctance towards BC, Creoles are far from being proud of their native language; they are at best apologetic, and often openly critical about it. Thus PE (17), a socially successful Creole, says "Creole is nothing to be proud of, really." Asked why, he abruptly shifts from linguistic to ethnic and cultural considerations: "From my mother side, I am of African descent; on my father side, I am of Spanish descent. Now, if I was to pick the two evils, I prefer the Spanish, not because of colour, but because of the moral fibre of people. We should erase as much of the Creole way of life as possible..." And ED (16), also questioned about his attachment to his native language, begins by stating that most people in his village are light-skinned, and continues: "The darker the skin, the worse the Creole...You still close to the African." Such derogatory statements are of course vestiges of colonization, which contributed to the stigmatization assigned to the language of the lower socio-economic strata in West Indian societies.

More contemporary reasons can be found in the ethnic attitudes which hold between Creoles and Caribs. There is a network of profound racial, economic, political and religious differences between the two communities: for example, Placencia Creoles are very diverse physically, but predominantly light-skinned, which reflects the mixed origin of the settlement - Portuguese and English pirates, Spaniards, Africans, - whereas Caribs are uniformly black, the African element having prevailed over the Indian element; Placencia is a relatively prosperous fishing community, unlike Seine Bight whose inhabitants face severe economic problems, some working in a neighbouring banana-shipping port, others taking menial jobs in Placencia. Furthermore, the two villages favour rival political parties, and have different religious affiliations, Creoles being Anglican, and Caribs Catholic. Finally, Creoles tend to make deprecatory statements about Garifuna, the Caribs' native language, which they consider as a primitive dialect, and this is in keeping with the slightly amused, superior attitude that they affect towards the Caribs (Carib jokes in Placencia are the equivalent of Polish jokes elsewhere). Caribs retaliate through feelings of linguistic superiority, and they have developed a strong drive for success. Their use of English mirrors a very real desire to overturn what they consider to be an unfair ethnic balance favouring the Creoles. The economic/linguistic tension thus creates a unique situation which determines a great deal of the variability observed in repertoire selection.

Creole as Prestige Variety

Among young people, however, both Creoles and Caribs, Creole constitutes a fashionable *lingua franca*: "taakin raas" is as prestigious as American disco music and blue-tinted "shades" (sunglasses) but borrows some lexical items from Black English - phrases like "Dig?", "Check it out!", for example. The prestige of Creole is part of the general reaction against the Establishment (parents and teachers have insisted that the use of English is the door to social success). A modification of this reaction is reflected in the following statement made by KA, 23, which is more representative of the attitude of the city youth: "I like the broken English, I don't like speaking Creole; it sounds too bad."

CONCLUSION

Status and prestige considerations are extremely important in analyzing code selection in the Belizean multi-lingual society where the acrolect is not the native language of any ethnic group, and the basilect is the native language of only one ethnic group (Creoles). For a given speaker of Creole who controls a substantial segment of the linguistic continuum, "raw Creole" may be prestigious in a situation of shared identity, comradeship, whereas WIS will be appropriate in a formal situation, or if the speaker wishes to maintain social distance or project an

impressive self-image, which is typical of diglossic situations. For Caribs interacting with Creoles, the continuum ranges mostly across mesolectal and acrolectal
varieties, and the overall frequency of prestige WIS features, as well as the occurrence of hypercorrected forms in their speech is related to feelings of ethnolinguistic insecurity. Measurements of specific phonological and syntactic features have revealed the pattern of linguistic variation in intra-group (Creole) and
intergroup (Creole/Carib) communication, and its correlation to ethnic factors.

REFERENCES

Bickerton, D. (1975) Dynamics of a Creole system, Cambridge University Press,
    Cambridge.

DeCamp, D. (1971) Towards a generative analysis of a post-Creole speech continuum,
    in D. Hymes (ed.): Pidginization and creolization of languages, Cambridge
    University Press, Cambridge.

R. Fasold, Two models of socially significant linguistic variation, Language, 46,
    3, 551-563 (1970).

R. French, An ethnography of speaking of the Belize Creole speech community, Un-
    published dissertation, Harvard University (1975).

M. Hellinger, Aspects of Belizean Creole, Folia Linguistica, 5-6, 118-134 (1973).

Hymes, D. (ed.) (1971) Pidginization and creolization of languages, Cambridge
    University Press, Cambridge.

Labov, W. (1966) The social stratification of English in New York City, Center
    for Applied Linguistics, Washington, D.C.

Labov, W. (1972) Language in the inner city, University of Pennsylvania Press, Pa.

Le Page, R. (1960) Jamaican Creole: Creole language studies I, MacMillan, London.

R. Le Page, Preliminary report on the sociolinguistic survey of multi-lingual
    communities, part I: Survey of Cayo District, B.H., Language in Society, 1,
    155-172 (1972).

R. Le Page, et al., Further report on the sociolinguistic survey of multi-lingual
    communities: Survey of Cayo District, B.H., Language in Society, 3, 1-32 (1974).

Taylor, D. (1951) The Black Carib of British Honduras, Viking Fund Publications
    in Anthropology, New York.

Taylor, D. (1977) Languages of the West Indies, The Johns Hopkins University Press,
    Baltimore.

Valdman, A. (1977) Pidgin and Creole linguistics, Indiana University Press.

Wolfram, W. (1969) A sociolinguistic description of Detroit Negro Speech, Center
    for Applied Linguistics, Washington, D.C.

Wolfram, W. (1973) Sociolinguistic aspects of assimilation of Puerto-Rican English
    in East Harlem, Center for Applied Linguistics, Washington, D.C.

Wolfram, W. & Fasold, R. (1972) <u>Social dialects in American English</u>, Prentice Hall, Englewood Cliffs.

C. Young, A sociolinguistic study of Belize Creole, Unpublished D.Phil. dissertation, University of York, England (1973).

LANGUAGE IN ETHNIC INTERACTION: A SOCIAL PSYCHOLOGICAL APPROACH[1]

R. Y. Bourhis

McMaster University, Hamilton, Ontario, Canada

The focus of this paper will be on language and ethnic interaction as it occurs in the immediacy of interpersonal encounters. In this sense the paper will focus mainly on the micro-individual aspect of ethnic interaction. This is not to say that the macro-collective aspect of ethnic relations will be ignored. The dynamics of interpersonal encounters between speakers of similar or contrastive ethnolinguistic groups can be greatly influenced by intergroup processes occurrring at the macro-collective level of society (Fishman, 1977; Jackson, 1977). Indeed it is through a social psychological approach that an attempt can be made to better integrate linguistic phenomena occurring at the micro-individual level of ethnic interaction with those occurring at the macro-collective level of ethnic group relations (Giles, Bourhis and Taylor, 1977).

The stuff of the dynamics of language in ethnic interaction is how speakers of similar or contrastive ethnic groups modulate both the *content* and the *form* of their utterances to communicate effectively and to express varying degrees of solidarity or distance with their interlocutors. Although the verbal content of an ethnic interaction may be crucial in determining the nature of the/a particular intergroup encounter, one of the assumptions of this paper is that the linguistic medium in which the interaction takes place may also be important in determining the flavour of such encounters.

Interpersonal encounters between speakers of similar or contrasting ethnolinguistic groups usually entail the use of two or more languages, dialects or accents during communication. Also, such encounters usually imply that one or more interactants in the encounter are bilingual or bidialectal. Thus, it is difficult to study language in ethnic interaction without referring to the notion of "code switching" as developed in sociolinguistics.

Code switching can be defined as:

> "...the use of two or more linguistic varieties in the same
> conversation or interaction...The varieties may be anything
> from genetically unrelated languages to two styles of the
> same language". (Scotton and Ury, 1977).

---

[1] I am grateful to Fred Genesee for his comments on an earlier draft of this paper.

117

Linguistic varieties or speech styles are particularly important in *ethnic* interaction since language, dialect and accent cannot only label speakers as members of
particular ethnic groups (Giles and Powesland, 1975) but can serve as an important
symbol of ethnic group identity (Bourhis, Giles and Tajfel, 1973; Fishman, 1977;
Haugen, 1971)[2]. For example, in intergroup contexts such as Québec and Wales where
language spoken is often used as a cue for categorizing people as ingroup and outgroup members, it has been found that language can be the most salient dimension of
ethnic identity (Giles, Taylor and Bourhis, 1977; Taylor, Bassili and Aboud, 1973).

What then are the sociolinguistic and social psychological determinants of speech
behaviour in intragroup and intergroup encounters? The focus of this discussion
will be on code switching behaviour which occurs mainly from one language, dialect
or accent to another, in encounters between speakers of similar and contrasting
ethnolinguistic groups.

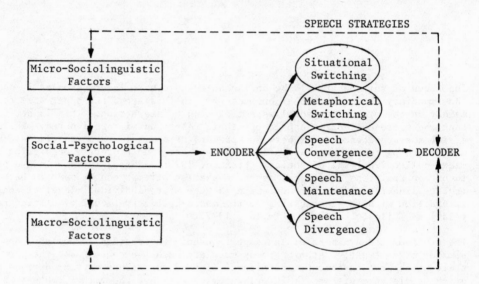

Fig.1.   Determinants of code switching strategies in
intragroup and intergroup encounters.

As can be seen in Fig. 1, and for the purpose of the present review, the determinants of code switching and associated speech strategies can be grouped under three
main headings, namely, Micro-sociolinguistic factors, Social-psychological factors
and Macro-sociolinguistic factors.

---

[2]Of course, accent, dialect and language can also identify speakers as members of
a particular social class or regional background (Giles and Powesland, 1975).

Micro-sociolinguistic factors are those traditionally described by sociolinguists who study speech behaviour using a taxonomic approach. These include the topic, setting and purpose of conversation as well as characteristics of the interlocutors. The speech strategies most commonly influenced by these factors have been referred to as "situational switching" and "metaphorical switching" (Blom and Gumperz, 1972; Fishman, 1972a; these will be defined later).

Social-psychological factors help explain why individual speakers use the speech strategies they do in terms other than just social norms and rules. These factors may consist of speakers' moods, motives, feelings, beliefs, and loyalties in ethnic interaction, as well as their perception of the intergroup relation situation and their awareness of existing sociolinguistic norms. The speech strategies most commonly encoded as a result of these social psychological factors have been described in the context of Giles's model of interpersonal speech accommodation (Giles, 1973, 1977; Giles, Taylor and Bourhis, 1973). As will be seen later these strategies include speech convergence, speech maintenance and speech divergence.

Macro-sociolinguistic factors refer to sociostructural factors which may affect individual's speech strategies in ethnic interaction. These can include the description of the intergroup relation situation in terms of diglossia and bilingualism (Fishman, 1967), ethnic cleavage, linguistic territories, language planning, and language legislation (Rubin and Jernudd, 1975; Weinreich, 1974). This category of factors can also refer to the description of individual speakers as *group members* in terms of their sex, socioeconomic status, regional origin, and the "vitality" of the ethnolinguistic group to which they belong (Giles, Bourhis and Taylor, 1977). Macro-sociolinguistic factors are likely to influence the encoding of the speech strategies enumerated in Fig. 1 (cf., Inglehart and Woodward, 1972).

The inclusion of the variables under the three categories of factors is somewhat arbitrary and no doubt different poolings of the variables could be equally valid. Nevertheless it is hoped that the present conceptualization will prove to be of some theoretical and practical value for the purpose of this over-view.

Three mean points can be made on the basis of the above conceptualization. The first point is that it may not be sufficient to use the traditional sociolinguistic approach to account for all instances of code switching in intragroup and intergroup encounters. A brief review of the literature suggests that social norms and rules as defined in sociolinguistics can account for only some speech strategies commonly encoded in ethnic interaction: namely, situational switching and metaphorical switching. The aim here is to demonstrate that to account for other speech strategies such as speech convergence and speech divergence, one must complement the Micro-sociolinguistic approach with a social psychological one. Furthermore, one can argue that even when a speech behaviour is most likely to be due to the influence of Micro- or Macro-sociolinguistic factors, one must assume that the behaviour was also determined by social psychological processes operating within both the encoder and decoder of the speech act. Thus, the assumption must be that a speaker's behaviour is never completely determined by social norms and rules within a situation, nor by the effects of sociostructural factors in society. In each instance, individuals' needs, motives, perceptions, and attributions must play some part in determining the speech strategy finally encoded or decoded in ethnic interaction.

The second point to be made is that an awareness and understanding of how social psychological factors affect individual's speech behaviour in intragroup and intergroup encounters may eventually help explain how sociolinguistic norms change or emerge in speech communities. In turn, patterns of speech strategies observed to be encoded in ethnic interaction may not only reflect subtle changes in the nature of a particular encounter between individual speakers but may also reflect changes emerging in the nature of a particular intergroup relation situation.

Thirdly, as seen from Fig. 1, the present author suggests there are grounds for identifying Macro-sociolinguistic factors as a third group of independent variables determining the encoding and decoding of speech strategies in ethnic interaction. Although a number of sociolinguists have paid attention to the role of sociostructural variables on code switching behaviour (cf., Fishman, 1972b), it may now be useful to consider their effects under this common rubric of Macro-sociolinguistic factors.

In this paper variables in each of the above three categories will be described in terms of how they can affect the encoding and decoding of speech strategies in ethnic interaction. In the closing part of the paper an attempt will be made to illustrate how variables from these three categories may combine in specific types of intergroup settings to influence speech strategies encoded in ethnic interaction. To this end a number of hypotheses will be proposed which could be explored empirically in future research.

MICRO-SOCIOLINGUISTIC FACTORS

What can sociolinguistics tell us about the determinants of code switching strategies in general and in ethnic interaction in particular? Sociolinguistics has developed from a need to determine how language and social setting interact (Gumperz, 1972). Hymes (1972) developed a taxonomy of situational determinants of speech behaviour including the topic of conversation, the social setting in which it occurs, the purpose of the verbal exchange and the characteristics of the interlocutor. There is empirical evidence which demonstrates that these variables do in fact influence speech strategies in both intragroup and intergroup encounters. As many of these have been reviewed elsewhere (Dittmar, 1976; Giles and Powesland, 1975; Gumperz and Hymes, 1972; Pride, 1971; Robinson, 1972; Trudgill, 1974), only some selected examples will be discussed here. Most of the code switching strategies that will be described under this rubric may be labelled as "situational switching". Code choice in these cases is assumed to be largely determined by social norms and rules in particular situations and settings.

Situational Switching

Although there is little doubt that *setting and topic* variables affect code switching in both intragroup and intergroup encounters, much of the evidence gathered so far has been obtained in intragroup encounters (i.e., in encounters between speakers of the same ethnolinguistic groups rather than in encounters between speakers of contrasting ethnolinguistic groups). Much evidence suggests that code switching is often determined by the setting of an encounter. As regards accent and pronunciation changes, the classic studies by Labov (1964, 1966) demonstrated that speakers in New York's lower East side used more prestigious forms of pronunciation when interviewed in a formal setting than in a casual one. In general, studies in numerous cultural contexts have shown that non-standard accents and dialects are considered most appropriate in informal and semi-formal settings whereas more standard speech styles are perceived to be most appropriate in formal settings (Giles and Powesland, 1975).

Setting can also influence code choice at the level of language. In the U.S., a study by Edelman, Cooper and Fishman (1968) with Puerto Rican children showed that these children reported using more Spanish than English when talking to other bilingual Puerto Ricans in the informal setting of the home and neighbourhood, but used more English than Spanish in the formal setting of the church. Many studies in the U.S. with immigrant and minority groups have shown that English is considered the standard language used in formal and public settings, while the immigrant's native language is considered most appropriate in private or informal intra-

group settings and situations (Kimble, Cooper and Fishman, 1969). Studies with
Spanish and Swedish immigrants (Barker, 1947; Hasselmo, 1961) as well as with
Mexican Americans (Ryan and Carranza, 1977; Sawyer, 1965) and Chinese immigrants
(Kuo, 1974) have shown that changes in social setting can dictate appropriate
language switching in the U.S. (cf., Fishman, Nahirny, Hoffman and Hayden, 1966).

The effect of setting on language switching has been observed in numerous other
cultural contexts. For example, in both the Philippines and Paraguay it was observed that while still courting, couples were expected to use only the impersonal
cosmopolitan language (English and Spanish respectively) while a switch to their
native language (Tagalog and Guarani respectively) was allowed only once the
couples were wedded (Rubin, 1962; Sechrest, Flores and Arellano, 1968). In both
these cultural contexts, and in numerous others, the local vernacular is restricted to the role of informal communication in private settings, while the more prestigious cosmopolitan language is considered the voice of intellect and of public,
formal communication. Similar situational determinants of language choice have
been observed in St.Lucia (Midgett, 1970), in Tanzania (O'Barr, 1971), in Paraguay
(Rubin, 1968), in Israel (Herman, 1961), and in various former British and French
colonies as regards the use of pidgins and creoles (Descamp and Hancock, 1974;
Hall, 1972). Other characteristics of setting affecting code switching such as
occasion, physical setting, privacy and purpose of the interaction have been reviewed by Giles and Powesland (1975). The above represent instances of what is
called "situational switching" since each reflects normative demands in the situation dictating appropriate code switching behaviour.

Topic of conversation may also affect code switching behaviour. Research in
Britain (Brook, 1963) and Israel (Herman, 1961) has shown that speakers tend to
revert to their native accent, dialect or language when they are discussing an
exciting or stressful topic. In Tanzania, a study by Beardsley and Eastman (1971)
showed that Swahili-English bilinguals used a lower proportion of English words
in their speech when they talked about topics that were relevant to life in Tanzania than when talking about topics that were not. Similarly, a study by Ervin-Tripp
(1964) with bilingual Japanese wives of Americans showed that they were quite fluent
in English except when discussing topics relevant to Japanese life. These studies
demonstrate that the topic of conversation can influence code switching behaviour.

The nature of a preceding speech act may also determine subsequent speech behaviour
in consistent and systematic ways that have been viewed as sociolinguistic rules
(Ervin-Tripp, 1969). Preceding speech acts can affect code switching behaviour.
For instance, in a study with multilingual Montréal Italian families, it was found
that language switching was more frequent when interlocutors answered questions
formulated as queries of a general nature or as declarative sentences than when
they had to answer questions of a very specific nature (di Sciullo, van Amerigen,
Cedergren and Pupier, 1976).

Other important determinants of code switching behaviour which have been well documented are those due to the attributes of individual speakers and listeners, such
as age, sex, assumed knowledge, social status and ethnicity (for reviews, see
Ervin-Tripp, 1969; Giles and Powesland, 1975).

One of the most important determinants of code switching behaviour in ethnic interaction is the linguistic competence of each speaker. As regards language competence, it may be useful to describe speakers in terms of both their encoding and
decoding skills in each of the various languages used in a particular multilingual
conversation. Thus, one can describe speakers as being dominant in one language
and weaker in another, or as being equally fluent in two or more languages. In
interaction between two or more speakers of different mother tongues, it is often
expected that the language of communication will be determined by that which is

best known by each of the interlocutors, in order to maintain optimal communication efficiency. Although this is often the case, some studies show that this is much too simplistic a view. In Spain a recent study in the province of Valencia inquir- ed about the reported code switching strategies of monolingual and bilingual Spanish and Valencian speakers in a variety of multiple group settings (Ros and Giles, in press). Preliminary results indicated that code switching was determ- ined by the linguistic competence of each interlocutor in only 50% of these en- counters. It was suggested that language choice in the remaining encounters was affected by the formality/informality of the setting and by the prestige position of Spanish compared to the Valencian language in Spanish society. In another study, the code switching strategies of members of two multilingual Montréal Ital- ian families were investigated by tape-recording a series of family interactions in which combinations of French, English and Italian were spoken (di Sciullo, et al., 1976). In this study, each code switching instance was systematically tab- ulated and analyzed, both in terms of its frequency of occurence relative to other types of speech strategies, and in terms of the context in which it occurred. As in the study in Valencia, it was found that a knowledge of the speaker's encoding competence and that of the target listener's decoding competence could account for only 52% of the total number of language switches observed in the recorded conver- sations. In half the remaining cases, it was found that language switching was more likely to occur when a speaker addressed a new interlocutor than when he main- tained the conversation with the same interlocutor. The likelihood of language switching occurring in a conversation was also increased when a new speaker took the floor in the conversation.

It may be argued that the results from both the Valencian and Québec studies were obtained in what one may consider amiable intragroup settings, since the encounters took place among friends or during family reunions which were pleasant and agree- able. There is reason to believe that linguistic competence alone would account for an even lower percentage of language choices in encounters between speakers of competing ethnolinguistic groups which may have negative dispositions towards each other, Indeed, Taylor and Simard (1975) as well as Segalowitz (1977) and Taylor (1977) have pointed out that linguistic competence is only one of the many factors determining language choice in intragroup and intergroup encounters. As we shall see in the next section, Social Psychological factors such as ethnic identity, ethnic threat, ethnocentrism and intergroup attitudes may each combine to influen- ce code switching behaviour in ethnic interaction.

One of the consequences of speakers being bilingual or bidialectal is that such speakers often generate social norms about the appropriateness of code switching which are different from those found amongst monolinguals (Gumperz and Wilson, 1971). This has been found to be the case for Chicano (Gumperz and Hernandez, 1969) and Puerto Rican bilinguals in the U.S. (Ma and Herasimchuk, 1968), for bi- dialectal speakers in Norway (Blom and Gumperz, 1972) and for Buang speakers in New Guinea (Sankoff, 1972). In each of these cultural settings, a number of code switching strategies are commonly found. First, when bilingual or bidialectal speakers interact with salient outgroup speakers they are commonly observed to switch from their local mother tongue speech style to that of the outgroup speaker. Amongst themselves in intragroup encounters, these bilingual or bidialectal speak- ers usually maintain the conversation in their shared mother tongue. As seen pre- viously, the above speech strategies in both intragroup and intergroup encounters can be subsumed under the rubric of "situational switching" since the code switches are mostly determined by setting variables and perceived socio-demographic char- acteristics of the interlocutors.

Norms concerning appropriate code switching behaviour can also be shared by bi- linguals from contrasting ethnolinguistic groups. This would most likely occur in multilingual contexts where the languages have roughly equal status and where a large majority of speakers are bilingual, multilingual, or share a common lingua franca. Settings where bilingual or multilingual speakers from different ethno-linguistic groups share common social norms concerning appropriate code switching behaviour (including translation) have been found in New Guinea (Salisbury, 1962), in the North West Amazon (Sorenson, 1972), and in parts of India (Gumperz and Wilson, 1971). In the above cultural contexts, situational switching based on setting and listener-speaker variables such as sex and linguistic competence is most common.

There are also contexts where speakers from different ethnolinguistic groups are uncertain about which social norm should dominate in governing appropriate language behaviour in a particular cross-cultural encounter. Scotton (1976) observed such instances in three African cities and found that in numerous cases speakers adopted an ethnically neutral language in order to avoid defining the interaction in eth-nically salient terms. Another, more complex, strategy of neutrality was also ob-served in these circumstances. In some cases it was found that speakers would make a point of code switching in each of the languages known by the interlocutors in the conversation. As will be seen in the next section, these linguistic strategies of neutrality may be best understood as forms of mutual "speech convergence" as described in the context of Giles's model of Interpersonal Speech Accommodation (Giles, 1973).

It is interesting that few sociolinguistic studies have been conducted in bilingual or multilingual contexts where speakers of contrasting and ethnolinguistic groups have conflicting social norms concerning appropriate speech behaviour in ethnic interaction. It is precisely under such circumstances that it may be most useful to investigate language in ethnic interaction, not only from a sociolinguistic point of view, but also from a social psychological point of view. Indeed, a Social Psychological approach may help understand code switching behaviour, not only in cases where speakers have conflicting social norms concerning appropriate speech behaviour but also in cases where speakers break sociolinguistic norms, in cases where speakers are uncertain about which sociolinguistic normal should apply, and in cases where sociolinguistic norms in all probability are not operative.

Metaphorical Switching

Although there are constant normative pressures for bilingual and bidialectal speakers to use their shared mother tongue in intragroup encounters, such speakers have been observed to intersperse their conversations with utterances in one or more outgroup languages or dialects. Blom and Gumperz (1972) labelled this type of code switching strategy "metaphorical switching". This is an important speech strategy since it seems to occur frequently amongst bilingual and bidialectal speakers who feel that a few words or sentences uttered in an outgroup language or dialect may be more efficient or potent for expressing a particular thought, feel-ing, or meaning than attempting to achieve the same effect in the ingroup speech style. Conversely, speakers using an outgroup language or dialect in a particular conversation may switch back to their ingroup speech style to express a particular thought or feeling more vividly. It would also appear that metaphorical switching can be a frequent speech strategy not only in intragroup encounters but also in intergroup encounters between speakers of contrasting ethnolinguistic groups. More generally, according to Scotton and Ury (1977), "metaphorical switching de-pends for its effect on a *departure* from the societal consensus on code allocation. As such, it is used to draw attention or to emphasize." The clearest instances of metaphorical switching have been observed in the speech of bidialectal intellect-uals in Norway by Blom and Gumperz (1977).

In this brief review, we have seen how various Micro-sociolinguistic factors can influence code switching strategies in ethnic encounters. Variables such as setting, topic of conversation, and listener-speaker characteristics have been observed to influence code switching strategies in numerous cultural contexts. The enumeration and description of these variables and how they combine to influence code switching strategies has been integrated by sociolinguists such as Ervin-Tripp (1969), Hymes (1972), and Fishman (1972a,b). This is usually done in terms of implicit and explicit rules and social norms which dictate how individuals should speak in various contexts and situations. Although it is reasonable to expect that much speech variation and code switching can be attributed to these Micro-sociolinguistic factors that combine as social norms, Giles, Taylor and Bourhis (1973: 178) pointed out that:

> "a great deal of work on monolingual speech diversity at
> the interpersonal level has been more concerned with dem-
> onstrating that often speakers adapt or accommodate their
> speech towards that of their interlocutors when social norms
> in all probability are not operative..."

The above authors depart from the usual approach to speech diversity when they focus their attention on the actual dynamics of the psychological processes that occur between speakers and listeners in social interaction. In the next section we will describe how social psychological factors may influence language behaviour in social interaction.

SOCIAL PSYCHOLOGICAL FACTORS

A social psychological model which helps account for the dynamics of speech behaviour in social interaction is known as Interpersonal Speech Accommodation (Giles, 1973; Giles, Taylor and Bourhis, 1973; and Giles and Powesland, 1975). This social psychological model can best account for three types of speech strategies in social interaction, namely, speech convergence (Giles, 1973; Giles, et al., 1973), speech maintenance (Bourhis, 1977b), and speech divergence (Bourhis and Giles, 1977). These three speech strategies will be discussed especially as they apply to the dynamics of ethnic interaction.

Speech Convergence

According to Giles (1977: 28), speech convergence refers to "the process whereby individuals adapt to each other's speech on a number of linguistic levels and in a manner that is not easily explicable simply in terms of normative demands of the situation". Numerous studies have shown that in interpersonal encounters, speakers often adopt the speech patterns of their interlocutor on a number of linguistic dimensions including speech rate, pause and utterance length, vocal intensity, regional accent, and language (Giles and Powesland, 1975).

It does appear that such speech shifts can occur in many types of social encounters and may reflect speakers' conscious or unconscious needs for social integration with their interlocutors. It is also argued that speech convergence can occur in the absence of or in spite of social norms concerning appropriate language behaviour in a particular situation or setting. Of course, such patterns of speech convergence may have their desired effect only if speakers have the linguistic repertoire to do so realistically. Three social psychological processes may help account for speech convergence in interpersonal encounters; these are Similarity Attraction theory, Social Exchange and Attribution theory.

Basically, Similarity Attraction theory (Byrne, 1969) suggests that the more similar our attitudes and beliefs are to certain others, the more likely we will be attracted to them. Through speech convergence linguistic dissimilarities between

two speakers can be attenuated. Thus, through an increased interpersonal similarity
on a linguistic dimension one can in turn increase mutual liking (Giles, et al.,
1973), intelligibility (Triandis, 1960), and predictability (Berger and Calabrese,
1975). Speech convergence may be an efficient strategy for facilitating interethnic encounters where linguistic dissimilarities may have been an important stumb-
ling block for effective cross-cultural communication and ethnic harmony. In
addition, speech convergence may reflect speakers' need for social approval in both
intragroup and intergroup encounters. Indeed, Natale (1975) found that speakers
with a high need for social approval converged more to another's pause length than
speakers with low need for social approval.

Social Exchange theory, as developed by Homans (1961), may also help account for
the phenomenon of speech convergence. Most succinctly, Social Exchange theory
states that before one engages in an action one weighs up its potential rewards
and costs. This suggests that people have a tendency to engage in behaviours which
reap rewards and avoid behaviours that result in negative or unpleasant outcomes.
From this perspective one would expect speech convergence to occur only when it
entails more potential rewards than costs. In ethnic interaction rewards for converging to the outgroup language could include being better perceived or accepted
by the outgroup interlocutor, while potential costs may include linguistic effort,
the possible loss of ingroup identity and possible rejection by ingroup peers for
having spoken in the outgroup speech style. Indeed, studies in a number of cultural settings have shown that in ethnic interaction people react more favourably
to outgroup speakers who converge towards them (in accent, dialect, or language)
than to outgroup speakers who do not (Bourhis, 1978; Bourhis and Giles, 1968; Giles,
et al., 1973; Harris and Baudin, 1973; Simard, Taylor and Giles, 1977).

In addition, studies in numerous cultural settings have shown that speakers who use
prestigious accents, dialects, or languages are more favourably perceived on dimensions of competence, self-confidence, and intelligence than speakers who use less
prestigious, non-standard speech styles (Giles and Powesland, 1975). Furthermore,
messages voiced in a standard prestigious speech style are often perceived to be
more persuasive, of better quality and more likely to elicit co-operation than messages voiced in a non-standard speech style. Thus, still according to Social Exchange theory, one would expect some definite social rewards for convergence to
some prestige speech styles and possible disadvantages for switches to less prestigious speech styles (Giles, 1973; Giles, Baker and Fielding, 1975). Nevertheless,
convergence to a prestige speech style in the "wrong social setting" or situation
may be disadvantageous (Bourhis, 1977a; Bourhis and Giles, 1976).

Favourable reactions to speech convergence may also depend on how the intent of
the convergent speech act is attributed. Results of studies on Causal Attribution
theory (Heider, 1958; Jones and Davis , 1965; Kelley, 1973) have shown that people
attribute others' behaviour not only in terms of their immediate outcome but also
by considering the actor's effort, abilities, intentions, and the influence of
external circumstances. Similar processes may influence the perception of a convergent speech act in ethnic interaction. For example, a study by Simard, Taylor
and Giles (1977) in Québec has shown that when French Canadian (FC) listeners attributed English Canadians' (EC) convergence to French as being due to a genuine
desire to communicate, convergence was perceived very positively. But when convergence to French was perceived as the product of external pressures in the situation,
FCs' reactions to the switch were not as favourable. Thus, evaluative and behavioural (Giles, et al., 1973) reactions to speech convergence in ethnic interaction
may depend on how the intent of this strategy is attributed by the interlocutors.

From the above discussion of speech convergence it can be seen that not all speech
strategies can be explained simply in terms of social norms dictating appropriate
language behaviour in ethnic encounters. As was suggested earlier, speakers' motives, perceptions, and attitudes may be as important in determining speech behav-

iour as the presence of implicit or explicit norms in the situation.

Speech Maintenance and Speech Divergence

Although individuals in ethnic interaction may wish to converge linguistically towards each other to reduce the psychological distance separating them, this tendency represents only one aspect of the Speech Accommodation process. In other circumstances, speakers may choose (consciously or unconsciously) not to converge linguistically but to maintain their own speech style (Bourhis, 1977a). The motivational tendencies of speakers who use speech maintenance can be especially evident in ethnic interaction where speakers use it as a symbolic tactic for maintaining their ethnic identity and cultural distinctiveness in the presence of salient outgroup interlocutors.

A form of speech maintenance may also occur when speakers who must learn a second language view this as a possible threat to their ethnic identity. Such feelings can be related to the notion of "substractive" bilingualism as developed by Lambert (1974, 1977) and Taylor, Meynard and Rheault (1977). In such circumstances, second language learners may make a point of maintaining a strong ethnic accent in their second language as a way of remaining ethnically distinct from native speakers of the target second language. For example, Lambert and Tucker (1972) found that a group of EC school children learning French through an immersion programme adopted more Anglicized phonological features after a few years in the scheme. The maintenance of these linguistic markers perhaps reflected the students' fears that fluency in the outgroup language could detract from their feelings of ingroup identity. Similarly, Segalowitz and Gatbonton (1977) found in phonological analysis of FC learners of English that those bilinguals who identified less closely with Québecois nationalism were more native-like in certain of their English pronunciations than those who expressed more nationalistic aspirations.

In a more recent exploratory study in a language laboratory setting, there was some evidence to suggest that FC learners of English not only maintained their French accents in English but also accentuated it and even used French words when replying to an EC interlocutor asking ethnically-threatening questions in English (Bourhis and Gatbonton, in preparation). These latter strategies demonstrate what is known as "speech divergence". Thus speakers may not only attempt to maintain their ethnic identity through speech maintenance, but may also emphasize it by using the strategy of speech divergence (Bourhis, Giles and Lambert, 1975; Doise, Sinclair and Bourhis, 1976).

For a long time much of the evidence for the existence of what can be called speech maintenance and speech divergence was either anecdotal and observational (Gumperz and Hymes, 1972; Scotton and Ury, 1977), or drawn from literary sources (Friedrich, 1972; Shuy, 1976). Recently studies have shown that these speech strategies could also be demonstrated empirically. In Wales, a study in a language laboratory setting showed that Welsh subjects who valued their national language and group membership highly diverged linguistically by accentuating their Welsh accent in their English when responding to a threatening English outgroup interlocutor. In contrast, Welsh Ss who did not value their group membership as highly were found to converge to the outgroup interlocutor in these circumstances (Bourhis and Giles, 1977).

Speech divergence was demonstrated more dramatically in a recent study carried out in Belgium in a language laboratory setting (Bourhis, Giles, Leyens and Tajfel, 1979). In this study, trilingual French informants responded to a series of neutral and threatening questions voiced by a Francophone outgroup speaker. As expected, language divergence was encoded by numerous Flemish informants when they

switched to Flemish in responding to ethnically-threatening questions posed in
French by the outgroup speaker. Recently, language maintenance, language convergence, and language divergence were observed in less artificial settings in a
series of field experiments in Québec, involving various types of inter-ethnic
encounters between FC and EC speakers (Bourhis, 1978).

Although speech maintenance and speech divergence are linguistic strategies which
form an integral part of the process of Interpersonal Speech Accommodation, there
are instances in which these strategies cannot be fully explained just in terms of
the three social psychological theories used to account for speech convergence.
In speech divergence speakers engage in a behaviour which is the opposite of speech
convergence in that the speaker modifies his speech away from his interlocutor in
order to sound least like him. Through speech divergence speakers can accentuate
the differences between themselves and others. This strategy may be used as a
result of speakers' desire to dissociate themselves from the listener's real or
apparent attributes and may also reflect speakers' desires to assert their ethnic
identity in intragroup or intergroup encounters. It is by considering Tajfel's
theory of intergroup relations (1974a; Tajfel and Turner, 1978) that one can expect speech divergence and speech maintenance to be more frequently occurring
speech strategies than one could predict only on the basis of the social psychological theories reviewed thus far.

In its simplest terms, Tajfel's theory proposes that intergroup social comparisons
occur when individuals define themselves as group members and when such group members are in the actual or perceived presence of salient outgroup members. It is
suggested that these social comparisons occur on dimensions which are important
to group members such as personal attributes, abilities, material possessions, and
so forth. Tajfel suggests that these intergroup social comparisons will often lead
group members to search or even create dimensions on which they can be sure to compare favourably with the outgroup, thus making themselves positively distinct from
the outgroup. The perception of such a positive distinctiveness by the ingroup
will ensure that they have an adequate and positive social identity. Implied in
Tajfel's theory is that group members experience satisfaction in belonging to a
social group, to the degree their group compares favourably with others on one or
more salient dimensions (cf., Giles, Bourhis and Taylor, 1977).

In ethnic interaction with an outgroup interlocutor, Tajfel's theory would suggest
that ingroup speakers who value their group membership highly, would have a strong
desire to make themselves distinctive on a valued dimension. Since a speaker's
language, dialect or accent can be an important and valued dimension of ethnic identity (Fishman, 1977), one could expect speech divergence and sometimes speech
maintenance to be important strategies for asserting positive group distinctiveness in ethnic encounters. In addition, Tajfel's theory takes into consideration
speaker's relative position in the intergroup status hierarchy in terms of being
dominant or subordinate group members. Tajfel and Turner (1978) also consider
group members' subjective perception of their position in the intergroup hierarchy.
Thus in Giles, Bourhis and Taylor (1977) it was argued that variables such as the
speakers' perception of the stability-instability of the intergroup situation as
well as the perception of its legitimacy-illegitimacy could influence the encoding
and decoding of speech strategies by both dominant and subordinate group speakers
in ethnic interaction.

Tajfel's notions allow one to account for speech maintenance and speech divergence from a truly social psychological perspective, since it takes into account
not only the speakers' objective position in the intergroup hierarchy but also the
speakers' needs for positive identity, their attitudes and stereotypes towards outgroup speakers as well as their perceptions and beliefs about the intergroup relation situation. The empirical evidence demonstrating the occurrence of these
various speech strategies indicate that Interpersonal Speech Accommodation is a

dynamic psychological process. As a social psychological phenomenon, Interpersonal Accommodation can be considered as the process by which individuals in social
interaction can at the linguistic level symbolize their mutual (or unilateral)
psychological solidarity in some instances or their mutual (or unilateral) distance
in other circumstances. This dynamic process has also been noted by Peng (1974)
using his notion of "communicative distance". Here Peng has argued that speakers
through their choice of words, expressions, and forms of address in an encounter
can either create an atmosphere of "closeness" with their interlocutor or one of
"remoteness". Peng described how through the various forms of address used in
Japan, speakers can either increase or decrease the communicative distance between
themselves and their interlocutors, depending on how they feel towards each other
and sometimes in spite of social norms governing appropriate use of address forms
in specific situations. Other studies on the use of forms of address in different
cultures could also be interpreted in this way (e.g., Bates and Berrigni, 1975;
Brown and Gilman, 1960; Ervin-Tripp, 1969; Haugen, 1975; Lambert, 1967; Lambert
and Tucker, 1976). More recently Lukens (this volume) elaborated the notion of
"communicative distance" to apply to inter-ethnic encounters in the U.S. and linked
these notions with those developed in Interpersonal Speech Accommodation.

It must be noted that speech convergence, speech divergence, and speech maintenance
may be used at more than one speech level at the same time including pitch, loudness, speech rate, syntax, lexical elements, content, and accent dialect or language. Speech change may be more conscious at some speech levels than others. For
instance, one could suggest that a strategy of speech divergence occurring in the
form of an actual language switch would be a more overt, conscious, and potent form
of divergence than if it occurred at the level of an accent, pitch, or intonation
shift. In addition, one could suggest that contrasting speech strategies may occur
simultaneously in the same speech utterance but on different linguistic dimensions
reflecting both conscious and less conscious motivations speakers may have towards
each other (Bourhis and Giles, 1977). For instance, a speaker may be forced to
converge to a high status interlocutor by using a certain form of address due to
powerful social norms, but may betray or symbolize his dislike of the interlocutor
by diverging at the accent or vocal level of speech. Such processes may reflect
the mood of cross-cultural encounters between speakers of rival ethnolinguistic
groups. Also, during the course of a conversation, speakers may adopt more than
one code switching strategy depending on both how they feel towards the interlocut-
or and on how satisfied they are with the progress of the conversation. For example, in an inter-ethnic encounter a speaker may first diverge linguistically to
assert his group identity vis à vis the outgroup interlocutor but later resort to
situational switching in order to pursue the interaction more efficiently in a
shared language, thus satisfying the demands of the particular communication situation. No doubt numerous combinations of code switching strategies remain to be
documented in both intragroup and intergroup encounters across different cultural
settings (cf., Whiteley, 1974; Giles, 1977).

The social psychological approach to language in social interaction takes into
consideration not only the existence of social norms and rules governing verbal
behaviour, but also seeks to explain how speakers perceive and internalize these
norms depending on their psychological needs and aspirations. Thus, sociolinguistic norms and rules may be obeyed or broken depending on how they interact with
speakers' motives, feelings, attitudes, and beliefs towards themselves (as individuals or as group members) and towards their interlocutors and the intergroup
relation situation. In addition, since Interpersonal Speech Accommodation deals
with the effects of individuals' changing motives and beliefs on their speech
behaviour, this approach may help account for how sociolinguistic norms eventually
change within speech communities. Indeed, the consistent and coherent use of
speech strategies contrary to existing sociolinguistic norms by a distinctive minority of speakers (Moscovici, 1977; Moscovici and Nemeth, 1974) may be instrumental in changing or redefining sociolinguistic norms concerning appropriate speech

behaviour within a speech community. Thus Interpersonal Speech Accommodation not only helps to account for how individuals break sociolinguistic norms but may also help to explain how sociolinguistic norms themselves may eventually be changed in the course of social interaction.

MACRO-SOCIOLINGUISTIC FACTORS

Although the influence of Macro-sociolinguistic factors on the encoding of speech strategies in ethnic interaction is sometimes difficult to demonstrate empirically, it is nevertheless important to briefly discuss the role of these factors in the hope that they will be more fully incorporated in future studies. The nature of an intergroup relation situation may affect the type of speech strategy encoded or decoded in ethnic interaction. In turn, both the nature of an intergroup relation situation and speech strategies encoded during ethnic interaction may be affected by the respective vitality of ethnolinguistic groups in contact. In a chapter by Giles, Bourhis and Taylor (1977) the vitality of an ethnolinguistic group was defined as "that which makes a group likely to behave as a distinctive and active collective entity in intergroup situations". From this it was argued that ethnolinguistic groups that had little or no group vitality would eventually cease to exist as distinctive groups. Conversely, the more vitality a linguistic group had, the more likely it would survive and thrive as a collective entity in an intergroup context. The structural variables most likely to influence the vitality of ethnolinguistic groups were grouped under three main headings, namely: the *status* factors, the *demographic* factors, and the *institutional* support factors. The numerous variables listed under these three headings will only be briefly enumerated here since they were discussed at length in Giles, Bourhis and Taylor (1977).

The status variables are those which pertain to a configuration of prestige variables of the linguistic group in the intergroup context. It was proposed that the more status a linguistic group is recognized to have, the more vitality it can be said to possess as a collective entity. The status factors were listed as follows: economic status, social status, socio-historical status, and language status. Each were described in terms of how they could contribute to the vitality of an ethnolinguistic group.

The demographic variables are those related to the sheer number of members included in the ethnolinguistic group and their distribution through the national or regional territory. It was suggested that ethnolinguistic groups whose demographic trends are favourable are more likely to have vitality as distinctive groups than those whose demographic trends are unfavourable and not conducive to group survival. The demographic factors were grouped under two headings: distribution factors and number factors. The distribution factors refer to the concentration of group members in various parts of the territory, their proportion relative to outgroup members, and whether or not the group still occupies its national territory. The number factors were comprised of various factors such as the group's absolute group numbers, their birth rate and their patterns of immigration and emigration.

Institutional support factors (Breton, 1971) were referred to as the extent to which a language group received formal and informal representation in the various institutions of a nation, region, or community. It was suggested that the vitality of a linguistic group was related to the degree its language was used in various institutions of the government, church, business, and so forth.

It was argued in Giles, et al. (1977) that each of these factors under the various headings may affect, in one direction or the other, the vitality of an ethnolinguistic group. It was suggested that linguistic groups could be meaningfully grouped according to the above three-factored view of vitality, such that ethnolinguistic groups could, for example, be classified as possessing low, medium, or high vitality.

Furthermore, individual speakers in ethnolinguistic groups which have little collective vitality could not be expected to behave in the same way in intergroup encounters as individuals whose group has much vitality. Indeed, the type of speech
strategy used by ethnolinguistic group speakers in intergroup encounters may well
differ according to whether the groups in question had high, medium, or low vitality. For example, one could expect that speakers from groups which have high vitality may feel more inclined to encode speech divergence in a wider range of social
situations and settings (private to public) than speakers from groups which have
low vitality. Thus speakers from high vitality groups may feel free to use their
own language in both informal and formal inter-ethnic settings whereas speakers
from low vitality groups may feel free to use their own language only in informal
private intragroup settings.

How can the notion of ethnolinguistic vitality and its influence on speech strategies be integrated with more traditional sociolinguistic descriptions of intergroup
relation situations? As an example of how this could be done one could choose the
notion of diglossia and bilingualism as developed by Fishman (1967). When considering speech communities in terms of diglossia and bilingualism one is implicit-
ly describing linguistic groups in terms of both their relative ethnolinguistic
vitality and the range of speech strategies they have available to them in intragroup and intergroup encounters. Usually in diglossia and bilingualism at least
two speech styles are used for different purposes, each of which are equally valued
by members of the speech community. One speech style is used for formal public
purposes, (the H form) while the other is used for common, everyday pursuits (the
L form). In such societies one could expect that both situational and metaphorical
switching would be most common since norms for code choice would be shared by most
speakers and would be determined mainly by the setting and purpose of the intragroup
or intergroup encounter (e.g., Paraguay, Rubin, 1968).

In societies where two ethnolinguistic groups are of uneven "vitality", diglossia
without bilingualism or bilingualism without diglossia may often prevail. Diglossia without bilingualism is often found in underdeveloped countries where the "élite"
speaks both a higher prestige cosmopolitan language and a local vernacular, whereas
the unmobilized masses speak one or more vernaculars. In such cases the élites
rarely interact with the masses such that there is both a class and linguistic
cleavage which reduces the frequency of intergroup contact. Thus intergroup communication may be more frequently mediated through bilingual "linguistic brokers"
than by dominant group speakers who would use speech convergence by communicating
in one or more of the vernaculars spoken by the masses.

A rapid rate of modernization may upset traditional social norms governing code
switching if the masses become politically and culturally mobilized. This often
occurs through widespread education and urbanization. If in the beginning the
cultural consequences of modernization are accepted and social mobility is not
blocked, bilingualism without diglossia may develop. In this case the masses become bilingual, mastering the modern language, while the old vernaculars and cultures lose their status and value in the speech community. Social norms governing
the use of the vernacular in the informal home domain gradually change in favour
of the modern language. Thus, through a phase where the masses are bilingual, the
new language of work and advancement may also become the language of the home. In
this transition phase of bilingualism without diglossia, a number of social patterns may emerge. The masses may completely drop the vernacular and stress the advantages of the newly acquired modern language such that unilingualism in the
modern language is achieved within a few generations. Alternatively, some may react by seeking to replace the modern language by creating an elaborate modernized
version of one of the old vernaculars (Fishman, 1972). If the above two patterns
develop simultaneously within the same speech community or within two speech communities in contact, competing social norms concerning appropriate code switching
behaviour in various types of intragroup and intergroup settings (public vs. pri-

vate, etc.) will develop. Code switching strategies encoded most frequently in
ethnic interaction may reflect which of the patterns will eventually prevail. If
assimilation to the modern language is perferred, speech convergence towards speakers of the modern (dominant) language will be common and may develop as a norm for
situational switching. Eventually situational switching in favour of the modern
language may generalize across a wider range of settings and situations including
those formerly occupied by the vernaculars in the private and informal home domain.
If maintenance of an updated form of the vernacular(s) is more important, then
speech maintenance and speech divergence from speakers who use the modern language
may occur more frequently. Eventually speech maintenance and speech divergence
may occur more frequently and across an increasing range of social settings (ranging from private and semi-formal settings to public and formal ones such as on the
mass communication networks).

In cases where modernization has mobilized the masses but where social mobility is
blocked (due to a lack of knowledge in the modern language or in spite of bilingualism in the modern language) bilingualism without diglossia may lead to secession-
ist movements. Such movements are likely to be composed of unilinguals in the
vernacular language(s), and bilinguals with a knowledge of the modern language but
whose social mobility has been blocked. The ideological tendencies of speakers
who belong to such groups may be reflected in the code switching strategies they
adopt in ethnic interaction. For such speakers confronted with salient outgroup
interlocutors, one may find speech maintenance and speech divergence to be more
frequently encoded speech strategies than speech convergence and situational
switching. Indeed such speakers may make a point of using their ingroup speech
style in as wide a range of intragroup and intergroup settings as possible.

In contexts where ethnolinguistic groups are of roughly equal strength in terms of
vitality, but have strong conflicts of interests, linguistic legislation with
powerful sanctions may be the only means of abating linguistic conflicts. In some
cultural contexts institutional bilingualism may be adopted as a way of encouraging
speakers to converge to each other's native tongue in ethnic interaction across a
wide range of social settings and situations (Gannon, 1978; Pool, 1974; Verdoodt,
1973). In other cultural contexts, ethnolinguistic conflict may be defused through
linguistic legislation which institutionalizes ethnic cleavage through the establishment of linguistic territories. This latter type of legislation restricts
inter-ethnic contact to settings where code switching norms may be shared by both
ingroup and outgroup speakers, thus reducing the likelihood of unpleasant interethnic encounters. Such linguistic territories are usually proclaimed unilingual
so that outgroup speakers in each territory expect to converge to the linguistic
norms of the native population.

The above are only some of the Macro-sociolinguistic factors which may affect code
switching strategies in ethnic interaction. Future studies should demonstrate how
these and other sociostructural factors may affect the encoding and decoding of
speech strategies in ethnic interaction.

SUGGESTION FOR FURTHER RESEARCH

Micro-sociolinguistic factors as well as Macro-sociolinguistic ones may combine
with Social Psychological factors to influence the type of speech strategy encoded
in ethnic interaction. To illustrate how this could occur, a number of variables
mentioned previously will be included for consideration in this section (although
the choice of these may appear somewhat arbitrary given the state of our knowledge).
To narrow the scope of the discussion the choice of the variables will be limited
to those likely to be most relevant in a context of high intergroup tension. The
type of intergroup situation to be examined is that in which contrasting ethnolinguistic group members view language both as a salient dimension of their ethnic

group identity and of the intergroup conflict situation. Thus as regards *Macro-sociolinguistic* factors one would be dealing with intergroup relation situations that are tense and conflictual rather than harmonious and amiable. Here one could be referring to ethnolinguistic conflict situations such as those found in Belgium, Canada, Wales, and Catalonia in Spain.[3] In such cases speakers could be categorized as dominant or subordinate group speakers on the basis of the relative vitality of the ethnolinguistic groups to which they belong. A *Micro-sociolinguistic* factor chosen for consideration at this juncture will be the setting (private vs. public) in which speech strategies are encoded and decoded by speakers in ethnic interaction. An important *Social Psychological* variable worth considering in such contexts is the effect of ingroup and outgroup sanctions on the encoding of speech strategies by dominant and subordinate group speakers. The above list of variables is by no means sufficient to account for the dynamics of linguistic behaviour in ethnic interaction, even when one restricts the discussion to intergroup contexts that are tense and conflictual.[4] Nevertheless, one may venture some hypotheses about how the above variables may combine to affect the encoding and decoding of speech strategies in tense intergroup relation situations.

As a first hypothesis dealing with Macro-sociolinguistic variables one may suggest (perhaps simplistically) that in contexts of high intergroup tension neutral or accommodative strategies such as "situational switching" and "speech convergence" may be less frequently encoded than dissociative strategies such as speech divergence and speech maintenance. The above trend may indicate that in a context of strong ethnolinguistic group tension speakers from conflicting speech communities may each strive to use their own speech style in as wide a range of intragroup and intergroup encounters as possible. This may be so since in such contexts speakers may not only wish to dissociate themselves from outgroup interlocutors but may strive to assert their group distinctiveness through speech divergence from outgroup speakers.

Intergroup encounters often occur in the presence of both ingroup and outgroup interactants who are often in the position to either "reward" or "punish" (attitudinally and behaviourally) ingroup and outgroup speakers, depending on the speech strategy they encode in intergroup encounters. Ingroup and outgroup sanctions can be an important Social Psychological variable, since for many members of ethnolinguistic groups, feelings of "group belonging" and being accepted as an "ingroup member" may become crucial for the maintenance of positive group identity. This may be the case especially in situations of heightened intergroup tension and competition. Ingroup and outgroup sanctions can be important variables also because once they have operated, it is quite likely that their effects (as rewards or punishment) can influence the types of speech strategies encoded by ingroup and

---

[3]The role of social psychological variables such as speakers' positive or negative social identity as well as their beliefs concerning the legitimacy and stability of the intergroup relation situation have also been postulated to play a major role on the encoding of speech strategies in ethnic interaction (Giles, Bourhis and Taylor, 1977).

[4]Recently, Giles (1978) completed a very useful survey describing various types of ethnolinguistic group contact situations. The above discussion pertains to only some of the ethnolinguistic contact situations described by Giles and does not imply that a study of speech strategies encoded in other types of inter-ethnic contact situations is less important.

outgroup speakers in future intergroup encounters. In the long-run, ingroup-outgroup sanctions may determine speakers' speech strategies in a wide range of intergroup encounters which in turn may result in the formation of new sociolinguistic
norms in ethnic interaction. Furthermore, the severity of ingroup and outgroup
sanctions may also depend on Macro-sociolinguistic factors such as the ethnolinguistic vitality of the groups in contact.

As a Micro-sociolinguistic factor, the setting in which intergroup encounters take
place is also important. For instance, it is likely that the importance and severity of ingroup and outgroup sanctions may increase or decrease as a function of
how public or private the intergroup encounter happens to be. Indeed, the setting
of intergroup encounters may range from a pole denoting very private situations
(and informal) to ones denoting very public (and formal) situations. How then
could the present selection of factors combine to influence the encoding and decoding of speech strategies in intergroup encounters? To summarize how the variables could combine the following additional hypotheses may be proposed.

Speech communities or ethnolinguistic groups that are dominant and have high vitality will be able to create more positive rewards for ingroup and outgroup speakers who use speech strategies in favour of the dominant group than ethnolinguistic
groups that are subordinate and have low vitality. Examples of speech strategies
in favour of the dominant group may be subordinate outgroup speakers converging
linguistically towards dominant group speakers or dominant group speakers asserting ingroup identity by diverging linguistically from subordinate outgroup interlocutors. Similarly, dominant ethnolinguistic groups can impose stronger sanctions on ingroup and outgroup speakers who use speech strategies against the dominant group than can subordinate groups. Examples of speech strategies encoded
against a speaker's own group may be ingroup speakers using speech convergence
towards outgroup interlocutors (in this context, a form of linguistic treason) or
outgroup speakers diverging from speakers of one's own group. As a result, it may
be proposed that dominant group speakers may be in a better position to encode
speech strategies of their choice in favour of their own group, than subordinate
group speakers that have low vitality.

Dominant group speakers with high ethnolinguistic vitality should be in a position
to reward speech strategies in favour of their own group in a wider range of social situations and intergroup settings (from private to public) than subordinate
group speakers with low ethnolinguistic vitality. Thus dominant group speakers
will be more likely to encode speech strategies in favour of their own group in a
wider range of social situations and intergroup settings than subordinate group
speakers.

Both the ethnolinguistic vitality of group speakers and the effects of rewards
and sanctions must play a part in determining which speech strategy will be most
commonly encoded between representative speakers of conflicting ethnolinguistic
groups. In the long term, the combined effects of the above variables may determine which ethnolinguistic groups will succeed in expanding the range of social
situations in which they can encode speech strategies in favour of their own group.

From the suggestions proposed above, it emerges that an important variable to consider is the nature of the rewards and sanctions that can be bestowed on speakers,
depending on the speech strategy they encode in intergroup encounters. Of course,
in the immediacy of intergroup encounters, the most obvious and spontaneous type
of reward or sanction that could be considered is the type of speech strategy encoded by a speaker replying to the interlocutor. It is at this immediate level
that Giles's Interpersonal Speech Accommodation model would operate most directly.
It was seen, for example, that when outgroup speakers converge towards ingroup
speakers, the latter have a strong tendency to converge in return (a form of reward) even though communication effectiveness may be reduced in the process

(Giles, Taylor and Bourhis, 1973; Simard, Taylor and Giles, 1977). Similarly, when the outgroup speaker diverges, the ingroup speakers tend to diverge also, perhaps as a form of retaliatory strategy (Bourhis, et al., 1979).

Nevertheless, sanctions and rewards may occur at other levels than speech behaviour. These may occur at the level of social evaluations of speakers or may manifest themselves in terms of favourable or unfavourable behavioural reactions towards ingroup and outgroup speakers. There is empirical evidence which suggests that speakers can be rewarded or sanctioned evaluatively depending on the speech strategy they encode in intergroup encounters. Such patterns of results were obtained for strategies of speech convergence, speech divergence, and speech maintenance in at least three cultural settings, namely, in Québec (Bourhis, Giles and Lambert, 1975; Bourhis and Genesse, 1978), in Wales (Bourhis, 1977a), and in Switzerland (Doise, Sinclair and Bourhis, 1976). In these studies rewards and sanctions consisted of speakers being rated more or less favourably (as individuals or as group members) depending on the speech strategy they encoded in intergroup encounters. No doubt similar patterns of results could emerge for strategies of situational and metaphorical switching encoded in various types of inter-ethnic encounters. At the behavioural level, a number of studies indicate that what could be viewed as speech convergence and situational switching in ethnic interaction tends to elicit higher rates of helping responses than strategies of speech maintenance and speech divergence (Bourhis and Giles, 1976; Feldman, 1968; Giles, Baker and Fielding, 1975; Harris and Baudin, 1973).

It is by using techniques such as sociolinguistic surveys, field observations, unobtrusive measures, and experimental procedures (such as variations of the matched-guise technique, Giles and Bourhis, 1976) that one may arrive at a better understanding of why and how certain speech strategies are used by ingroup and outgroup speakers in various types of intragroup and intergroup encounters. In turn, such understanding may provide valuable insights into the dynamics of intergroup relations in general, and inter-ethnic group conflict in particular. Indeed, it may be found that patterns of speech strategies occurring in inter-ethnic encounters could reflect the nature of a particular intergroup relation situation. By monitoring changes in the pattern of speech strategies used by ingroup and outgroup speakers in various types of inter-individual encounters, one may even detect subtle changes emerging in the overall pattern of relations between ethnolinguistic groups. For instance, in a particular intergroup context, one may detect that speech divergence from outgroup speakers is encoded by speakers more frequently across an increasing range of social situations than was the case in the past. In the absence of other more overt signs of emerging intergroup tension, the above patterns could be taken as the first signs that the pattern of relations between the groups are indeed changing. Conversely, speech convergence may be encoded more frequently between ingroup and outgroup interlocutors in an increasing range of social settings and may thus reflect the emergence of more amiable relations between ethnolinguistic groups in contact. Furthermore, by investigating ingroup and outgroup reactions to various patterns of speech strategies portrayed by stimulus ingroup and outgroup speakers on tape (as was done by Bourhis, et al., 1975; Doise, et al., 1976) one may eventually be in a position to predict trends likely to develop in the pattern of relations between contrasting ethnolinguistic groups.

The purpose of this paper was to illustrate ways in which a social psychological approach could contribute to a better understanding of the dynamics of speech behaviour in ethnic interaction. Further research may indicate how other social psychological models and variables could serve to better integrate linguistic phenomena occurring at the micro-individual level of ethnic interaction with those occurring at the macro-collective level of ethnic group relations.

REFERENCES

G.C. Barker, Social functions of language in a Mexican-American community, Acta Americana, 5, 185-202 (1947).

E. Bates & L. Berrigni, Rules of address in Italy: A sociological survey, Language in Society, 4, 271-288 (1975).

R.B. Beardsley & C.M. Eastman, Markers, pauses, and codeswitching in bilingual Tanzanian speech, General Linguistics, 11, 17-27 (1971).

C. Berger & R. Calabrese, Some explorations in initial interaction and beyond: Towards a developmental theory of interpersonal communication, Human Communication Research, 1, 99-112 (1975).

Blom, J.P. & Gumperz, J.J. (1972) Social meaning in linguistic structures: Code-switching in Norway, in J.J. Gumperz & D. Hymes (eds.): Directions in sociolinguistics, Holt, Rinehart and Winston, New York.

R.Y. Bourhis, The language of treason and loyalty in Wales. A paper presented at the 39th International Communication Association Convention, Berlin, West Germany (1977).

R.Y. Bourhis, Language and social evaluation in Wales. Unpublished doctoral dissertation, University of Bristol (1977a).

R.Y. Bourhis, Code-switching in Montréal, McGill University Mimeo (1978).

R.Y. Bourhis & E. Gatbonton, Language convergence and divergence in Québec (in preparation).

R.Y. Bourhis & F. Genesee, Evaluative reactions to code switching in Québec, McGill University Mimeo (1978).

R.Y. Bourhis & H. Giles, The language of co-operation in Wales, Language Sciences, 42, 13-16 (1976).

Bourhis, R.Y. & Giles, H. (1977) The language of intergroup distinctiveness, in H. Giles (ed.): Language, ethnicity and intergroup relations, Academic Press, London.

R.Y. Bourhis, H. Giles & W.E. Lambert, Social consequences of accommodating one's style of speech: A cross-national investigation, International Journal of the Sociology of Language, 6, 53-71 (1975).

Bourhis, R.Y., Giles, H., Leyens, J-P. & Tajfel, H. (1979) Psycholinguistic distinctiveness: Language divergence in Belgium, in H. Giles & R. St.Clair (eds.): Language and social psychology, Blackwell, Oxford.

R.Y. Bourhis, H. Giles & H. Tajfel, Language as a determinant of Welsh identity, European Journal of Social Psychology, 3, 447-460 (1973).

Breton, R. (1971) Institutional completeness of ethnic communities and personal relations of immigrants, in B.R. Blishen, F.E. Jones, K.D. Naegels & J. Porter (eds.): Canadian society: Sociological perspectives, MacMillan, Toronto.

Brook, G.L. (1973) Varieties of English, MacMillan, London.

Brown, R.J. (1978) Divided we fall: An analysis of relations between sections of a factory workforce, in H. Tajfel (ed.): Differentiation between social groups: Studies in the social psychology of intergroup relations, Academic Press, London.

Brown, R. & Gilman, A. (1972) The pronouns of power and solidarity, in P.P. Giglioli (ed.): Language and social context, Penguin Books, Harmondsworth.

Byrne, D. (1969) Attitudes and attraction, in L. Berkowitz (ed.): Advances in experimental social psychology, Academic Press, New York.

Decamp, D. & Hancock, I.F. (1974) Pidgins and Creoles: Current trends and prospects, Georgetown University Press, Washington, D.C.

A.M. di Scuillo, A. van Amerigen, H. Cedergren & P. Pupier, Étude de l'interaction verbale chez des Montréalais d'origine Italiènne, Cahier de Linguistique: La Sociolinguistique au Québec, 6, 127-153 (1976).

Dittmar, N. (1976) Sociolinguistics, Edward Arnold, London.

W. Doise, A. Sinclair & R.Y. Bourhis, Evaluation of accent convergence and divergence in co-operative and competitive intergroup situations, British Journal of Social and Clinical Psychology, 15, 247-252 (1976).

M. Edelman, R.L. Cooper & J.A. Fishman, The contextualization of schoolchildren's bilingualism, Irish Journal of Education, 2, 106-111 (1968).

Ervin-Tripp, S.M. (1968) An analysis of the interaction of language, topic and listener, in J.A. Fishman (ed.): Readings in the sociology of language, Mouton, The Hague.

R.E. Feldman, Response to compatriots and foreigners who seek assistance, Journal of Personality and Social Psychology, 10, 202-214 (1968).

J.A. Fishman, Bilingualism with and without diglossia: Diglossia with and without bilingualism, The Journal of Social Issues, 23, 29-38 (1967).

Fishman, J.A. (1972) Language and nationalism, Newbury House, Rowley, Mass.

Fishman, J.A. (1972a) The sociology of language, Newbury House, Rowley, Mass.

Fishman, J.A. (1972b) Domains and the relationship between micro- and macro-sociolinguistics, in J.J. Gumperz & D. Hymes (eds.): Directions in sociolinguistics, Holt, Rinehart and Winston, New York.

Fishman, J.A. (1977) Language and ethnicity, in H. Giles (ed.): Language, ethnicity and intergroup relations, Academic Press, London.

Fishman, J.A., Nahirny, V.C., Hoffman, J.E. & Hayden, R.G. (1966) Language loyalty in the U.S., Mouton, The Hague.

Friedrich, P. (1972) Social context and semantic feature: The Russian pronominal usage, in J.J. Gumperz & D. Hymes (eds.): Directions in sociolinguistics, Holt, Rinehart and Winston, New York.

R. Gannon, The French-language unit: A key instrument in Canada's Official Language Policy, Language Problems and Language Planning, 1, 131-139 (1978).

H. Giles, Evaluative reactions to accent, Education Review, 22, 211-227 (1970).

H. Giles, Accent mobility: A model and some data, Anthropological Linguistics, 15, 87-105 (1973).

H. Giles, Social psychology and applied linguistics: Towards an integrative approach, ITL Review of Applied Linguistics, 35, 27-42 (1977).

Giles, H. (ed.) (1978) Language, ethnicity and intergroup relations, Academic Press, London.

Giles, H. (1978) Linguistic differentiation between social groups, in H. Tajfel (ed.): Differentiation between social groups: Studies in the social psychology of intergroup relations, Academic Press, London.

H. Giles, S. Baker & G. Fielding, Communication length as a behavioural index of accent prejudice, International Journal of the Sociology of Language, 6, 73-81 (1975).

H. Giles & R.Y. Bourhis, Methodological issues in dialect perception: Some social psychological perspectives, Anthropological Linguistics, 18, 294-304 (1976).

Giles, H., Bourhis, R.Y. & Taylor, D.M. (1977) Towards a theory of language in ethnic group relations, in H. Giles (ed.): Language, ethnicity and intergroup relations, Academic Press, London.

Giles, H. & Powesland,P.F. (1975) Speech Style and Social Evaluation, Academic Press, London.

H. Giles, D.M. Taylor & R.Y. Bourhis, Towards a theory of interpersonal accommodation through language: Some Canadian data, Language in Society, 2, 177-192 (1973).

H. Giles, D.M. Taylor & R.Y. Bourhis, Dimensions of Welsh identity, European Journal of Social Psychology, 7, 165-174 (1977).

Gumperz, J.J. (1972) Introduction, in J.J. Gumperz & D. Hymes (eds.): Directions in sociolinguistics, Holt, Rinehart and Winston, New York.

Gumperz, J.J. & Hernandez, E. (1971) Bilingualism, bidialectism and classroom interaction, in S. Dil (ed.): Language and social groups: Essays by J.J. Gumperz, Stanford University Press, Stanford.

Gumperz, J.J. & Hymes, D. (eds.) (1972) Directions in sociolinguistics, Holt, Rinehart and Winston, New York.

Gumperz, J.J. & Wilson, P. (1971) Convergence and Creolization: A case from the Indo-Aryan/Dravidian border in India, in S. Dil (ed.): Language and social groups: Essays by J.J. Gumperz, Stanford University Press, Stanford.

Hall, R.A. (1972) Pidgins and Creoles as standard language, in J.B. Pride & J. Holmes (eds.): Sociolinguistics, Penguin Books, Harmondsworth.

M.B. Harris & H. Baudin, The language of altruism: The effects of language, dress and ethnic group, Journal of Social Psychology, 97, 37-41 (1973).

N. Hasselmo, American Swedish: A study in bilingualism. Unpublished doctoral dissertation, Harvard University (1961).

Haugen, E. (1971) Instrumentalism in language planning, in J. Rubin & B.H. Jernudd
    (eds.): Can language be planned?, The University Press of Hawaii, Honolulu.

E. Haugen, Pronominal address in Icelandic: From you-two to you-all, Language in
    Society, 4, 323-339 (1975).

Heider, P. (1958) The psychology of interpersonal relations, Wiley, New York.

S. Herman, Explorations in the social psychology of language choice, Human
    Relations, 14, 149-164 (1961).

Hobart, C.W. (1977) Language planning in Canada: Politics and practices, in W.H.
    Coons, D.M. Taylor & M.A. Tremlay (eds.): The individual, language and society
    in Canada, The Canada Council, Ottawa.

Homans, G.C. (1961) Social behaviour, Harcourt, Brace and World, New York.

Hymes, D. (1972) Models of the interaction of language and social life, in J.J.
    Gumperz & D. Hymes (eds.): Directions in sociolinguistics, Holt, Rinehart and
    Winston, New York.

Inglehart, R. & Woodward, M. (1972) Language conflicts and the political community,
    in P.P. Giglioli (ed.): Language and social context, Penguin Books, Harmonds-
    worth.

Jackson, J.D. (1977) The functions of language in Canada: On the political economy
    of language, in W.H. Coons, D.M. Taylor & M.A. Tremlay (eds.): The individual,
    language and society in Canada, The Canada Council, Ottawa.

Jones, E.E. & Davis, K.E. (1965) From acts to dispositions: The attribution pro-
    cess in person perception, in L. Berkowitz (ed.): Advances in experimental
    social psychology, Academic Press, New York.

H.H. Kelley, The process of causal attribution, American Psychologist, 28,
    107-128 (1973).

J. Kimble, Jr., R.L. Cooper & J.A. Fishman, Language switching and the interpret-
    ation of conversations, Lingua, 23, 127-134 (1969).

E. Kuo, Bilingual patterns of a Chinese immigrant group in the United States,
    Anthropological Linguistics, 16, 128-140 (1974).

Labov, W. (1966) The social stratification of English in New York City, Center
    for Applied Linguistics, Washington, D.C.

W. Labov, Phonological correlates of social stratification, in supplement to
    American Psychologist, 66, 164-176 (1964).

W.E. Lambert, A social psychology of bilingualism, The Journal of Social Issues,
    23, 91-109 (1967).

Lambert, W.E. (1977) The effects of bilingualism on the individual: Cognitive and
    sociocultural consequences, in P.A. Hornby (ed.): Bilingualism: Psychological,
    social and educational implications, Academic Press, New York.

Lambert, W.E. & Tucker, G.R. (1972) Bilingual education of children: The St.
    Lambert experiment, Newbury House, Rowley, Mass.

Lambert, W.E. & Tucker, G.R. (1976) Tu, Vous, Usted: A social psychological study of address patterns, Newbury House, Rowley, Mass.

Ma, R. & Herasimchuk, E. (1971) The linguistic dimensions of a bilingual neighbourhood, in J.A. Fishman (ed.): Bilingualism in the barrio, Language Sciences Monographs, no.7, Indiana University, Bloomington.

D. Midgett, Bilingualism and linguistic change in St. Lucia, Anthropological Linguistics, 12, 158-170 (1970).

Moscovici, S. (1977) Social influence and social change, Academic Press, London.

Moscovici, S. & Nemeth, C. (1974) Social influence II: Minority influence, in C. Nemeth (ed.): Social psychology: Classic and contemporary integrations, Rand McNally, Chicago.

M. Natale, Social desirability as related to convergence of temporal speech patterns, Perceptual and Motor Skills, 40, 827-830 (1975).

W.M. O'Barr, Multilingualism in a rural Tanzanian village, Anthropological Linguistics, 13, 289-300 (1971).

F. Peng, Communicative distance, Language Sciences, 31, 32-38 (1974).

Pool, J. (1974) Mass opinion on language policy: The case of Canada, in J.A. Fishman (ed.): Advances in language planning, Mouton, The Hague.

Pride, J.B. (1971) The social meaning of language, Oxford University Press, London.

Robinson, W.P. (1972) Language and social behaviour, Penguin Books, Harmondsworth.

M. Ros & H. Giles, The Valencian language situation: An accommodation perspective, ITL Review of Applied Linguistics (in press).

J. Rubin, Bilingualism in Paraguay, Anthropological Linguistics, 4, 52-58 (1962).

Rubin, J. (1968) National bilingualism in Paraguay, Mouton, The Hague.

Rubin, J. & Jernudd, B.H. (1975) Can language be planned?, The University Press of Hawaii, Honolulu.

Ryan, B.E. & Carranza, M.A. (1977) Ingroup and outgroup reactions to Mexican-American language varieties, in H. Giles (ed.): Language, ethnicity and intergroup relations, Academic Press, London.

R.F. Salisbury, Notes on bilingualism and linguistic change in New Guinea, Anthropological Linguistics, 4, 1-13 (1962).

Sankoff, G. (1972) Language use in multilingual societies: Some alternative approaches, in J.B. Pride & J. Holmes (eds.): Sociolinguistics, Penguin Books, Harmondsworth.

J.B. Sawyer, Social aspects of bilingualism in San Antonio, Texas, American Dialect Society, 41, 7-16 (1965).

C.M. Scotton, Strategies of neutrality, Language, 52, 913-941 (1976).

C.M. Scotton & W. Ury, Bilingual strategies: The social functions of code switching, International Journal of the Sociology of Language, 13, 5-20 (1977).

L. Sechrest, Flores, L. & L. Arellano, Language and social interaction in a
bilingual culture, Journal of Social Psychology, 76, 155-161 (1968).

Segalowitz, N. (1977) Bilingualism and social behaviour, in W.H. Coons, D.M.
Taylor & M.A. Tremlay (eds.): The individual, language and society in Canada,
The Canada Council, Ottawa.

Segalowitz, N. & Gatbonton, E. (1977) Studies of the non-fluent bilingual, in
P.A. Hornby (ed.): Bilingualism: Psychological, social and educational implications, Academic Press, New York.

R.W. Shuy, Code switching in Lady Chatterly's Lover, Working papers in Sociolinguistics, no.22, Austin, Texas, Southwest Educational Development
Laboratory (1975).

L.M. Simard, D.M. Taylor & H. Giles, Attribution processes and interpersonal
accommodation in a bilingual setting, Language and Speech, 19, 374-387 (1977).

Sorenson, A.P. (1972) Multilingualism in the Northwest Amazon, in J.B. Pride &
J. Holmes (eds.): Sociolinguistics, Penguin Books, Harmondsworth.

H. Tajfel, Social identity and intergroup behaviour, Social Science Information,
13, 65-93 (1974).

Tajfel, H. & Turner, J.C. (in press) An integrative theory of intergroup conflict, in W.G. Austin & S. Worchel (eds.): The social psychology of intergroup relations, Brooks/Cole, Monterey.

Taylor, D.M. (1977) Bilingualism and intergroup relations, in P.A. Hornby (ed.):
Bilingualism: Psychological, social and educational implications, Academic
Press, New York.

D.M. Taylor, J.N. Bassili & F.E. Aboud, Dimensions of ethnic identity: An
example from Québec, Journal of Social Psychology, 89, 185-192 (1973).

Taylor, D.M., Meynard, R. & Rheault, E. (1977) Threat to ethnic identity and
second-language learning, in H. Giles (ed.): Language, ethnicity and intergroup relations, Academic Press, London.

D.M. Taylor & L.M. Simard, Social interaction in a bilingual setting, Canadian
Psychological Review, 16, 240-254 (1975).

H.C. Triandis, Cognitive similarity and communication in a dyad, Human Relations,
13, 175-183 (1960).

Trudgill, P. (1974) Sociolinguistics: An Introduction, Penguin Books, Harmondsworth.

J. C. Turner & R.J. Brown, Ingroups, outgroups and social identity: Just how
rational is social conflict?, Mimeo, University of Bristol (1977).

Verdoodt, A. (1973) La protection des droits de l'homme dans les états pluri-
lingues, Editions Labor, Bruxelles.

Weinreich, U. (1974) <u>Languages in contact</u>, Mouton, The Hague.

Whitely, W.H. (-974) <u>Language in Kenya</u>, Oxford University Press, Nairobi.

INTERETHNIC CONFLICT AND
COMMUNICATIVE DISTANCES

J. G. Lukens

University of Wisconsin-Milwaukee, Milwaukee, Wisconsin, U.S.A.

Language can have much influence on the attitudes of those employing it as well as on the attitudes of those towards whom it is directed. Racist language may be purposefully used to perpetuate racist attitudes among ingroup members and to instil feelings of inferiority in members of the outgroup. Where prejudice and feelings of antipathy towards an outgroup are relatively weak, speech may be only subtly racist and reflect the ingroup members' insensitivity and indifference towards the outgroup. It may include the use of phrases conforming to "symbolic racism" such as (1) "Blacks should not push themselves to where they are not wanted"; (2) "Over the past few years, blacks have gotten more than they economically deserve"; (3) "More attention is paid to the requests of blacks than to those of whites"; and (4) "Many blacks who are on welfare could get along without it" (McConahay and Hough, 1976). More intense racism, by contrast, is marked by more blatantly racist language and frequently includes the use of ethnophaulisms, derogatory nicknames for different racial and ethnic groups, (Palmore, 1962), as well as other forms of intense verbal abuse.

Since language behaviour encompasses many dimensions it, therefore, is not sufficient to be concerned only with how certain lexical items and idiomatic expressions reflect racism and ethnocentrism. In a broader context, one should examine how racism and ethnocentrism may affect many facets of language behaviour including choices of phonological variants, syntactic structures, idiomatic expressions, discourse structures and lexical items. An important sociolinguistic concept which is concerned with the way in which speakers manipulate linguistic variants either to increase or to decrease the psychological distance between one another is "communicative distance" (Peng, 1974). In order to provide an increased understanding of how speakers may set up different kinds of communicative distances in interethnic interaction, this writer extended Peng's concept to include three distances. Each distance in the order indicated reflects a greater intensity of ethnocentrism than the preceding one. The three distances include: (1) the distance of indifference; (2) the distance of avoidance; and (3) the distance of disparagement. Differences between dominant and subordinate groups with regard to the types of linguistic characteristics and speech styles associated with the distances are discussed in the paper. Yet, prior to presenting the three distances, several related theoretical frameworks concerning the interrelationship between language behaviour, ethnic identity and ingroup-outgroup attitudes as evidenced in interethnic interaction will be considered.

ETHNOCENTRISM AND LINGUISTIC VARIATION

Ethnocentrism has been defined in a variety of ways. It was defined by Downs
(1971) as the tendency to apply the standards of one's own culture to human activities in other cultures. LeVine and Campbell (1972) recently have maintained
that ethnocentrism is the belief that one's own culture is the paragon of value.
This belief structure may result in a display of strong feelings of ingroup loyalty and antipathy towards outsiders. Sumner's classic definition of ethnocentrism (1906:13) maintains that:

> "Ethnocentrism is the technical name for the view of things
> in which one's own group is the centre of everything, and
> all others are scaled and rated with reference to it...Each
> group nourishes its own pride and vanity and looks with con-
> tempt on outsiders...Each group thinks its own folkways are
> the right ones; and if it observes that other groups have
> other folkways, these excite its scorn."

The dissimilarities present in these definitions may be attributed to these
scholars' academic backgrounds. In addition, the dissimilarities also may be
reflective of actual differences in intensity of ethnocentrism. Thus, Down's
definition, besides reflecting a low intensity of ethnocentrism, also may represent the influence of the cultural relativism viewpoint of anthropologists during
the 1960's on it, while those of LeVine and Campbell and Sumner, on the other
hand, would seem to correspond to a greater intensity of ethnocentrism resulting
in the expression of ingroup-outgroup antagonisms in conflict situations.[1] Whereas Frech (1973) contended that a low level of ethnocentrism is vital in preserving
a culture, in its more extreme forms it results in feelings of superiority, intolerance and chauvinism. Fishman (1977) has claimed that racism is one of the
excesses into which ethnocentrism can develop.

The relationship between language and ethnocentrism to the present has not been
adequately studied. As a result, many contradictory findings exist in the literature. Most studies concerned with language behaviour as related to ethnic identity and nationalism have not been fully conclusive as they primarily investigated single aspects of language. Also, most sociolinguistic studies were only
concerned with linguistic phenomena as they prevail in particular cultures and
did not involve worldwide comparisons (Fishman, 1966). While some scholars have
maintained that ethnic identity influences language behaviour (McDavid, 1951;
Lieberson, 1970; Fishman, 1972), other researchers have found that some aspects
of language behaviour, such as language loyalty, may not be directly related to
ethnic identity (Riley, 1975). Riley's research revealed that feelings of ethnic
identity and ethnocentrism among Guamanians did not necessarily result in a strong

---

[1]Many psychological dimensions of ethnocentrism (and its ingroup-outgroup functions) were largely ignored by anthropologists during the 1960's who defined ethnocentrism as the tendency to indiscriminately apply the standards of one's own
culture to other societies. Not reflecting the cultural relativism viewpoint
assumed by many anthropologists in defining ethnocentrism, psychologists, on the
other hand, have regarded it as the tendency to accept the culturally "alike"
(values and life-style of the ingroup) and to reject the culturally "unalike"
(values and life-style of the outgroup).

adherence to the indigenous language. Weinreich (1974), however, noted, "It is in the situation of language contact that people become aware of their language as against others, and it is there that the purity of the standardized language most easily becomes the symbol of group integrity".

Nonetheless, another area of language usage related to ethnocentrism and racism has concerned the relationship between lexical items containing the term "black", which exhibit a negative connotation, and those containing the term "white", which have a positive connotation, and ethnocentrism. Some writers, essentially, have claimed that terms such as "black magic", "to blacklist" and "blackhead" are the result of longstanding prejudice against blacks, whereas terms such as "white lie", "white magic" and "Snow White" have been attributed to attitudes of cultural superiority by whites (Burgest, 1973; Williams, 1965; Williams and Stabler, 1973). On the other hand, other writers have denied a racist basis for these terms (Akintola, 1973; Barnes, 1973; Bosmajian, 1974). More recently, Holt (1972) has suggested that blacks may reverse the meanings of terms used towards them in a derogatory way by whites in order to rebuff the racist implications. Examples of terms that may be used with a sense of endearment to counteract the meanings ascribed to them by whites include labels such as "bad niggers", "dirty niggers" and "uppity attitude". The above research suffers because of its nearly exclusive concentration on single aspects of language as opposed to its assuming a broader multi-dimensional approach. Besides focusing primarily on "words and expressions", another weakness has consisted of its failure to consider the dynamics of interethnic interaction and how conflict in assymetrical relationships between members of majority and minority groups will affect language behaviour. G. Williams (this volume) has contended that if a fuller understanding of language behaviour in relationship to ethnocentrism, ethnic identity and varying intensities of racism is to be achieved, linguistic variation must be investigated from the vantage point of a power struggle between dominant and subordinate groups. Indeed, the moods, motives and hostilities of the interlocutors that give rise to different types of linguistic variation ultimately are influenced by inequalities implicit in the majority-minority relationship.

An approach constituting several social psychological concepts which offers much promise for providing a better understanding of the dynamic aspects of language behaviour in intergroup situations is "accommodation theory". This approach encompasses the linguistic strategies of (1) speech convergence and (2) non-convergence (speech maintenance and speech divergence).

ACCOMMODATION THEORY AND LANGUAGE BEHAVIOUR IN INTERETHNIC INTERACTION

Sociolinguists have long been interested in the social backgrounds of speakers and hearers and the types of linguistic diversities they produce. They have been mostly concerned with the impact of variables, such as social class, occupation, age, sex and attitudes on linguistic structures (Labov, 1966, 1972). Only recently it has been recognized that more research is needed concerning the psychological and social psychological variables that may underlie much linguistic variation. Lindenfeld (1972), for example, has maintained that important psychological variables such as personality makeup, moods and anxieties must receive more research attention. Giles (1977) claimed that to neglect people's moods, motives, feelings and loyalties would give the false impression of the speaker as "some kind of sociolinguistic automaton".

In response to the need to consider the impact of social psychological variables on language behaviour in intergroup situations Giles, Bourhis and Taylor (1977) developed several theoretical notions regarding possible factors underlying various linguistic strategies. These strategies are speech convergence (the modification of speech - dialect, intensity, length of pauses and loudness, etc - in a direction

towards that of another interlocutor); speech maintenance (the neutral condition
in which a speaker will retain his/her regular pattern of speech without consciously or unconsciously altering it towards or away from that of another party); and
speech divergence (the shifting of speech in a direction away from that of another
interlocutor). In order to account for the manipulation of language in intergroup
encounters the conceptual framework known as "accommodation theory" encompassing
the four interrelated social psychological concepts of (1) similarity attraction;
(2) social exchange; (3) causal attribution; and (4) intergroup distinctiveness
was adopted. With respect to linguistic variation in interethnic and interracial
encounters, the fourth concept, intergroup distinctiveness, seems the most app-
licable. The above researchers have maintained that ingroup speech (and sometimes
ingroup-influenced outgroup speech) frequently serves to symbolize ethnic identity
and cultural solidarity. Indeed, linguistic analyses utilizing "accommodation
theory" to account for linguistic diversity have provided greater explanatory power
for the modification of speech in intergroup situations, than has been the case
with most other types of sociolinguistic studies.[2]

In order to account for the linguistic selections of speakers of different cultural backgrounds, Giles, Bourhis and Taylor (1977) developed a theory of language
behaviour in interethnic interaction. They contended that the decision to either
employ speech convergence or speech divergence (upward or downward) or speech maintenance by members of different racial or ethnic groups will depend on: (1) the
position of the speaker's group in the power structure - dominant or subordinate;
(2) the extent to which the speaker perceives the position of his/her group (dominant or subordinate) as legitimate or illegitimate; and (3) the extent to which
a speaker perceives or does not perceive cognitive alternatives to the existing
intergroup situation. For example, a speaker who perceives the subordinate position of his/her group as legitimate may upwardly converge, while another individual may either employ speech maintenance or downwardly diverge if he/she perceives
the group's subordinate position as being illegitimate. Essentially, downward
speech divergence and a rejection of the dominant culture - "the cultural rejection hypothesis" - may account for the accentuation of a distinctive black speech
style by some blacks in interracial encounters (Giles and Bourhis, 1976). Likewise, the use of speech maintenance, downward convergence or upward divergence by
members of the dominant culture will depend on their assessments of the legitimacy
or illegitimacy of their high status positions in relationship to persons belonging
to various subordinate groups.

To date there has been little research concerning a hierarchy of strategies of
psycholinguistic distinctiveness. Yet Giles, Bourhis and Taylor (1977) have
suggested that interethnic conflict situations may be distinguished by different
types of speech divergences - some more or less dissociative of outgroups than
others.

> "...perhaps both from the perspective of ingroup encoder
> and outgroup decoder, putative, pronunciation and content
> differentiation may be considered instances of low psycho-
> linguistic distinctiveness, whereas various forms of accent
> and dialect divergence may be considered instances of strong-
> er ethnic dissociation. Verbal abuse, the maintenance of

---

[2]In contrast to many sociolinguistic studies, those employing "accommodation
theory" attempt to discover the reasoning underlying the manipulation of language
as opposed to merely providing a description of linguistic variation. Much language behaviour can be attributed to rational choices in which speakers attempt
to minimize risk and to maximize favourable outcomes.

or switch to another language in the face of an outgroup
speaker (in a bi- or multi-lingual setting) may be among
the most potent of psycholinguistic distinctiveness.
...Language spoken can, therefore, be used as a tactic to
maximize the differences between ethnic groups on a valued
dimension in the search for a positive distinctiveness"
(Giles, Bourhis and Taylor, 1977:330-331).

A recent study by Bourhis, Giles, Leyens and Tajfel (1979) revealed that different
types of speech divergences may result from varying intensities of perceived threat
from outgroups. Their research involved an experiment in order to determine how
different types of speech divergences, including accent and content divergence as
well as the switch to another language in the face of an outgroup speaker in a bi-
or multi-lingual setting could result from different degrees of perceived "ethnic
threat" from outsiders. It was found that the switch to Flemish (the ingroup language) from English in the face of outgroup members (non-speakers of the ingroup
language) occurred under conditions where "ethnic threat" from Walloons (Francophones) was perceived as most intense. On the other hand, under conditions where
"ethnic threat" was perceived as less intense content and accent divergence occurred.

While the linguistic research associated with "accommodation theory" advanced the
state of knowledge regarding the dynamics of language behaviour in interethnic
interaction, particularly concerning choices of linguistic strategies, the majority of investigations have been experimental and, therefore, it must not be indiscriminately assumed that the findings can be generalized to all settings. Rather,
other approaches are needed to provide greater insight concerning the dynamics of
language behaviour in various naturalistic settings involving speakers of different ethnic and racial backgrounds. An approach that demonstrates much potential
for facilitating this understanding is the concept of "communicative distance"
(Peng, 1974). Thus far this approach has been primarily concerned with language
behaviour in intra-ethnic interaction. However, it also offers much potential
for enhancing the understanding of how speakers of different ethnic and racial
backgrounds may manipulate language in interethnic situations.

COMMUNICATIVE DISTANCE AND LINGUISTIC VARIATION

The introduction of the concept of "communicative distance" generated much interest in how speakers may manipulate language in various intergroup encounters.
Until recently, much linguistic variation which could not be accounted for in
terms of various demographic variables, and corresponding sociolinguistic norms
and rules was ascribed to what once were regarded as "free variations". However,
over the past decade it has been increasingly recognized that many seemingly
anomalous variants, those not specifically governed by sociolinguistic norms or
rules, may be deliberately employed by interlocutors to lengthen, shorten or maintain a given communicative distance. Consequently, many so-called deviant linguistic variants, such as those not accounted for in accordance with the rules of
power semantics or solidarity semantics (Brown and Gilman, 1972), in actuality,
may represent the devices used for establishing and altering communicative distances. For example, while persons of lower status in general are expected to
employ relatively formal forms of address with those of higher status than themselves, in some instances they may intentionally use seemingly inappropriately
familiar forms in order to counteract the hierarchical differences reflected in
speech. Where the use of the latter is not the outcome of longstanding feelings
of amity, it, indeed, might represent a desire to lengthen communicative distance.
The addressee in perceiving the use of such inappropriately familiar forms as an
attack on his/her authority, in turn, may decide to manipulate language to rein-
stitute the previous communicative distance or to establish an altogether new one.

Unlike Hall (1966), who differentiates between the four spatial or proxemic distances of (1) intimate distance; (2) personal distance; (3) social distance; and
(4) public distance in terms of feet and inches, Peng has not so operationally
defined "communicative distance" nor, for that matter, suggested how different communicative distances might have proxemic counterparts. He also did not attempt to
designate particular psychological meanings which might be associated with different communicative distances (emotional feelings between speakers and hearers) or
discuss the way in which these feelings might be linked with particular proxemic
distances. More recently Leginski and Izzet (1973) found that linguistic styles
(similar to communicative distances) do not necessarily exhibit a one to one correspondence with proxemic distances. Perhaps, unanticipated findings such as very
informal linguistic styles discovered in association with the longer proxemic distances - the social distance (four to seven feet between speakers) and the public
distance (twelve to twenty-five feet between speakers) - could signal the establishment of a new distance in which the proxemic-linguistic norms are intentionally
violated. Although Peng has maintained that communicative distances are not directly measurable, he does maintain that they definitely exist. Moreover, he contends
that they are subjectively very real for both speakers and hearers.

> "A communicative distance cannot be measured directly. It
> is not even visible. But we can be sure of its presence
> when we hear certain words and expressions or detect the
> omission of certain expected words and expressions. In
> other words, our awareness of the existence of a communic-
> ative distance in the midst of a conversation depends to a
> large extent on certain linguistic devices which serve from
> the speaker's point of view, to set up the communicative
> distance, or, from the hearer's point of view to let the
> hearer know that it has already been set up by the speaker"
> (Peng, 1974:33).

While much of the research concerning communicative distance has been in respect
of misunderstandings of the use of linguistic variants by members of different ethnic groups in interethnic encounters (Yashiro, 1973; Peng, 1974), much too little
attention has been directed towards investigating the dynamics of language behaviour and the manipulation of speech by dominant and subordinate groups with one
another in interethnic conflict situations. Indeed, it is evident that ethnic consciousness and class interests will greatly influence the nature of linguistic variation. The following example involving the use of demeaning address forms by a
white police officer to a black doctor illustrates how certain linguistic strategies may be used by members of the dominant culture to keep the outgroup subordinate.

> "What's your name, boy?" the policeman asked..."
> "Dr. Pouissant. I'm a physician..."
> "What's your first name, boy?..."
> "Alvin." (Ervin-Tripp, 1967:4).

In recognition that ethnocentrism will influence linguistic variation in interethnic encounters, Lukens (1978) extended the concept of communicative distance to
encompass three types of communicative distances. These reflect varying degrees
of ethnocentrism and differences in the sharpness of contradictions in interethnic
interaction. It is suggested that depending on the intensity of ethnocentrism of
the dominant group and ethnic stratification involving domination, mystification
and manipulation, different types of linguistic variation will be manifested in
intergroup conflict situations. Additionally, members of subordinate groups, consonant with their class and ethnic consciousness, will adopt certain linguistic
strategies to counterpoise the various communicative distances established by dominant group members. Essentially, it can be assumed that linguistic strategies
employed by speakers will conform to one of three possible communicative distances

depending on which of the below takes precedence in a situation: (1) feelings of indifference and insensitivity towards an outgroup - (lowest intensity of ethnocentrism and intergroup conflict); (2) a desire to avoid interaction with an outgroup - (moderate intensity of ethnocentrism and intergroup conflict); and (3) feelings of ethnic and racial superiority or hostility towards an outgroup - (highest intensity of ethnocentrism and intergroup conflict). The communicative distances that are consonant with the above mentioned variables (predispositions of ingroup members towards the outgroup) include: (1) the distance of indifference; (2) the distance of avoidance; and (3) the distance of disparagement. With respect to the lengthening of communicative distance, these three distances should be seen as representing qualitatively distinct aspects of a larger process - namely, that of speech divergence.

THE THREE COMMUNICATIVE DISTANCES AND INTERETHNIC CONFLICT

Hediger (1955) suggested that animals in defending their territories from lurking dangers frequently will react to these by successively establishing the following distances as perceived threat increases: (1) flight distance; (2) critical distance and (3) attack distance. Just as animals set up various distances in response to different intensities of threat, humans will react similarly to perceived threat from those below them, or, in the case of subordinate groups, to that from those in powerful positions. While physical escape and brute force are two possible means for handling a threatening situation, a human being may also employ various linguistic strategies in order to contend with different intensities of perceived threat from outgroups. As conflict and ethnocentrism increase under changing social conditions the linguistic selections of speakers will vary accordingly. This writer has suggested, for example, that under conditions of low "ethnic threat" the language behaviour of interlocutors, particularly that of members of the dominant culture, will be influenced by their insensitivity towards the outgroup as well as by their desire to perpetuate the inequalities implicit in the majority-minority relationship. However, in situations in which threat from an outgroup is perceived to be moderate in intensity ingroup members may adopt linguistic strategies that tend to accentuate differences between themselves and the outgroup. Finally, in the event that an outgroup is seen as extremely threatening, speech may be altered in a myriad of ways by ingroup members in order to devalue and to attack the outgroup (symbolically annihilating it).

Indeed, the three communicative distances which reflect ethnocentrism and ingroup-outgroup antagonisms in conflict situations of varying intensities -(1) the distance of indifference; (2) the distance of avoidance; and (3) the distance of disparagement - represent the "far side" of communicative distance. The successive establishment of these distances implies a lengthening of communicative distance as opposed to a shortening of it. Yet, it is apparent that as ingroup members lengthen communicative distance with members of various outgroups, it will be shortened among themselves. Thus, in actuality, the "near" and "far" sides of communicative distance exist simultaneously with each side presupposing the other.

The distinction between the three distances as suggested earlier could be related to the concept of speech divergence. Each distance could be regarded as a specific type of speech divergence contained in a hierarchy of strategies of psycholinguistic distinctiveness (see Giles, Bourhis and Taylor, 1977). The distance of indifference would entail the use of the least potent strategies of psycholinguistic distinctiveness. The distance of avoidance, on the other hand, reflecting a moderate intensity of interethnic tension would involve moderately potent strategies of psycholinguistic distinctiveness. Finally, the distance of disparagement, established in situations characterized by extreme intergroup conflict, would involve the most potent strategies. Essentially, these distances will tend to be realized in two distinct types of situations - (1) members of different ethnic and racial groups personally confronting each other and (2) members of different ethnic and racial groups making references to a given outgroup in conversing with a third party. A discussion of the three communicative distances and their respective linguistic characteristics and speech styles is presented below.[3] It is suggested that the linguistic phenomena associated with the various distances will differ in both degree and kind for each of them.

1. The Distance of Indifference (Low Interethnic Conflict)

The distance of indifference is established in situations in which intergroup tension is low and there is little perceived threat from outgroups. Members of the majority culture frequently will establish this distance with subordinate group members in order to maintain their dominant position and to prevent the latter from gaining greater political leverage. Where intergroup antagonisms are low, ethnocentrism will also be minimal and will result in linguistic selections reflecting much insensitivity towards the culture of the outgroup. Here, the linguistic characteristics and speech styles used by speakers represent the view that their own culture or subculture is the centre of everything. Thus, many statements may be made about the outgroup which amount to little other than "glittering generalizations" with little or no basis in fact. Members of subordinate groups will only tend to establish this distance under conditions in which they would be thwarted from overtly expressing antipathy towards the outgroup. Yet, regrettably, their use of linguistic characteristics and speech styles associated with this distance may be misperceived as reflecting a state of apathy. In actuality, the distance of indifference and its characteristics should be regarded as a linguistic repertoire of the dominant group. It is only occasionally used as an adaptive strategy by subordinate group members.

The linguistic selections of members of the dominant culture in reference to a given outgroup may result from insensitivity or a reluctance to demonstrate feelings of empathy for the outgroup. Some expressions used by dominant group members to describe a subordinate group which would exemplify the above include demeaning phrases like "illegal aliens", "the Negro problem", and "culturally deprived". Rich (1974), moreover, has maintained that the following so-called "bristle statements" including - "I must help these people as they cannot help themselves", "to raise them up to our level", and "to remove the white man's burden" - result from the assumption that the outgroup is to be blamed as opposed to being viewed as a victim of the system. The distance of indifference also may entail the use of terms, such as "unambitious", "unmotivated", and "non-goal oriented" to characterize various ethnic and racial groups. As Gearing (1970) has pointed out, these "nondescriptions" (adjectives containing the "un" or "non" prefix) reveal very little about the culture of the outgroup. Indeed, such speech forms represent the insensitivity and obliviousness of ingroup members concerning the outgroup. Their use also may reflect a desire of dominant group members to keep members of subordinate outgroups mystified with regard to the inegalitarian majority-minority relationship.

---

[3]For a more detailed treatment of the nature of the three communicative distances and the linguistic characteristics and speech styles associated with each one, see Lukens (1978). The present paper is more concerned with how variables such as the position of a speaker's ethnic or racial group in the power structure and extent of class and ethnic consciousness influence the linguistic variation associated with each of the distances than the earlier paper.

Besides the use of the aforementioned types of lexical items and idiomatic expressions, the distance of indifference also frequently entails the use of distinct
speech styles which in-as-such may be quite patronizing towards minorities. According to Fanon (1961), for example, whites may recurrently behave towards blacks
as adults do with children by "smirking, whispering, patronizing and cozening".
In addition, speech patterns (especially the syntax) used in conversing with foreigners and others of different ethnic backgrounds may be overly simplified. Here,
the assumption is that the foreigner or "ethnic" would be unable to grasp the complexities of Standard English despite their possibly having demonstrated much fluency. Finally, in other instances speakers' vocal qualities and intonations may
become muffled and indistinct. This again may reflect indifferent feelings and a
lack of rapport between ingroup and outgroup members.

A means by which members of minority groups may establish the distance of indifference is through the use of linguistic selections corresponding to a discourse
style referred to as "pretence" (Else, 1969). Here, a form of speech may be used
by members of subordinate groups that is incongruent with their real intentions.
Such use of language will represent cynical role performances in which members of
subordinate groups appear to be ceding to the dominant culture. More specifically,
subordinate group members' utilization of "double-entendres" and similar forms may
serve to defy the dominant culture and the "false consciousness" it deploys. Both
"shucking" and "signifying" as used by blacks in interacting with whites, hence,
often stem from feelings of indifference and pretence. While on the surface
blacks' speech patterns may often appear as accommodating to the dominant culture,
double messages frequently are conveyed. Mitchell-Kernan (1971), accordingly, has
reported that explicit and implicit contents of messages of blacks to whites may
differ and often are purposefully ambiguous. With respect to "signifying" she
states:

> "Such messages, because of their form - they contain both
> explicit and implicit content - structure interpretation in
> such a way that the parties have the option of avoiding real
> confrontation...Alternately, they provoke confrontations
> without at the same time exposing unequivocally the speaker's
> intent. The advantage in either case is for the speaker be-
> cause it gives him control of the situation at the receiver's
> expense. The speaker, because of the purposeful ambiguity
> of his original remark, reserves the right to subsequently
> insist on the harmless interpretation rather than the provoc-
> ative one...the addressee faces the possibility that if he
> attempts to confront the speaker, the latter will deny the
> message or intent imputed, leaving him in the embarrassing
> predicament of appearing contentious"(1971:103).

2. The Distance of Avoidance (Moderate Interethnic Conflict)

The distance of avoidance is established by both dominant and subordinate groups
in situations in which ethnocentrism and intergroup conflict are of a moderate intensity. The linguistic characteristics and speech styles associated with this
distance, however, will be inherently different with respect to whether a speaker
is a member of the former or the latter. This distance as established by members
of the dominant culture will reflect a moderate degree of "ethnic threat" from
subordinate outgroups, whereas, as set up by subordinate group members, it may
serve to challenge the hegemony of the dominant group. As for its use with the
latter, ingroup members may exaggerate their own distinctive linguistic patterns
in order to resist the dominant group and possible assimilation into the so-called
"melting pot concept" of American society. Specifically, the establishment of the
distance of avoidance by members of subordinate groups may reflect the "cultural

rejection hypothesis" or a turning away from mainstream values by oppressed groups
which feel estranged. Thus, persons belonging to subordinate groups may emphasize
their unique speech styles and dialects as a means of reviving their ethnicity and
for "psycho-social liberation".

Both dominant and subordinate group members may establish the distance of avoidance through emphasizing their unique dialect characteristics and specific solidarity terms. Whereas members of dominant groups may accentuate their "prestigious"
dialects and pronunciation patterns (hypercorrection), subordinate group members,
on the other hand, may emphasize what members of the dominant culture regard as
"stigmatized" forms (Ryan, 1979). In addition to accentuating their linguistic
patterns, ingroup members, according to Giles, Bourhis and Taylor (1977) on occasion, may also scrupulously avoid various phonological patterns or syntactic
characteristics associated with a given outgroup. They have pointed out that
middle class Anglos in the southwestern part of the United States frequently will
avoid the {a} pronunciation as in "father" in pronouncing other lexical items such
as *patio* in order to distance themselves from the Spanish pronunciation of these
words.

Besides the use of hypercorrection and omission of specific phonological patterns
various lexical items may be used to emphasize ingroup solidarity. Among these
lexical items used to distinguish the ingroup from the outgroup are "us" versus
"them", "we" versus "they", and "you people". Dominant group members also may
employ phrases such as "real Americans of the old stock" or "we must maintain our
White Christian heritage and the principles upon which our nation was founded".
Conversely, some solidarity expressions used by members of the outgroup to counteract domination by the majority culture include phrases such as "viva la raza",
"Chicano power", "brother", "right on sister" and "black is beautiful". Holt
(1972) has contended that the use of these and similar phrases crystallizes self-
awareness and ideological direction while solidifying bonds of the national black
(or other minority) experience in confrontation with white domination. Holt has
also suggested that members of minority groups often resort to the strategy of
"linguistic inversion" in order to distance themselves from the majority culture.
Kochman describes the use of linguistic inversion by blacks as follows:

> "In essence, the idea is to make any word of denigration used
> by the power group take on shades of meaning known only to
> the inverter, reflecting a determination to call themselves
> by any name other than that used by whites...This serves as
> a defensive mechanism to fight linguistic, and thereby psy-
> chological entrapment. Thus "nigger" when used by whites
> ...has only one meaning, though the degree of degradation
> may vary with the users. When used by blacks the word is
> often used as a term of affection, admiration, approval: it
> is a word of positive connotation, a contradiction of orig-
> inal intent" (1976:271).

A characteristic associated with the distance of avoidance which is likely to be
more frequently used by the subordinate culture than the dominant group is the
"restricted code" (Bernstein, 1967, 1973) and other forms of abbreviated speech.
Unfortunately, as Rosen (1972) has claimed, these speech forms (sociolinguistic
codes) have not been properly understood from the perspective of oppressed groups
and their desire to possibly withhold information and feelings from members of
the dominant culture. Rather, their use has often been attributed to "basic cognitive defects" or seen as the natural outcome of situations in which feelings,
ideas and thoughts are extensively shared among ingroup members. In actuality,
however, the latter's use of the "restricted code" and other abbreviated speech
forms generally serves to lengthen communicative distance with the dominant group
as intended.

3. The Distance of Disparagement (High Interethnic Conflict)

The distance of disparagement is established in situations in which interethnic conflict and ethnocentrism are extremely intense. It will be established where members of the dominant group perceive subordinate group members as highly threatening and as exhibiting very high degrees of ethnic and class consciousness. Subordinate group members, on the other hand, may establish this distance upon realizing that the dominant culture has illegitimately assumed a position of authority and that through collective action it can be subverted. Essentially, the speech styles and linguistic characteristics associated with these distances, whether established by subordinate or dominant group members, will serve to derogate and deride members of the outgroup.

In intergroup conflict situations in which the dominant culture is perceived as highly oppressive to minorities, the latter may resort to speech patterns that conform to the rhetorical strategy of "confrontation polarization" (Lanigan, 1970). Here, the dominant group is portrayed as exhibiting characteristics and values polar opposite of those of the ingroup. While subordinate groups may employ speech styles reflecting their desire to verbally assault and annihilate the dominant group, members of the latter will do likewise in their desire to symbolically debase the subordinate group. In essence, the linguistic characteristics and speech styles associated with this distance will serve to belittle and deride outgroup members. Specifically, linguistic selections representing "confrontational polarization" will vary in accordance with the position of a speaker's racial or ethnic group in the power structure.

With respect to the desire of dominant and subordinate group members to attack one another, both will employ verbal abuse and "flettoric" (four letter rhetoric) to denigrate the other. As with most linguistic phenomena, its nature will also differ depending on the position of a speaker's group in the power structure. With regard to its use at the time of the Russian revolution Trotsky in 1923 made the following statement:

> "Russian swearing in "the lower depths" was the result of
> despair, embitterment and, above all, slavery without hope,
> without escape. The swearing of the upper classes, on the
> other hand, the swearing that came out of the throats of the
> gentry, the authorities, was the outcome of class rule, slave-
> owners' pride, unshakeable power" (Trotsky, 1973:52).

As Trotsky had speculated that the nature of swearing would differ with respect to social class, it will also vary with regard to power differences between racial and ethnic groups in relation to each other. It was found that subordinate groups in perceiving that they have little to lose due to their lowly position, will be more "vulgar" in their use of flettoric, while members of the dominant culture, on the other hand, will be much more discerning in their use of it (Baumdicker, 1973). The former will be more apt to use "flettoric" which is "dirtier, uglier and rougher" - namely, that which more frequently refers to sexual, visceral and gastro-excretory activities - than the latter.

Yet another characteristic associated with the distance of disparagement and one which is employed by members of dominant and subordinate groups alike is the use of "ethnophaulisms" (see Palmore, 1962). Again ethnophaulism may be used as much by members of the dominant culture as by subordinate group members. However, here too, their nature will differ as is true concerning other linguistic characteristics. Kochman (1976), accordingly, has suggested that terms used by the dominant culture (whites) in reference to blacks will primarily distinguish between them in terms of their various physical attributes. For example, some racial epithets used

by whites for blacks include "spook", "darky", "Sambo", "burr-head", "spade", and
"monkey". Those used by blacks in reference to whites, on the other hand, distinguish between whites with respect to differences in their conduct and mode of interaction. Accordingly, the term "honky" is used to denote a white racist, while "The
Man" and "Mr. Charlie" are used in reference to whites in positions of power such
as law enforcement officials. Kochman claims that the differences between epithets used by blacks for whites and those by whites for blacks reflect the political
inequities in society. Whereas the former reflects the tendency for blacks to
perceive whites as actors or agents of power, the latter suggests that many whites
even today still tend to regard blacks as less than human - that is, as objects or
chattels.

Quite frequently highly derogatory expressions intended to devalue an outgroup will
be employed by ingroup members in establishing the distance of disparagement. Some
examples of these include phrases like "good people - but nobody", "snobs trying
to push their way up", and "people not our kind" (Davis, Gardner and Gardner, 1941).
In addition, ethnic or national slurs also may be used to deride outgroup members.
For instance, puns such as "Philadelphia is the city of "soul brotherly" love" (in-
sinuating that blacks are to blame for the high crime rate in Philadelphia) and "to
get the man to show his true colour" (in reference to a black who is not being "up
front" about his genuine concerns or who is skulking) could be used to attack the
outgroup.

Another characteristic associated with the distance of indifference is the tendency
for speakers to use their ingroup language in the presence of outgroup members who
are unfamiliar with it. Through their use of the ingroup language in the latter's
presence, ingroup members may counteract the communicative distances already established by the outgroup. Moreover, subordinate group members in interacting with
the dominant culture may employ extremely informal speech patterns and slang expressions. Berman (1978) has claimed that extreme informality and slang expressions
may be used with an interlocutor as a means of establishing power and equality - the
idea that the person with whom one is communicating is an equal, or, in many instances, an inferior. While these characteristics will serve to strengthen bonds among
ingroup members, their use in relationship to the outgroup lengthens communicative
distance.

Finally, the use of "Marxist rhetoric" by subordinate group members also may serve
to attack the outgroup - that is, the dominant culture. Marxist slogans will arise
primarily in situations in which economic exploitation is seen as the main factor
responsible for the subordinate group's plight. Revolutionary rhetoric along with
other linguistic characteristics associated with the distance of disparagement may
be reinforced through the use of downward speech divergence.

At this point the linguistic characteristics and speech styles suggested for the
various distances are largely speculative and thus, a comprehensive research effort
must be undertaken in order to determine their validity. Data must be collected
through both participant observation and tightly controlled experiments. In order
to generalize the findings concerning these distances data should be collected in
a wide variety of naturalistic settings.

IMPLICATIONS AND DIRECTIONS FOR FUTURE RESEARCH

The theoretical framework concerning the three distances as they apply in interethnic interaction offers much potential for improving the current understanding of
language as it is manipulated by speakers in dynamic intergroup situations. Much
research, however, must be conducted in order to determine how different types of
interethnic encounters may affect the nature of linguistic variation associated
with these distances. For example, an effort must be exerted to identify those

linguistic characteristics and speech styles that would seem to apply most consistently in diverse interethnic encounters versus those that might be more ephemeral
and unique to specific kinds of situations. In the latter instance, the given
characteristics might not all necessarily reflect the longstanding components of
ethnocentrism - oblivion to cultural differences, desire to avoid interaction with
outgroup members and a demonstration of hostility towards a given outgroup - or
specific differences in the intensity of interethnic conflict.

Another area in which research should be undertaken would be to determine whether
interethnic interaction in which co-operation is sought by different groups might
involve distinctly different communicative distances which, unlike the aforementioned three, may reflect the "near side" of communicative distance. This research
might bear some similarity to a theory developed by Lanigan (1970) concerning two
interrelated sets of concepts: (1) "isolational polarization" and "confrontational
polarization" and (2) "isolational communication" and "confrontational communication". With respect to the former, individuals may employ, first, either isolational polarization (offensive and involving avoidance of the outgroup), or, second,
confrontational polarization (defensive and defining the outgroup as "evil" or as
"the enemy to be destroyed"). Here, it is suggested that the communication styles
and linguistic characteristics will reflect different intensities along the "far
side" of communicative distance. In essence, Lanigan's isolational polarization
and confrontational polarization could be equated, respectively, with the distance
of avoidance and the distance of disparagement. However, in the case of his second
set of concepts, isolational communication and confrontational communication, they
would seem to represent the "near side" of communicative distance entailing the
usage of speech styles and linguistic characteristics intended to encourage dialog-
ue and intergroup understanding. In view of the fact that persons of different
ethnic and racial backgrounds frequently attempt to enhance intergroup understanding, future research efforts might be directed towards identifying particular types
of linguistic characteristics and speech styles associated with the shortening of
communicative distance in interethnic encounters. Perhaps distinct types of communicative distances might be specified here, as has been done concerning the three
types associated with the lengthening of communicative distance.

In view of the speculative thinking that the position of a speaker's group in the
power structure as well as the extent of his/her ethnic and class consciousness
will have much impact on the nature of linguistic variation associated with the
three distances, more research attention must be focused in this direction. As
already indicated, the manifestation of the three communicative distances, likewise, might be influenced by the same variables which Giles, Bourhis and Taylor
(1977) have suggested may underlie a speaker's selection of particular linguistic
strategies, whether they be speech convergence, speech divergence (either in an
upward or downward direction) or speech maintenance. These variables consist of
the following: (1) the position of a speaker's group in the power structure; (2) the
extent to which a speaker perceives the dominant or subordinate position of his/her
group in the power structure as legitimate or illegitimate; and (3) the extent to
which a speaker perceives cognitive alternatives to the present position of his/her
group in the power structure.

Essentially, an increased understanding of the three communicative distances as established by subordinate groups and of the linguistic variants and speech styles
associated with these distances could assist in dispelling some of the false infer-
ences drawn concerning the linguistic selections of various minority groups. All
too often, the use of "stigmatized speech forms" has been attributed to "low cognitive abilities" or to "poor motivation" (Labov, 1975; Giles and Bourhis, 1976;
Rosen, 1972). Instead, with regard to blacks, the emphasis of a distinctly black
speech style in interracial encounters may result from their desire to distance
themselves from whites (Labov, 1966; Giles and Bourhis, 1976). Similarly, Ryan
and Carranza (1975) have suggested that the use of so-called "stigmatized forms of

speech" of Mexican Americans may ensue from a comparable motivation. Certainly
more research must be directed towards enhancing the current state of knowledge
concerning the functions of the various linguistic selections and speech styles
used by speakers of different racial and ethnic backgrounds in intergroup conflict
situations. The concept of three communicative distances and suggested differences
in their manifestation with respect to the position of a speaker's group in the
power structure provides an impetus for increased investigation of linguistic variation in interethnic encounters. This area of research could be referred to as
either "linguistic proxemics" or "proxemic linguistics".

REFERENCES

K. Akintola, Response to "Racism in everyday speech and social work jargon",
   Social Work, 18, 102-104 (1973).

J. Barnes, Response to "Racism in everyday speech and social work jargon", Social
   Work, 18, 101-102 (1973).

D. Baumdicker, Flettoric - a view of four-letter rhetorical status indicators
   based on depersonalizing and personalizing interactions in an industrial organization, Mimeo, University of Wisconsin-Milwaukee (1973).

L. Berman, Slang of the 70's, Detroit Free Press, p.18 (January 9. 1978).

Bernstein, B. (1967) Elaborated and restricted codes: An outline, in S. Lieberson
   (ed.): Explorations in sociolinguistics, Indiana University Press, Bloomington.

Bernstein, B. (1973) Class, codes and control: Applied studies towards a sociology
   of language, Routledge and Kegan Paul, London.

Bosmajian, H. (1974) The language of oppression, Public Affairs Press, Washington,
   D.C.

Bourhis, R.Y., Giles, H., Leyens, J-P. & Tajfel, H. (1979) Psycholinguistic distinctiveness: Language divergence in Belgium, in H. Giles and R. St.Clair (eds.):
   Language and social psychology, Blackwell, Oxford.

Brown, R. & Gilman, A. (1972) The pronouns of power and solidarity, in P.P. Giglioli
   (ed.): Language and social context, Penguin Books, Harmondsworth, Middlesex.

D.R. Burgest, Racism in everyday speech and social work jargon, Social Work, 18,
   20-25 (1973).

Davis, A., Gardner, B. & Gardner, M. (1941) Deep South: A social anthropological
   study of caste and class, University of Chicago Press, Chicago.

Downs, J.F. (1971) Cultures in crisis, Glencoe Press, Beverly Hills, California.

J.F. Else, A sociological consideration of pretence, Unpublished M.A. Thesis,
   University of Nebraska, Lincoln (1969).

Ervin-Tripp, S. (1967) Sociolinguistics, Language-Behaviour Research Laboratory,
   University of California-Berkeley, Berkeley.

Fanon, F. (1961) Black skin, white masks, Grove Press, New York.

J.A. Fishman, Some contrasts between linguistically homogeneous and linguistically heterogeneous polities, Sociological Inquiry, 36, 146-158 (1966).

Fishman, J.A. (1972) Language and nationalism, Newbury House, Rowley, Mass.

Fishman, J.A. (1977) Language, ethnicity and racism, in M. Saville-Troike (ed.): Linguistics and anthropology, Georgetown University Press, Washington, D.C.

W.P. Frech, Jr., An analysis of the effect of the anthropology curriculum project material, The concept of culture, on the ethnocentric attitudes of fourth grade students, Unpublished doctoral dissertation, University of Georgia, Athens (1973).

Gearing, F.O. (1970) The face of the fox, Aldine, Chicago.

H. Giles, Social psychology and applied linguistics: Towards an integrative approach, ITL Review of Applied Linguistics, 35, 27-42 (1977).

H. Giles & R.Y. Bourhis, Voice and racial categorizations in Britain, Communication Monographs, 43, 108-114 (1976).

Giles, H., Bourhis, R.Y. & Taylor, D.M. (1977) Towards a theory of language in ethnic group relations, in H. Giles (ed.): Language, ethnicity and intergroup relations, Academic Press, London.

Hall, E.T. (1966) The hidden dimension, Doubleday, New York.

Hediger, H. (1955) Studies in the psychology and behaviour of captive animals in zoos and circuses, Butterworths, London.

Holt, G.S. (1972) "Inversion" in black communication, in T. Kochman (ed.): Rappin' and stylin' out: Communication in urban black America, University of Illinois Press, Champaign-Urbana.

T. Kochman, Perceptions along the power axis: A cognitive residue of interracial encounters, Anthropological Linguistics, 18, 261-273 (1976).

Labov, W. (1966) The social stratification of English in New York City, The Center for Applied Linguistics, Washington, D.C.

Labov, W. (1972) Sociolinguistic patterns, University of Pennsylvania Press, Philadelphia.

Labov, W. (1975) The logic of non-standard English, in P. Stoller (ed.): Black American English: Its background and usage in the schools and in literature, Dell Publishing Co., New York.

R.L. Lanigan, Urban crisis: Polarization and communication, Central States Speech Journal, 21, 108-116 (1970).

W. Leginski & R. Izzet, Linguistic styles as indices for interpersonal distance, Journal of Social Psychology, 91, 291-304 (1973).

LeVine, R.A. & Campbell, D.T. (1972) Ethnocentrism: Theories of conflict, ethnocentric attitudes and group behaviour, John Wiley, New York.

Lieberson, S. (1970) Language and ethnic relations in Canada, John Wiley, New York.

J. Lindenfeld, In search of psycholinguistic factors of linguistic variation, Semiotica, 5, 350-361 (1972).

J.G. Lukens, Ethnocentric speech: Its nature and implications, Ethnic groups: An international periodical of ethnic studies, 2 (1978).

J.B. McConahay & J.C. Hough, Jr., Symbolic racism, Journal of Social Issues, 32, 23-45 (1976).

R.I. McDavid, Dialect differences and intergroup tensions, Studies in Linguistics, 9, 27-33 (1951).

Mitchell-Kernan, C. (1971) Language behaviour in a black urban community, Language-Behaviour Research Laboratory, University of California-Berkeley, Berkeley.

E.B. Palmore, Ethnophaulism and ethnocentrism, The American Journal of Sociology, 67, 442-445 (1962).

F.C.C. Peng, Communicative distance, Language Sciences, 31, 32-38 (1974).

Rich, A.L. (1974) Interracial communication, Harper and Row, New York.

G.A. Riley, Language loyalty and ethnocentrism in the Guamanian speech community, Anthropological Linguistics, 17, 286-292 (1975).

Rosen, H. (1972) Language and class: A critical look at the theories of Basil Bernstein, Falling Wall Press, Bristol.

Ryan, E.B. (1979) Why do low-prestige language varieties persist? in H. Giles & R. St.Clair (eds.): Language and social psychology, Blackwell, Oxford.

E.B. Ryan & M.A. Carranza, Evaluative reactions towards speakers of Standard English and Mexican American accented English, Journal of Personality and Social Psychology, 31, 855-863 (1975).

Sumner, W.G. (1906) Folkways, Ginn and Company, Boston.

Trotsky, L. (1973) Problems of everyday life, Monad Press, New York.

Weinreich, U. (1974) Languages in contact, Mouton, The Hague.

J.E. Williams, Connotations of racial concepts and colour names, Journal of Personality and Social Psychology, 3, 531-540 (1965).

J.E. Williams & J.R. Stabler, If white means good, then black..., Psychology Today, 7, 50-54 (1973).

K. Yashiro, A study of communicative distance in English and Japanese, Unpublished M.A. Thesis, International Christian University, Tokyo (1973).

INSIDERS, OUTSIDERS, AND RENEGADES: TOWARDS A CLASSIFICATION OF ETHNOLINGUISTIC LABELS

B. B. Khleif

Department of Sociology and Anthropology, University of New Hampshire, U.S.A.

1. INTRODUCTION

This paper explores the use of language in maintenance of ethnic boundaries, that is, in regulating interaction between groups. It deals with labels of inclusion, exclusion, and desertion. It draws upon work done by the author and by others, utilizing data pertaining to ethnic groups in North America, Welsh-English relations, and religious communities.

The paper rests on the following assumptions:

1. Boundaries are part of the human experience: they mark off groups from one another; they enable the person, as Berger would say (1963:67), to live within his group-given co-ordinates, to have an identity. If ethnic groups are essentially "categories of ascription"; if it is the boundary that determines the group (Barth, 1969:10, 15); if identity is basically a matter of social location, socially bestowed and socially nurtured (Berger, 1963:66-68, 98); if boundary maintenance is the *sine qua non* of group survival, then we can see how boundaries are inextricably linked to two issues of group life: socialization and social control, that is, the regulation of interaction for members and non-members.

2. If boundaries define belonging, if identity itself is anchored in boundaries, then a decreasing emphasis on, or a blurring of, boundaries would be regarded as a threat to group existence, that is, to allegiance, social coherence, and conformity - a harbinger perhaps of anonymity, anomie, and marginality (cf., Ross, 1975:56-58). As Douglas says, "...all margins are dangerous. If they are pulled this way or that the shape of fundamental experience is altered. *Any structure of ideas is vulnerable at its margins*" (1966:121, emphasis added).

3. Language forms our thoughts. It determines the categories by which we experience the world. It reflects and reinforces the structure of social relations. It makes reality a matter of definition, a socially constructed activity; it makes identity a deadly game of recognitions, non-recognitions, and counter-recognitions (cf., Berger, 1963:84, 118). If ethnicity is a "primordial tie" (Shils, 1957); if boundaries create insiders and outsiders and separate - even through pollution barriers - in order to unite the ingroup, then language becomes, by definition, the chief marker of boundaries and ethnolinguistic labels the symbols and arbiters of distinctiveness.

4. Socialization, perhaps, is usually done in terms of three groups: an ingroup, an outgroup, and a non-group. The ingroup is the object of praise; the outgroup, of blame; and the non-group may have nothing for it or against it, that is, be somewhat of a neutral valence until experience shifts it to be an "in" or an "out".

There are often gradations for ingroups and outgroups, but the most pervasive thing is their dichotomy. As Douglas maintains with reference to boundaries and margins, "It is only by exaggerating the difference between within and without, above and below, male and female, with and against, that a semblance of order is created" (1966:4). Language imposes such order.

5. Ethnolinguistic labels are prescriptions for interaction (cf., Goffman, 1959; Barth, 1969:16); they are stereotypes deliberately manufactured to enhance a sense of collective identity, to express stratification, to support an ideology that buttresses socioeconomic and sociopolitical interests, to signal identity and membership, to exorcize the group - so to speak - from an assumed filth or pollution, to prevent boundary transgression. Pollution beliefs express claims and counter-claims to status; moral values and social rules are upheld by beliefs in *dangerous contagion* (Douglas, 1966:3). Ethnolinguistic boundary indicators connote "purity and danger" (cf., the title of the 1966 Douglas book); perjorative labels focused on enemies and on renegades who identify with enemies are an embodiment of the notion of dangerous contagion, of the commandment to live within group boundaries.

6. Following Bernstein, we can say that ethnolinguistic labels are a special form of "restricted code" in that they condense communication and force it into an unbridgeable dichotomy; they induce closure in interaction; they refer directly to position and hierarchy; they do not facilitate the verbal elaboration of meaning, making their meaning richly implicit; they narrow the perceptual sphere; they reaffirm unquestioned boundaries and psychologically link the speaker to his kin and community, giving him personal and social integration at the same time (Bernstein, 1965, 1970, 1971; discussed in Douglas, 1973:41-48, 54-55, 77-82, 191).

These assumptions will be examined with reference to a variety of data; at times, to two or more languages.

2. LANGUAGE ITSELF AS AN ETHNIC BOUNDARY

Regardless of what is said in any given language or languages for ingroups or outgroups, language itself - in the sense of being claimed as a precious possession particular to a given group - has often served as the chief indicator of ethnicity, as a major boundary marker akin to religion or skin colour. Examples are:

1. The Welsh point out how their bards have constantly identified their language with their nation - "ein hiaith, ein gwlad, ein cenedl" (our language, our country, our nation). Some contend that the word for language in Welsh, *Iaith*, originally meant both language and nation (community) and that the word for "foreigner" was *Anghyfiaith*, literally, "not of the same language"; for compatriot or countryman, *Cyfiaith*, that is, "of the same language" (Khleif, 1975:53). In this context, two other examples can be cited:

> (a)   The pre-Islamic Arabs referred metaphorically to their
>   language as *Lughet-id-Dhad*, the "language of the *Dhad*",
>   that is, of a hard "d" symbolizing consonantal eloquence,
>   a sound that others cannot pronounce accurately, a sound
>   supposedly unique to Arabic; they called non-Arabs (their
>   "Goyim", so to speak) *Ajam*, literally, "mute", i.e., mute
>   or non-communicative foreigners (the word in modern daily
>   usage now simply means Persians). (Other examples of ad-
>   oration of the ingroup language are: *Kultursprache* for
>   German; *la langue de la conversation, la conversation
>   elle même* for French; and *la bella lingua* for Italian).

(b) In the Sephardic-accented Hebrew of Israel, there is a
dichotomy between *Ivrit*, i.e., Hebrew or the native
tongue, and *Lo'azit*, foreign language. The latter word
is actually derived from the ancient root which indicates
undue mystification, lack of clarity, a muddling up, a
puzzle or riddle (cf., "It is *Greek* to me"). In daily
use, *Lo'azit* is neutral in tone, but its derivations,
e.g., verb forms, have a strongly negative connotation.

So much for the language of others!

2. Some ethnic groups have used different languages for different types of nationalism and as a means for differentiating themselves from their own past as well as
from others. Examples are:

(a) Whereas in Eastern Europe prior to 1914, the "Jewish
Labour Bund of Russia, Lithuania, and Poland" emphasized
Yiddish, the Zionist movement emphasized Hebrew, the
two languages subsequently colliding in what came to be
known as "Riv Haloshoynes" (language conflict), with
Hebrew becoming the language of daily life outside the
Diaspora (Fishman, 1968:49-50; Milosz, 1975:345-348).

(b) Whereas the official language of the Ottoman Empire for
about 400 years was *Osmanlija* (a blend of Turkish, Per-
sian and Arabic), a language in which the founders of
the Turkish nationalist movement expressed themselves,
the leaders of the post-1922 Turkey deliberately and
punitively dismantled *Osmanlija* in favour of a new form
of language, modern Turkish, that emphasized Altaic word
roots, a linguistic identification with Central Asia,
and a deliberate utilization of peasant language, *Kaba
Turkche*, to emphasize etymological purity.

A people can be "born again" through language. A revitalized ancestral language
is thought to be both a language of cultural regeneration and of the new self (cf.,
Welsh). Language, like dress, marks the new identity, sets it off from others.

3. Language can be used not only to mark off external boundaries but also internal
lines; not only to praise the ingroup and isolate the outgroup but also to single
out renegades - those of the ingroup who break cultural ranks to identify with
outgroups. The labels used for outgroups and for renegades express a fear of
contamination, a disavowal of those who desert or betray the ingroup.

As usual in the cases of identity maintenance revolving around the language there
are various grades of authenticity. For example (Khleif, 1975:404-406, 1976c:14),
for the pro-Welsh Welshman, an authentic Welshman is *Cymro-Cymraeg* (Welsh-Welsh-
man), *Cymroi'r Carn* (Welshman to the core, Welshman through and through), or
Cymro Ronc (true Welshman, a Welsh-speaking Welshman). The English are *Saeson*
(derived from "Saxons" - cf., the Scottish "Sassenach"): the person is *Saesneg*
when he is English in speech; *Saesnig* when he is English in spirit. The Anglo-
Welshman who is anti-Welsh as a language is, on the other hand, called *Sais-o-
Gymro* (an English-speaking Welshman - literally, an Englishman of a Welshman, i.e.,
part of "Englishry" in Wales). He is also called *Cymro-heb-Gymraeg* or *Cymro-di-
Gymraeg*, both expressions meaning literally a "Welshman without Welsh, a Welshman
stripped of his Welsh", *Cymro-di-Gymraeg* being the stronger of the two and conn-
oting a sense of loss as well as shaky identity (its negative connotation is somewhat as unpleasant as the "un" in "Un-American", with an equivalent sense of be-
trayal).

4. Some embattled minorities - religious or cultural - have a combination of *diglossia* (two forms of the same language, high and low, for different social

domains) and *bilingualism* (two different languages) to differentiate themselves
internally and externally. (Some writers would say this is a special form of
triglossia). Examples are:

(a) The French Canadians of Québec who use standard French
     for writing, *Joual* (Québec French) for conversation,
     and consider English the language of the outgroup that
     threatens their cultural existence (Khleif, 1975b).

(b) Members of the Hasidic community of Williamsburg, Brook-
     lyn, who use *Loshen Kodesh* (Talmudic Hebrew, literally
     the "Holy Tongue") for the religious life, *Mame Loshen*
     (literally "Mother Tongue")or Yiddish for secular aff-
     airs, and regard English as the language of the non-
     sacred outer environment. The Williamsburg group even
     uses a former Diaspora language, Hungarian - more used
     by women than men - for the secular and mundane, which
     points out an overall combination of diglossia and tri-
     lingualism (Poll, 1969)!

(c) The Neturei-Karta, an ultra-orthodox religious group in
     Jerusalem use *Loshen Kodesh* (Talmudic Hebrew, which they
     pronounce in the Ashkenazi manner) for religiously orien-
     ted decrees and other aspects of the religious life;
     Yiddish for secular matters, and consider *Ivris* (their
     term for the modern Hebrew of Israel which is pronounced
     in the Sephardic manner, which borrows from other lang-
     uages and which - in their eyes - is distorted and de-
     formed because it is also used for secular affairs) a
     defiliation of the holy and a threatening instrument of
     assimilation (Poll,1976, 1977).

In the case of the French Canadians of Québec, the Hasidim of Williamsburg, and
the Neturei-Karta of Jerusalem, language distinctiveness is the *sine qua non* for
safeguarding traditions, prolonging group life, and thwarting assimilation. Socialization of the young through controlling all aspects of local education and a
constant attention to *Shemiras Haloshon* (language protection - Poll, 1977:8) are
aspects of the tight social control upon which religiously or culturally embattled
groups seem to insist.

3. CULTURAL RENEGADES, APOSTATES, AND TURNCOATS

Not only does the ingroup punish the linguistic renegade through labelling him a
double-outsider, so to speak - cf., *Sais-o-Gymro*, an Englishman of a Welshman,
and *Cymro-di-Gymraeg*, a Welshman stripped of his linguistic core, a "déraciné
Welshman", - but it perhaps reserves its wrath to the ingroup member who betrays
what it considers its fundamental way of life. Some of the most perjorative labels
are not only manufactured to put outsiders "in their place", but also to heap un-
told contempt on the cultural Quisling, the betrayer of the ingroup's integrity
and self-respect. If we agree with Shils (1957) that ethnicity may be considered
a "primordial trait" and with Barth (1969:17-18) that ethnicity - especially for
embattled groups - seems to be an "imperative status" that constrains the person
in most of his activities, then we can perhaps appreciate the fury an ingroup
directs towards the cultural deserter or betrayer. Examples of labels against
apostates and turncoats - highly intense labels that warn of pollution and contamination, of dirt and danger, or in Bernstein's vocabulary, "restricted code"
labels - are:

(a) *Meshummed*: Jewish convert to Christianity, i.e., to the

religion of those who had historically persecuted one's
ancestors.

(b) *Yiddishe Goyim* (as distinct from "Goyishe Goyim"): a
Hasidic label for those born Jewish but who are not
religiously observant. Literally, "Jewish Gentiles".

(c) *Apple Indian*: an American Indian who identifies with
Whites - Red on the outside, White on the inside.

(d) *Oreo Black*: an American Black who identifies with Whites
- like the "Oreo" cookies that have a cream filling;
Black on the outside, White inside.

(e) *Uncle Tom; Uncle Tomahawk;* and *Uncle Tomas*: a subservient
Black, American Indian, or Mexican-American. (Cf., "Yehudi
Galluti" - used by Israeli "Sabras" to condemn the Diaspora
-type behaviour of a person; "Die Siôn Dyfed" - Dick,
Johnny, Dave - Welsh for "Uncle Tom").

(f) *Un-American*: someone who is not up to the ideals on which
America is based and to which fellow Americans are deeply
attached.

Ethnolinguistic labels, such as the above, are essentially *prescriptions for
interaction* (cf., Goffman, 1959; Barth, 1969:16), are rules for avoidance or
contact.

4. THE INGROUP vs. THE OUTGROUP: PRAISEWORTHY vs. REPREHENSIBLE CHARACTERISTICS

An ingroup cannot be understood apart from an outgroup; both are interlocked into
a unity of opposites; one cannot be understood apart from the other; one cannot
be understood except in terms of the other (cf., virtue vs. vice, men vs. women,
and other dichotomies). If such an overall assumption is true, if we can say that
technically there is no sociology of Blacks, for example, but a sociology of
Black-White relations (cf., Banton, 1974:86), then ethnicity becomes a study of
ethnic *relations*, a dialectical concept with variant manifestations, not a property
of a group viewed in isolation from the context or social system of which it is
merely a constituent part. In matters of identity and historical memory, language
becomes a boundary for inclusion or exclusion, degradation or aggrandizement.
Ethnolinguistic labels, then, become a key to understanding boundaries and sub-
boundaries, a clue to historical interaction and socioeconomic arrangements, an
embodiment of the ideology that supports both interaction and stratification.

Ethnolinguistic labels enable us to see not things, but *things in their relationships* - how an ingroup cannot be defined apart from an outgroup, how both form a
social system, *how an outgroup is so necessary for an ingroup to be itself!*

We shall clarify these matters as follows:

1. An ingroup may think of its language as divinely inspired, as superior to any
other language (cf., the attitude of the French to their language). Some languages are considered holy in the sense that God hath chosen to speak in them, that
holy books are written in them, e.g., the three holy languages of (a) Hebrew, in
which the Bible is written; (b) Arabic, the Koran; and (c) even American English
- the Book of Mormon. The non-holy languages, obviously, enhance the holiness of
one's own.

2. An ingroup may tend to believe that it is its language, and only its language,
that contains key words or concepts that cannot be easily translated. An example

from Welsh is *Hiraeth*, a longing for the land, people, and culture of Wales
(Khleif, 1975:405). Or, an ingroup may think that it is only its language which is
fluent, expressive, and a joy to speak! As Bailik, the twentieth-century Hebrew
poet is purported to have said: *Hebraish Retmann, Ober Yiddish Retzich* (one can
speak Hebrew, but Yiddish speaks itself)! It may be disconcerting to ingroups to
find out that other groups think the same of their own languages.

3. Language is social history: at times an ingroup goes out of its way to discredit
an outgroup and its language, thereby attempting self-enhancement through belitt-
ling or degradation of others. Examples are:

    (a)   Because of erstwhile naval competition between England
    and Holland, many words damning the Dutch have crept
    into daily use in English, e.g., "Dutch treat", "Dutch
    uncle", "Dutch courage", "Dutch wife", "in Dutch with",
    and "go Dutch". (Cf., to "take a French leave", "Russian
    roulette", and so forth. For examples from the era of
    Mercantilism, enshrined in an earlier form of Anglican
    prayer, see Trench, 1958:254-255. For American-English
    examples of damnation of the true natives, cf., "Indian
    giver", and "Indian summer").

    (b)   From the sixteenth-century onwards, the English coined
    a lot of words to slander the Welsh, as Vol.10, Part 2,
    pp.308-310 of the multi-volume *Oxford New English Dict-
    ionary* shows. Examples are: "Welsh cricket", to "Welsh"
    on a deal, and "Welsher"; also variations of the nursery
    rhyme "Taffy was a Welshman" publicized against the Welsh
    (Khleif, 1975:26-28). Such labels may be termed "Ling-
    uistic Golliwogs" or "Genoslander" - words aimed at the
    generic caricature of outgroups (Khleif, 1975:iii, xi).

    (c)   Like American Indians, the Welsh were named by their con-
    querors: whereas the "Indians" owe their name to Colum-
    bus's mistake, the Welsh owe theirs to the rather exclus-
    ive or intolerant spirit of their invaders, the Anglo-
    Saxons. "Welsh" comes from Old English *Waelise*; "Wales"
    from Old English *Wealnas*, perjorative terms meaning
    "foreigners" and "land of foreigners" respectively. For
    the non-native Saxons, the natives were foreigners. (A
    modern cognate of the two Old English words is "Wallace",
    originally applied to other Celts and surviving as a
    surname). The Welsh, in their own language, call them-
    selves *Cymry* (singular, *Cymro*); their country *Cymru* -
    cf., "Cumberland" and "Cambrian" in English (Khleif,
    1975:31-32).

A redefinition of boundaries means a new self-appellation, e.g., from "Negro" to
Black; "Mexican" to *Chicano* (derived from the U.S. Spanish dialect for "Mexican"
- "Mechicano"); "American Indians" to *Native Americans* or *Original Americans*.

4. Assimilation means the breakdown of boundaries between dominant and subordinate
entities, between ingroups and outgroups. Hence, groups that feel encroached
upon (as well as encroachers) have a stake in boundary maintenance. This is done
through extensive self-praise on the one hand, and denigration of the outgroup or
outgroups on the other. Examples are:

    (a)   Among the elaborate categories for ingroup and outgroup
    types used by the Hasidic Jews of the Williamsburg sect-
    ion of Brooklyn - a religious group devoted to strict
    observance of their faith amidst secular encroachments
    from both Gentiles and non-Orthodox co-religionists -

are the following: "Erlicher Yidden durch und durch",
or "Frumer Yidden" (i.e., honest through and through,
pious, or religiously observant) for themselves, but
"Goyishe Goyim" for outright Goyim (the Gentile Gentiles)
and "Yiddishe Goyim" for the half-Goyim (non-religious
Jews considered Gentiles). Also "Begleibter Yidden",
"Sheiner", "Ferlislicher", or "Obgehitener" to indicate
trustworthiness, being a beautiful person - i.e., religiously observant - or being extremely conscientious,
a guardian of faith (Poll, 1969:280-287).

(b) Among the Neturei-Karta of Jerusalem, ingroup vs. outgroup distinctiveness is conveyed by such expressions as
the following: "Darkei Avoisenu" (ways of our fathers)
vs. "Shemad" (forced conversion); "Benei Torah Amisiyim"
(authentic sons of the Torah) vs. "Minim" or "Kofrim"
(idolators or infidels); "Temimesidige Yidden" (complete
or flawless, full of piety) vs. "Avoideh Zoreh" (idolatry)
- see Poll, 1976:9-12; 1977:7.

5. AN EMBARRASSMENT OF RICHES: OUTGROUP DESIGNATIONS IN AMERICAN ENGLISH

The U.S.A. is considered one of the most multi-ethnic societies on earth, composed
of close to 200 ethnic groups and mixtures thereof. There are in American English
close to 300 perjorative words against groups (a sort of linguistic overkill),
most of which were coined between 1890 and 1924 at the height of the Great Immigration to America. Some of these ethnolinguistic labels are not currently used
(e.g., "Heine"); some are used in a totally positive way ("turning the minus into
a plus" - e.g., "Yankee", especially in New England); some are being shed and
forgotten as particular groups move up the social ladder; some are coined by outgroups in an attempt to even the scales, return the compliment. The abundance of
derogatory labels for groups in American English is akin to the abundance of words
for snow in the Eskimo languages or for reindeer among the Lapps! Analysis of
these words highlights the boundaries erected by "natives" (Anglos) around themselves and around generations of immigrants; it also highlights issues of American
identity, stratification, socialization, and social control.

We begin with a quotation to convey the flavour of what may have permeated American life and literature prior to 1945, a sort of brief taxonomy of outgroups:

>   "Love thy neighbour if he's not a Seventh-Day Adventist or a
>   nigger or a greaser or a ginzo or a hunkie or a bohunk or a
>   frog or a spik or a limey or a heine or a mick or a chink or
>   a jap or a dutchman or a squarehead or a mockie or a slicked-
>   up grease-ball from the Argentine... (Wolfert, Underworld,
>   1943:484 - quoted in Wentworth and Flexner, 1960:341).

Perhaps one of the earliest prejudice words coined on the North American continent
was Yankee: Dutch "Jan-Kees", meaning Johnny-Come-Lately or Johnny-Cheesehead
(cf., "Kasskop" in modern Dutch), to express resentment of members of the New
Netherlands Dutch Colony on Manhatten for English settlers. "Yankees", however,
has had an interesting history: acquiring a highly positive meaning and becoming
a badge of honour for the Old Stock; becoming, for people overseas, a synonym for
all Americans (as in "The Yanks Are Coming" and "Yankee Go Home"); and, since the
American Civil War of the 1860's, becoming for Southerners surgically fused with
an epithet to designate, in one word, their former enemies, the Northerners ("Dam-
yankees").

Some of the latest words of opprobrium to be coined against groups have perhaps been two: (a) "WASP's" (White Anglo-Saxon Protestants - also spelled not as an acronym but as a common noun, "Wasps"), coined in the late 1950's by rising White Ethnics (non-Protestant Whites) who after the end of World War II and by the time John Kennedy, a Catholic, was elected President in 1960, were already in competition with Anglos for mobility into the middle-class and beyond (Allen, 1975 - cf., Schrag, 1970; Novak, 1971); and (b) "Honkies", coined during the Black Civil Rights Movement of the 1960's to symbolize, as an outgroup, all Whites (it is thought that "Honkies" is a corruption of "Hunkies", an older word which used to be hurled at Central Europeans or Hungarians). With new events and conflicts, new terms are devised or old terms are dusted up and re-used (cf., "Gooks" for the South Vietnamese in the late 'sixties and early 'seventies).

Analysis of American Ethnolinguistic Labels

In the U.S., the ingroup has been that which has supplied the Pilgrim Fathers, "British-Americans". From the very start, they alone were synonymous with America, calling themselves Americans, Old Americans, or Native Americans (the Indians had not yet claimed such Nativity as a group name). In the nineteenth-century, in an age of Manifest Destiny, expansionism, and industrialization, they called themselves Anglo-Saxons (see Gossett, 1965:310-338) and Old Stock. But with the cultural and economic rise of White Ethnics and non-Whites in America after World War II, Anglos have been rediscovered as an ethnic group, so to speak (at times now called "British Ethnics" - formerly everybody else was "ethnic" except themselves). Being American, even a "100% American", was no longer confined to them; their cultural landlordism ("Balabustishkeit") was modified (cf., Schrag, 1970; Hacker, 1971; Novak, 1971; Greeley, 1977).

Between the Civil War and the end of World War II, close to 300 perjorative group names were coined by Americans to put successive waves of immigrants "in their place", especially at the height of the Great Immigration, between 1890 and 1924. Both World War I and World War II helped develop a number of derogatory labels, e.g., for Germans. What are the categories of all these perjorative American group names? How can they be classified?

An inspection of 286 prejudice words for American ethnic groups, culled from various literary and lexical sources, shows the following characteristics:

1. By far, most disparaging words are aimed at American Blacks, Chicanos, Indians, and Chinese. Colour, in America, seems to be the supreme boundary (cf., Warner's "Scale of Subordination and Assimilation", Yankee City, 1963:416-417, 423).

2. World War I seems to have supplied more perjorative words than any other war, before or since.

3. A number of perjorative words are now obsolete, unfamiliar to the average American.

4. Subordinate groups, e.g., Blacks, at times returned the compliment, coining perjorative words for Whites, (e.g., "Peckerwood", i.e., like a wood-pecker, and "Hay-eaters").

5. At times, one word was used to damn more than one group, e.g., "Dingbat" (for both Italians and Chinese); "Moke" (for both Negroes and Filipinos - derived from "Mocha"); "Spik" (for Italians, Mexicans, even Germans - supposedly derived from the faulty pronunciation, by these groups, of the English word, "speak").

6. At times, the same word was used as a boomerang, e.g.,
    "Spook" (used by Whites against Blacks); "Oil-Hair Spook"
    (used by Blacks against Whites).

7. In a preliminary attempt to construct a typology, we can
    say that the principal categories of American ethnoling-
    uistic labels seem to be the following (they are herewith
    presented in a somewhat ascending order of intensity):

    (1) A proper noun in a foreign language is made to sym-
         bolize the whole group (or a group supposedly akin
         to it) and damn it in the eyes of the ingroup, e.g.,
         "Fritz"; "Hans"; "Paddy"; (cf., "paddy-wagon");
         "Mick"; "Dago" (actually from the Spanish "Diego");
         "Tojo".

    (2) Derogation based on reference to a geographic area,
         e.g., "Bohunk" (Bohemian-Hungarian); "Canuck".

    (3) Derogation through deliberate mispronunciation of
         the group's name or shortening it to one closed
         syllable, e.g., "Eyetalians"; "Jap"; "Mex".

    (4) Use of pseudo-onomatopoeic alliteration in double-
         syllable combinations as a put-down, e.g., "Dee-
         Donk" (a Frenchman); "Goo-goo" (Filipino).

    (5) Derogation through belittling a national symbol of
         a group, e.g., "Harp" (for Irishmen - from the
         Celtic harp on the Irish flag).

    (6) Turning a frequently used word in a foreign lang-
         uage, a word with an honourable meaning, into one
         with which the whole group is defamed. "Guapo" (in
         Sicilian, a tough brave man) and "Shain" (Yiddish
         for beautiful person, i.e., humane or pious, or used
         in describing merchandise as beautiful) become "Wop"
         and "Sheenie", respectively (see Rosten, 1970:338-
         339).

    (7) Derogation in relation to food habits or favourite
         ethnic food, e.g., "Rice-belly" (Chinese); "Chilli-
         eater" or "Pepper" (Mexican); "Frog" or "Frog-eater"
         (Frenchman); "Sausage" or "Kraut" (from Sauerkraut,
         German); "Spags" (from spaghetti, Italian). (Cf.,
         "Mackerel Snappers", used by Protestants for Cath-
         olics).

    (8) Derogation on the basis of an occupation deemed lowly
         by the natives (and for which others may import "Gast-
         arbeiter" or "Braceros"), e.g., "Chilli-pickers"
         (Mexicans).

    (9) Derogation in relation to the way supposedly members
         of an ethnic group may have entered the country,
         e.g., "Wetbacks" (from swimming the Rio Grande to
         cross the border, Mexicans).

    (10) Derogation based on newcomership, e.g., "Green-horn".

    (11) Failure to speak American English correctly, e.g.,
         "Spik" (also spelled "Spic" and "Spick" - Italians
         and others).

(12) Derogation in relation to dress, e.g., "Hand-
      kerchief Head" (a subservient, old-fashioned
      Negro).

(13) Derogation linked to a musical instrument, e.g.,
      "Jew's Harp" (i.e., harmonica - originally "jaw's
      harp", a harp for the jaws); "Wop Stick" (i.e.,
      clarinet, thought at one time to have been a fav-
      ourite of Italian musicians).

(14) Derogation in relation to physical characteristics:
      (a) with regard to thick, black, oily hair that
      people from Mediterranean countries supposedly have
      more than others, e.g., Italians, Spaniards, and
      Greeks; also, South Americans; "Greaseball";
      "Greaser"; "Oiler". (b) with regard to skin colour
      head, or face: "Square-head"; "Hook-nose"; "Blue
      Gum"; "Burr-head"; "Chocolate Drop"; "Moke";
      "Yellow". (c) some sort of assumed similarity to
      an animal or bird: "Monkey"; "Ape"; "Coon"; "Skunk";
      "Geese". (d) reference to both geographic area and
      colour: "Zulu".

(15) Derogation through association with dirt or excre-
      ment, e.g., "Bucket Head" (for WWI German soldier,
      from the shape of his helmet).

Because of their scope and variety, American ethnolinguistic labels could, for
purposes of quantification, be subjected to scalogram analysis to get at their
common core of content (cf., Edwards, 1957) or to a Lazarsfeldian reduction to a
one-dimensional "attribute space" (cf., Lazarsfeld and Barton, 1965) to get at
their interlinked manifestations.

Perhaps the fundamental fact about America is its ethnicity and, especially since
1945, its somewhat shifting ethnic boundaries.

6. DISCUSSION

This is a preliminary study of the importance of ethnic terminology in marking off
group boundaries and the consequences of such boundaries for group organization,
group identity, socialization, and social control. The sociocultural framework
for this study is anchored in the notions of social boundaries and their dichotom-
ization and trichotomization, group symbols and their maintenance, and the treatment of language as a social institution, that is, as a determinant of the structure of social relations, of its stability and change (cf., Douglas, 1973:42).

A comparative approach has been adopted; a variety of data examined. Three or four
case studies have been interlinked.

What is true of ethnic groups, their boundaries, and boundary markers, could,
mutatis mutandis, be applied to occupational groups, religious groups, or groups
whose boundaries are those of age, sex, class, or caste.

In particular, the vocabularies that are used by various occupations and profess-
ions to structure their worlds and differentiate them from adversaries and allies
merit special attention (cf., Khleif, 1978). Case studies of occupational renegades, for example; ingroup and outgroup relations - and such matters as the structure of dominance in clusters of occupations; occupations that serve as orienting

or "significant others"; border raids for vocabularies, concepts, and models -
would further highlight the essence of that part of sociology which is called
symbolic interaction (cf., Simmel's *Wechselwirkung* or reciprocal effect), that
is, the role of language in everyday life, the labelling process, and what humans
take for granted or are led to take for granted.

In this paper, we have dwelt on boundary maintenance and boundary protection, alluded to boundary straddling and boundary crossing, and, as a case in point, singled
out the phenomenon of the renegade. Our approach has been social psychological
rather than social organizational or social structural: we have emphasized the
role of language in "definition of the situation" for ingroups and outgroups, in
construction of reality for them. In this context, we assert that the essence of
reality is that it is socially defined, a negotiated order, and that power, in
group life, is precisely *the capacity to define reality for others* (cf., Khleif,
1975:17). We have attempted to extend "labelling theory" - a framework usually
arbitrarily confined within American sociology to studies of mental illness and
other forms of exceptionality, e.g., to inmates of total institutions - to society
at large, to day-to-day ethnic interaction. It is because of ethnic hegemony and
ethnic competition that there are prejudice words, ethnolinguistic labels, that
act as we-they markers, or, in Allport's terms (1958:176), as "labels of primary
potency".

We would like to sketch out a variant way of viewing our data, the other side of
the coin, so to speak. Had we taken a social-structural approach, we would have
in particular emphasized the following: (a) issues of social class within and
between ethnic groups; (b) ethnic groups, or language groups, as *estates* in
Weber's sense of the term, as *Staende*, in contradistinction to *Klassen* (to trans-
late the former as "status groups", as is often done in American sociology, is but
to disregard the long history of "estates" in Medieval stratification in Europe,
nay, even in modern America - Khleif, 1978a:103-104; 1978b:54-55); (c) an examination of the relation of ethnic groups to the economy and the issues of collective
- i.e., ethnic, rather than personal - mobility; and (d) a discussion of ethnic
stratification as a case of internal colonialism, as the structural *sine qua non*
for certain interactive processes, group-boundary demarcations, and associated
tensions of superordination-subordination - all obviously with a bearing on ethno-
terminology! The psychological can thus be seen as a reflection of the structural,
not vice versa. In the final analysis, perhaps, there is no psychology without a
sociology, no sociology without an anthropology, and none without linguistics,
especially sociolinguistics!

REFERENCES

I.L. Allen, WASP: From sociological concept to epithet, Ethnicity, 2, 153–162 (1975).

Allport, G.W. (1958) The nature of prejudice, Doubleday Anchor Books, New York.

Ashworth, G. (ed.) (1977) World minorities, Quartermaine House, Sunbury, Middlesex and Minority Rights Group, London.

M. Banton, Race in the American sociological tradition: From Park to Parsons, Jewish Journal of Sociology, 26, 85–93 (1974).

Barth, F. (1969) Introduction, pp.9–38, in F. Barth (ed.): Ethnic groups and boundaries. Little, Brown, Boston.

Berger, P.L. (1963) Invitation to sociology: A humanistic perspective, Doubleday Anchor Books, New York.

Bernstein, B. (1965) A sociolinguistic approach to social learning, pp.144–168, in J. Gould (ed.): Penguin survey of the social sciences, (1965), Penguin Books, Baltimore.

Bernstein, B. (1970) A sociolinguistic approach to socialization. In J. Gumperz & D. Hymes (eds.): Directions in sociolinguistics. Holt-Rinehart & Winston, New York.

Bernstein, B. (1971) Class, codes, and control, Vol.I: Theoretical studies towards a sociology of language, Routledge and Kegan Paul, London and Boston.

Brewer, E.C. (1962) Brewer's dictionary of phrase and fable. Revised and enlarged edition, Harper & Row, New York.

Douglas, M. (1966) Purity and danger: An analysis of concepts of pollution and taboo, Praeger, New York.

Douglas, M. (1973) Natural symbols: Explorations in cosmology, Vintage Books, New York.

Edwards, A.L. (1957) Techniques of attitude scale construction, Appleton-Century-Crofts, New York.

Fishman, J.A., et al. (eds.) (1968) Language problems of developing nations, Wiley, New York.

Goffman, E. (1959) The presentation of self in everyday life, Doubleday Anchor Books, New York.

Gossett, T.F. (1965) Race: The history of an idea in America, Schocken Books, Books, New York.

Greeley, A.M. (1977) The American Catholic: A social portrait, Basic Books, New York.

Hacker, A. (1971) The end of the American era, Athenaum, New York.

Bud B. Khleif, Ethnic boundaries in Welsh-English relations, Paper read at the annual meeting of the Society for the Study of Social Problems, Montréal, Canada, August 24, 1974, Mimeo., pp.25. A revised version of this paper is published in Spanish in Revista de Ciencias Sociales, 20, 2 (1978).

Bud B. Khleif, Ethnic boundaries, identity, and schooling: A sociocultural study of Welsh-English relations, Washington, D.C., N.I.E., Lithographed, pp.464. Available from Center for Applied Linguistics, ERIC Clearinghouse on Languages and Linguistics, 1611 North Kent Street, Arlington, Virginia 22209 (1975).

Bud B. Khleif, Cultural regeneration and the school: An anthropological study of Welsh-medium schools in Wales, International Review of Education, UNESCO, Hamburg, 22, 2, 117-192 (1976a).

Bud B. Khleif, Language as identity: Towards an ethnography of Welsh nationalism, Paper read at the annual meeting of the American Anthropological Association, Washington, D.C., 1976, Mimeo., pp.21 (1976b).

Bud B. Khleif, The political economy of language problems: Wales, Québec, and other cases, Paper read at the annual meeting of the Society for the Study of Social Problems, New York, August 29, 1976, Typescript, pp.32 (1976c).

Khleif, B.B. (1978a) Ethnic awakening in the first world: The case of Wales, pp. 102-119, in G. Williams (ed.): Social and cultural change in contemporary Wales, Routledge and Kegan Paul, London and Boston.

Bud B. Khleif, A sociocultural framework for understanding race and ethnic relations in schools and society of the U.S.A., Sociologus, 29, 1, 54-69 (1978b).

Bud B. Khleif, Towards an ethnography of occupations: Cases and a framework, Typescript, pp.35 (1978c).

Bud B. Khleif, Language as an ethnic boundary in Welsh-English relations, Special issue on Language and Identity, International Journal of the Sociology of Language, in press (1979).

Lazarsfeld, P.F. & Barton, A.H. (1965) Qualitative measurement in the social sciences: Classification, typologies, and indices, pp.155-192, in D. Lerner, et al. (eds.): The policy sciences: Recent development in scope and method, Stanford University Press, Stanford.

Milosz, C. (1975) Vilnius, Lithuania: An ethnic agglomerate, pp.339-352, in G. De Vos & L. Romanucci-Ross (eds.): Ethnic identity: Cultural continuities and change, Mayfield, Palo Alto, California.

Novak, M. (1971) The rise of the unmeltable ethnics, MacMillan, New York.

Poll, S. (1969) The Hasidic community of Williamsburg, Schocken Books, New York.

S. Poll, The sacred-secular conflict in the use of Hebrew among the ultra-orthodox Jews of Jerusalem. Paper read at the annual meeting of the American Sociological Association, New York, August 31, 1976, Mimeo., pp.22 (1976).

S. Poll, Sociolinguistics and stratification of a religious community in Jerusalem, Typescript, pp.12 (1977).

Partridge, E. (1961) A dictionary of the underworld: British and American, Bonanza Books, New York.

Partridge, E. (1963) A dictionary of clichés, Dutton, New York.

Partridge, E. (1970) A dictionary of slang and unconventional English. Seventh Edition. MacMillan, New York.

J-K. Ross, Social borders: Definitions of diversity (with a "Comments" section), Current Anthropology, 16, 1, 53-72 (1975). (Further "Comments" on Ross's paper are published in Current Anthropology, 16, 3, 468-470 (1975).

Rosten, L. (1970) The joys of Yiddish, Pocket Books, New York.

Schrag, P. (1970) The decline of the WASP, Touchstone Books, New York.

E. Schils, Primordial, personal, sacred, and civil ties, British Journal of Sociology, 8, 130-145 (1957).

Stephens, M. (1977) Linguistic minorities in Western Europe, Gomer Press, Llandysul, Wales.

Trench, R.C. (1958) Dictionary of obsolete English, Philosophical Library, Wisdom Library, New York.

Warner, W.L. (ed.) (1963) Yankee city, One volume, abridged edition, Yale University Press, New Haven.

Wentworth, H. & Flexner, S.B. (1960) Dictionary of American slang, Crowell, New York.

LANGUAGE AND ETHNIC INTERACTION IN
RABBIT BOSS: A NOVEL BY THOMAS SANCHEZ

P. A. Geuder

University of Nevada, Las Vegas, U.S.A.

The purpose of this paper is two-fold: to posit that a sociolinguistic analysis of a novel can aid in the theoretical understanding of interethnic relations; and to present a methodological perspective for the analysis.

The novel is *Rabbit Boss* by Thomas Sanchez. The setting is Washo Indian territory (the extreme Western part of Nevada and Eastern California), a microcosm of the last frontier of the United States. The time commences with the entrapped Donner Party in the High Sierra Mountains in the winter of 1846-47 and terminates in 1931. The characters include four generations of Washo and numerous Whitemen who come to and pass through, who "invade" and destroy, a small, remote American Indian tribe and its territory.

Theoretically, *Rabbit Boss* extends far beyond one geographic location, four generations, and one writer's interpretation of interethnic relationships; it exceeds the relationships between just the Washo and the Whiteman. In the novel, *Washo* specific becomes *Indian* general. And the invaded become the minority, the suppressed minority universal. The Donner Party is *White* specific; the *Whitemen* who follow become *Whites* general. The invader becomes the majority - the oppressor universal. Therefore, the interethnic conflict in *Rabbit Boss* can be considered representative of universal interethnic processes between the invaded and the invader.

Rabbit Boss serves well as source material for analysis of interethnic conflict. The Washo themselves did not maintain written tribal records or produce printed fiction. The Whiteman's history and fiction of the Western movement, or the "settlement" of the West, treat the Washo ahistorically, scantily, or demeaningly. Study of the few remaining and scattered Washo could not produce sufficient or accurate data about and insights into the impact of an "invasion" which started shortly prior to 1850 (and presumably continues). *Rabbit Boss* is the ONLY novel which spans four generations of Washo. It is the ONLY novel that features an omnipresent and omnipotent observer-narrator who reconstructs historical facts within a credible fictional framework through the eyes, ears, and thoughts of the Washo counterbalanced with the words and the actions of the Whiteman.

The novel incorporates language and ethnic interaction from the beginning - a Washo's witnessing of the cannibalism of the Donner Party in the winter of 1846-1847 - to the end - the Whiteman's decimation of the Washo tribe. The novel examines the ethnic interaction primarily between Whites and Indians. Sanchez juxta-

173

poses ethnic interaction from two sociolinguistic vantages: the Indians' view of the Whiteman and the Whiteman's view of Indians. These two vantages provide the methodology.

Ethnic interaction from the Indian perspective occurs in three major sociolinguistic forms. The predominant form is the more than 250 italicized personal pronouns in reference to the Whiteman: namely, *they*, *them*, and *their*. The italicized pronouns visually and stylistically establish and sustain the dichotomy between the Whiteman and the Indian. The lone Washo witnessing the cannibalism of the Donner Party opens the first chapter. Sanchez writes, "The Washo watched. The Washo watched through the trees, on him, on *them*". (p.3). The lone Washo's account to his father is prophetic: "I have seen the way before me and followed it as I was taught, but my eyes have now seen new things, things for which I have no teaching, no power". (p.11). When his father asks, "For what new things are you without power?" the response is "*them*". (p.11).

The second major form is the more than 65 uses (and capitalization) of *White* in reference to the Indian perspective of the Caucasian encroachment and multi-faceted destruction.

> "These Whitemen had in their rolling tents small children,
> and women who would clean their bodies in the still waters
> and cook foods in the black-iron baskets...Each time a line
> of the tents rolled off from the lake some of the Whites
> stayed and built high flatsided shelters to protect them
> against the cold of the coming white days. The people set
> up their own small shelters around those of the Whites and
> waited for the things the Whites no longer had use for to
> be given to them. The time was past when the people could
> go out into the still water and capture the Birds...the
> Birds were gone, taken by the Whites who killed from the
> muddy shore with loud noises from metal sticks..." (pp.206-
> 207).

The destruction of Indian land is evident when "The Whiteman had come with the power of his chainsaw" which "could tear the hide off a tree as old as the rivers and slice through its flesh in minutes". The destruction continues with "The Whiteman had cut the river. A bank of concrete across the full current robbed the power of great waters". (p.483). The Whiteman destroys the Indian way of life and finally decimates the number of Washo through tuberculosis.

> "They died out the old way with the sickness of the Whites
> spreading in their lungs. Their lungs were on fire. The
> last of the people in those days became dead or dying. The
> life was being choked from them by the sickness of the
> Whites, by the T-burkulur. Then they were all dead. The
> Whites threw kerosene into the shacks with the bodies of
> the people piling up inside...Then the Whites rode out to
> burn all the Indian peoples." (p.338).

The third major form is found in the more than 35 adjectival uses of *white* which complement and reinforce pronoun references to the Whiteman and noun uses of *White*. The use of *White Ghosts* serves as an initial and ominous reference to Caucasians: "He returned with no meat weighing down his shoulders but only talk of the *White Ghosts* of the lake yonder...he told of the White Ghosts that ate of *themselves*". (p.101). "The turning houses covered by a white cloud" refers to the invading settlers' covered wagons. (p.297). The English language of the invader is the "White tongue". (p.338). The oblique use of "white burden" in a number of passages suggests the crushing totality of the Whiteman: "The white burden had followed the rain". (p.506). Throughout four generations of Washo, "The White power is strong".

(p.329). The Washo have no immunity to the "white death", an epidemic of tuberculosis. (p.519). That "The White beast was a flesheater" is an all-consuming com-
mentary on the Caucasian destructive capability. (p.491). And through the collective adjectival use of *white*, the Caucasian is, indeed, the "White Beast, mad White
Beast, wild White *Musege*" (evil power). (p.507).

Ethnic evaluation from the Whiteman's perspective begins with a factual report.
Before the opening of *Rabbit Boss*, Sanchez quotes the Twenty-eight Annual Report
of the Commissioner of Indian Affairs to the Secretary of the Interior (Superint-
endent Parker) in 1886. The report sets the stage for the language and ethnic
interaction from the Whiteman's perspective.

> "The Washo is a small tribe of about 500 Indians, living in
> the extreme Western part of Nevada, and Eastern California.
> They are usually a harmless people, with much less physical
> and mental development than the Paiutes, and more degraded
> morally. They are indolent, improvident, and much addicted
> to the vices and evil practices common in savage life. They
> manifest an almost uncontrollable appetite for intoxicating
> drinks. They are sensual and filthy, and are annually dim-
> inishing in numbers from the diseases contracted through
> their indulgences. A few have learned the English language
> ...There is no suitable place for a reservation in the
> bounds of their territory, and, in view of their rapidly
> diminishing numbers and the diseases to which they are sub-
> jected, none is required."

Ethnic interactions from the Whiteman's perspective occur in two forms. One form
is perjorative names in references to Indians including these categories: ethnicity, degree of ethnicity, tribe, age, sex, and colour. Ethnicity is designated
by the use of *Indian* and *Injun*. The narrator consistently and objectively uses
Indian, but Caucasians rarely do. The use of *Injun* is predominate and negative,
whether spoken to or about an Indian. The following excerpt illustrates a thorough devaluation according to "White law":

> "Now I realize that in this free land of ours this redskin
> heathen standing before you is not considered by Law a man.
> This Country does not recognize him as one of its own, he
> is not a citizen of the United States of America. He can't
> vote, he can't get married legal, his children are all Bas-
> tards, he is by Law an Injun." (p.380).

Injun is used not only by itself but in two additional patterns. One is in combination with negative traits: for example, "lying Injun" (p.67); "loco Injun" (p.74);
"filthy Injun" (p.74); "conniving Injun" (p.384); and "warring Injun" (p.391). The
other pattern is the adjectival use of *Injun*: for example, "Injun blood" (p.188)
and "Injun trouble" (p.214). Ironically, the terms "Injun fever" (p.90) and "Injun
plague" (p.92) are references to tuberculosis, a Whiteman's disease transmitted to
the Indians.

Even the degree of ethnicity becomes a case in point at the Golden Nugget Casino
in Reno. The sign "INDIANS NOT ALLOWED" does not deter the old Caucasian Mr. Fixa
from entering with Bob, the Indian lad whom he is rearing. Fixa tells the casino
guard, "Bob's my son. That makes him half-breed. Your sign doesn't say HALF-
BREEDS NOT ALLOWED". (p.242). As they enter, the guard reminds Fixa about the Reno
Sundown Ordinance which prohibits Indians from being "on the streets within the
town limits after dark. Indians on the street after sundown are fined 500 dollars,
shot on sight, or both". (p.242). Shortly after dark, the guard tells Fixa,
"Mister, it's after sundown", and Fixa and Bob exit rapidly.

The Whiteman ranks ethnicity within ethnicity, and the Washo ranks at the bottom. The tavern scene in Genoa, Nevada, clearly states the rank of the Washo:

> "Ain't too many of you bucks left around these parts, is there Chief. I mean you Washo don't get shot out of the saddle like the Paiute. You Washo like to die in bed with one hand on your pecker and the other around a bottle of firewater. What I mean to say is Chief, you Washo don't got no Paiute blood in you, it's mostly Digger blood, ain't it Chief. I mean the Paiute whooped you Washo pretty bad before we whites even got here, didn't they Chief? You got nothing to say, do you? No sabe, huh Chief? You bucks no sabe anything except how to ask for whiskey. You bucks don't ever say a word cept *whiskey*." (pp.212-213).

A man in the tavern crowd concurs with and extends the previous comments that

> "Washos ain't got no devil in him...Washos is nothing but Diggers! Root Diggers! They ain't like the Paiute and Shoshone, they won't fight. They're like John Chinaman, all they got in them is squaw blood! Squaw blood and a rabbit heart!" (p.214).

Age and sex are also used deprecatingly in reference to Indians. *Boy*, for instance is frequently applied to an Indian male obviously beyond boyhood. Yet *old squaw* is applied to an elderly Indian woman obviously of advanced age. Rather than using sex designations of *man* and *woman*, Caucasians customarily use *buck* and *squaw*. Sex references particularly denigrate the Indian woman to "squaw meat".

Caucasians uniformly insult Indians through the use of *red*; these insults encompass at least eight non-mutually exclusive categories. (1) The Indian is referred to and addressed by the colour of his skin. The Indian is called *Redman*: "You're in a pack of trouble Redman. You're in more trouble than you ever thought you could get in outside of your T-pee". (p.68). (2) "Red body", "red belly", and "red balls" refer to Indian anatomy. (3) "Red devil" and, more specifically, "Washo red devil" suggest Indian evil. (4) "Inebriate red devil" identifies Indian drinking habits. (5) "Lying red devil", "thieving red snake", and "lying thieving redskin" indicate the Indian lack of honesty. (6) "Red snake" and "red devil snake" imply the age-old abhorrence of the lowliest of creatures. (7) "Red rabbit" connotes the Washo lack of courage, or bravery. (8) "Red heathen" and "red skin heathen" connote the Indian lack of Christianity.

The second form is perjorative remarks. The 532 pages of *Rabbit Boss* contain over 140 negative remarks made to and about Indians. Collectively, the following remarks signify that - to Caucasians - Indians are unquestionably inferior.

1. "Hell, that's the only way you can communicate, with one word grunts". (p.32).

2. "...you got to change your ways if you aim a whole lot to get along with civilized man". (p.45).

3. "...he knew like everyone else how Indians were born to drink". (p.148).

4. "The old boys up there don't take to no bucks mixing their time with a white as snow woman. And don't you never try it neither Cap. You get a rise on you just better find some donkey to plug, cause if you don't those boys will cut your berries off and leave em to cook in the sun." (p.193).

5. "Red devils is red devils. They're all the same. Get a little liquor in them and they'll sneak up in the night and cut the top of you head off." (p.214).

6. "You mean you father was an Indian *and* a Christian?" (p.370).

7. "Gents, Injuns is all the same, wherever there is troubled waters, an Injun will be fishing them." (p.381).

8. "...you know how cunning these Injuns are, they can walk twelve months with nothing but a cheap tobacco chew and spit on their chin". (p.385).

9. "Have you ever noticed how all Injuns look alike? I can't tell one from the other." (p.413).

10. "I've never met an Indian yet who didn't have at least three names." (p.428).

11. "...I think you should stick to horses like the rest of your kind. No Indian in town has a car, no need for you to be the first. Besides you can't drive a nail straight let alone a car". (pp. 440-441).

12. "He's like a dog, he ain't partial to Indian scents, specially you Washo. He's been jackin' up in Washington Country around the Wenatchee Injuns, course they don't have no stink since it goes and rains everyday up in that country so they gets a bath whether they want it or not." (p.498).

13. "No sir, these modern squaws ain't up to much, I don't see much value in them, they're just like tobacco, no nourishment and highly injurious to health." (p.502).

Within the novel, the perjorative names and comments lead to one conclusion about the Whiteman's evaluation: the Indian is not only significantly different from but significantly inferior to the Whiteman. In *Rabbit Boss*, the two sociolinguistic perspectives cumulatively suggest that the "savage" Indian is civilized; the "civilized" Whiteman, savage.

If, in fact, this novel functions as a mirror of reality, the future use of novels as source material for identifying and delineating interethnic relationships may serve as fruitful and revealing complements to sociolinguistic studies based on bona fide and recorded interethnic encounters.

REFERENCE

Sanchez, T. (1972/1973) Rabbit Boss, Ballantine Books, New York.

SOCIAL IDENTITY AND THE LANGUAGE OF
RACE RELATIONS

C. Husband

University of Leicester, Leicester, U.K.

It will be the purpose of this paper to examine the press reporting of race
relations in Great Britain during the 1960's and 1970's and in particular to pose
questions about the implications of the particular language used to describe the
situation during that period. This paper offers a somewhat speculative discussion
in relation to theory and represents a continuation of an earlier analysis which
presented a greater body of empirical data (Husband, 1977). This analysis will
proceed in relation to Tajfel's (1974) statement on "Social identity and intergroup behaviour" which offers a valuable theoretical structure within which to
develop the argument.

Tajfel offers a framework for the analysis of social identity, "understood as deriving in a comparative and 'relational' manner from an individual's group membership" (Tajfel, 1974:77). Social identity is thus defined as "that part of an individual's self concept which derives from his knowledge of his membership of a
social group (or groups) together with the emotional significance attached to that
membership" (Tajfel, 1974:69). Since for Tajfel social identity is achieved in
respect of perceived group memberships existing in relation to a universe of potential groups wherein one may or may not find membership, then a necessary prerequisite for such a social world is the prior existence in society of social categories which provide a structuring of the social environment through social categorization. Thus, social categorization, by segmenting an individual's social environment into membership and non-membership groups, facilitates social identity and
defines the context within which that identity will be sustained, for social identity only possesses meaning in comparative relation to elements of other groups.
Tajfel therefore argues that a social group will be capable of preserving its contribution to those aspects of an individual's social identity which are positively
valued by him only if it manages to keep its positively valued distinctiveness from
other groups (Tajfel, 1974:72). Clearly inherent in social identity is social comparison. Importantly, this social comparison does not proceed as a passive cognitive accountancy but is a dynamic activity in which the psychological distinctiveness
of membership groups is enhanced in relation to dimensions valued in the ingroup.
It is the dynamic relationships between social categorization, social identity,
social comparison and psychological distinctiveness which forms the creative core
for Tajfel's further discussion of social identity and intergroup behaviour, and it
is in relation to this core of analytically distinct elements that this particular
argument will proceed.

SOCIAL CATEGORIZATION: HISTORY AND VALUED DIMENSIONS OF IDENTITY

One advantage of a post hoc analysis such as this is that one can proceed to outline the relevant antecedents to the events under discussion with a degree of
economy which might otherwise be difficult. Following Tajfel's theory it is appropriate to start an analysis of intergroup behaviour in 1960's Britain with an
account of relevant social categorizations in operation at the time. With the
advantage of hindsight, it is clear that the role which race was to play in these
events was a reflection of the salience of racial categorization within British
society and of its incorporation through social comparison into British social
identity.[1] Racial distinctions based upon skin colour have a long and remarkably
consistent existence within British culture (Hunter, 1967). In Elizabethan
Britain, when black persons first came to this country, there was already available
a social categorization which set them apart as bestial, lascivious, primitive and
inferior (cf., Jordan, 1969; Walvin, 1971). Indeed, at the time of this first
black presence in Britain, perversely, English identity was particularly tied to
a system of aesthetics which polarized a black-white social comparison (Lyons,
1975).

From this inauspicious beginning, the de facto relations between white British
society and black people either dwelling in Britain or elsewhere, has been such as
to maintain skin colour as a potent basis of social categorization wherein the
essential assumed inferiority of black in relation to white identity has remained
intact (cf., Hunter, 1967; Davis, 1970; Bolt, 1971; Kiernan, 1972; Hartmann and
Husband, 1974; Dummett, 1973).

If British identity now is closely associated with membership of a white social
category, then we should not forget that the social categorization of individuals
sharing a certain geographic boundary as "British" has itself been generated
through time. The incorporation of Irish, Welsh and Scots identities within the
British (English) nationality was only achieved through military conquest and
cultural imperialism (e.g., Johnson, 1975; Hechter, 1975). Evidence of the continuing reality of this English hegemony was found in the perception of the greater status of an English identity amongst Scots school children (Tajfel et al.,
1972). There is evidence, however, that British identity has been threatened in
recent years by the increasing potency of Scots and Welsh nationalism and the independence struggle in Ireland (e.g., Brown, 1975; Webb, 1977; Williams, 1978).

British identity has throughout its existence had to counter the potentially dis-
ruptive forces within itself and one familiar phenomenon has been the enhancement
of British identity in comparison to clearly specified outgroups. Wars against
European opponents have served to focus national identity through uniting regional
identities in the superordinate task of vanquishing the common enemy (cf., Sherif,
1966). Within Britain a similar end has been achieved in relation to identifiable

---

[1]The idea of "British" identity is at one level of analysis a fiction, and yet
within a continuing political-economic state entity it has a substantial common
historical core which allows the notion a mythic viability. It is indeed a myth
which has been actively promoted as an ideological adjunct to the political viability of Britain as a nation state. Particularly in an analysis of the national
press where regional variation is obscured it is appropriate to discuss British
social identity.

immigrant groups entering Britain (cf., Gartner, 1959; Garrard, 1971; Foot, 1965; Holmes, 1978).

The development of a British social identity as outlined so far indicates the location of skin colour and racial categorization as fundamental within that identity. Also, a unique sense of British worth has been maintained in relation to "aliens" and immigrants. Apparently paradoxically, but consistent with social comparison theory, the denigration and oppression of outgroups has helped to generate as salient dimensions within British identity belief in the superior civilized culture of British society, (cf., Lyons, 1978; Jordan, 1969; Kiernan, 1972) and belief in the centrality of tolerance in British intergroup behaviour, (cf., Husband, 1975). These beliefs do not exist in isolation from each other, or other dominant images such as Britain as the quintessence of democracy; and hence of fairness and rational reasonableness. The significance of these interlocking images is well expressed by Hall et al.:

> "We would argue that all social ideologies contain powerful
> images of society at their heart. These images may be diff-
> use, quite untheorized in any elaborate sense; but they
> serve to condense and order the view of society in which the
> ideologies are active, and they constitute both its unquest-
> ioned substratum of truth - what carries conviction - and the
> source of its collective emotional force and appeal. Toget-
> her, these images produce and sustain an uncodified but imm-
> ensely powerful conservative sense of Englishness, of an
> English "way of life", of an "English" viewpoint which -
> by its very density of reference - everyone shares to some
> extent." (Hall et al., 1978:140).

Whilst not wishing to specify a definitively British identity, it remains the case that these beliefs in balance, fairness, tolerance and rationality can be found variously interlocking with themselves and with notions, long established, of a highly civilized British culture. Interestingly, Chibnall has identified these images as being powerfully represented within the dominant values of British press ideology (Chibnall, 1977). Thus, we see valued dimensions of British identity being expressed in the values of professional journalism. It should not be surprising that this is so since the British press is essentially staffed by Britons socialized into a "British identity" themselves; and also is significantly lacking in staff with a black skin (Morrison, 1975). Also, we should anticipate that the interests of the dominant élite whose hegemony is reflected in the ownership and control of the news media are well served by the mystifications of reality inherent in these salient images of our national identity (Hall, 1973, 1977; Murdock and Golding, 1977).

However, it would be wrong to see the ownership and organization of news media as in itself sufficient to guarantee the visibility of these national images within the news media. A significant force in sustaining these images is the creative process of generating news itself. News as a distinct entity does not occur in the natural world; news is a post hoc construal of an event, rather than the event itself. In determining which events should be isolated and translated into their constructed representations - "news" - journalists are guided by a body of professional criteria (cf., Galtung and Ruge, 1965; Halloran, Elliott and Murdock, 1970; and Chibnall, 1977). Dominant among these are: the extent to which the event is unusual, the extent to which the event contains negative elements of, for example, disaster or loss of conflict, and the presence of already established personalities in the events. Whatever the criteria invoked in identifying the event to be translated into news, the problem remains for the journalist to render an account of the event which will be intelligible to his audience. This requires that the

journalist shares the language and more specifically a common stock of cultural
knowledge with his audience. Thus, the news media in the very nature of its task
must concern itself with the social categorizations and valued images of the audience it serves; though constraints towards emphasizing those categorizations and
those values which serve a dominant élite lie, as we have noted, within the control and ownership of the media.

RACE RELATIONS: STRUCTURAL PRESSURES AND SOCIAL IMAGES

The race relations situation, which the British press have reported, represents
the human consequences of previous imperialism and colonization of other societies,
largely black, and the more immediate needs of British capital. In post-war Britain there was a great demand for labour which could not be met from indigenous
sources, and Britain, therefore, recruited from her colonial pool. Thus Britain
in the 1960's and '70's has been a society undergoing a redistribution of the indigenous labour force, accompanied by the settlement of a minority black population.
This settlement has become the focus of animated political discussion, and the essential hostility felt towards this black presence has been reflected in the passage
of Acts of Parliament intended to selectively exclude black immigrants from Britain.

In the absence of a full description of the development of race relations in Britain
over the last 30 years, it is important to recognize the progressive accumulation of
individual experiences of separation from kin, humiliation and de facto stateless-
ness which these Acts have meant for black persons with historical and legal claims
on Britain (cf., Foot, 1965; Humphry and Ward, 1974; Moore and Wallace, 1975; Akram,
1974). These Acts of Parliament represent a practical demonstration of the strength of British identity and of its inherent linkage with images of white racial categories. They are an indication also of the political élite's willingness to affirm racial intolerance when this is advantageous to their interests. Though there
has been grass roots pressure for racial discrimination, there is good reason to
believe its power has been allowed for reasons of political expediency (cf., Foot,
1965; Dummett and Dummett, 1969; Sivanandan, 1976).

Britain during the 1960's has been a society under change, not only through immigration. Both Chibnall (1977) and Hall et al. (1978) identify the challenge to consensus politics and established "cultural hegemony" during this time. Both seek to
locate their different analyses within this larger perspective; and it is appropriate to accept the relevance of this stance for the argument here: particularly as
this sense of flux permeated both popular understandings, political anxieties and
inevitably media news frameworks where Chibnall suggests that:

> "The implications of the analysis are that interpretations
> generated in one domain of newspaper discourse (e.g., crime
> news) can easily be, and have been, transposed through link-
> ing concepts (e.g., the violent society) to other domains
> (e.g., political and industrial news)." (Chibnall, 1977:75).

"Society under threat" was the leitmotif of the times and as a "linking concept"
its wide range of perceived relevance ensured its own vitality by demonstrating
its legitimacy through "moral panics" relating to criminal violence, political
violence, industrial anarchy, sexual permissiveness and drug abuse. It required
little to invoke its potent symbolism in relation to that valued dimension of
British identity, race, and the structural forces hinted at above were more than
sufficient to raise race to visibility.

Thus, throughout the 1960's, in Tajfel's terms, white Britons perceived themselves
to be a consensually superior group whose position was threatened by an inferior

outgroup. This threat followed from the denial of equal opportunities and rights
to black citizens and hence, in areas of black immigrant settlement, there was a
perceived threat from black competition for employment and other major sources of
housing, education and welfare (cf., Rex and Moore, 1967; Bagley, 1970). Catalyzed
by this local "threat" there was also a more diffuse sense of cultural threat experienced throughout the country; a fear of cultural dilution which Enoch Powell
tapped with such resonant phrases as - "Caravans encamped in our cities". Thus,
white Britons having assumed the "lesser entitlement of black" (Hartmann and
Husband, 1974:50) experienced a perceived direct threat to their status from the
"inferior" immigrant group. The response to this threat was consistent with
Tajfel's theory - "an intensification of precautions aimed at keeping the superior
group in its position", central to which was the immigration legislation. However,
Tajfel's theory also notes that "superior" groups may experience insecure social
comparisons arising from a conflict of values as when the "superior" status is
exposed as being based upon "unfair advantages, various other forms of injustice,
exploitation, illegitimate use of force, etc." (Tajfel, 1974:79). And this was
exactly the case in the 1960's when the response to the perceived direct threat
became increasingly racist, thus embarrassingly exposing the injustice and prejudice of British race relations - injustice which was, of course, inimical to the
officially espoused value of tolerance in our national imagery. If much of the
response to the direct threat was an exercise of power, it was important that the
threat experienced to dominant values be negotiated through the exercise of influence (cf., Moscovici, 1976:62). The gross nature of institutional and grass
roots discrimination (cf., Moore, 1975; Smith, 1977) required the cultivation of
salient imagery which would facilitate the generation of a definition of the situation wherein such behaviours became apparently reasonable and apparently inevitable. Since the evidence exists to indicate that the news media furnished just
such a definition of the situation (ref., Hartmann and Husband, 1974) it is significant to note Cohen's statement that:

> "Communication, and especially the mass communication of
> stereotypes, depends on the symbolic power of words and
> images". (Cohen, 1973:40).

THE PRESS COVERAGE OF RACE RELATIONS

In discussing the press reporting of race relations in Britain during the 1960's
and '70's it will be my intention to provide only sufficient material to sustain
the general argument; whilst more complete data can be found in Hartmann, Husband
and Clark (1974); Critcher, Parker and Sondhi (1977); Evans (1976) and Runnymede
Trust (1971): related analysis can also be found in Hartmann and Husband (1974)
and Husband (1977).

In their analysis of the reporting of race relations in four national daily papers
(The Times, The Guardian, The Daily Mirror and The Daily Express) from 1963 to
1970, Hartmann et al. concluded that:

> "Race, as the press sees it, is predominantly about immig-
> ration, and immigration is not only a matter of people com-
> ing into the country, it is about keeping them out. Race
> is also about the relations between white and black which is
> presented as a matter of concern; coloured people appear as
> the objects and victims of hostility and discrimination by
> whites, and particularly in later years there is some indic-
> ation of reciprocal hostility from the black side. Both
> immigration and the relations between white and black are
> the subjects of legislation and statutory machinery and of
> debate and controversy. The picture of race in the press
> has been like this throughout the period, but as the period

> has worn on it has become progressively more like this. In
> addition a minority of material has portrayed coloured
> people more or less as ordinary members of society, or as
> engaged in the ordinary run of crime. These latter aspects
> have not changed much over the period. There has, however,
> been a marked increase in the emphasis given to a number of
> coloured people in the country over the period." (Hartmann
> et al., 1974:13).

What was particularly significant in this coverage was the remarkable similarity
in the definition of the situation which emerged from these four papers having
very different style and market position.[2] This homogeneity reflected the function of the press in mirroring "significant" events, but also indicates the shared
professional judgements operating in selecting these events, and a common value
structure in interpreting them. The salient images which were elicited and the
social categorizations which became ossified in the definition of Britain's "immigration problem" arose from a culturally overdetermined common stock of knowledge.

The "symbolization" (Cohen, 1973) of the immigration issue shifted the focus of
public debate from internal structural crisis and indigenous white racism to an
external problem of black migration. I have argued elsewhere (Husband, 1977) that
the words "immigrant" and "immigration" were already heavily penetrated with the
resonant images of prior "invasions" and "floods" of aliens. They were potent
condensation symbols (Graber, 1976) which came to dominate the press conceptualization of race relations. Empirical evidence of the press crystallization of meanings in headlines was found in the content analysis of the national press (Hartmann
et al., 1974) which demonstrated the narrow range of words used in association with
"immigration" and "colour" such that cumulatively they were associated with conflict, threat and opposition to the black presence. This phenomenon not only reflected the habitual journalistic predilection for conflict and hyperbole; but in
ways capable of multiple example, expressed the salience of British *white* identity.
For example, illegal immigration, itself a moral panic indicative of this sensitivity – threw up an example when the discovery of 40 Indians in a cellar was cap-
tioned: *"Police Find Forty Indians in Black Hole"* - a subtle reference back to a
potent symbol of perceived Indian barbarity (and an example which necessitously
requires British schooling to provide the necessary historical "facts" and affective response).

It is difficult to exaggerate the centrality which this symbolization of immigration had for the interpretation of race relations in the period 1963-70. It was
the fulcrum around which related images pivoted and it was the purpose of my
earlier paper to identify these images within the context of their historically
determined meanings and their particular salience during a period of heightened
intergroup tension. Nor should it be thought that the role of culturally charged
language in the press reporting of race relations has been demonstrated only for
the period 1963-70 (Hartmann et al., 1974; Critcher et al., 1977). Whereas in 1970
there were, for example, such headlines as "Invasion of Migrants" and "40 Indians
Invade", in 1976, in response to the arrival of a few Malawi Asians, there was a
comparable response in headlines such as "Asian Flood Warning as More Fly In" and
"Mass Expulsion of Malawi Asians Fear". In January this year, Mrs. Thatcher, the
leader of the Opposition, shifting the linking symbol of threat from "numbers" to

---

[2]When the number of column inches falling under different topic headings were
ranked for each paper, the coefficient of concordance calculated across all four
papers was 0.86.

culture - a dimension previously skilfully exercised by Enoch Powell - made headlines with her reference to the possibility that "this country might be rather
swamped by people with a different culture". Both *Race and Press* (Runnymede Trust,
1971) and *Publish and be Damned* (Evans, 1977) provide accounts of the emotive language used by the British press in reporting race relations. That the language of
threat, floods and invasions is cued by race and not immigration per se has been
recently admirably illustrated in the example of yet another African exodus. However, it is the absence of such powerfully emotive symbolism in response to the
information carried in the *Sunday Times*, of London (August 8th, 1978), that 10,000
Rhodesians are reported to have already booked flights to Britain, and that a
further 150,000 "have a constitutional right to enter" which is so telling. The
critical element in this potential influx of immigrants is that they are white;
and indeed are perceived as kith and kin rather than representative of an illegal
colonial regime.

Clearly the language of intergroup relations is crucial in its construction of the
perception of the situation and equally significant is the non-random determinat-
ion of the language used. Tajfel's (1974) statement is valuable in providing a
framework which can contain an analysis of the forces operating in generating the
lexicon employed in encoding messages; for example, press accounts of race relations. Equally that same framework can inform our comprehensions of the decoding
of that language within different audiences. In an analysis of the press reporting of race relations in the 1960's and '70's this framework requires that we first
locate the membership groups in interaction, and establish the nature of their
relationship. In Britain we have seen the white majority population as a "consensually superior group whose position was threatened by an inferior outgroup".
We have noted the differential modes of response to the perceived direct threat,
and to the conflict of values arising from the response to the direct threat. The
identification of the threat in racial terms, it is argued, has emerged from the
historically rooted social identity of "the British": which with its inherent am-
biguities, requires continuing construction. This definition of threatened British identity, itself located in a "society under threat", has been observed to
exist in a dynamic process of social comparison wherein valued dimensions of ingroup identity are cued to salience, and reinforced. Given the sociopolitical
hegemony of the white majority, the definition of race relations emerging in the
press has been seen to reflect the content of, and interests of, the dominant
white British group.[3] In particular, the language use significantly reflects
dominant images of British identity and illustrates the existence of consistent
social comparison directed toward maintaining the distinctiveness of the valued
ingroup.

The particular strength of Tajfel's framework is perhaps in linking the forces
operating at the encoding of messages to those operating at decoding. In viewing
the white majority we have seen political interest link with individual social
identity. For, though the media were operating to mystify a structural crisis,
it was seen that this was mediated through the co-option of powerful images linked
to salient aspects of social identity. This process was itself aided by the cul-

---

[3]In an adequate analysis it should also be shown how this process of sustaining
white British identity has simultaneously excluded black minority groups from
entry into "British" social identity and has thereby added a black response to
rejection as an amplifier to white identity maintenance, thus adding an additional
element to the process of "increased psychological differentiation along valued
dimensions" which Tajfel postulates.

tural predispositions of the predominantly white media personnel. It is the shared cultural assumptions and social identity - within the domain of race if not of
nationality or class - which facilitates the correspondence of meaning at the
point of audience decoding of newsprint. However, what Tajfel's framework makes
inescapable is the acutely dynamic process of decoding the press accounts of race
relations. Thus the audience's acquisition of a shared definition of the situation is not merely the consequence of exposure to a monolithic press product (ref.,
Hartman and Husband, 1974): it is not passive exposure learning, but rather it is
a dynamic personal process in which meanings are constructed in relation to salient aspects of a threatened social identity. Therefore it is important to note
that much of the mystificatory "work" of the press can be seen to be achieved by
the dynamic psychological investment of the individual consumer of newsprint;
rather than there being a passive acquisition of an over-determined definition of
the situation.

Having looked briefly at some aspects of language use in the press reporting of
race relations I wish now to extend the analysis by examining further interactions
between press routines and the creation of a specific universe of discourse for
reporting race relations. In particular I wish to ask *whose language was it anyway?* and thereby make further links between the structural properties of institutions of mass communication and the social psychology central to Tajfel's framework.

RACE IN THE PRESS: WHOSE LANGUAGE?

The press operate in relation to "events" taking place at any particular time and,
given the press's role of setting the agenda for their audience's concerns, their
linkage to the consensus ideology of élite interests make the press necessitously
sensitive to those events which might have "political" significance. As we have
seen, the 1960's was marked by a dominant image of society under threat and this
at a time when changes in economic and social patterns was generating a growing
intergroup tension between the indigenous white population and migrant black population. The political necessity to acknowledge the grass roots expression of
feeling, and the political capital to be made from exploiting this feeling (cf.,
Foot, 1969; Foot, 1965; Smithies and Fiddick, 1969; and Seymour-Ure, 1974) resulted in race becoming a central issue in political discussion and particularly party
political pursuit of the marginal vote has provided the motive power to sustain
this issue since it emerged substantially in the early years of the 1960's. This
debate has existed in relation to grass roots scapegoating of the black immigrant
threat and the political pragmatism of successive governments seeking to control
the supply of labour to meet the changing demands of capital (cf., Peach, 1968
and Sivanandan, 1976). Thus, much of the reality - the events - which became news
were reflections of the political activity of the era. Indeed, empirical evidence
of the extent to which press reporting paralleled political activity was provided
in the content analysis of the national press (Hartmann and Husband, 1974:127-139)
where fluctuations in the visibility of different topics in the press was seen to
map the flow and ebb of race in political and Parliamentary activity.

It is a fundamental element of the analysis here that the overlap of political
"event" and press "news" coverage is no passive consequence of journalists merely
reflecting current events. As Moscovici notes: "Societies..., carefully separate
the instruments of their power from those of their influence" (Moscovici, 1976:
62). Legislation since 1962 has represented the exercise of power in keeping the
superior group in its position faced with direct conflict; but the press have operated critically as a medium of *influence* to defend the superior groups against
the conflict of values which was contingent upon the exercise of power in this
discriminatory manner. Thus we come to the question of whose language is being
used in the press accounts, and in terms of press routines, the operation of

structured access is immediately critical.

Just as events become news through a non-random professional structure and routine, so too those events which achieve initial visibility are not in themselves random. The structure of the journalistic world with specialists (e.g., political correspondents, home affairs correspondents, etc.) generates a professional territory which must needs be productive, and this of itself creates a need for established and reliable sources. Since news deals reputedly with "fact" and not opinion, there is a corresponding pressure to maintain sources who have access to where the action is. These forces constitute a filter which tend to exclude the average man and retain the expert, the accredited source, for information (ref., Rock, 1973; Murdock, 1974; Tunstall, 1971). An independent pressure toward structured access to the news media comes from the press commitment to objectivity, impartiality and fairness (ref., Carey, 1969; Tuchman, 1972) whereby the journalist, in order to demonstrate his independence from "the facts" seeks out the "expert" and, lest there is a doubt as to the fairness and balance of the resulting news, then two expert views may be opposed. It is the highly selective access to the press which results from forces such as these which leads Hall to talk of primary definers.

> "The result of this structured preference given in the media
> to the opinions of the powerful is that these "spokesmen"
> become what we call the primary definers of topics... The
> important point about the structured relationship between
> the media and the primary institutional definers is that it
> permits the institutional definers to establish the initial
> definition or *primary interpretation* of the topic in question.
> This interpretation then "commands the field" in all sub-
> sequent treatment and sets the terms of reference within
> which all further coverage or debate takes place." (Hall et
> al., 1978:58).

One hypothesis which readily arises from the structured access of individuals to the media is that the "man in the street" has a minimal chance of becoming a primary definer. In the area of race, the man in the street had the power to create events such as the 1958 disturbances in Notting Hill but they lacked access to the media to generate definitions. The interpretation, given the grass roots "events", stemmed from primary definers who occupied different positions in society. From the beginning, grass roots resentment has had members of Parliament, who because of their institutional power and position, have been accredited sources for the media. As early as 1954, Cyril Osborne and Norman Pannell demanded legislation to control Commonwealth immigration to Britain. Though their status gained them access to the press, they lacked the power to achieve the status of primary definers which fell to their political masters who, at that time, chose to define the issue in terms of a commitment to "Civis Britannicus Sum". Similarly though individuals may act through marches or switching votes to express their views on race relations, the control of this mechanism of influence lies beyond them. The events of the times are defined in the terms of the political élite. The remarkable agreement in the press reporting of race attested to this hegemony.

However, access alone was not the sole variable facilitating the penetration of politicians' definitions into press accounts. The language of Parliament itself bears within it properties which render it compatible with journalistic style. Parliamentary language is a particular entity – where utterances, and their source are evaluated as much for the stylistic properties evident in the speech as for the sense it contains. Hence politicians have a professional investment in language use, and a need to develop a capacity for replicating styles suitable for statements in the House of Commons, at election meetings, for self-selected gatherings of party members; and increasingly to the mass media. Thus politicians and journalists share a professional concern for language and its use. News media language tends

to operate with a limited lexicon, and particularly in the construction of headlines we have seen the power of conservative words (Osgood, 1971) constraining the
constructed reality. In headlines too we find a particularly concentrated form of
the news media's attraction for language which has pace, hyperbole, conflict and
cultural reference. The analyses of Hartmann, Husband and Clark (1974) and Critcher, Parker and Sondhi (1977) have demonstrated the prevalence of conflictful and
emotive language in news headlines referring to race relations items. We may speak
of the press habitually demonstrating a linguistic style which employs hyperbole,
- "Race, row, rumpus" - is a debate in Parliament, and which tends to amplify conflict. Thus we may note the ways in which the linguistic styles of politicians
have operated in relation to the general press style (though there are variations
between individual papers in the extent to which they embody these tendencies, cf.,
Martin, 1964; Hall et al., 1978).

Sivanandan has made the general point that:

> "In British race policy, the philosophy, the rationale comes
> first - then to be taken up and embellished by sections of
> the media - thereby creating a "climate of opinion" - demand-
> ing legislation." (Sivanandan, 1978:80).

What his statement does not reflect is the extent to which, at varying times, the
philosophy emanating from politicians has been expressed in terms which served to
counter the tendency toward sensationalization within the press and at other times
has presented that philosophy in terms entirely compatible with press linguistic
style. In the early 1960's, as the political machinery began to respond to grass
roots disquiet, the philosophy was presented in quiet terms as a sad but necessary
eventuality. The press, however, were already amplifying the grass roots feeling
with provocative headlines and occasionally, scandalously inflammatory articles
(cf., Butterworth, 1962). When in 1964 Peter Griffith ran an explicitly anti-imm-
igration election campaign, he was vilified by the then Prime Minister as a "Parliamentary leper". Here a primary definer was using evocative, powerful language
to underscore a "liberal" position. The fact that Griffith's campaign was successful had important repercussions for the party political thinking about race, but
the use of moderate language by political primary definers continued. In 1966, even
Enoch Powell, who came to personify rabid opposition to a black presence in Britain
- "While advocating even stricter control, (he) did not attempt to whip up popular
support on the subject" (Foot, 1969:94). Thus, although by 1966 the actions of
government were discriminatory, and though their collusion with the symbolization
of the "immigration" issue was racist, the denotative message of commitment to a
liberal integration emanating from political primary definers (ref., Rose, 1969)
was enhanced by the moderation of their language.

The shift to political rhetoric matching press values and style came dramatically
with Enoch Powell's speeches in 1968. Such was the potency of Powell's *language*,
which itself demonstrated a fine sensitivity for the cultural resonance of the
words he used, that exceptionally large quotations from his speeches were printed
verbatim in the press (ref., Seymour-Ure, 1974). It is this cultural resonance
which bridges the world of the politician and the "common man"; it is the cueing
of images which define identity, which reassert dominant values within that identity
and which express commitment to that identity through the suspension of sobriety in
language and the use of emotive language. Powell created remarkably potent images
(ref., Foot, 1969; Smithies and Fiddick, 1969) and, like others before him, he
appealed directly to the people in a language which bore a semblance to their own
- "we must be mad, literally mad" and which in the tenor of its expression, acknow-
ledged the intensity of their shared fears - "I see the Tiber flowing with much
blood". The speeches of Enoch Powell were all the more a triumph of language use
in that, as a primary definer rather than a maverick backbench M.P. like Cyril
Osborne, he used emotive language which rang all the louder for the constraint

which preceded it. Powell's intervention created a new universe of discourse for
political discussion, and one which more closely tapped the sentiments of the electorate. If Powell's style acted as a releaser for grass roots affect, he also
generated a style which was more amenable to press news values. From 1968, the
political debate was conducted in a style which could not act as a moderating influence upon press predilections, but rather both were now in an amplificatory
feedback loop.

Clearly there is an interaction between the language per se, - (and we must remember that the English language is no neutral medium for the transmission of meanings
in multiracial Britain, (ref., Husband, 1977: 212-215); - the context of its use,
- (structural crisis defined as "Society under Threat"); - and the weighting which
may be given the words is, itself, contingent upon their source. A more recent
example than Powell to illuminate this process came in January 1978, with the
leader of the Opposition's reference to the possibility that English culture might
be "swamped" by alien cultures. As on previous occasions there is nothing unique
in this view; it is, for example, reflected in the growth of the *National Front*
in Britain. What was critical was the structured access of this particular source
and the use by this source of a word with such "immoderate" potency which made it
more newsworthy and signalled to the audience the intensity of the source's feeling for the issue. The word itself is redolent of the images of threat, invasion,
flood (society under threat) which has typified press frameworks for reporting
race, and was amplified in its effect by the eminence of the source.

What is being argued here is that political primary definers have operated two
channels of meaning; the one essentially denotative has conveyed the constructs,
the definition of the situation, the "philosophy"; the other channel, essentially
expressive, has conveyed the appropriate affect to qualify the denotative meanings.
The denotative channel would itself seem to represent the use of a familiar political rhetorical style, what Graber calls the rhetoric of the statesman - "The
statesman appeals to value judgements on intellectual rather than emotional planes.
In cultures which prize notions of rationality, people do not fear the statesman's
talk as defined here; they consider his type of speech making as an exposition of
facts and clearly labelled opinions which leaves the audience free to draw its own
conclusions" (Graber, 1976:182). Perhaps it is the inherent appeal to rationality
within this style which limits its expressive range and thereby creates a base line
against which an expressive channel can be all the more potent in its appeal to
values on an emotional plane. Such different channels of communication could be
hypothesized to have differential impacts upon different audiences. In their study
of white Briton's response to the black communities in Britain, Hartmann and Husband (1974) found that though affect (hostility) varied from area to area in
Britain, there was a uniform perception of race relations in Britain in which there
was a ubiquitous acceptance of the "immigration problem". Thus many individuals
with no particular hostility toward black people accepted as factually inevitable
an essentially racist definition of the situation. It could be hypothesized that
the rational appeal of the denotative channel facilitated the acceptance of this
definition among "liberal" whites. Whereas it would seem appropriate to hypothesize that the affective channel was more active in promoting the illiberal convictions of those who were racially hostile; for whom the racial aspect of their
social identity would be particularly salient.

Continuing a discussion of the two channels employed by political primary definers,
it is instructive to reflect on party political philosophy on race in 1978. With
legislation against black immigration virtually as inhumanely restrictive as possible, the options available for further repressive legislation are heavily contingent upon the party leaders' willingness to generate an acute conflict of values
by shedding the last vestige of racial tolerance. Thus the actual policies on
immigration were virtually identical. It is of interest to note, therefore, that
when the denotative channel conveyed comparable policies, there appeared to be a

differential use of the expressive channel. The Labour Government presented its programme in considered tones and employed emotive language to reassert Britain's tolerant liberal tradition, to stress the therefore limited legislative potential. The Tory party, on the other hand, appear to have presented a programme comparable in major essentials but experimented with emotive language to suggest the possibility that their policy was different because it recognizes the disquiet and threat experienced by the electorate faced with a black presence in Britain. The virtue of this strategy is that both parties, when challenged, can deflect attacks by directing attention to the "legitimate" denotative channel alone: an inversion of the traditional - "It is not what you say, it's the way that you say it". Labour can claim to be as tough as the Tories, while the Tories can claim to be no more restrictive than Labour. And of course they have!

CONCLUSION

We have seen that the national press reporting of race relations has been closely linked to political events; and the structured access of politicians has greatly amplified their contribution to the description of race relations in Britain. The recent *Royal Commission on the Press* (H.M.S.O., 1977) has indicated that news about what the Government is doing is second only to news about what is going on in the respondent's own part of the country as a priority of interest in news content, (H.M.S.O., 1977:37). The same report also indicates that the national press is second only to television as the most valued source of such information, (H.M.S.O., 1977:31). It has also been demonstrated that press definitions of race relations in Britain have penetrated significantly into popular definitions of the situation (Hartmann and Husband, 1974). Within this framework it is important to note that politicians, as "primary definers", were unable to generate a cognitive alternative to the symbolization of "immigration" since, in responding to grass roots "events", themselves contingent upon structural pressures, these individuals predominantly shared the same social identity as white Britons ; and the same salient values in, for example, accepting the normality of white preferment and the reality of British tolerance. Increasingly in the exercise of legislative power to contain the crises of the 1960's, these same people were reiterating and reasserting British identity, and to a significant extent, white identity, through the exclusion of black people from Britain. Thus, the symbolization of the "immigration problem" was a necessary exercise in social influence which promoted, or, rather more accurately, given the essential grass roots genesis of this definition, facilitated the emergence of an ideology which defended British identity against an embarrassing conflict of values.

Tajfel's theory has been seen to provide a valuable framework within which to locate the construction of this ideology: and in particular demonstrates the crucial vitality of social psychological processes mediating structural pressures. Indeed an analysis with social identity as a central variable proves remarkably heuristic in the further questions it throws up. For example, it remains a possibility that the use of such potent condensation symbols, which cued the racial imagery of British identity so effectively, may, through the very dynamics of social comparison, directed toward enhancing ingroup identity, have relocated racial categorization more centrally within British identity. Racial identity thereby may ultimately threaten national identity, for 40 per cent of the black population are now British born, and yet it seems unlikely that the press or politicians can easily relinquish the "immigrant" scapegoat: for two reasons. Firstly because the cueing of *white* British identity over the last 20 years has successfully activated the dynamics of social identity maintenance which may now be regarded as a social psychological process operating independently of its original stimulus. Secondly the national press, for commercial reasons, cannot promote regional identity (Martin, 1964) and Parliament, for political reasons, must submerge regional identity; and given the ambiguous nature of "British" identity it is

difficult to construct a positive condensation symbol of British identity. Therefore, we must hypothesize that the scapegoating of the "immigrant" outgroup will
continue. Tajfel's theory provides a framework in which it is possible to locate
press accounts of race relations as being not only structurally functional, but
also social psychologically potent in their reference to individual identity. It
can be argued that the autonomous consequences of this psychological dynamic can
ultimately become dysfunctional for the needs of capital and the state.

The implications of this analysis are not limited to the British situation.
Tajfel's theory indicates that wherever the mass media, in operating as an arm of
state ideological influence, employ language which cues valued aspects of social
identity then the consequences of such activities may be difficult to predict or
control. The potentially autonomous psychological dynamic of identity maintenance
can no longer be left out of any analysis of mass media functioning within situations of intergroup contact.

REFERENCES

Akram, M. (1974) Where do you keep your string beds?, Runnymede Trust, London.

Bagley, C. (1970) Social structure and prejudice in five English boroughs, Institute of Race Relations, London.

Beharrell, P. & Philo, G. (1977) Trade Unions and the media, MacMillan, London.

Bolt, C. (1971) Victorian attitudes to race, Routledge and Kegan Paul, London.

Brown, G. (ed.) (1975) The red paper on Scotland, E.U.S.P.B., Edinburgh.

E. Butterworth, The smallpox outbreak and the British press, Race, VII, 4 (1962).

J. Carey, The communications revolution and the professional communicator, Sociological Review Monograph, 13 (1969).

Chibnall, S. (1977) Law and order news, Tavistock Publications, London.

Critcher, C., Parker, M. & Sondhi, R. (1977) Race in the provincial press: A case study of five West Midlands newspapers. In Ethnicity and the media, U.N.E.S.C.O. (1977).

Cohen, S. (1973) Folk Devils and Moral Panics, Paladin Books, London.

Cohen, S. & Young, J. (1973) The manufacture of news, Constable, London.

Davis, D.B. (1970) The problem of slavery in Western culture, Pelican Books.

J. Downing, Class and "race" in the British mass media, Paper given to the Working Convention on Racism in the Political Economy of Britain, London (1971).

Dummett, A. (1973) A portrait of English racism, Penguin Books, Harmondsworth.

Dummett, M. & Dummett, A. (1969) The role of government in Britain's racial crisis. In L. Donnelly (ed.): Justice first, Sheed and Ward, London.

Evans, P. (1977) Publish and be damned, Runnymede Trust, London.

Fanon, F. (1970) Black skin, white masks, Paladin Books, London.

Foot, P. (1965) Immigration and race in British politics, Penguin Books, Harmondsworth.

Foot, P. (1969) The rise of Enoch Powell, Penguin Books, Harmondsworth.

J. Galtung & R.H. Ruge, The structure of foreign news, Journal of Peace Research, 1 (1965) and in J. Tunstall (1970) Media Sociology.

Garrard, J.A. (1971) The English and immigration 1880-1910, Oxford University Press, London.

Gartner, L.P. (1959) The Jewish immigrant to England 1870-1914, George Allen and Unwin, London.

Goodman, M.E. (1964) Race awareness in young children, Collier Books, New York.

Graber, D.A. (1976) Verbal behaviour and politics, University of Illinois Press, Urbana.

S. Hall, The structured communication of events, Occasional paper, No.5, Centre for Contemporary Cultural Studies, University of Birmingham, England (1973).

Hall, S. (1977) Culture, the media and the "ideological effects". In J. Curran et al. (eds.): Mass communication and society, Edward Arnold, London.

Hall, S., Critcher, C., Jefferson, T., Clark, J. & Roberts, B. (1978) Policing the crisis, Macmillan, London.

Halloran, J.D., Elliott, P. & Murdock, G. (1970) Demonstrations and communication: A case study, Penguin Books, Harmondsworth.

H.M.S.O. (1977) Attitudes to the press, Royal Commission on the press, H.M.S.O. London, Comnd., 6810-3.

Hartmann, P. & Husband, C. (1974) Racism and the mass media, Davis-Poynter, London.

Hartmann, P., Husband, C. & Clark, J. (1974) Race as news: A study in the handling of race in the British national press from 1963-1970. In Race as news, U.N.E.S.C.O. Press, Paris.

Hechter, M. (1975) Internal colonialism, Routledge and Kegan Paul, London.

Holmes, C. (1978) Immigrants and minorities in British society, George Allen and Unwin, London.

Humphry, D. & Ward, M. (1974) Passports and politics, Penguin Books, Harmondsworth.

Hunter, G.K. (1967) Othello and colour prejudice. In The Proceedings of the British Academy, LIII, Oxford University Press, London.

Husband, C. (1975) Racism in society and the mass media: A critical interaction. In C. Husband (ed.): White media and black Britain.

Husband, C. (1977) News media, language and race relations: A case study in identity maintenance. In H. Giles (ed.): Language, ethnicity and inter-group relations, Academic Press, London.

Johnson, P. (1975) The offshore islanders, Penguin Books, Harmondsworth.

Jordan, W.D. (1969) White over black, Penguin Books, Harmondsworth.

Kiernan, V.G. (1972) The lords of human kind, Pelican Books, Harmondsworth.

King, J. & Stott, M. (1977) Is this your life?, Virago, London.

Lyons, C.H. (1975) To wash an Aethiop white, Teachers College Press, Columbia University, New York.

Martin, G. (1964) The press. In D. Thompson (ed.): Discrimination and popular culture, Penguin Books, Harmondsworth.

Milner, D. (1975) Children and race, Penguin Books, Harmondsworth.

Moore, R. (1975) Racism and black resistance in Britain, Pluto Press, London.

Moore, R. & Wallace, T. (1975) Slamming the door: The administration of immig-
    ration control, Martin Robertson, London.

Moscovici, S. (1976) Social influence and social change, Academic Press, London.

Murdock, G. (1974) Mass communication and the construction of meaning. In
    N. Armistead (ed.): Reconstructing social psychology, Penguin Books,
    Harmondsworth.

Murdock, G. & Golding, P. (1971) Capitalism, communication and class relations.
    In J. Curran et al.: Mass communication and society, Edward Arnold, London.

Osgood, C.E. (1971) Conservative words and radical sentences in the semantics
    of international politics. In G. Abcarian & J.W. Soule: Social psychology
    and political behaviour: Problems and prospects, Charles E. Merrill,
    Columbus.

Peach, C. (1968) West Indian migration to Britain: A social geography, Oxford
    University Press/I.R.R., London.

Rex, J. & Moore, R. (1967) Race, community and conflict, Oxford University Press/
    I.R.R., London.

Rock, P. (1973) News as eternal recurrence. In S. Cohen & J. Young (eds.):
    The manufacture of news, Constable, London.

Rose, E.J.B. et al. (1969) Colour and citizenship, Oxford University Press,
    London.

Runnymede Trust (1971) Race and the press, Runnymede Trust, London.

Seymour-Ure, C. (1974) The political impact of the mass media, Constable, London.

Sharf, A. (1964) The British press and Jews under Nazi rule, Institute of Race
    Relations / Oxford University Press, London.

Sherif, M. (1966) Group conflict and co-operation, Routledge and Kegan Paul,
    London.

A. Sivanandan, Race, class and the state: The black experience in Britain,
    Race and Class, XVII, 4, 347-368 (1976).

A. Sivanandan, From immigration control to "induced repatriation", Race and
    Class, XX, 1, 75-82 (1978).

Smith, D.J. (1977) Racial disadvantage in Britain, Penguin Books, Harmondsworth.

Smithies, B. & Fiddick, P. (1969) Enoch Powell and immigration, Sphere, London.

H. Tajfel, G. Jahoda, C. Nemeth, Y. Rim & N.B. Johnson, The devaluation by
    children of their own national and ethnic group: Two case studies, British
    Journal of Social and Clinical Psychology, II, 3, 235-243 (1972).

H. Tajfel, Social identity and intergroup behaviour, <u>Social Science Information</u>, <u>13</u>, 2, 65–93 (1974).

G. Tuchman, Objectivity as strategic ritual: An examination of newsmen's notions of objectivity, <u>American Journal of Sociology</u>, <u>77</u>, 4 (1972).

Tunstall, J. (1971) <u>Journalists at work</u>, Constable, London.

Walvin, J. (1971) <u>The black presence</u>, Orbach and Chambers, London.

Webb, K. (1978) <u>The growth of nationalism in Scotland</u>, Pelican Books, Harmondsworth.

Williams, G. (ed.) (1978) <u>Social and cultural change in contemporary Wales</u>, Routledge and Kegan Paul, London.

WHITE REACTION TO THE BLACK HANDSHAKE
UNDER THREE EXPERIMENTAL CONDITIONS[1]

W. von Raffler-Engel, M. Stewart and J. C. Elliott *

Vanderbilt University, U.S.A.
***Tennessee State University, U.S.A.**

INTRODUCTION

People are generally aware of verbal differences in intercultural communication and accept these as given, even when they exhibit a marked dislike for some, if not all, of the so-called substandard dialects. The nonverbal component of the speech act needs a much higher threshold to attain conscious awareness, and some aspects never reach full consciousness (von Raffler-Engel, in press). Experiments involving nonverbal behaviour are therefore especially suited for testing attitudes in intercultural relations.

In the study of dialects and subcultures, it is important "never to consider one as basic and match the others against it" (von Raffler-Engel, 1974:759). In attitudinal studies, such as this one, the focus of the research is on what the subjects say and how they approach the description, whether they are ethnocentric or not.

PURPOSE

We wished to discover to what extent the perception and description of an outgroup kinesic behaviour is influenced by the viewer's preconveived notion of how such behaviour related to his ingroup. The goal of the research was to test the impact of preconceptions in short-term memory on the quantity and the quality of body motions by members of the outgroup. In addition, we wanted to analyze the body movements and facial expressions of persons while observing the outgroup behaviour from different preconceived viewpoints.

A total of 10 subjects, five white and five black, were asked whether they believed that telling white subjects that the black persons they would view on the screen had a friendly or a hostile attitude towards them would influence the manner in which they would perceive the movements of those persons. All white subjects emphatically said that this certainly would make a considerable difference. All black subjects immediately stated that it could not possibly make a difference because the encounters the subjects would see on the screen were between blacks only,

---

[1]The authors acknowledge the help of the Vanderbilt Media Centre and especially its video-technician, Robin Foster.

and there were no instances of communication across racial lines.

RESEARCH DESIGN

The third author who is black and professor of foreign languages at Tennessee
State University, a predominantly black university, video-taped three pairs of
black students at her university in the process of greeting each other with the
soul handshake. (In this paper the term *soul handshake* is used for the entire
greeting ritual. In the black culture this expression is reserved for one particular phase of the greeting ritual called the *thumblock*, as practiced in Handshake II. For a detailed treatment of the subject, see Cooke, 1972:61). Each
pair used another style of this typical Black-American greeting ritual. The third
author had a cameraman stationed on a busy crossing on her campus. She then walk-
ed up to a passing male student and asked him to shake hands with the next male
student that would pass by in front of the camera. After the two students had
done their handshaking, she waited until another pair was in sight. All six students complied gracefully and - luckily - each pair performed a different type of
soul handshake. None of the participants happened to know each other previously.
When they had finished their handshaking, each continued to walk in his own way.
While all this was going on, some onlookers gathered around joking about the situation. No white person was in sight at any time.

A step-by-step description of the classic ritual was prepared. In the analysis of
the test results, this description was used as a base to compare the responses of
the subjects.

The Sony video band with the three encounters was then transferred to a Sony cassette at the Vanderbilt University Media Center, allowing for a three minute interval between each encounter, each new encounter being preceded by a beep signal.
At the completion of the third encounter there was another three minute interval
followed by a beep signal to announce the end of the experiment, and allowing for
a three minute interval before the next and final beep.

The edited video cassette was shown to white students at Vanderbilt University, a
predominantly white university, by the second author who is white and a research
assistant to the first author, who is also white and professor of linguistics at
that university. All subjects were shown the video cassette with each encounter
run once at normal speed, immediately thereafter once again at slow speed. Subjects were asked to describe in as much detail as possible the hand movements
which they saw on the screen. Then they were asked to make some general comments
during the last three minutes. Subjects were video-taped throughout the experiment after they had given their written consent before the start of the experiment.

The total number of subjects was 47, of which 45 were utilized in the analysis,
(for demographic data, see Appendix). Subject no.5 had to be disqualified because he is the son of the first author. Subject no.36, who is black, was disqualified because he would be interpreting the gestures from ingroup status. The
subjects were divided into three groups. The first group was not given any information besides the instructions to describe the movements of the soul handshake
as they saw it on the tape. The second group was given these same instructions
and told that the black handshake was an assertion of hatred for the white man.
After the completion of this particular experiment, the subjects were immediately
informed of the truth. The third group, in addition to the usual instructions,
was told that the soul handshake was a friendly greeting among blacks without any
thought of antagonism towards whites. Subjects in this group were told that the
soul handshake was intended as a friendly, brotherly greeting among black sold-
iers, which eventually was interpreted as a gesture of defiance against white
society by their officers in the U.S. Army during the Viet Nam War (Elliott, 1977).

No attempt was made to determine beforehand what the subjects thought the soul hand-shake represented, or what their attitude was towards blacks in general. The neut-ral group was neutral only with regard to any pre-testing influence by the exper-imenter, and the other groups were under a hostile or friendly influence only with reference to the period immediately preceding the test. The subjects being chosen at random, it was assumed that their original attitudes would even out among them. What transpired, eventually, from the test results was that all subjects, without exception, had basically a friendly attitude towards black people. Even though sometimes this attitude was naively condescending, there never seemed to be any conscious ill disposition. Subjects ranged from the pluralistic attitude of sub-ject no.11 for whom "other groups or societies also have 'secret' handshakes" to the melting pot approach of subject no.31, who felt "like it will eventually fade as the blacks are able to integrate more and more into society and feel more secure about themselves, so they don't have to remain so close as a group".

Two subjects (16, 17) remarked in their comments that they would not conceive that any of the greeters they had seen on the screen had any sort of hostile feelings in them. "I did not perceive any black rebellious/contre-white sentiment in the gesture" (17). "One aspect of what was told us that stayed with me was "the hos-tility" of the gesture. Yet I felt no response that would indicate that." Still another subject (30), after remarking that the handshake is meant to keep outsiders out, goes on in saying that the greeters feel very contented.

The test was administered within a span of three weeks time to small numbers of subjects ranging from one to 10. All subjects were self-selected from students coming out of various regular classrooms when they were asked whether they were willing to spend some 15 minutes in an experiment for the Linguistics Program. At the start of the experiment, the subjects were seated in a regular classroom, horseshoe style and facing the camera. Each subject was provided with two pages of lined paper on which to write comments and the following information:

        sex   place of family residence
        birthdate   class standing
        birthplace   academic major

There was considerable variation in the time each student used for the completion of each of the four tasks. Some students remarked that three minutes was "just about right" for the time they needed; very few thought they needed more time, and the majority of students did not utilize the full time span available to them. After completing their writing they sat quietly waiting for the next phase of the experiment at which time they resumed their writing. From the video-tapes, all timings could be easily reconstructed if one wanted to correlate the time spent on the writing and the actual length of the descriptions and comments.

EVALUATION PROCEDURES

As the subjects did not come in complete groups, but in very small groups as their time permitted, the total footage of the video-tape of the subjects was extremely long. Therefore, we randomly selected a manageable portion of the master-tape by transferring on a second tape portions of one-half minute each at intervals of five minutes. The portions of the five minute interval were edited out, but the full master-tape has been preserved for possible future use. Then an adjustment was made to equal the time of duration of each edited section of tape. The three edited tapes were shown to a total of three coders to check for inter-coder agree-ment. The coders ranged from 25 to 63 years of age, two females and one male. The rating test was conducted by the second author in the same classroom where the experiment had been conducted. The edited tapes were shown in the following seq-uence: neutral, negatively-influenced, positively-influenced. The tape lasted a total time span of fifteen minutes, each section being five minutes long.

In addition to the evaluation of the subjects' nonverbal behaviour during the test, the 45 unmarked test papers which had been written by the subjects were given to five independent judges. These raters were requested to sort the papers according to which of the three groups they seemed to belong to. The sorters ranged from 13 to 33 years of age, all female.

ANALYSIS OF SUBJECT RESPONSES

In general, several of the subjects did not grasp the instructions, probably because they had never been asked previously to describe a nonverbal communication. Although the students said they understood the instructions of only describing the scene and reserving comments for the end, they constantly introduced interpretative observations, even when they started initially with an objective description. The three groups did not differ in that respect.

The analysis of the test results was done jointly by the first and second author. A series of comparisons was established. The comparisons were of two distinct types: one consisting of a series of selected interpretations such as aggressiveness and happiness, and one being attention to details of body motions. The analysis following general remarks will be divided into:

Interpretative Comments

    I. Categories of sentence meaning
    II. Categories of lexical meaning

Descriptive Observations

    I. Number of kinesic details reported in descriptions
    II. The fist

Finally, the evaluation by the coders of nonverbal behaviour and the judges of written papers will be covered as a further contrast of the descriptive interpretative categories, respectively. The papers were divided by the sex of subjects, geographic distribution, and by their academic major. Of interest was whether or not any of the means of perception and report were related to sex, place of origin or academic major.

GENERAL REMARKS

All subjects identified the greeters as males with the exception of subject no.7, who thought that one of the greeters in the third picture was a girl, probably because this greeter carried a large shoulder bag which she mistook for a woman's handbag.

All of the greeters were fellow-students at Tennessee State University but they did not know each other personally. The majority of the subjects believed that the greeters were old friends. Some subjects distinguished between friends, "not so close friends", and "casual acquaintances". Except for two instances there was no verbal exchange between the two greeters. In Handshake I the following exchange occurred: *What's happening?* and *Hey, buddy*. The second instance occurs in Handshake II. Only one of the greeters speaks, saying *Hey*.

Several subjects commented to the experimenter after the test, telling her that the almost total lack of verbalization was strange. But in the written response, they only reported the fact without evaluative comments. After the test some (a total of 6 – one from the neutral and five from the negatively-influenced group) asked

the experimenter whether the greeters did or did not know that they were being
video-taped. The test papers themselves were quite contradictory. Frequently, the
same subject categorized one encounter as obviously natural, while the next one was
viewed as certainly staged. Whether the subjects regarded the greetings as spontaneous or planned was not considered relevant to the research goal: subjects' responses were not classified in this regard.

It is difficult to find a rationale between the length of the response and its relation to pre-test influence. A word count of each paper showed that a mean number
of words for the neutral and negatively-influenced group was almost identical,
while the positively-influenced group showed 36% fewer words than the other two.
Ten students in this group had just come from a class where they had viewed a lengthy film; as a result they were probably tired prior to the experiment. The visual fatigue may have diminished their interest in still another visual objective,
resulting in shorter papers.

Mean number of words per paper:	Neutral group	Negative group	Positive group
	212.6	215.1	138.2

INTERPRETATIVE COMMENTS

(The complete meaning of the interpretative statements in some test papers becomes
clear only when read within the full context of the description of all the three
phases of the test - Handshakes I, II and III. This is particularly true for subjects nos.23, 24 and 26).

Neither linguists nor psychologists have yet at their disposal a procedure for the
analysis of meaning that is truly objective. In an attempt to double-check the
interpretation, test responses were systematized on two different levels. Two sets
of semantic categories were established. One set consisted of a series of categories formed on the basis of sentence meaning (Categories A-F). Another set was determined by groups of vocabulary items (List of Qualifying Words). In the sentence based system, the statement, "One aspect of what was told us that stayed with
me was the 'hostility' of the gesture. Yet, I felt no response that would indicate that" (Subject 16) was grouped with, "This was a friendly handshake" (Subject
1) - while in the lexically determined system the words *hostility* and *friendly* belong to two entirely different categories. In the List of Qualifying Words, lexical items were grouped into categories with common meaning such as *brotherhood* and
unspoken bond. If a single subject made repeated mention of the term, whether
within the description of a single handshake or when describing more than one handshake, the multiple occurrence of the term was still considered as only one unit.
The total number of occurrences of each term was established by counting the number of subjects that mentioned it at least once. Comparative qualifiers such as
more intimate and *less friendly* were listed as simple qualifiers, *intimate, friendly*. Synonomous terms such as *typically black* and *typical of black, aggressive* and
aggression were listed only in one form, but were counted according to use by different subjects.

1. Categories of Sentence Meaning

A series of significant categories was established in order to compare the three
groups. Under each category heading the subject responses were transcribed verbatim for each of the three encounters and the general comment which the subjects
wrote at the end of the test.

     Category A: Mention of soul handshake as a form of ingroup identificat-
ion. All groups mention the ingroup function of the handshake. The number of

subjects who refer to the bonding nature of the soul handshake for each group are
as follows: (numbers in each list denote the number assigned the subject, not the
number of subjects):

Neutral Group	Negative Group	Positive Group
1	13	32
2	14	33
3	15	34
4	17	39
7	23	40
8	27	42
11	28	43
20	29	44
21	30	45
		47
9*	9*	
		10*

*Denotes total number of subjects

There is a striking difference between the groups. Only the negatively influenced
subjects mention the fact that an ingroup identification mark by definition also
serves the function of keeping the outgroup outside. The excluding function is
mentioned by four subjects (14, 23, 27, 30). In only one instance (30, general
comments) this is referred to in a manner clearly hostile to whites; but, interestingly, the subject adds that the black culture "retaliates against the majority"
who does "not let them into jobs and keeps them from making as much money as whites
which holds them back from the educational achievement and social status of whites".

Category B: Mention of fact that other groups, too, have special types
of handshakes. Here, too, there is a marked difference between the groups. The
fact that blacks are not the only ones to practice "secret" handshakes is mentioned
three times each in the neutral group (3, 11. 20) and in the positive group (32,
44, 47), but only once (30) in the negatively-influenced group.

Category C: Comparison of the soul handshake with the average white
handshake. Several subjects remarked that the grip is not the "standard" (18),
"conventional" (33) way to shake hands. Their number divided by groups is as follows: (numbers in each list denote the number assigned to the subject, not the
number of subjects):

Neutral Group	Negative Group	Positive Group
1	12	33
3	15	35
6	22	37
8	31	38
10		39
18	4*	42
19		45
20		46
8*		8*

*Denotes total number of subjects

In the neutral and in the positive group the comparison came more easily than in
the negatively-influenced group, which mentioned it half as often.

The subjects fall into two types: those that adopt the anthropological and those

that adopt the sociological model for their cross-cultural comparison. For the
anthropologist all forms of behaviour are described in their own right, as independent units, whereas sociologists tend to establish a norm, and behaviours are
described in relation to their conformity or deviance from said norm.
A good example for the anthropological model is subject no.39: *I see nothing wrong
with the handshake other than it is different from what many people are accustomed
to.* The sociological model is used by subject no.31: *I personally feel like it
will eventually fade as the blacks are able to integrate more and more into society.*

Given the brevity of the comments one cannot always be fully certain about their
classification. Keeping this proviso in mind, the following dichotomy must be
considered only tentative.

Anthropological Model	Sociological Model
1 (neutral)	6 (neutral)
3 (neutral)	8 (neutral)
12 (negative)	18 (neutral)
15 (negative)	19 (neutral)
22 (negative)	20 (neutral)
32 (positive)	31 (negative)
39 (positive)	37 (positive)
44 (positive)	
	7*
8*	

*Denotes total number of subjects

Among the negatively-influenced subjects, three (12, 15, 22) followed the anthropological model and only one (31) utilized the sociological model. From the neutral group, on the contrary, five subjects (6, 8, 18, 19, 20) selected the sociological model against two (1, 3) who favoured the anthropological model. Fewer
subjects in the negatively-influenced group than in the neutral group had compared
the black handshake initially. Therefore, the preference for the anthropological
model could possibly be explained in reason of a greater detachment, but no firm
conclusion can be drawn from the data. All comments, independent of whatever group
the subjects belong to, show genuine friendliness towards the black people.

     Category D: Physical qualities. One subject (15) wrote that "blacks
have traditionally been very physically-oriented people. Therefore, we can expect
this type of handshake". This remark prompted a search for comments on physical
movements that would be considered peculiar to blacks.

Four subjects in the neutral group (2, 4, 21, 22) and four subjects in the negatively-influenced group (12, 15, 23, 30) made some mention of physical qualities.
In the neutral group only one such mention (by subject no.2) gave specifics, while
in the negatively-influenced group three very specific movements were mentioned
(by subjects nos.12, 23, 30). The positively-influenced group included only two
subjects (32, 47). One might conclude that the negatively-influenced subjects
were more perceptive, possibly because they looked for more differentiating features. The physical motions mentioned in detail are the following:

Neutral Group

   Subject no.2: *The fluidity of motion is combined with imagination.*

Negatively-influenced Group

   Subject no.12: *In this handshake the participants seem to be more vigorously
               expressing emotion. It passes a current from one man to the other.*

Subject no.23: *the grace and fluidity of the handshake...very dance-like quality.*

Subject no.30: *Something rhythmic.*

Positively-influenced Group

Subject no.32: *They are really the same as kisses.*

Subject no.47: *Hands in slow motion were very expressive - sensual.*

      Category E: Mention of friendliness or happiness. Throughout the test papers, the greeters were seen as full of joy in the first encounter. The other two encounters were occasionally perceived as joyous, but still replete with contentment. When the papers were divided by groups it appeared that the strongest statements in that sense came from the negatively-influenced group (13, 15, 23, 24, 26, 27, 28, 30). In the neutral group only two subjects (1, 9) actually made such observations against the eight in the negative group. In the positive five subjects (32, 33, 34, 37, 41) mention happiness and laughter, but on the whole their wording is not as strong as in the negative group.

Similar to the findings for Category D, the negatively-influenced subjects are those who see the most attractive traits in blacks as they greet each other. They find these black encounters "jubilant" (23), full of "mutual happiness" (13), and a "euphoric feeling of satisfaction, approval and acceptance" (15); whereas the subjects in the neutral group do not go beyond such quiet statements as "very friendly" (22), "laughing, smiling and sharing humour" (9).

      Category F: Mention of aggressiveness in the behaviour of the greeters. The first and second author and two among the judges who were asked whether they thought that the three different pre-testing approaches would produce significantly different test results, hypothesized that the negatively-influenced subjects would transfer the feeling of hostility and discover traits of aggressiveness and violence in the personality of the greeters. This hypothesis was not borne out by the data. The three subjects in the negative group (24, 26, 30) who made mention of aggressive features were equally matched by three subjects in the neutral group (4, 8, 18) and by two in the positively-influenced group (37, 44). There were four remarks indicating very strong hostility; *vented anger* (no.30 from the negatively-influenced group), *disguised aggression* (no.4 from the neutral group), *enthusiasm for the hitting* (no.37 from the positive group) and *wrestler's grip - no fooling* (no.44 from the positive group). It is in the neutral group that the most violent of all descriptions can be found. *This seems like a greeting of rival gang members that one sees in Harlem when they occasionally meet to discuss the territory* (4).

The culture norms for courtesy vary greatly among white and black Americans. Cross-cultural misunderstandings did indeed happen when observing the third encounter. The young man on the right ends the handshake by turning his back to the other while their fingers are still clasped. This motion causes the other's fingers to slide from his hand. Although the manner was graceful, the departure could be considered abrupt.

One subject (no.18 from the neutral group) noticed that "he breaks off interaction by turning away, not backing away. They had a very aggressive handshake at first." One subject from the positive group wrote: "Jerk passes ending in a sort of slide away from the other person."

2. Categories of Lexical Meanings

Similar to the test results from the sentence-based categorization, the results
from the lexically-based categorization do indicate that pre-testing influences
have little, if any, influence on the judgement of the subjects.

Key words were selected for the comparison of qualifying attributes. When mentioned at least once (disregarding repeated occurrences by the same subject) the ratio
for the qualifying terms in the three groups is as follows:

Key Word/s	Neutral Group	Negative Group	Positive Group
Racial difference	20	17	12
Strangeness	4	3	1
Ritualistic aspect	20	16	11
Brotherhood	39	37	22
Creativity	13	10	11
Happiness	9	17	12
Bodily movement	9	15	6
Aggressiveness	7	12	3
Social status	3	0	0
Feelings	2	9	5

In this particular test the subjects' opinion was not consistently swayed in one
direction or the other by what the experimenter had told them (see sentence categories). The experimenter did, however, have a significant impact on the attention subjects paid to the task, or rather, on the manner in which they approached
their task (see word categories).

The comparison of the qualifying words yielded the following results between the
neutral and the negative groups:
No significant difference emerged between terms denoting *racial difference* (20:17),
brotherhood (39:37) and *strangeness* (4:3). A slight difference emerged between
terms denoting *ritualistic aspects* (20:16) and *creativity* (13:10). The difference
was significant between terms denoting *happiness* (9:17), *bodily movement* (9:15),
aggressiveness (7:12), *social status* (3:0) and *feelings* (2:9).

If any conclusion can be drawn from these data it is that the negatively-influenced
group was more emotionally involved when viewing the tapes. This group has a consistently higher ratio of terms that carry an emotional content than any other
group. Terms of *feeling* occur three times as often as in the neutral group; terms
denoting *happiness* occur almost twice as frequently; terms of *aggressiveness*, equally, occur almost twice; and terms referring to *bodily movements* occur one-third
more often. *Social status* mentioned three times in the neutral group was totally
ignored by the group which had been negatively influenced. In conclusion, a
greater emotional involvement does not imply that subjects lose their sense of
judgement. It only implies that they judge with a heightened degree of involvement.

Given the disparity in the length of the papers of the positive group compared to
the two other groups, it is difficult to establish a fair ratio for the use of
qualifying words. As it is uncertain whether the brevity of the papers from the
positively-influenced group was significant or accidental it could not be justified to adjust the ratio of qualifying words by 36%. Nonetheless, one feature is
starkly apparent - the low number of aggressive terms. The neutral group has
seven aggressive terms; the negatively-influenced group jumps to thirteen; and the
positively-influenced group only has three. The final conclusion from the test
results is that pre-test influencing of subjects does not necessarily affect their
judgement, but has a strong bearing on their strategy. With reference to judgement, one can safely conclude with a quote from the general comments of subject

no.35: *No big deal! I mean, really - so what?*

DESCRIPTIVE OBSERVATIONS

The analysis of the description of the hand motions performed by the greeters was
divided into two parts. In Part I the step-by-step description of the physical
events was evaluated. Part II gives special consideration to the mention of the
word *fist* to denote the formation of the hand into the balled position.

1. Number of Kinesic Details Reported in Descriptions

The various motions were divided into units, with each unit being assigned one
point. The responses were evaluated for the frequency of units reported. Some
subjects did not recall the exact sequence of the units. Credit was given for the
total number of units without regard for the proper sequencing or when some minor
detail was missing in the unit. Erroneous interpretations were disregarded (neither given credit nor deducted any number of points). Eye contact was mentioned by
three subjects, but these observations were not credited as a kinesic unit. Time
constraint made it impossible to evaluate eye gaze, proxemics and other nonverbal
aspects. The only facial mimicry that was included was laughing at Handshake I
because of its frequent mention by the subjects. The frequent mention of the smiling face is due to the fact that when looking at somebody it is natural to look at
his face first of all. Facial mimicry seems to be the most important aspect of
nonverbal behaviour which is observed and evaluated by the viewer. This fact may
also explain the absolute frequency of the word *friendly* in the list of qualifying
terms.

The following represents the list of kinesic units for each of the three handshakes.
Some motions that technically could have been considered as separate units were
combined because their sequence was so rapid that they were best judged as a single
motion. The narrative description of the three communicative events is available
in Appendix 2.

DESCRIPTIVE OBSERVATIONS

1. Number of Kinesic Details Reported in Descriptions

Handshake I

A   Thumblock: greeters interlock right thumbs with one another, laying
    fingers on each other's wrist.
B   Single shake.
C   Thumbs open; fingers slide against each other.
D   Interlock ends of fingers in cupped or curled position.
E   Single shake in that position.
F   *Blood knock*: hands balled to fist.
G   Each hits top and bottom of other's fist.
H   Start to repeat *Blood knock* and miss.
I   Exit laughing.

Handshake II

A   *Give me some skin* or *Give me five*: one person holds out the palm
    of the hand and the other person slaps his hand.
B   Thumblock: the persons lock the thumbs while placing the fingers
    on each other's wrist.
C   Thumbs open and palms slide against each other.
D   A firm grip is made with each other's finger tips.

DESCRIPTIVE OBSERVATIONS continued

Handshake II

E *The Pound:* shake in that position as they bring left hands and hit other's backhand. One greeter holds a briefcase with the hand that hits the backhand.
F *Give me skin.*
G *Give me skin.*

Handshake III

A *Give me some skin:* one person holds out the palm of the hand and the other person slaps his hand.
B Thumblock. Palms glide against one another to C position.
C Cupped fingers.
D Shake.
E *The Pound:* left fist hits other's backhand still in clasp. The hit occurs as clasped hands are in downward movement of shake.
F Pocketbook drops off right shoulder of one greeter. He reaches across with left hand, but maintains clasp.
G The clasp turns over with one backhand on top during the pocketbook adjustment. One greeter begins turning around causing the shake to end by:
H The index and middle fingers sliding slowly through the other's hand.

In all three groups, the hand positions most frequently noticed were those requiring a hitting of fists: the Blood Knock and the Pound. Their distribution in kinesic points is as follows:

	Handshake I	Neutral group	-ve group	+ve group		Handshake II	Neutral group	-ve group	+ve group		Handshake III	Neutral group	-ve group	+ve group
Blood Knock														
Pound	F	7	5	9		E	8	6	10		E	8	9	12

The total of kinesic points earned in the neutral group and in the negatively-influenced group are about equal (77:71). The total for the positively-influenced group is 35.6% greater than the other groups (113). The higher ratio of the positively-influenced group is particularly significant in view of the fact that these papers are shorter than those of the other two groups. There again, the pre-testing influence has affected the subjects' strategy. Contrary to an original prediction that the negatively-influenced group would be the most perceptive, it was the positively-influenced group whose perception was keenest. In the positively-influenced group, there were fewer students majoring in the humanities. This fact may have some bearing on their greater precision in describing physical detail objectively. The distribution of humanities majors across the groups was not clear-cut enough to indicate any effect on descriptive ability. One can safely conclude that the pre-testing influence determined the strategy of the subjects.

2. The Fist

All three pairs of greeters perform the Blood Knock or the Pound. Although Cooke (1972:61) includes the formation of the fist in association with the black power salute, none of the black persons interviewed by the three authors thought there was a relationship between the black power salute (with raised fist) and the Blood Knock or Pound. The greeting fists have nothing in common with the power fist except the physical shape of the hand which is incidental. White people may not be

aware of this. Some subjects did not appear to relate the fists they saw on the
screen with the black power fist. Subject no.10 from the neutral group jokingly
wrote of "a lot of bumping of fists (cf., one potato, two potato)". Subject no.17
from the negatively-influenced group describes the motion in similar, friendly
terms: "When they hit fists, laughing, a collision of friends." Many subjects, on
the contrary, did indeed relate the greeting fists of the Blood Knock and the
Pound to the fists of the black power salute.

One subject in the negatively-influenced group (12) actually recalled the fist seen
on the screen in the exact terms of the power salute. In her paper this "last step
before departure is the commonly used gesture of the closed fist with raised elbow."
In actuality, there was no raised elbow, only a slight forward thrust of the fore-
arm in order to hit the other's hand.

Divided by groups, the following subjects associated the fist of the soul shake
with the fist of the power salute:

Association of Fist with Power Salute
(The numbers in each list denote the code number assigned the subject, not the
number of subjects).

Neutral Group	Negative Group	Positive Group
3	12	
4	14 (by implication)	
6	17 (by implication)	
18		
4*	3*	0*

*Denotes total number of subjects

No relevant difference can thus be established among the groups except for the
fact that the neutral group is more explicit in actually using the word *power* more
frequently than the other group.

Not all subjects mention the word *fist* in their descriptions. Those that mention
it are equally distributed among the groups. The following chart shows the number
of times the word *fist* is used at least once in the description of each encounter.
(Each occurrence of the word *fist* was counted regardless of whether it was repeated
by the same subject or across subjects. Number 4 could indicate that one subject
referred to the word four times or that four subjects referred to it once each).

Mention of Fist
(The numbers in each list denote the code number assigned the subject, not the
number of subjects).

Neutral Group	Negative Group	Positive Group
6	4	8 in Handshake I
4	1	2 in Handshake II
4	7	9 in Handshake III
0	2	1 in General Comm-
		ents
14*	14*	20*

*Denotes total number of occurrences

There was, however, one significant difference between the groups. It is only in
the negatively and positively-influenced groups that mention is made of violence
in this connection. In the negatively-influenced group subject no.26 writes that
"the way they clinch their fists and drew them back towards themselves indicates
some hostility, or at least some reservation between the two." Subject no.14

comments that it "could symbolize the brutality of the white from the outside". In the positively-influenced group, subject no.37 states "more violent quality, fists this time". Comparison of the three groups is totally inconclusive.

The report from the three coders of the video-taped subjects in the process of taking the test was extremely interesting. All three coders correctly identified the neutral and the positive groups. Coder no.1 (F, 25 years old) identified all groups correctly. Coder no.2 (M, 63 years old) thought that the second group was positive-to-neutral and Coder no.3 (F, 50 years old) classified the second group with the neutral one.

The two erroneous interpretations of the second group, most probably, are due to the fact that the subjects qua persons had no negative attitude towards what they saw. As stated earlier, their judgement was not affected by the pre-test influence, only their strategy.

Subsequently, the 45 unmarked papers were given to five independent judges. They were requested to sort the papers into three files, each file representing the original group. The judges, all female, ranged in age from 13 to 33. The result of their sorting is totally random. Two sorters classified 46.6% correctly; one subject classified 35.5% correctly; and, two classified 33-1/3% correctly. The group percentage for correct identification is 39.06%.

Comparison of percentage of correct responses between the three groups showed complete randomness. As stated above, the comparison of the sentence-based meanings with lexical usage resulted in the distinction of judgement and strategy on the part of the subjects. Comparing the results from the rating of the video-tapes with the results from the ratings from the writing papers, the same conclusion was apparent. The subjects' judgement as expressed in their written test papers was not affected by pre-testing influence. On the contrary, subjects' approach to the task, manifested in their nonverbal self-expressions, was affected by pre-testing influence.

Given the small number of coders of nonverbal behaviour, the interpretation presented here may not be fully conclusive, but certainly warrants further investigation of the subject utilizing a larger number of judges.

Categorizing the subjects by academic major, the following distribution emerged:

	Social Science	Natural Science	Humanities	Undeclared
Neutral Group	3	1	7	4
Negative Group	5-1/3*	3	3-2/3*	3
Positive Group	4-1/2*	5	4-1/2*	1

*Fractions represent multiple majors by one person

The distribution by sex was the following:

	Male	Female
Neutral Group	10	5
Negatively-influenced Group	4	11
Positively-influenced Group	10	5
Total	24	21

Sex did not appear to be a significant factor in over-all subject response.

CONCLUSIONS

The sympathetic disposition towards this particular form of greeting was practic-
ally unanimous. There was no difference in attitude between the three groups.
The experimenter had no effect on the subjects' judgement. The experimenter was
influential with regard to the strategy by which the students approached the task.
The subjects in the negatively-influenced group were the only ones that mentioned
that a symbol intended to foster ingroup solidarity is also meant to exclude the
outgroup. In the positively-influenced group the subjects were more co-operative
in following the instructions carefully and obviously had a heightened sense of
perception.

The basic similarity of evaluation of events among the subjects explains why the
raters who sorted the papers into three groups totally failed at the task. The
difference in strategy among the subjects explains how the coders asked to assign
them to the pertinent groups by the way subjects looked during the test were successful.

Neutral and negative clustered together against the positive. The positively-influenced group would be likely to assume the pre-testing statements as true, since
no personal challenge of their white status quo position was made. Usually people
will eagerly accept statements that are favourable to them. However, the negatively-influenced group, when told the gesture was antagonistic to the white culture,
would be likely to challenge this statement as it involved them. To assume a negative statement to be true would be unlikely, as it is not fashionably intelligent
within the college community to accept racial bias. Theoretically, it could not
be ruled out that apparent unconcern with supposed hostility may indicate an attitude of racial superiority that had no concern for the opinion of the people who
have traditionally been considered inferior. The degree of either of these attitudes is impossible to assess.

It appears that the judgement of the subjects was not affected by pre-testing influence. Subjects in all groups showed a friendly attitude towards the soul handshake. The pre-testing influence, however, affected their strategy in evaluating
the tapes in order to arrive at that identical conclusion. Papers from the positively-influenced group contain only three aggressive terms, where the neutral group
has seven such terms. In the negatively-influenced group the number of aggressive
terms jumps to thirteen. Saying that a greeting is *not aggressive* implies that the
speaker considered the possibility of aggressiveness before deciding against it.

REFERENCES

Cooke, B.G. (1972) Nonverbal communication among Afro-Americans: An initial class-
    ification, pp.32-64, in T. Kochman (ed.): Rappin' and stylin' out, University
    of Illinois Press, Urbana, Ill.

Elliott, J.C. (1977) The soul handshake, pp.287-290, in W. von Raffler-Engel &
    B. Hoffer (eds.): Aspects of nonverbal communication, Trinity University,
    San Antonio, Texas.

von Raffler-Engel, W. (1974) Language in context: Situationally conditioned style
    change in Black English, pp.757-763, in L. Heilmann (ed.): Proceedings of the
    XIth International Congress of Linguists, University of Bologna, Italy, 1972,
    Il Mulino, Bologna, Italy

von Raffler-Engel, W. (in press) Kinesic awareness in intercultural interaction,
    in R. St.Clair & H. Giles (eds.): The social and psychological context of
    language, Laurence Erlbaum, New York. A preliminary version of the article
    appeared in A.G. Lozano (ed.): Proceedings of the VIIth Southwestern Area
    Languages and Linguistics Workshop, University of Colorado at Boulder, 1978,
    University of Colorado, Boulder, Colo.

APPENDIX 1

SUBJECTS' DEMOGRAPHIC DATA

1. neutral	2. neutral	3. neutral	4. neutral	6. neutral
Female 1952	Male 1956	Male 1958	Female 1958	Male 1958
Rochester, NY	Bethpage, NY	Atlanta, Grg.	Pensacola, FL	Albany, Grg.
Junior	Graduate 1	Junior	Senior	Junior
Classics	English	Econ./Eng.	Philosophy	Eng./History

7. neutral	8. neutral	9. neutral	10. neutral	11. neutral
Female 1958	Male 1958	Male 1942	Male 1949	Female 1950
Kansas City, Mo.	Elkhart, Ind.	Brooklyn, NY	Bronx, NY	St.Louis, Mo.
Junior	Sophomore	Unclassified	Unclassified	Unclassified
Psychology	Undeclared	Indep. Study	Indep. Study	Indep. Study

12. negative	13. negative	14. negative	15. negative	16. negative
Female 1959	Male 1957	Female 1959	Male 1956	Female 1953
Huntsville, Ala.	Winston Salem, NT	Houston, TX	Barranquilla,SA.	Sayre, Pa.
Sophomore	Freshman	Sophomore	Senior	Graduate 3
Undeclared	Eng./History	Undeclared	Chem. Eng.	Philosophy

17. negative	18. neutral	19 neutral	20. neutral	21. neutral
Female 1956	Male 1958	Male 1957	Male 1957	Male 1957
Birmingham, Ala.	Nashville, TN	Humboldt, TN	Ashland, KY	Fayetteville,NC
Senior	Junior	Senior	Senior	Senior
French	Eng./Geology	History	Business Adm.	Physics/Sociol.

22. neutral	23. negative	24. negative	25. negative	26. negative
Female 1957	Female 1956	Male 1954	Female 1959	Female 1956
Lookout Mount. TN	Houston, TX	Houston, TX	Olney, Ill.	Dallas, TX
Senior	Graduate 1	Senior	Sophomore	Junior
History	Anthropology	Civil eng.	Undeclared	Political Sci.

27. negative	28. negative	29. negative	30. negative	31. negative
Female 1958	Female 1959	Female 1959	Female 1957	Male 1956
Washington, DC	Louisville, KY	Nashville, TN	Athens, TN	Colorado Spr.
Junior	Sophomore	Sophomore	Senior	Senior
Sociol./Psychol.	German	Economics	Business Adm.	Biomedical Eng.

APPENDIX 1 continued

32. positive	33. positive	34. positive	35. positive	37. positive
Male 1961	Female 1962	Male 1958	Male 1957	Female 1958
New York City, NY	Columbia, Mo.	Denver, Co.	Oradell. NJ	Little Rock,Ark
Rising Freshman	Rising Freshman	Junior	Senior	Senior
Bus. (Film-making)	English	Econ./Bus.	English	Drama

38. positive	39. positive	40. positive	41. positive	42. positive
Male 1960	Male 1957	Female 1959	Female ?	Male 1956
Huntsville, Ala.	Nashville, TN	Hyattsville, Md.	Alexandria, VA	Memphis, TN
Freshman	Senior	Sophomore	Senior	Senior
Physics	Civil Eng.	Undeclared	English	Business

43. positive	44. positive	45. positive	46. positive	47. positive
Male 1958	Male 1958	Male ?	Male 1957	Female 1958
Nashville, TN	Winchester, KY	Boston, Mass.	Arlington, Eng	Louisville, KY
Sophomore	Junior	Junior	Senior	Junior
Mech. Eng.	Business	Comp. Science	Psychology	Psychology

APPENDIX 2

A STEP-BY-STEP DESCRIPTION OF THE SOUL HANDSHAKES

Most of the handshakes are a combination of different motions with the hands and
the fingers.

Handshake I:

The acquaintances quickly approach each other. The young man to the left calls
"What's happening?" The other answers, "Hey, buddy", raising his hand first for
the *thumblock*. They grasp right hands, interlocking thumbs and laying fingers on
the wrist of the other person. One shake occurs in this position. Then the hands
glide over the palm, pulling hand back towards oneself, thumbs up, until one another's fingertips are touching. The fingertips are grasped in a curled or cupped
manner; and then they shake once in same position. Afterwards each person balls
his fist and hits the top and bottom of the other's fist. This hand motion is
called the *Blood Knock*. An attempt is made to repeat the *Blood Knock*, but the
young men do not make contact with the fists. The person on the right bends forward and is laughing as he exits, crossing to the left.

Handshake II:

The two young men approach one another, raising hands near chest level. They stop
a couple of feet apart with extended hands dropped just above the waist. They use
the handshake which accompanies the expression, *Give me some skin*, or *Give me five*.
One person extends the hand, palm upward, horizontally, while the other person
slaps it. Then the two persons use the soul handshake. After the thumblock, where
the fingers are placed on the other's wrist with interlocking thumbs, there is no
shake, but a gliding motion where the fingers are pulled backwards across the palm.
A firm grip is made with the fingertips. *The Pound* follows: the outer left hands
are brought in hitting against the backhand of the clasp. *The Pound* occurs while
the finger clasped right hands are shaking. (The young man to the right holds a
briefcase in his left hand. He brings the case in and taps the clasped hands; this
article obscures the other's fist during the pound). Then the two acquaintances
slap hands twice in "Give me skin" fashion. They step backwards facing each other.

Handshake III:

While walking towards each other the young man on the left slowly raises his right
hand in an overhand stroke. They begin the greeting with the slapping of the hand
which is generally referred to as "Give me some skin". They drop hands briefly
and rejoin hands in the *Thumblock*. Each person locks his hand around the other's
thumb and makes a firm grip. The palms slide against one another until the fingertips join in a curled grasp. *The Pound* follows: the left hands, fisted, swing in-
ward and rap the backhand of the clasp twice on the downward movement of the shake.
A pocketbook drops off the right shoulder of the person on the left. He reaches
across with his left hand to pick up the strap. The clasp is maintained during
this adjustment. When placing the strap on his shoulder, the clasped hands turn
over from a sideward to top-bottom position. The young man on the right begins
turning his back to the other which causes the grip to loosen. The young man on
the left lets his index and middle fingers slowly slide from the other's hand.

LANGUAGE RESURRECTION: A LANGUAGE PLAN FOR ETHNIC INTERACTION

C. M. Eastman

University of Washington, Seattle, U.S.A.

Many scholars see language as crucial to the maintenance of ethnic identity and some even feel it to be *the* most singular mark of distinctive ethnicity. Yet as DeVos (1975:15) observed "...ethnicity is frequently related more to the symbol of a separate language than to its actual use by all members of a group". Gaelic, as a symbol of Celtic ethnicity, is important to the Irish but the ability to speak it is not a requisite of group membership (op.cit.). This point has some interesting ramifications for sociolinguists and for the purpose of this paper.

Sociolinguistic research is concerned with describing speech use in context and with examining phenomena such as relative prestige values attached to different styles of speech or to social dialects. It is the purpose of this paper to broaden the scope of concern of sociolinguistics - particularly the branch dealing with language policy and planning - to include a different definition of language. This "language" is a set of speech elements which reflects culturally-specific items.

Such a definition of language differs from the structuralist's idea of *parole* as instances of a particular linguistic system (*langue*) and also differs from *performance* as what people do with their linguistic knowledge or *competence*. While this "language" like *parole* and *performance* refers to language's use functions, it reflects cultural or behavioural usage concepts rather than linguistic or speech usage concepts.

This definition of language is implicit in DeVos's comment (1975:16) that:

> "Group identity can even be maintained by minor differences
> in linguistic patterns and by styles of gesture. There are
> a wide variety of ways in which language patterning fluency
> or lack of fluency in a second language is related to ident-
> ity maintenance. Changing patterns within groups are relat-
> ed to the sanctioning positively or negatively of specific
> dialects..."

Modern societies, necessarily heterogeneous, are striving to preserve the ethnic identity of their components while at the same time they are endeavouring to instil socio-cultural consciousness in the interest of a unified and functional visibility in the world. To be effective, such societies generally adopt a single language, a language of wider communication (LWC), whether designated national, official or standard, which is then encouraged by government policy and represents a linguistic avenue to individual and societal success politically and socio-econ-

215

omically. Such LWC are often either alien or unknown to a large number of the society's population. For example, in the Pacific southwestern part of the United
States, in the late 19th and early 20th century, English as an LWC was alien to
many American Indian groups. Today, many Spanish-speaking persons in the United
States do not know English. In East Africa, English was an LWC not known by many
Kenyans and Tanzanians. Today Swahili is being encouraged there and it, too, is
unknown by many persons in non-coastal areas of Kenya and Tanzania.

Still, at the sub-societal or sub-cultural level, language remains a factor of
ethnic identity. In Kenya, Kikuyu people are those who know, or whose parents know
Kikuyu, whether or not they also know and use Swahili and/or English. In New York
City, Spanish is a factor of ethnic identity among many people while various groups
on the northwest coast of the United States value their linguistic heritage - even
if their particular languages are rapidly becoming extinct. The American Indian
situation is different from the Spanish-speaking and Kikuyu-speaking situations in
the midst of an English or Swahili-dominant society. The distinction is important
to the plan being proposed here. What we will see to be *language resurrection* is
a plan that is particularly suited to languages (unlike Spanish and Kikuyu) which
no longer are used communicatively but which are important aspects of group ethnic
identity.

Such languages that function as a factor of ethnic identity do not involve speech
in communicational use, but rather a stock of vocabulary reflecting cultural concepts. These languages, at non-state-wide levels of society, which function in
ethnic identity are symbolic of cultural "languages". It is the Gaelic of the
ethnic Celt yet non-Gaelic speaking Irish person of DeVos's example cited above.
It is also the language that various groups in the English-speaking United States
have that contributes to their self-definition and also to their American-ness -
a status that *all* Americans have, as the airline commercial says, symbolizing their
"two heritages" (cf., Pan American Airways television commercials, Winter, 1978).

Language resurrection refers to the elaboration of an idea in some previous papers
(Eastman, 1976, 1978) that in certain non-nation/state-wide or sub-sociocultural
unit contexts, a feasible language plan can be devised which can function both to
facilitate the preservation of individual ethnic identities in complex societies
and to simultaneously foster the requisite ethnic interaction needed for such societies to function as unified wholes. What follows is an outline and further development of this idea that where a number of groups exist in a heterogeneous society which has a designated LWC and where these groups within the society no longer possess their indigenous, mother or native tongues as a means of communication,
it is practical and productive to resurrect the groups' languages as a way to institute a sense of group culture and to effect ethnic interaction.

Where language resurrection plans are feasible, it is necessary that some persons
must be available who still know the language but who rarely, if ever, use it. In
Pacific northwestern North America there are a number of older American Indians
who know their respective native languages but who seldom have an opportunity to
use them. A language resurrection plan is particularly feasible in this context.
In general, among ethnic groups where the groups' languages are not used for communication but nevertheless are retained by some members and valued by others as a
part of their cultural heritage, resurrection plans might be considered. Conversely, such plans are not advocated where group languages remain communicationally
viable yet differ from the LWC.

THE PLAN

In the field of general linguistics, one period in the 1950's is marked by a notion
that there are certain words in all languages that are "culture-free" (e.g.,

Swadesh, 1952). Such words comprise the part of vocabulary which was thought to
be unlikely to change - pronouns, numerals, body parts - in any language. Unfortunately, it appears unlikely that any such list of words can be compiled due to
problems of translation from one language to another, non-overlapping ranges of usage for lexical items in the different languages, and so forth. There is also no
way to empirically validate an assumption that a culture-free vocabulary exists.
But, on the other hand, it might be valid to conceive of different languages as having instead specific "culture-loaded" vocabularies. Items in such a vocabulary, as
culture-free items were meant to be, would be "words" but not of any general Basic
Vocabulary but rather culturally specific terms peculiar to different ethnic groups
rather than common to all. Instead of being translatable cross-linguistically, they
would be the items for which there is usually no equivalent term in translation or
lexical range in the LWC fostered by the sociocultural entity. Included would be
monolexemic items in the groups' languages for which the dominant linguistic entity
would require a phrase, a number of vocabulary items or a periphrastic construction.
A vocabulary for Eskimo language groups, to exploit Whorf's classic example, would
include each of the words for snow as separate items, not just a single word equivalent to match the one word in English.

In fact, in some cases, even words thought to be culture-free such as body parts
(e.g., where hand and arm are a single lexical item in the non-dominant language
but separate in the LWC) and pronouns (e.g., where gender is distinguished pronom-
inally in one language but not in the other) would occur in a culture-loaded word
list instead. Other likely items in a culture-loaded word list would be names of
characters, spirits or beings from particular cultural groups' lore or mythology,
terms of reference for different kin types reflecting the different systems of kin-
ship rather than those all cultures share, labels for items of folk art, crafts,
cosmology and the like.

For example, in the North American Indian language Haida[1], there is a word *(xəgith)*
which designates the legendary Alaskan version of the Abominable Snowman or Big
Foot creature. All Haida know about *(xəgith)* yet the word defies translation into
English connotatively, denotatively and emotionally. Another Haida word *(dəgwan)*
which is roughly translatable as *darling* has a range of reference far wider than
that of English such that it refers to either sex when spoken by either sex and may
be used reciprocally across generations. Other types of culturally loaded vocabulary include the words for moiety[2] and clans and their labelled sub-categories (e.g.,
Eagle, Raven, Bear, etc.), the words for bentwood box, oolichan oil, herring eggs,
halibut hook, and the vast number of dialect monolexemic labels for salmon.

What constitutes such a cultural vocabulary may often be gleaned, in part at least,
from the ethnographic literature dealing with the culture of the language's speakers
where mention is made of customs, practices and "things" deemed exotic or worth describing in that culture by early explorers and/or ethnographers. Further, this
vocabulary includes what the first generation of non-native speakers retains of vocabulary stock from their native-speaking parents.

---

[1]Haida is a linguistic isolate spoken on the Queen Charlotte Islands of British
Columbia, Canada and on Prince of Wales Island in southeast Alaska, U.S.A. Some
Alaskan Haida also live in Seattle, Washington, U.S.A.

[2]The term *moiety* refers to each of two units or tribal divisions based on unilineal
descent. Among the Haida there are the Eagle and Raven moieties and clans such as
Bear, Frog, Killer Whale and so forth.

Once the vocabulary is amassed, it is necessary to write it down. Often the vocabularies come from languages which are unwritten and even undescribed linguistically. As observed elsewhere, (Eastman, 1978) the resurrection or revival of a language in this way is feasible only where the group that no longer possesses the language as a means of communication desires to know it in order to achieve a sense of the heritage of group culture. To accomplish this, then, the next procedure in language resurrection after determining its cultural vocabulary is to develop a practical orthography.

Since the orthography of the LWC accommodates that language, as we might expect, there would be sounds in the vocabulary items retained by ethnic groups from their ancestral language which would require symbols for which there is no obvious orthographic representation. It would be impractical to expect persons who are literate in an LWC to learn IPA (the International Phonetic Alphabet) to solve this problem. Phonetic transcription is also not desirable as a means of recording culture-loaded vocabulary since there are far too many symbols available than needed and the virtue of the alphabet is that it is responsive to changes in pronunciation of spoken vocabulary rather than to standardization. So, practical orthographies are devised which adapt the orthography of the dominant language.

In the Haida word *(ɣəgitʰ)* mentioned above and transcribed phonetically, we have a back post-velar or laryngeal fricative followed by a lower-midcentral vowel, a voiced velar stop, a high front vowel and a final aspirated dental stop. Since Haida people are, for the most part, literate in English, a practical orthographic representation of the word for this creature which is a part of Haida cultural heritage would produce a more familiar looking form /ǥagiit/, with the only symbol unfamiliar to English literate persons being the /g/ with a /-/ through its stem to represent the post-velar or back laryngeal fricative. The "letter" is called "g-line" (gee-line) and the word is spelled "gee-line", a, g, double-ii, t". The /a/ used for the phonetic schwa *(ə)* occasions a double-a to be used for the phonetic *(a)* elsewhere. The double-i is used for a tense or long /i/, that is for the phonetic *(i)* while a single-i represents the lax *(I)*. The word *(dəgwan)* then is orthographically /dagwaan/. For Haida this particular practical orthography was developed at the Haida Language Workshop in Ketchikan, Alaska (1972) by Professor Jack Osteen and Ms. Erma Lawrence.

Often the development of such practical orthographies provides the first instance of a written form for such languages. Once an orthography exists, a cultural vocabulary can be incorporated into the literate world of the general culture bearers. What would occur next in the resurrection process is the training of persons who wish to know and use the orthography to prepare cultural materials. That is, after devising a vocabulary and adapting an orthography for it, the next task is to see that persons gain literacy in the newly defined culture language.

Language resurrection as a plan, to this point in its execution, is a process amounting to a *strategy of reorientation* (cf., Eastman, 1976). In environments (e.g., North America) where native languages were suppressed in the last century in the interest of assimilation, what is being proposed here is that people now be encouraged to find out about and learn an aspect of the language of their ancestors or of the ancestors of their locality in written and usable form if they so desire.

The final step in the resurrection process is to develop "material on the history, literature and culture of the area in the language and to make already existing materials usable and accessible" (Eastman, 1978:10). This constitutes *cultural revival*.

In earlier discussions (Eastman, 1976, 1978) the experience of Powell (1973, 1976)

was cited in a programme ostensibly designed to teach the Quileute[3] language to
Quileute children of Quileute parents who were native speakers of English. Powell's
language project became a culture project and he developed a *de facto* language policy of language reintroduction where what was being asked for was bilingual education in the interest of preserving the Quileute language. There was no Quileute
parole or communicable speech any longer in use in the community. Though the grandparents consisted of some remaining speakers of the language, they had grown up at
a time when, though the speech community shared a Quileute *langue*, its use was
discouraged. When these language-bearers in turn had children, they did not encourage them to learn Quileute so as to protect them from ridicule in the community
now expanded to include English-speaking settlers. In Powell's class in the 1970's
were children who only heard occasional "words" or phrases of Quileute cultural
vocabulary at home. Rather than teaching these children how to speak Quileute,
they were taught about their cultural heritage by means of language resurrection.

> "What the project produced consists of a history booklet and
> guide to the region (in English), a practical orthography
> for the language, children's books (pictures labelled with
> native words), a reading, writing and pronunciation work-
> book for the language, films (e.g., of people performing
> songs in the language), a dictionary and a calendar. In
> the planning stages are books on myth and cultural activit-
> ies and there is now a distant plan to produce a language
> book with lessons and tapes using the audio-lingual approach
> and an ethnography." (Eastman, 1978:12, reporting on Powell,
> 1976).

What Powell did was carry out a programme of redefining Quileute not as language
but culture, by developing a way to write it down, and by training the children
(and young adults) to use the vocabulary and gather new examples of it from their
Quileute-speaking but non-Quileute communicating elders. It might be desirable to
set up programmes expressly to accomplish language resurrection. If the language
resurrected is overtly defined as culture, such a "language" has a practically-
written "culture-loaded" vocabulary used in materials on the history, lore and literature of the area where speakers of the language, now no longer communicationally
used, dwelled and where their descendants remain and retain a non-linguistic ethnicity.

Such a programme to resurrect a language (and transform it from a reflection of
langue to a reflection of a part of a particular culture's ideational code perhaps)
is a form of Language Planning and is best accomplished by sociolinguists - who
would here focus on the *use* of this "culture-language" rather than on the *use* of
"speech language" in culturally significant settings.

Ideally a language programme of this type ought to go on simultaneously with the
analysis and description of the grammar of the language. If possible, descriptive
linguists, working with the remaining speakers (but non-communicators) of the language, should be encouraged in their work for scholarly objectives. In addition,

> "The analysis and descriptive account of the grammar done by
> the descriptive linguist for analytical purposes would en-
> hance the sociolinguist's ability to produce grammar lessons

---

[3]*Quileute* is a Chimakuan language of Pacific northwestern North America spoken by
approximately 10 persons over 60 years of age in La Push, Washington, U.S.A.
(Powell, 1973:41).

in a practical orthography and to consider the language as
a whole in an accurate presentation of the language as culture for pedagogical purposes." (Eastman, 1978:15).

The resurrection of language(s) through language planning activity, when occurring
in multi-ethnic societies, would serve to foster ethnic interaction. In the examples briefly mentioned here, it is already the case that the knowledge of Quileute
"culture language" as resurrected in the State of Washington has increased the
awareness of the English-speaking Americans of the state (including Quileute people) as to the "other" heritage of some state residents and of part of the heritage
of the region's history. The practical orthography and emerging culture vocabulary
of the Haida in southeast Alaska is beginning to facilitate their interaction in
the larger complex culture.

In summary, a Language Resurrection plan in terms of the activities involved and
the outcomes expected can be schematized as follows:

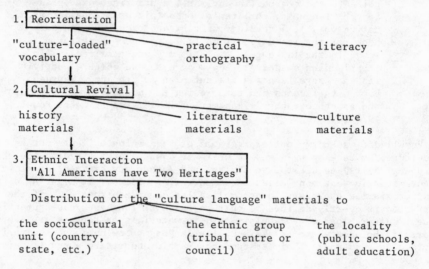

1. Reorientation

"culture-loaded"   practical   literacy
vocabulary   orthography

2. Cultural Revival

history   literature   culture
materials   materials   materials

3. Ethnic Interaction
"All Americans have Two Heritages"

Distribution of the "culture language" materials to

the sociocultural   the ethnic group   the locality
unit (country,   (tribal centre or   (public schools,
state, etc.)   council)   adult education)

CONCLUSION

Clearly the scheme proposed here would work only where an LWC is established and
literacy in that language is already established. The idea of language resurrection is also only practical or practicable where, with regard to language policy,
no other options any longer exist. That is to say, language resurrection as a way
to foster ethnic interaction can only be accomplished where ethnic groups are unlikely to be in a position to demand "recognition as a nationality" (Brass, 1976:
38). The northwest coast of North America where *the* policy had long been to supp-
ress native languages in an effort to accomplish assimilation is such a place.

Language resurrection as reorientation (see diagram above), except for the added
notion of "culture-loaded" vocabulary, conforms precisely to Haugen's definition
of language planning as "the activity of preparing a normative orthography, grammar
and dictionary for the guidance of writers and speakers in a non-homogeneous speech
community" (1959:8). The added facet of cultural revival is what leads to the outcome of ethnic interaction. The chief innovation of the planner in a language
resurrection scheme is the empirical transformation of language seen as instances
of *parole* used in a speech community where a *langue* is shared as a *langage* of communication (cf., DeSaussure, 1916) to language seen as instances of labelled behaviour used in a community which shares an ideational code (cf., Goodenough, 1964).

As noted earlier, what is being proposed here would occasion the broadening of the definition of language used by the sociolinguist. Likewise, where the goal of sociolinguistics is to understand and make explicit the nature of *communicative competence*, the definition of it might be seen to broaden as well. Where, to the sociolinguist, communicative competence is "what a speaker needs to know to *communicate* effectively in culturally significant settings" (Gumperz and Hymes, 1972: vii, italics mine), to the person interested in language resurrection what is to be described is an ability to *behave* appropriately in culturally significant settings - to use culturally significant labels appropriately even when the labels are no longer part of a communicational speech system.

Language resurrection as outlined here would succeed best where literacy in an LWC is well-established and widespread. If the standard form of the LWC is too new and literacy still emergent, practical orthographies are premature. Likewise, a programme of resurrecting a language can only succeed where the language to be resurrected has, for all practical purposes, died out as communicated speech yet still survives in a passive way in a bilingual grandparent generation which continues to pass on cultural traditions. Again the northwest coast is an ideal setting. But, it might be the case that modifications of such a scheme leading to language resurrection might be a useful plan to consider as a means of implementing language for ethnic interaction in other parts of the world.

Language resurrection plans can be implemented by sociolinguists at the request of a particular ethnic group (as the Quileute asked Powell to do) or in co-operation with school systems. It is unlikely that either ethnic communities or local school officials would specifically request a resurrection programme. But, both communities and schools are beginning to seek out linguists more and more to help them either learn their own language (in the case of communities) or deal with multi-lingual/multicultural diversity (in the case of schools). Language resurrection is an option that we, as scientists, may offer communities and schools when both ethnic identity and skill in an LWC are desired goals.

If the notion of a "culture-loaded" word list as the foundation of a language which can be "resurrected" is workable, parameters would need to be worked out and flexibility built in to account for and accommodate change. That is, language planning will need to be done both at a general and a theoretical level as well as at a specific and applied one. We are suggesting here that the sociolinguistic definition of language be broadened to include behaviouro-cultural usage as well as speech-communicational usage. Thus, it would seem that language planners would have a wide new area in which to work towards exploring the relationship between language and ethnic interaction - indeed towards planning for successful ethnic interaction.

REFERENCES

P.R. Brass, Ethnic groups and nationalities: The formation persistence and trans-
    formation of ethnic identities over time, Paper presented at the Conference on
    ethnicity in Eastern Europe, University of Washington (June, 1976).

DeSaussure, F. (1966) Cours de linguistique générale (Course in general linguist-
    ics), Ist Edition, 1916, McGraw-Hill, New York, The Philosophical Library.

DeVos, G. (1975) Ethnic pluralism: Conflict and accommodation, Chapter I in Part
    I of G. DeVos & L. Romannucci-Ross (eds.): Ethnic identity: Cultural continuit-
    ies and change, Mayfield, Palo Alto, California, pp.5-41.

C.M. Eastman, Language reintroduction on the northwest coast as a factor of
    ethnicity and modernization: A suggestion for language policy, Paper presented
    at the Northwest Coast Studies Conference, Simon Fraser University, Vancouver,
    British Columbia (May, 1976).

C.M. Eastman, Language reintroduction: Activity and outcome language planning,
    to appear in General Linguistics, University Park, Pennsylvania (1978).

Goodenough, W. (1964) Introduction, Explorations in cultural anthropology, McGraw-
    Hill, New York.

Gumperz, J.J. & Hymes, D. (1972) Directions in sociolinguistics: The ethnography
    of communication, Holt, Rinehart and Winston, New York.

E. Haugen, Planning for a standard language in modern Norway, Anthropological
    Linguistics, 1, 8-21 (1959).

J.V. Powell, Preparing a second language programme for teaching a Washington
    Indian language, Lecture to Language Learning Colloquium, University of
    Washington (February, 1976).

J.V. Powell, Raising pidgins for fun and profit: A new departure in language
    teaching, Proceedings of the Pacific Northwest Conference on Foreign Lang-
    uages, XVII, 40-43 (1973).

M. Swadesh, Lexico-statistic dating of prehistoric ethnic contacts, Proceedings
    of the American Philosophical Society, 96, 453-462 (1952).

ETHNICITY, VALUES AND LANGUAGE POLICY IN THE UNITED STATES

G. Drake

San Diego State University, San Diego, California, U.S.A.

During the 1960's minority relations in the United States seemed to undergo a dramatic change. As a result of this, language planning policy has become an important activity, especially with respect to bilingual education. There has been massive planning towards the training of populations of students in two languages, either towards the purpose of maintaining the minority tongue or towards the purpose of teaching some skills within a minority tongue in order to assure the educational success of the non-English speaking students. This effort has been supported by massive federal and state funding and by facilitative and, to some extent, coercive legislation and judicial rulings (Epstein, 1978). As in all such movements, the social, economic, and political motivations are complicated. However, it seems to me that one major impetus for the bilingual education movement in the United States has been the widespread assumption that a new social situation has asserted itself in the last two decades as regards the tension between assimilation values - that is, the so-called melting pot notion - and what is generally termed "cultural pluralism". This assumption is embedded in the larger assumption of the "new America". One commentator has written of this assumption:

> "From some time early in the 1960's, perhaps even before the assassination of John F. Kennedy, it was common to believe that the times were exceptional, that events were moving with unaccustomed speed, and that the United States would never again resemble what it had once been. That sentiment became even more pronounced as the decade proceeded; in the late 1960's and early 1970's, when new violence erupted, public confidence and trust were shaken. A host of established institutions, conventions, and opinions seemed suddenly threatened, and there was talk of "revolutionary" change touching much that once seemed permanent and inviolable. No innovation seemed impossible. Why not believe, as many did, that we were witnessing the beginning of a "new" politics, the creation of a "new" generation animated by "new" ideals and values, and responsive to "new" social demands? There was talk of a "new" morality; indeed, of a "new" liberty. The mass media, intentionally or unwittingly, abetted all such expectations; their shortened time horizons contributed to the illusion that institutions were malleable, indeed vulnerable, and that they would necessarily collapse before the violence and passions that were being reported." (Graubard, 1978:v).

As regards ethnicity in this light, here is a typical statement by a social scientist:

> "I am assuming that the 1960's...constitutes a water-shed of
> the 20th century...Cultural pluralism and separatism capture
> the imagination of countless persons...Minorities of every
> kind are now resonating to the claim of the right to be
> different...authenticity (sic), independence, autonomy, self-
> determination or self-sufficiency." (Schemerhorn, 1974:3-4).

And here is a typical statement by a linguist proclaiming a tilt in the social landscape:

> "The social movement (of the last decade) involves...the liq-
> uidation of the assimilationist's mythos...in favour of an
> identificatory policy that seeks out in the social fabric
> that which is unique - ethnically, racially, and most pert-
> inently, linguistically." (Keller, 1976:18).

Thus, there is widely proclaimed a major shift in the values and ideology of the American system.

A bilingual education policy is necessary to the U.S. at this time, but inasmuch as the bilingual education movement is built on the assumption of a major value shift, it is built on shifting sand. The assumption flows from a serious mis-reading of social developments. Furthermore, in this misreading are the seeds for the failure of the bilingual education movement as it is now conceived, a failure that may be just beginning to become apparent. This article suggests how this misreading comes about, why it may be fatal to the bilingual education policy, and, very briefly, alternative bases for establishing bilingual policies.

This discussion focuses on the United States, but the situation may not be unique to the United States, as the problem of pluralism versus assimilation is becoming more and more general in cultures where modernity has invaded and settled.

First, what about the events of the 1960's and 1970's as regards American values? To what extent was the shift in ideology a media event, and to what extent is it rooted in social reality? There is widespread evidence that American values have changed since the 1960's to reject *restrictions* based on race, religion, or nation-ality (Sowell, 1978:220). These changes are signalled by social behaviour, survey responses and voting data. The same pattern and trend are seen in all three areas. In general, there has been a breakdown of employment, educational and intermarriage barriers. Many black officials have been elected by white constituencies. We have had a Catholic president and oriental senators. Other such examples could be cited (Sowell, 1978:218-220).

In the light of these developments, intellectuals in general and those in biling-ual education, in particular, have sweepingly dismissed the "melting pot" notion. *The paradox is that as this once popular concept has been rejected by intellect-uals such as the ones I have quoted above it is actually becoming closer to real-ity* (Sowell, 1978:213). Values have shifted towards tolerance of ethnics but not necessarily in favour of pluralism. Attitudes favouring ethnic inclusion do not necessarily favour the maintainance or even the acknowledgement of ethnic diff-erence. The fact that language planners have not realized this makes plain the crisis in bilingual education today.

For, at the same time that there has been growing acceptance of race and ethnicity in some respects, there is growing evidence of impatience with programmes provid-ing benefits based upon similar ethnic categories. Impatience with quotas and goals in affirmative action programmes has just recently been manifested in the

U.S. Supreme Court in the Bakke case. The widespread opposition to busing to achieve racial balance is another example of impatience with ethnic lines. In addition, there is growing opposition to present bilingual education policies. The
press is increasingly questioning the efficacy of bilingual education programmes.
An example appeared in the *Christian Science Monitor* recently (Henderson, 1978).
This careful, well-researched, and balanced article raises questions about the
government's role in bilingual education and about the lack of evidence of success
of the programmes. A journalist, Noel Epstein (1978) has recently published in
book form an exhaustive historical and policy analysis of bilingual education programmes. In the book, Epstein questions the national government's role in promoting pluralism, as the term is used here. The most damning development of all has
been the release of a recent research report on the impact of a major (Title VII)
national Spanish/English bilingual education programme. This report, the first of
its kind, was prepared by the American Institute for Research and commissioned by
the United States Office of Education. The report shows a lack of significant
gains in the performance or attitudes on the part of children in bilingual education programmes as compared to children in regular classrooms (Epstein, 1978:10-11;
Scott-Blair, 1978).

All of this is evidence of a growing national debate about bilingual education
which signals a crisis in bilingual education policy. The growing opposition to
bilingual education represents a strong continuity of American values that has
been ignored in the general euphoria of the bilingual education movement in the
last several years.

How could language planners have made such a dangerous misreading? For one thing,
in a sense bilingual education advocates have participated in the very events that
they have been investigating. We have become victims of what in the sociology of
knowledge is known as Mannheim's Paradox (Drake, 1978). Our own values have structured our perception of the data or our own seeking after the social good we believe to be the consequence of bilingual education has affected our treatment of
the data. As is usual with ideologies, the central concepts remain fuzzy. Thus,
the concept "bilingual education" can mean many things to many groups. Bilingual
programmes may be acceptable to the society insofar as they facilitate inclusion
of ethnics into the main-stream culture and unacceptable insofar as they set ethnics off from the majority culture. This could help to explain why the aims of
bilingual education have always been so fuzzy. The aim has been in the eye of the
beholder. For assimilationists the aims are seen as transitional, i.e., to provide a transition from the mother tongue to English. Pluralists see linguistic
maintenance as the aim. The programmes are coming under fire now not primarily
because this ambiguity has been exposed, but because of the lack of evidence that
even transition programmes are working. Sociolinguists and other linguists involved in the movement are interested in language diversity, tolerant of it to the
point of celebrating it, and convinced of the general benefit and social good to
be derived from bilingual behaviour. These elements began as scientific inferen-
ces, evolved into values and beliefs, and ended as an ideological system. In such
a subtle and generally nonconscious process it becomes increasingly difficult for
the scientific side to account for evidence that does not accord with ideology.
Objectivity declines in the heat of social passion, except in those sociolinguists
who have cultivated the ability to be at once critical and apologetic towards the
same situation.

Moreover, there have arisen and spread organizations administering to or "representing" racial and ethnic groups in various ways (Sowell, 1978:233). These range
from government organizations such as U.S. Office of Education to such private
groups as El Congresso (National Congress of Hispanic American Citizens) and many
others. The organizations, on the one hand, serve the useful purpose of defining
heretofore incomprehensible social situations, of calling attention to serious
problems, and mobilizing groups to political action. On the other hand, they

create large constituencies with "a vested interest in social pathology and even
aversion to consideration of ethnic success, advance, and development" in the
traditional manner. "Ethnic groups are thus constantly presented to the public in
terms of "minority problems" to be "solved" by spending large sums of tax money."
There may be political advantages in this, but "it has obvious intellectual disadvantages as an approach to reality" (Sowell, 1978:233). In general, these groups
have contributed to the scholarly misperception of the situation.

The general approach to ethnicity in the U.S. by most, but not all, sociolinguists
may be out of touch with reality as well. For example, there has been a failure
to take into account the attitudes of ethnic groups about themselves. Their attitudes differ sharply from the media image in being clearly more main-stream and
assimilationist (Sowell, 1978:219) than generally believed by language planners.

Most importantly, the bilingual education movement tends to be ahistorical. This
accounts in part for the tendency of bilingual education advocates to see the tension between assimilation and pluralism as a "new" phenomenon emerging in the
1960's. In point of fact, the fundamental tension, devoid at first of ethnic factors, is as old as the beginning of U.S. civilization. The tension was crucial to
the New England Puritan who faced the task of maintaining a unified society while
guarding the purity of the independent congregation. The U.S. Constitution has
the problem built in as the tension between national supremacy and state and local
rights (Higham, 1975:231). Thus, the problem of the one and the many had formed
an importance *before* the ethnic issue added the dimension of reconciling ethnic
diversity with national unity. Indeed, the dialectic between pluralism and assimilation was much discussed in the 19th and early 20th centuries. Pluralism was
generally submerged during most of the 19th century to the quest for unity. The
pluralist's ideology probably had its greatest impact not in the recent decades but
in the late 19th century and early 20th century (without its linguistic component
as primary, however). The ideology has had strong intellectual advocacy in the
persons of such scholars as William James, Horace Kallen, and W.E.B. DuBois. The
pluralist's theory of group relations attained its widest vogue prior to the present time in the post World War I era. This vogue was apparently fueled by opposition to a monolithic enemy that seemed to call for a pluralistic alternative.
During this period intellectuals such as Louis Adamic joined professional historians in denouncing the melting pot as a false ideal (Higham, 1975:211-22).

During the 1950's, of course, this pluralist fervour waned. It is curious that it
waned in part for the same reason that bilingual education is being challenged
now: the absence of empirical evidence of its existence. Scholars were unable to
describe and identify evidence of the persistence of ethnic sub-culture (Higham,
1975:223-24) in much the same way that scholars are at present unable to find evidence of success of bilingual education in achieving its stated goals.

Among the lessons of this long history are some ironies that are compounded by
recent experiences with the continuity of the ethnic dilemma which is today manifested in the bilingual education argument. For example, the general 20th century
experience shows us that:

> "...cultural pluralism would appeal to people who are al-
> ready strongly enough positioned to imagine that permanent
> minority status might be advantageous. It was congenial to
> minorities spokesmen often enough to visualize themselves
> at the centre rather than the periphery of American exper-
> ience. Accordingly, cultural pluralism proved most attract-
> ive to people who were already largely assimilated. It was
> itself one of the products of the American melting pot"
> (Higham, 1975:211).

The major differences between the argument prior to the 1960's and 70's and since is that the linguistic issue is now central and that otherwise the issue changes from a cultural one to, in the present time, one of power and status. Essentially, however, the present argument about bilingual education represents a continuity with a dilemma with which Americans, old and new, have struggled since the Puritan founded his city on the hill in the 17th century.

If we were to be more historical in our approach, the detachment that results from the historical view might show that both the assimilationist's model and the pluralist's model leave much to be desired, so far as a just society is concerned. Both positions are undesirable and unrealistic. This is the reason for the dilemma and for the alternation between the two models throughout our history. Neither has been found satisfactory.

The social historian John Higham (1975) has enumerated the shortcomings of both models. The assimilationist in seeking the elimination of ethnic boundaries - and language is seen as a boundary maintenance device - teaches the rejection and contempt for things that resist rejection and deserve respect. The assimilationist trades affection and loyalty for autonomy and mastery. The assimilationist achieves the pursuit of individual success at the cost of identity. The assimilationist assumes that an individual needs only the opportunity to prove his worth. This leads to alienation and self-hatred on the part of those who fail to prove their worth in the assimilationist's terms (Higham, 1975:235-36; Abrahams, 1972).

Pluralism, on the other hand, insists on a rigidity of boundaries and a commitment to group that American society simply will not permit. Pluralism limits the autonomous, the adventurous, and the ambitious. Pluralism breeds suspicion, narrowmindedness, and prejudice against the outside world - a deadly environment in which to educate. This individual is at the mercy of the group. Thus, in our zeal for spreading benefits of linguistic diversity, many of us have defined a conflict and picked a side that assures that we will lose even if we win. As Higham has noted (1975:240) all during the 20th century there has been a tendency for writers to seize exclusively on one side of the American ethnic dilemma. This tendency remains strong with writers of bilingual education. Perhaps if these writers were more historically informed, they would be more cautious with their loyalty, more sceptical in their atttitudes, and more efficient with their advice.

Other factors have led also to the misreading of the weakening of ethnic boundaries in the 60's and 70's. For one thing, there is evidence that ethnic mobilization and assimilation are alternating phases in the history of ethnic contact. There is no reason to assume that the pluralism of the present will be any more enduring than the integration of the 50's. The sociologist Robert E. Park (1950; cf., Higham, 1975:240-41) has posited that group solidarity such as we are seeing now becomes an essential but temporary stage in the progress for integration. Competition arouses nationalist or racial sentiments and the group acquires self-consciousness to challenge the distribution of power and status. This brings about the accommodation of perhaps the sort we are seeing now. This accommodation could be the motivation for the support of bilingual education manifest by legislatures and the courts in the last ten years. There follows mutual assimilation.

Another possibility for this seeming ethnic revolution and for the optimism about bilingual education may be explained by reference to the historian of ethnicity Marcus L. Hansen's law of "third generation return", the notion that "what the son wishes to forget the grandson wishes to remember" (Bender and Kayiwada, 1968:36). Glazer,(1954:171-73), in modifying this notion, points out that what occurs with the third generation is not a cultural return, but an ideal return to "a vague nostalgia and an undefined ideology" which is primarily a reaction to the conditions of life in the 20th century and which has no organic relation to the descendent's individual past.

There are other plausible explanations to explain the ethnic interest in the 60's and 70's as a continuity rather than as a change. For example, the notion, rather crucial to the bilingual education movement, that ethnic groups have internal solidarity may lead us astray and help account for our failure on this point. There is a strong possibility, as a result, that bilingual education as now conceived could turn out to be for a minority of the minorities (Epstein, 1978:45-47). Indeed, Higham (1975:246) believes that "...the ethnic revival of the 1960's may have to do with the strengthening of the nuclei rather than guarding of the boundaries". If this is so, it could have profound implications for language policy, inasmuch as language is often seen as a boundary maintenance device. It could also help explain such an anomaly as the assimilated ethnic leaders, as, for example, in the Chicano movement, who seem to be urging pluralism against their own example.

In truth, ethnicity per se or even language per se are much too general explanations for most of the phenomena dealt with in connection with bilingual education. Differences in the location and the age of ethnics are not controversial but may explain more in terms of income, education, or occupation than mere ethnic membership or language usage (Sowell, 1978:220ff.). The same may be said of religious and political factors. Indeed, the evidence regarding educational success can be read in such a way that social class has much more explanatory power than ethnicity (cf., Epstein, 1978:54; Paulston, 1974).

It is common to read in the sociolinguistics literature that we must choose either the assimilationist's or the pluralist's side for a policy base for bilingual education. Rubin (1977:288) and Kjolseth (1973) are distinguished statements of this point of view. How we as sociolinguists or planners can "choose" an alternative such as this in the face of such strong historical and ideological currents is an enigma to me, but, more importantly, history and the value system of the U.S. would suggest that bilingualism ought to be a policy instrument to *mediate* the tension of assimilation and pluralism. If, as has been claimed here, both assimilation and pluralism in their pure form are historically unacceptable and socially and psychologically limiting, then one aim of bilingual education ought to be to prepare students and communities to understand the dilemma posed here.

The question of the role of government or mandarin-like organizations in urging or coercing individuals and communities towards particular models of bilingual education needs to be addressed more seriously. It is unfortunate that, as Kjolseth (1973) points out, most bilingual programmes in the United States are assimilationist. However, this fact is not surprising given the dominant value structure of American society and its singular history of linguistic shift. Moreover, it would be just as unfortunate, or maybe more so, if the majority of bilingual programmes were pluralistic. Rubin (1977:289) is too quick to dismiss the fear that many Americans have that the country will lose its national unity in the face of widespread bilingualism. She dismisses this fear as a trait of the "silent majority". Many intellectuals and political élites, excluding linguist intellectuals, share this view. American historians as a rule think that the United States has been extremely fortunate in not having to deal with the intractable problems of some genuinely bilingual societies (e.g., Higham, 1975). While linguists may view bilingualism as liberating, many policy makers view language as one of the most crucial means of maintaining ethnic boundaries - as a means of keeping people in. At present, the mood of the country is not to keep people in.

Language planners in the United States have ample evidence of the social, psychological, attitudinal, cognitive, and intellectual benefits of bilingualism under some conditions. Planners should turn to research that assesses the presence of such conditions, both social and geographical, in the United States. Planners should perhaps seek domains for bilingualism other than or in addition to the school. Above all, planning should turn away from a policy basis that places bilingual education in the cross-fire of the assimilationist/pluralist tension.

With bilingual education rests the best hope of capturing for society some of the best features of both pluralism and assimilation and of avoiding some of the worst features of each of these ideals. Language above all other aspects of culture ties one to group. Through the use and retention of the mother tongue in a bilingual relationship with a competing language, one can refer to one's native group and at the same time achieve the more cosmopolitan outlook and behaviours of the larger society. It is clear from the number of studies that bilingual education can contribute to the enhancement of attitudinal and intellectual skills that the upwardly mobile middle class values and seeks in other ways in the education of its children. Of all the possible bridges between the emotional health and security of pluralism and the autonomy and adventure of assimilation, language is probably the sturdiest and most enduring. But this bridge can only be supported by a viable programme of bilingual education.

In terms of public policy in the U.S. the missing ingredient in bilingual education has been the notion of bilingual education as an enrichment process (cf., Fishman, 1976; Drake, 1975). Bilingual education has been presented primarily as a compensatory programme for deprived minorities and underclass ethnics.

The fundamental policy error, then, has been to argue that transitional programmes promote pluralism, thus loading the dice against bilingual education in general and causing tensions even within the rank of the advocates of bilingual education. Bilingual education needs to break out of the bounds of this narrow goal. It is for this reason that the recent experiments with the immersion programmes are of value; for these immersion programmes have demonstrated that bilingual education can be an enrichment process for students from all socio-economic levels, that bilingual education can blunt ethnic and intergroup discord under some circumstances and is thus a benefit to the community as well as to the individual.

It would be misleading to suggest that bilingual education would produce these results under all conditions, however (Drake, 1975). It is clear that high status groups will sometimes use bilingual education merely to enforce and maintain their superiority. For this reason, it would be useful for policy makers and planners in the United States to become more aware of the bilingual education situation world-wide in order to better gauge under what conditions bilingual education is functional within the value system of the culture of the United States (for excellent overviews of world-wide practices, see Ferguson, Houghton and Wells, 1977, and Fishman, 1976).

Only when bilingualism is seen as an enrichment process rather than as a social engineering scheme for minority ethnics; only when it is seen as a benefit to the entire community and as an asset for *all* individuals, will progress towards the goal of a genuine functional bilingualism in the United States be seen.

By means of such a development, however, *all* people could be better equipped to cope with the stresses and demands of modernity, to keep in touch with their past and in tune with their identity and to influence their environment in order to shape their future.

REFERENCES

Abrahams, R.D. (1972) Stereotyping and beyond, in R. Abrahams & R. Troike (eds.): Language and cultural diversity in American education, Prentice-Hall, Englewood Cliffs, N.J., 19-29.

E.I. Bender & G. Kayiwada, Hansen's "Law of third generation return" and the study of American religio-ethnic groups, Phylon, 29, 360-70 (1968).

G.F. Drake, Integrity, promise and language planning, Language Learning, 25, 2, 267-279 (1975).

Epstein, N. (1977) Language, ethnicity and the schools, Institute for Educational Leadership, Washington, D.C.

Ferguson, C.A., Houghton, C. & Wells, M. (1977), in B. Spolsky & R. Cooper (eds.): Frontiers of bilingual education, Newbury House, Rowley, Mass.

Fishman, J. (1976) Bilingual education: An international sociological perspective, Newbury House, Rowley, Mass.

Glazer, N. (1954) Ethnic groups in America: From national culture to ideology, in M. Berger, T. Abel & C. Page (eds.): Freedom and control in modern society, Van Nostrand, New York.

S.R. Graubard, Preface to the issue: A new America?, Daedalus, 107, 1, v-vi (1978).

K.J. Henderson, Bilingualism: Where to draw the line, The Christian Science Monitor, May 22, 16-17 (1978).

Higham, J. (1975) Send these to me, Athenaum, New York.

Keller, G. (1976) Contracting valid goals for bilingual and bidialectal education: The role of the applied linguist and the bilingual educator, in G. Keller, R. Teschner & S. Vicra (eds.): Bilingualism in the bicentennial and beyond, Bilingual Press, New York, 17-37.

Kjolseth, R. (1973) Assimilation or pluralism, in P. Turner & R. Tucson (eds.): Bilingualism in the Southwest, University of Arizona Press, Arizona, 3-27.

Park, R.E. (1950) Race and culture, Free Press, Glencoe, III.

Paulston, C.B. (1974) Implication of language learning theory for language planning: Concerns in bilingual education, Center for Applied Linguistics, Arlington, Va.

Rubin, J. (1977) Bilingual education and language planning, in B. Spolsky & R. Cooper (eds.): Frontiers of bilingual education, Newbury House, Rowley, Mass., 282-294.

R.A. Schemerhorn, Ethnicity in the perspective of the sociology of knowledge, Ethnicity, 1, 1-14 (1974).

M. Scott-Blair, 1990 "Ethnic Majority" report stirs debate in State, San Diego Union, 16 July, A-3 (1978).

T. Sowell, Ethnicity in a changing America, Daedalus, Winter, 213-337 (1978).

AT THE CROSSROADS OF RESEARCH INTO
LANGUAGE AND ETHNIC RELATIONS

D. M. Taylor and H. Giles *

McGill University, Montreal, Canada
*University of Bristol, Bristol, U.K.

In its formative stages, sociolinguistics represented a unique blending of the hithertofore separate domains of language and society. The search for systematic relationships between social and linguistic variables was, and is, an important legitimate endeavour, and the specific relationship between ethnicity and language has attracted its share of attention in this regard. Despite the embryonic state of sociolinguistic research into ethnicity and language, there would seem to have developed already certain norms regarding appropriate orientations to theory, method and the form of empirical questions posed.

The responsibility for serving as discussant and co-editor respectively for the present volume has provided us with a unique perspective from which to reflect, albeit as social psychologists, on the orientations and styles of research represented in the area of language and ethnicity. While we cannot help but be impressed by advances represented by the previous papers, we are struck by some of the implicit assumptions which appear to characterize and guide much of current research. In this final paper, we would like to address four issues with a view to hopefully expanding and, perhaps in a modest way, altering the thrust of sociolinguistic inquiry into the domain of language and ethnicity.

1. THE NATURE OF THE RELATIONSHIP BETWEEN LANGUAGE AND ETHNICITY

A common underlying theme to many of the papers in this volume, although by no means all of them, is that language is one indicator of some more fundamental underlying socio-psychological process. Appropriate aspects of language serve as a barometer of ethnocentrism (papers by Khleif and Lukens), of the potential for ethnic survival (papers by de Vries and Anderson), of institutional racism (Husband's paper) and of social integration and differentiation (papers by Escure and Bourhis), to name but a few. Viewing language as merely an "indicator" of social processes severely belittles the importance of language per se. Smith, Giles and Hewstone (1979) have made a similar observation about sociolinguistic research in general where they note that language is usually operationalized as a dependent rather than an independent variable. In short, the implicit causal link is that social structures and processes, in this case ethnicity, affect certain aspects of language, not so much the reverse.

There are two important implications of this trend. First, such a unidirectional causal assumption places an unwarranted bias on the focus for constructive theory

development. Thus, in the cases where language reflects ethnocentrism or racism in
the examples alluded to earlier, the key theoretical issues become understanding
the causes and structure of ethnocentrism and the genesis of racism respectively.
Language then remains at the level of a good index or measure of the operation of
these societal processes. Sociolinguistic inquiry in the area of language and ethnicity will likely have little to offer if this implicit causal assumption continues to guide the field. Any important theoretical advances will necessarily be
made by sociologists and social psychologists dealing directly with ethnicity;
language will serve as one index for supporting or refuting their progress.

The second implication, and one that follows directly from the first, is that this
unidirectional causal view not only emphasizes social theory to the exclusion of
language, but makes it impossible for sociolinguistic inquiry to make its unique
and distinctive contribution. Surely, language not only reflects social structure
and process but actively contributes to it in a dynamic fashion. Language must be
afforded a more central role in terms of creating, defining and maintaining social
categories. For example, consistent with the notions of symbolic interactionism,
language is the vehicle which permits shared meaning to emerge and for social categories to be formed (St.Clair, 1979). Ethnicity, then, to a great extent depends
upon language for its creation. This becomes all the more significant when the
emotional and attitudinal significance of ethnicity is considered, for emotional
meaning perhaps more than any other requires shared understanding of the most intimate kind (see papers by Eastman and Khleif) - the kind only the subtleties of language can provide (Fishman, 1977). Often it is assumed that one's ethnicity is inherited; a person is Black or White, Anglophone or Francophone, Welsh or Irish by
birth. As Reiger (1978) points out, however, one's ethnicity is a creative process
(see Ross's paper). She notes in the Canadian context that an individual may describe him or herself as a Canadian, Italian-Canadian, Anglophone or Italian to take
one example. All are legitimate ethnicities, but the implications of each are important and clearly language plays an active role in the creation of the particular
identity desired. Indeed, the paper by Mercer et al. demonstrates how different
ethnic ingroup descriptions are associated with different language attitudes and
values.

The important creative role of language can be further illustrated with reference
to listeners' social interpretations of ethnic speech styles, where there is ample
potential for mis-attribution. For example, a Welshman, a Black in the United
States or a Francophone in Canada may broaden or otherwise alter their speech in
order to denote their ethnic identity (see papers by Bourhis and Lukens). Perceiv-
ers, however, often equate these forms of speech with social class; indeed, a number of papers refer to the relationship between class and ethnicity (see Ross,
Drake, and particularly G. Williams). Thus, while a speaker may intend to emphasize ethnicity, the listener may well not consider ethnic features and may make in-
ferences about the speaker's social class. The listener then has redefined the
situation, categorizing the social context as well as structure on the basis of
class. Alternatively, of course, the speaker may be wishing to identify him or
herself with a particular social class and this may be interpreted by the listener
as a statement of ethnic identity (for a review of positions held about the class-
ethnic relationships, as well as a new model, see Sandlund, 1976).

The implications of the above can best be understood by conceptualizing the situation in the form of a two by two table simultaneously representing the speaker's
intentions and the listener's perceptions.

Cells A and D represent instances where there is congruence between the speaker's
intentions and the listener's attributions. Even in these contexts, however, the
role of language as a definer of social structure is evident. The speaker clearly
wishes to define the situation in terms of ethnicity or social class and it is precisely through language that this social structure and its meaning is created.

TABLE 1

Speaker's Intention

Perceiver's Attribution of Speaker		signal ethnicity	signal social class
	speaker's ethnicity	A	B
	speaker's social class	C	D

That is, the social structure of interaction is multi-dimensional involving many others: aspects of formality, purpose of interaction, group identity, interpersonal and intergroup attitudes. What features become salient and how the meaning of the social structure becomes created in the form of a shared understanding of the situation is to a large extent determined through language. This creative role of language is even more clearly evident in the case of the mis-attributions described in cells B and C which were outlined previously.

The role of language as a generator of social categorization and structure is not limited to ethnicity and social class. A speaker may, in an intergroup encounter, adopt a broad accent in order to denote affiliation with a particular ethnic group. This speech modification, however, may be perceived as a shift to a more informal style indicating increased intimacy or familiarity on the part of the speaker. In this case, the situation is again totally redefined through language and the attribution made to it (cf., Giles, Scherer and Taylor (1979) for a discussion of "ambiguous" or "equivocal" speech markers).

Our plea for considering language in a more fundamental and dynamic role is not aimed directly at the papers in this volume. They represent important contributions in their respective areas and some authors (particularly Ross, Husband and G. Williams) do highlight the creative role of language as a mechanism of social and political influence. As Doise (1978) says "ideology expresses most of its influence through language" (cf., Billig, 1976). As a whole, however, the volume does reflect the prevalent orientation to language and ethnicity; perhaps there is room for language to assume an expanded role along the lines proposed such that sociolinguistic research can make a unique theoretical contribution to the field of ethnic relations.

2. THE SOCIAL NATURE OF ETHNICITY

Ethnicity and ethnic relations are social processes involving actual or symbolic relations between individuals in an ethnic context. The sociolinguistic issues are social as well, focusing upon such topics as the survival of ethnic groups (C. Williams's paper), conflict between ethnic groups (von Raffler-Engel, et al.'s paper), the formation of ethnic identity (Ross's paper) and concerns for assimilation and cultural pluralism (Drake's paper). Unfortunately, micro-sociolinguistic research on these issues tends to be individualistic in emphasis, with little appreciation of their social nature. This individualistic bias is not limited to sociolinguistics and has been raised forcefully recently in the context of social psychological research on intergroup relations generally (see Tajfel, 1972; Moscovici, 1972; Sampson, 1977; Steiner, 1974); the views expressed here follow those outlined by Taylor and Brown (in press).

The issue in question is a complex one, and one not easily resolved. Most research designs involve examining, in natural or controlled conditions, a small number of informants or subjects. This in itself is not inappropriate since one of the major

goals of sociolinguistic inquiry is to understand the individual. The problem is
that in the context of ethnicity an important aim is to comprehend the individual
in a particular social context, ethnic, and it is precisely the social component
which is most often neglected. For example, when a person uses a derogatory term
about another to his or her face (Khleif's paper), or individuals converge or diverge in their speech (Bourhis's paper) or express various forms of ethnocentrism
(Lukens's paper), they may be interacting as two individuals, but they may also
be expressing important *collective*, social or political views. A Ukrainian, in a
one-to-one encounter, may well be making a statement for all Ukrainians, and indeed
if he or she construes the situation in that context, what appears as an individualistic encounter may well in fact be the expression of group attitudes (cf.,
Dustin and Davis, 1970; Billig and Tajfel, 1973). Unfortunately, there is nothing
directly observable in the encounter to indicate the extent to which social or
group processes are involved. Rather, the group aspects are a psychological symbolic process which grows out of a shared understanding among interlocutors of the
meaning of a particular interaction (cf., Rommetveit, 1976). Account must be taken
of these group features especially in an area involving language and ethnicity (see
Ross's paper, particularly identity stage 3). Such group features may be considered as representing the second extreme of the two types of interaction discussed
by Tajfel and Turner (in press):

> "At one extreme is the interaction between two or more indiv-
> iduals which is *fully* determined by their interpersonal rel-
> ationships and individual characteristics and not at all aff-
> ected by various social groups or categories to which they
> respectively belong. The other extreme consists of inter-
> actions between two or more individuals (or groups of in-
> dividuals) which are *fully* determined by their respective
> memberships of various social groups or categories, and are
> not at all affected by the interindividual personal relation-
> ships between the people involved."

Furthermore, the nearer are members of a group to this second (so-called "social
change") extreme of the continuum:

> "...the more uniformity will they show in their behaviour
> towards members of the relevant outgroup...(and)...the more
> they will tend to treat members of the outgroup as undiff-
> erentiated items in a unified social category rather than in
> terms of their individual characteristics" (Tajfel and Turner,
> in press).

This greater emphasis on the collective or social aspects of ethnicity and language can lead to whole new domains of inquiry. Two individuals from different
ethnolinguistic groups may well show consistent evidence of speech convergence in
a wide variety of situations. However, as soon as an individual interacts with a
member of another ethnolinguistic group in the presence of other members of his or
her own group, there may be pressure to "represent" the group and hence not converge to the other person (Giles, 1979). The numerous studies which have used the
"matched guise" procedure introduced by Lambert (1967) illustrate this point. Members of one ethnolinguistic group are typically presented with tape recordings of
individuals from their own group and a competitive outgroup (in fact, the recordings are made by the same person who is bilingual or bidialectal). The speech
characteristics of the person on the tape clearly marks the speaker's ethnolinguistic affiliation and the listeners are required to make attitudinal judgements of
the speaker *privately* on a questionnaire (see review, Giles and Powesland, 1975).
What if a group of listeners was required to publicly announce their attitudes towards the speaker in front of other members of their group? This subtle change
in the experimental methodology would highlight the group or shared aspect of ethnicity and may well lead to entirely different findings. Indeed, many of the att-

itudes expressed in such a public context may be more a statement of the listener's
beliefs about his or her own group, and an expression of group solidarity, than any
attitudinal statement towards the outgroup *individual* in the tape recording.[1] As
Blake and Mouton (1961:177) point out:

> "(a representative) is not entirely "free" to act in accord
> with fact or to engage in compromise, for to do so would be
> interpreted by group members as bringing them 'defeat'".

A new emphasis on the group or social aspect cannot only modify our approach to
established sociolinguistic inquiry but also provide a new impetus for neglected
areas of research. Language, for example, can be viewed as a fundamental collective resource for an ethnic group which can be employed in competitive power relations with rival outgroups. That is, language is a complex acquired skill and as
such those who have the skill can exploit it to their ends (see papers by Ross and
Husband). Recent developments in Canada illustrate the social power of language.
Historically, full participation in Canadian society required functioning in English, a norm which guaranteed advantages to the group whose mother tongue was English, and placed Francophones at a distinct disadvantage. Recent demands by Québec
at the federal level and the newly-passed language legislation making French the
official language of Québec for the first time has monumental implications for relations between the two groups. Thus, while this language legislation may be motivated in part by a need to affirm Francophone identity and express collective
pride, making French a requirement for full participation in Québec society dramatically alters the power relations between the two groups. And, the power motive
need not be expressed solely through legislation. Individual Francophones may well
reflect the same motivation at times in their individual encounters by speaking
French and believing that if enough members of their own group behave similarly the
same effect as official legislation might be realized.

Awareness of the collective or group aspects of sociolinguistic phenomena can perhaps lead to new insights. As Taylor and Brown (in press) have argued, the focus
of attention must remain at the level of the individual for it is the individual
who is the locus of speech. However, being cognizant that at times the individual
acts as an individual but at other times as a representative of an ethnolinguistic
group requires our attention; the challenge is to discover when persons are operating at one level or the other and how this is manifest linguistically.

3. THE FUNCTIONS OF LANGUAGE

Research on language and ethnicity has focused mainly on the affective or emotional
functions of language. Thus, language has been depicted as a mechanism for expressing ethnocentric attitudes (papers by Lukens and Khleif), for expressing attraction
or dislike for another individual or group (paper by Bourhis), a means of expressing racism (paper by Husband), or as an expression of ethnic solidarity (papers by
Mercer, et al., and C. Williams). While the importance of these emotional functions
of language cannot be overestimated, there is a second set of functions concerning
cognitive organization which have not received sufficient attention (see Giles,
Scherer and Taylor, 1979, and Taylor, forthcoming, for a more detailed discussion
of this function). Speech is often used by encoders and decoders to organize persons in terms of important social categories thus rendering the complex social en-

---

[1]See Smith, Giles and Hewstone (1979) and Hewstone (1979) for a discussion of the
as yet sociolinguistically-neglected, crucial role of cognitive structures in mediating between an individual's perceptions of the context/structure and his or her
language behaviour (Doise, 1978:114; Jaspars, forthcoming).

vironment manageable. The accommodation theory of Giles, outlined in the papers by
Bourhis and Lukens, illustrates the potential operation of the organizational function of language. Speech convergence, maintenance and divergence are described as
mechanisms by which interpersonal or intergroup attitudes are expressed. Social
desirability can be communicated by converging towards the speech of the other,
whereas social distance and intergroup distinctiveness can be transmitted through
speech divergence. There would seem to be an entire area left unexplored by accommodation theory, namely instances where the motivation for accommodation is not
to express attitudes but rather to help the interlocutor put order and meaning into the interaction, and provide a mutually understood basis for effective communication (cf., Runkel, 1956, 1963; Triandis, 1960; Lemaine, 1959).

A speaker may well adopt a certain accent, refer to certain topics or use key lexical items which communicate to the other certain shared bases of experience and
interest which can form the basis for effective interaction. Similarly, certain
speech divergences may be designed to help the interlocutor categorize the speaker
according to important social categories. In Britain, one of the authors may emphasize his Canadian speech in order to provide information to a British colleague of
what assumptions can be made about knowledge of local norms and topics of interest.
At the simplest level, such divergence might indicate that rugby league and ice
hockey are not shared aspects of experience. In this example, speech divergence
is less than an emotional statement of defiance but more a means of facilitating
the process of social categorization.

Lukens's emphasis on the emotional significance of language for expressing ethnocentrism provides a further example. But ethnocentrism involves categorization as
well as affect. It is often important to signify "who I am" as well as what my
intergroup attitudes may be. An extreme might be a case where one member of a
group, in the presence of other members, makes openly derogatory remarks about an
outgroup member. This behaviour may be motivated by a need to express belonging
and solidarity with the ingroup rather than any genuine negative feelings towards
members of the other group. In this case, the function of language would be more
one of cognitive organization in terms of the speaker rather than an expression of
affective or emotional needs regarding the outgroup.

A major theoretical and empirical challenge will be to determine for any given interaction which of the major functions, emotional or organizational, is most operative. Although language behaviour may be evoked mainly for organizational reasons
with no focus on emotional functions, and vice-versa, it is equally possible that
these two orthogonal functions may be operating simultaneously. For example, the
minority group member who adopts a distinctive accent may do so for two separate
purposes simultaneously: one, to have him or herself categorized (organization) and
secondly, to express negative attitudes towards the outgroup member (emotion);
whether they will be decoded as such is of course another problem akin to that discussed in relation to Table 1 earlier. Similarly, neither function may be especially salient as when uncontrolled aspects of language reveal ethnicity unwittingly
in a ritual interaction of little significance or consequence. Thus, the two functions operate simultaneously and independently for any particular speech encounter.

One qualification must be made with respect to the completely independent operation
of the two functions. It has been hypothesized (see Taylor, forthcoming) that where
emotional functions operate at a high level of intensity this is usually at the expense of organizational functioning. Thus, in a highly-charged intergroup encounter
where language is of the type Lukens and Khleif describe as maximally ethnocentric,
the high arousal involved in satisfying emotional needs may well be to the detri-
ment of careful attention to organizational cues through language. (Arguments between spouses are often characterized by verbal exchanges that are designed to satisfy the emotional needs of each, but in the process all potential for attending
to the subtle cues which reflect the needs of the other are lost). In general,

however, there has been little attention paid to the organizational function of
language in the context of ethnicity. Future research may hopefully expand to include the organizational function and its relationship to the emotional function
which has thus far been emphasized in the literature.

4. TOWARDS A FRAMEWORK FOR RESEARCH

The topic of language and ethnicity is at one level a very personal issue but, as
we have emphasized, it is also a social or group phenomenon. More specifically,
we view the individual, the locus of thought, language and action as the ultimate
unit of analysis although others prefer to focus on the level of the social group
(e.g., Sandlund, 1976). Social structures and processes are created by and through
the individual, and it is these issues, as they become represented in individuals,
that warrant attention. As Taylor and Brown state:

> "Clearly, social structures and processes may be examined in
> their own right. Nevertheless, these social realities do
> have psychological meaning for the individual, and, through
> commerce with the environment, the individual generates and
> participates in the very social processes he is in turn in-
> fluenced by."

The topic of language and ethnicity clearly involves intra- and inter-group processes (Escure's paper), where the groups in question are defined in terms of ethnicity. To date there have not emerged any conceptual frameworks in this field
that are sufficiently sociolinguistic in nature, although papers by Bourhis, Ross
and G. Williams are clearly important new contributions in this regard. The same
lack of understanding of intergroup dynamics can be levelled at more traditional
theories of intergroup relations (Billig, 1976; Tajfel, 1978a) and these have the
additional problem that language plays no active role in their propositions (Giles,
Bourhis and Taylor, 1977; Giles, 1978, 1979). In the absence of an integrated
theory, there is an immediate need for a framework which can at least enhance the
chances for research to be cumulative. Many excellent studies lose their impact
simply because there is no larger coherent framework within which to incorporate
research. At this stage it is not crucial that a framework be one that has been
supported by a lengthy tradition of research; rather, what is required is one that
is at least comprehensive in scope. It is in this spirit that we present a brief
overview of a theory developed by Taylor and McKirnan (1978) which attempts to predict the stages involved in all relations between groups. There are two further
reasons for presenting a brief description of this framework in the present paper.
First, the framework builds on current theorizing on intergroup relations within
social psychology (Tajfel, 1978a; Tajfel and Turner, in press), and, secondly, the
framework can be used to illustrate the previous three points developed so far in
this paper.

The framework posits four stages to relations between groups: *Stage 1: Stable hierarchically organized intergroup relations:* This arbitrary starting point represents the traditional dominant-subordinate group relationship typified by social
class structures and majority-minority group relations. The key theoretical issue
at this stage is the process by which such inequity can be maintained and at least
be tolerated if not accepted by members of the disadvantaged group (see Ross's
paper, the stage of "minority group status"). *Stage 2: Social mobility:* At this
stage individual members of the disadvantaged group attempt to pass into the advantaged one. Specifically, high status individuals within the disadvantaged group
initiate the passing process (see G. Williams's paper, cell 3 "individuals").
Stage 3: Consciousness raising: The disadvantaged individuals who attempt passing
may or may not be successful. Those few who do pass assimilate to the advantaged
group in the extreme (cf., Tajfel, 1978b). Those who do not or more accurately

are not permitted access to the advantaged group recognize that status enhancement
lies in efforts to increase the status of the disadvantaged group as a whole. As
an initial step, these key individuals attempt to persuade all members of the disadvantaged group that their status is collectively defined, that it is illegitimate
and that collective action is required. *Stage 4: Competitive intergroup behaviour:*
The disadvantaged group initiates collective action and using a variety of group
strategies (e.g., social competition, redefinition, social originality - see
Tajfel and Turner, in press) aim for what they believe to be a more equitable distribution of material and social rewards (see Ross's paper, the stage of "ethnic
identity status").

The theoretical psychological underpinnings to the framework are not presented here,
nor are the details of the modest evidence in support of the propositions. There
are, however, two assumptions regarding the relationships among the stages which
deserve brief elaboration. First, the stages are hypothesized to be sequential
such that they operate in order for any given intergroup context, although the time
spent at any one stage will vary depending upon a number of situational variables.
It is possible, then, for an entire generation to be born into an intergroup situation which has developed to Stage 3 and the shift to the next stage may vary in
time from months to generations. At no time is it possible to skip a stage despite
great variations in the time spent at the various stages. Secondly, once Stage 4
has been reached a new balance will be achieved between the groups in question.
The balance will never be total equality but as long as one group is not totally
dominant and the other inevitably disadvantaged, "healthy" competition will ensue
(cf., Apfelbaum and Lubek, 1976; Billig, 1976; Plon, 1974). If one group becomes
continually disadvantaged, the stages become cyclical such that there will be a
return to Stage 1 and the process will begin anew (see the historical continuity
perspective in Drake's paper). The present framework, however briefly described,
serves to illustrate perhaps how it may provoke sociolinguistic research which is
cumulative. Moreover, a brief stage by stage analysis may be used to demonstrate
the potential directions for research described in this chapter.

At Stage 1, the stable hierarchically organized intergroup relations involve fundamental social categorizations and these categorizations are both created through
and maintained by language. An important research issue is how through distinctive
language styles the disadvantaged group members become categorized and how their
language serves to reinforce the disadvantaged position (see Ross's paper). Research on this issue has begun to amass (e.g., see Ryan, 1979) and might be usefully
organized around the present framework. This issue involves not only a more dynamic role for language as was advocated at the outset of the present paper, but also
requires understanding of the organizational function of language. Finally, group
processes are the foundation for the framework and hence must feature prominently
in future sociolinguistic analyses.

Stage 2 is characterized by individual mobility by key persons within the disadvantaged group. To what extent will such individuals adopt a different ethnolinguistic style, specifically that of the advantaged group as part of the passing strategy? Will such language accommodation to the advantaged group be reacted to by
other members of the ingroup? If so, will the reaction be one of admiration or dis-
gust and how through language will these reactions be expressed? What are the language demands of the advantaged group for these accommodating individuals to be
acceptable? Do passing individuals become bidialectal or bilingual while in a tra-
nsitory position in order to maintain an identity with both groups? Answers to
these questions clearly involve a central role for language in an intergroup context where organizational as well as emotional functions operate.

Stage 3 involves within group language processes as key individuals actively seek
to generate an awareness among all disadvantaged group members of their collective
unjustly attributed status. Language changes might be expected here in the form

of a new lexicon which can serve as the pivotal or rallying point for consciousness raising (cf., Eastman's paper). Examples might include new labels to describe the group itself, for the advantaged group and for the treatment of the one by the other (see Khleif's paper). A new awareness of language distinctiveness may also develop and the distinctiveness may be made more salient as a means of enhancing group categorization.

Consciousness raising requires the transformation of an aggregate of individuals into a true collectivity. Such a transformation requires that individuals perceive that they share a common fate, a common set of objectives and have a shared rationale for their collective position; in short, have a shared meaning of their social environment (see Husband's paper). Language will play a central role in the genesis of this shared meaning. For example, it might be hypothesizied that the more physically dispersed and otherwise diverse the group to be transformed into a collectivity (see C. Williams's paper) the greater will be the need for a simply worded, appealing, distinctive "manifesto" to serve as the shared basis of the group. The rationale here is that only such a series of propositions could be focal enough to provide a true sense of sharedness among an extremely heterogeneous group (see Mercer, et al.'s paper).

At Stage 4 the expectation would be that intergroup competition would take the form of not merely linguistic change among selected individuals but collective change. Creating distinctive language styles, or a renewed pride in a linguistic style the group was previously ashamed of are examples of this process. As well, however, social and structural processes would become involved as for instance when changes in group language become institutionalized in education and business or when, as described earlier, language is used as a means of exerting social power (see papers by Anderson and G. Williams).

SUMMARY AND CONCLUSIONS

In this paper, we have advocated a more active role for the language side of the social-language equation as well as a more truly social or group approach to sociolinguistic inquiry. Without detracting from research on the emotional functions of language, we see the need for a renewed focus on the cognitive or organizational function. Finally, at the present crossroads a general framework in the context of language and ethnicity which can serve to organize existing research and provide direction for the future is required.

Our observations do not reflect weaknesses of the papers in this volume, nor indeed of sociolinguistic research on language and ethnicity in general. On the contrary, our conclusions grew out of reading the diverse offerings in this volume in a concentrated period of time. To advocate *new* directions it is necessary to have established directions and that, together with the emerging cross-disciplinary flavour of the field highlighted in the editors' preface, is an accomplishment at such an early stage of development in the study of language and ethnic relations. Finally, the framework described briefly in this paper is modest in its detail, articulation of propositions and empirical support, but broad in scope. It is this latter feature which perhaps complements the diversity of research represented in this volume.

REFERENCES

Apfelbaum, E. & Lubek, I. (1976) Resolution versus revolution? The theory of conflicts in question, in L.H. Strickland, F.E. Aboud & K.J. Gergen (eds.): Social psychology in transition, Plenum Press, New York.

Billig, M. (1976) The social psychology of intergroup relations, Academic Press, London.

M. Billig & H. Tajfel, Social categorization and similarity in intergroup behaviour, European Journal of Social Psychology, 3, 27-52 (1973).

R.R. Blake & J.S. Mouton, Loyalty of representatives to ingroup positions during intergroup competition, Sociometry, 24, 177-183 (1961).

Doise, W. (1978) Groups and individuals: Explanations in social psychology, Cambridge University Press, Cambridge.

D.S. Dustin & H.P. Davis, Evaluative bias in group and individual competition, Journal of Social Psychology, 80, 103-108 (1970).

Fishman, J.A. (1977) Language and ethnicity, in H. Giles (ed.): Language, ethnicity, and intergroup relations, Academic Press, London.

Giles, H. (1978) Linguistic differentiation between ethnic groups, in H. Tajfel (ed.): Differentiation between social groups: Studies in the social psychology of intergroup relations, European Monographs in Social Psychology, Academic Press, London.

Giles, H. (1979) Ethnicity markers in speech, in K.R. Scherer & H. Giles (eds.): Social markers in speech, Cambridge University Press, Cambridge.

Giles, H., Bourhis, R.Y. & Taylor, D.M. (1977) Towards a theory of language and ethnic relations, in H. Giles (ed.): Language, ethnicity and intergroup relations, Academic Press, London.

Giles, H. & Powesland, P.F. (1975) Speech style and social evaluation, Academic Press, London.

Giles, H., Scherer, K.R. & Taylor, D.M. (1979) Speech markers in social interaction, in K.R. Scherer & H. Giles (eds.): Social markers in speech, Cambridge University Press, Cambridge.

M. Hewstone, Social cognition and sociolinguistics: An alternative approach to conflict resolution, Working paper, Department of psychology, University of Oxford (1979).

Jaspars, J.M.F. (forthcoming) The double representation of social reality, Department of psychology, University of Oxford.

W.E. Lambert, The social psychology of bilingualism, Journal of Social Issues, 23 (1967).

J-M. Lemaine, Similitude cognitive et relations interpersonelles, Psychologie Française, 4, 102-116 (1959).

Moscovici, S. (1972) Society and theory in social psychology, in J. Israel & H. Tajfel (eds.): The context of social psychology, Academic Press, London.

M. Plon, On the meaning of the notion of conflict and its study in social psychology, European Journal of Social Psychology, 4, 389-436 (1974).

D.W. Reiger, Multiple group membership and definition of self, Unpublished M.A. Thesis, McGill University (1978).

Rommetveit, R. (1976) On the architecture of intersubjectivity, in L.H. Strickland, F.E. Aboud & K.J. Gergen (eds.): Social psychology in transition, Plenum Press, New York.

P.J. Runkel, Cognitive similarity in facilitating communication, Sociometry, 19, 178-191 (1956).

P.J. Runkel, Dimensionality, map-matching and anxiety, Psychological Reports, 13, 335-350, Monograph Supplement 3-vi3 (1963).

Ryan, E.B. (1979) Why do non-prestige language varieties persist?, in H. Giles & R. St.Clair (eds.): Language and social psychology, Blackwell, Oxford.

E.E. Sampson, Psychology and the American ideal, Journal of Personality and Social Psychology, 35, 767-782 (1977).

Sandlund, T. (1976) Social classes, ethnic groups and capitalist development: An outline of a theory, Svenska Litteratursällskapet i Finland, Abo.

Smith, P.M., Giles, H. & Hewstone, M. (1979) Sociolinguistics: A social psychological perspective, in R. St.Clair & H. Giles (eds.): Social and psychological contexts of language, Erlbaum, Hillsdale, N.J.

St.Clair, R. (1979) The contexts of language, in R. St.Clair & H. Giles (eds.): Social and psychological contexts of language, Erlbaum, Hillsdale, N.J.

I.D. Steiner, Whatever happened to the group in social psychology?, Journal of Experimental Social Psychology, 10, 94-108 (1974).

Tajfel, H. (1972) Experiments in a vacuum, in J. Israel & H. Tajfel (eds.): The context of social psychology, Academic Press, London.

Tajfel, H. (ed.) (1978a) Differentiation between social groups: Studies in the social psychology of intergroup relations, Academic Press, London.

Tajfel, H. (1978b) The social psychology of minorities, Minority Rights Group, London.

Tajfel, H. & Turner, J.C. (in press) An integrative theory of intergroup conflict, in W.G. Austin & H. Worchel (eds.): The social psychology of intergroup relations, Brooks/Cole, Monterey.

Taylor, D.M. (forthcoming) Stereotypes and intergroup relations, in R.C. Gardner & R. Kalin (eds.): A Canadian social psychology of ethnic relations.

D.M. Taylor & R.J. Brown, Towards a more social social psychology?, British Journal of Social and Clinical Psychology (in press).

D.M. Taylor & D.J. McKirnan, Four stages in the dynamics of intergroup relations, Unpublished ms., McGill University (1978).

H.C. Triandis, Cognitive similarity and communication in a dyad, Human Relations, 13, 175-183 (1960).

SUBJECT INDEX

Accent 118, 124-126
Acrolect 102-114
Adjectives 174-176
Africa 7, 15, 91, 123
Age 73
Amazon 123
Americans
  Black 143-155, 163, 166, 197-210
  Immigrant Groups 68, 121, 155, 163-168
Amerindians 41, 10, 101, 173-177,
  216-221
Analysis
  Behavioural 35-43
  Cohort 94
  Historical 164, 180-181, 224-229
  Scalogram 103, 168
  Spatial 27-43
Anglicization 29, 35
Anthropological 169, 203
Assimilation 8, 57-64, 68-78, 223-229
Audio-visual Approach 219
Belgium 9, 58, 75, 96, 126
Berlize 101-115
Bilingualism 33, 37, 74-75, 96-97, 126,
  130-131, 162, 228
Births 88, 90, 121
Black Handshakes 197-210
British Immigrants 15-25, 179-191
Burghers 64
Canada 9, 58, 67-78, 87-97
Canadian
  French 68, 70-77, 125-126, 162
  Indian 70, 95
  Italian 70-71, 92, 121, 232
  Other Immigrant Groups 67-77, 92, 95,
  121
Carib 101-115
Census 33, 88-96

Chicano 122, 228
Child-Woman Ratio 92
Code-switching
  Metaphorical 119, 123-124, 134
  Situational 37, 119-123, 134
Cognitive Organization 235-236
Collective Action 8-12, 234-239
Confrontational Communication/Polariz-
  ation 153, 155
Core 31
Creole 105-115, 121
Cultural
  Renegades 162-163
  Revival 220
Decreolization 112-113
Demographic 63, 70, 78, 87-97, 129
Dialects 76-77, 197
Diglossia 115, 130-131, 161
Distance
  Avoidance of 149, 151-152, 155
  Communicative 128, 143-156
  Disparagement of 149, 153-155
  Indifference of 149-151, 155
Domain 32
Doukhobors 71, 73
East European 72, 87, 161
Ecological 29-35, 78
Economic 1-13, 28, 57-64, 75, 114
Education 2, 9, 17, 28, 30, 32, 37,
  69-70, 228
  Bilingual 223-229
Emigration 11, 88-96, 121
Endogamy 92
Ethnic
  Boundaries 3, 7, 11, 57, 159-169
  Conflict 9, 62, 143-156, 184, 188
  Cuing 18

243

Differentiation/Distinctiveness 2-3,
127-134, 143-156, 179-191
Identity 4-13, 16-18, 25, 67-68,
57-64, 118, 126
Mobilization 4-13, 29
Mortality 88-96
Nuptiality 95
Ethnicity 1-13, 16-18, 159-160, 215,
231-235
Ethnocentrism 144-148, 236
Ethnolinguistic
Labels 143, 160-169
Vitality 28, 129-134
Ethnophaulisms 143, 153
Ethno-religious 68-78, 161-166
Experimental Method 197-210
Familiarity 233
Family Structure 15-25, 96
Fertility 89-96
Finland 9, 75, 87, 94
Fist 207-209
Fletoric 153
Formality-Informality 121-122, 233
Forms of Address 128
Geographers 27-43
Geographical Distribution 64
Government 225
Groups
Communal 4-13
Language 59-64
Representative 233-235
Guamanians 144
Hegemony 63, 180
Holland 164
Home Language 92-93
Hostility 189, 197-210
Hutterites 67, 71
Hyperbole 184, 188
Hypercorrection 113, 152
Ideological 28, 63, 163, 180, 224-229,
233
Immersion Programme 126, 229
Immigration 28, 68, 73, 76, 88, 121, 166,
179-191
India 2, 6, 15, 123
Industrialization 3, 28
Infra-structure 57-64
Institutional Completeness/Support 62,
70, 74, 129
Integration 40
Integrative/Instrumental Motivation 23,
42
Intelligibility 125
Intermarriage 73, 92, 95-96, 224
Intonation 7
Isolational Communication/Polarization
155
Israel 2, 162, 165
Italy 76

Jewish 162-165
Jokey 21, 114
Joval 162
Journalism 179-191, 225
Kinesic 197-210
Language
Attitudes 18-25, 36-43, 113-114
Emotive 152-155, 188, 201-205
Erosion/Shift 28, 57, 93-95
Functions 235-236
Loyalty 15-25, 37, 61, 69, 118
Maintenance 57, 69-77, 225
Planning 215-221, 223-229
Prestige 58, 114
Resurrection 215-221
Status 58-64
Wider Communication (L.W.E.) 215-221
'Languages
Arab 160
Buang 122
Czech 10
Eskimo 165
Flemish 58, 126
French 89-96, 126
German 70, 160
Guarani 121
Gujarati 15-25
Haida 217-221
Irish Gaelic 2, 10, 68, 215
Quileute 219
Scots Gaelic 10, 67-68, 161
Spanish 2, 101, 121-122, 216, 225
Swahili 121, 216
Swedish 70, 87
Tagalog 121
Turkish 161
Ukrainian 70-71
Yiddish 10
Langue 215
Law of Third Generation Return 227
Legislation 28, 182, 187-189, 223
Legitimization 63
Lexical 7, 128, 152, 205, 216-221
Perjorative 153-155, 165-168, 174-177
Likert Scale 19
Lingua Franca 10, 101, 114
Linguistic
Accommodation 74-77
Boundaries 60-62
Change 5, 27-43, 74-77, 227-228
Diversity 146, 227
Inversion 152
Linguistics 101-115, 156, 169, 215
Lutheran 72
Luxembourg 76
Macro-Sociolinguistics 129-134
Mannheim's Paradox 225
Mass Media 5, 15, 28, 37, 43, 180-191,
216, 224

Melting Pot 151, 223
Mennonites 71-101
Micro-Sociolinguistics 117-128, 133
Migration 91, 95, 186
Models
  Quasi-Population 87-97
  Population 87-89
Modernization 1-3, 7, 9, 28, 42, 58,
  130-131
Mother Tongue 67-78, 89, 93, 121
Name Change 77
Nationalism 10-11, 27-43, 87, 180
Neologisms 75-77
New Guinea 122-123
News 180-191
New Zealand 89
Nondescriptions 150
Nonverbal Behaviour 197-210
Norway 10, 72, 122
Novel 173-177
Occupational Mobility 60-64
Optimization 60
Oral 5, 21
Orthography 218-221
Parole 215
Paraguay 121, 130
Passing 8, 61, 238-239
Pauses 124-125
Periphery 32
Phillipines 121
Phonological 103-114, 152
Pidgin 7, 121
Pitch 128
Pluralism 75, 223-229
Political 1-13, 29-43, 57-64, 75,
  179-191
Preconceptions 197-210
Pretence 151
Primary Definers/Interpretation 187-189
Pronouns 152, 174
Pronounciation 152, 218
Protestant 166
Proxemics 148, 156
Psycholinguistic Distinctiveness 146, 149
Puerto Ricans 58, 120, 122
Puns 154
Racism 143, 179-191, 231
Relative Deprivation 60-62
Religion 3-6, 20, 30-43, 62, 68-78, 90,
  129, 224
Reorientation 220
Restricted Code 152
Rhetoric 154
Risk Minimization 63
Saskatchewan 67-77
Secularization 71, 74
Self-
  Government 39-40
  Identity 16-25, 164
Sentence Meaning 201-204

Separatism 28, 39, 224
Setting 120-122, 130
Sex 73, 176
Shucking 151
Signifying 151
Skin Colour 114, 180-181
Slang 154
Slogans 154
Social
  Categorization 180-182, 232-233, 236,
    238
  Class 3, 30, 58-64, 70, 228, 232-233
  Identity 171-191
  Influence 186-189, 233
  Mobility 7-8, 58-64, 70, 73, 237-238
  Psychological 64, 117-134, 145-147,
    169, 190, 231-239
  Structural 57, 64, 119, 169
Sociological 1, 57-64, 67, 169, 203
South Africa 75
Soviet Union 2, 9, 87
Speech
  Convergence 124-125, 145-146, 155, 236
  Divergence 126-128, 145-147, 149,
    154-155, 236
  Maintenance 126-128, 145-146, 155, 236
  Markers 104, 233
  Rate 124, 128
Status
  Congruence 63
  Factors 129
  Maximization 62
  Occupational 60-64
Stereotypes 183
Stigmatized 10, 107, 113-114, 152
St. Lucia 121
Switzerland 134
Syntactic 7, 10, 104, 128, 143-155
Tanzania 121
Title VII 225
Theory
  Accommodation 123-127, 145-147, 236
  Causal Attribution 125, 146
  Intergroup Distinctiveness/Social
    Identity 127, 146, 179-191
  Similarity Attraction 124-125, 146
  Social Comparison 181
  Social Exchange 125, 146
Topic 121
United States 9, 120-121, 165-168,
  223-239
Urbanization 5, 71, 74
Values 9, 183-191
Valencia 122
Vernacular 130-131, 224-229
Video 198-210
Vocal Intensity 124
Wales 27-43, 134
Written Observations 206-209

AUTHOR INDEX

Aboud, F.E.   118, 140
Abrahams, R.D.   227, 230
Akintola, K.   145, 156
Akram, M.   182, 192
Allen, I.L.   166, 170
Allport, G.W.   67, 79, 169-170
Almond, G.   2, 4, 12
Anderson, A.B.   69-73, 75-77, 79
Anderson, G.M.   69, 80
Anderson, J.T.M.   77, 80
Anderson, N.   74, 76, 80
Angle, J.   58, 65
Apfelbaum, E.   238, 240
Arellano, L.   121, 140
Armstrong, J.A.   6, 12
Bagley, C.   183, 192
Baker, S.   134, 137
Balandier, G.   6, 12
Ballard, C.   16, 20, 26
Ballard, R.   16, 20, 26
Banton, M.   163, 180
Barker, G.C.   121, 135
Barnes, J.   145, 156
Barth, F.   3, 12, 159-160, 162-163, 180
Barton, A.H.   166, 171
Bassili, J.N.   118, 140
Bates, E.   128, 135
Baudin, H.   125, 134, 137
Baumdicker, D.   153, 156
Beardsley, R.B.   121, 135
Bender, E.I.   227, 230
Berger, C.   125, 135
Berger, P.L.   159, 170
Berman, L.   154, 156
Bernstein, B.   152, 156, 160, 170
Berrigni, L.   128, 135
Bickerton, D.   102, 115
Billig, M.   233-234, 237-238, 240
Blake, R.R.   235, 240

Blalock, Jr., H.M.   6, 12
Blom, J.P.   119, 122-123, 135
Boissevain, J.   69, 80, 92, 98
Bolt, C.   180, 192
Borrie, W.D.   68, 73-74, 80
Bosmajian, H.   145, 156
Bourhis, R.Y.   17, 19, 24-26, 59, 61,
    63-65, 67, 74, 81, 117-119, 124-129,
    132, 134-137, 145-147, 149, 152, 154,
    156-157, 237, 240
Bowen, E.G.   27, 35-36, 44
Brah, A.   18, 26
Bram, J.   67, 69, 76, 80
Brass, P.R.   220, 222
Brass, W.   91, 98
Breton, R.   70, 80, 129, 135
Brook, G.C.   121, 135
Brown, G.   180, 192
Brown, R.   128, 136, 147, 156
Brown, R.J.   136, 140, 233, 235, 241
Burgest, D.R.   145, 156
Busteed, M.   30, 44
Butterworth, E.   188, 192
Byrne, D.   124, 136
Calabrese, R.   125, 135
Caldwell, J.C.   91, 98
Campbell, D.   69, 80
Campbell, D.T.   143, 157
Carey, J.   187, 192
Carranza, M.   19, 26, 121, 139, 154, 158
Carter, H.   27, 30, 35-36, 41, 44
Cedegren, H.   121-122, 136
Chibnall, S.   181-182, 192
Clark, J.   181-184, 187-188, 193
Cohen, A.   16, 26
Cohen, R.   2, 12
Cohen, S.   183-184, 192
Connor, W.   3-6, 9, 12, 74, 80
Cooke, B.G.   198, 207, 211

Cooper, R.L. 120-121, 136
Cox, K. 29, 44
Critcher, C. 180, 183-184, 187-188,
  192-193
Dalto, G. 87, 99
Davis, A. 154, 156
Davis, D.B. 180, 192
Davis, H.P. 234, 240
Davis, K.E. 125, 138
DeCamp, D. 102-103, 115, 121, 136
De Meyer, J. 74, 80
De Ruyter, B. 95, 98
DeSaussure, F. 220, 222
Deutsch, K.W. 2, 12, 74, 80
DeVos, G. 215, 222
de Vries, J. 69, 80, 89-90, 92, 94-96,
  98-99
Dion, L. 75, 80
di Scuillo, A.M. 121-122, 136
Dittmar, N. 120, 136
Doise, W. 126, 134, 136, 233, 235, 240
Douglas, M. 159-160, 168, 170
Downs, J.F. 144, 156
Drake, G.F. 225, 229, 230
Dressier, W. 69, 80
Driedger, L. 69, 71, 77, 79, 80
Dummett, A. 180, 182, 192
Dummett, M. 182, 192
Dustin, D.S. 234, 240
Eastman, C.M. 121, 135, 216, 218-220,
  222
Ebuchi, K. 6, 12
Edelman, M. 120, 136
Edwards, A.D. 74-75, 80
Edwards, A.L. 168, 170
Elliott, J.C. 198, 211
Elliott, P. 181, 193
Else, J.F. 151, 156
Emmerson, G.S. 69, 80
England, R. 71, 81
Enloe, C.H. 3, 12
Epp, F.H. 71, 77, 81
Epstein, N. 223, 225, 228, 230
Erwin-Tripp, S.M. 121, 124, 128, 136,
  148, 156
Evans, P. 183, 185, 192
Fanon, F. 151, 156
Fasold, R. 103, 109, 115
Feldman, R.E. 134, 136
Ferguson, C.A. 229-230
Fiddick, P. 186, 188, 194
Fielding, G. 134, 137
Fishman, J.A. 16, 26, 44, 59, 67, 69,
  74-75, 81, 117-121, 124, 127, 130, 136,
  144, 159, 161, 170, 229-230, 232, 240
Flexner, S.B. 165, 172
Flores, L. 121, 140
Foltz, W.J. 2, 12
Foot, P. 181-182, 186, 188, 192

Fougstedt, G. 96, 98
Frech, Jr., W.P. 144, 157
Freeman, E.A. 67, 81
French, R. 103, 115
Friedrich, P. 126, 136
Fuller, B. 18, 26
Furnivall, J.S. 4, 12
Galtung, J. 181, 192
Gannon, R. 131, 136
Gardner, B. 154, 156
Gardner, M. 154, 156
Gardner, R.C. 23, 26
Garrard, J.A. 181, 192
Gartner, L.P. 181, 192
Gatbonton, E. 126, 135, 140
Gearing, F.O. 150, 157
Genessee, F. 134, 135
Geertz, C. 2, 12
Gerth, H.H. 59, 65
Giles, H. 17, 19, 24-26, 59, 61, 63-65,
  67, 74, 81, 117-121, 123-129, 132,
  134-135, 137, 139-140, 145-147, 149,
  152, 154, 156-157, 231, 233-235, 237,
  240-241
Gilman, A. 128, 136, 147, 156
Glaler, N. 9, 12, 227, 230
Goffman, E. 160, 163, 170
Golding, P. 181, 194
Goldscheider, C. 88, 98
Goodenough, W. 220, 222
Gordon, M. 57, 63, 65, 67, 73, 82
Gossett, T.F. 166, 170
Graber, D.A. 184, 189, 193
Grabowski, Y. 69, 82
Graubard, S.R. 223, 230
Greenfield, L. 24, 26
Gross, P.S. 77, 82
Gumperz, J.J. 21, 26, 119-120, 122-123,
  126, 135, 137, 220, 222
Greeley, A.M. 166, 170
Hacker, A. 166, 170
Hall, E.T. 148, 157
Hall, R.A. 75, 82, 121, 137
Hall, S. 181-182, 187-188, 193
Halloran, J.D. 181, 193
Hancock, I.F. 121, 136
Handlin, O. 67, 82
Hansen, C.K. 87, 99
Harris, M.B. 125, 134, 137
Hartmann, P. 180, 183-184, 186, 188-190,
  193
Hasselmo, N. 121, 137
Haugen, E. 75, 82, 118, 128, 138, 220,
  222
Hayden, R.G. 121, 136
Hechter, M. 7, 12, 64, 65, 180, 193
Hediger, H. 149, 157
Heer, D.M. 73, 82
Heider, P. 125, 138

Hellinger, M. 103, 115
Henderson, K.J. 225, 230
Henripin, J. 75, 82, 91, 94, 98
Herasimchuk, E. 122, 139
Herberg, W. 73, 82
Herman, S. 121, 138
Herman, S.R. 74, 82
Hernandez, E. 122, 137
Hewstone, M. 231, 235, 240-241
Heydenkorn, B. 69, 84
Higham, J. 226-228, 230
H.M.S.O. 190, 193
Hoffman, J.E. 121, 136
Holmes, C. 181, 193
Holt, G.S. 145, 152, 157
Holt, R.T. 2, 13
Homans, G.C. 125, 138
Horowitz, D.C. 8, 11, 13
Hostetler, J.A. 77, 82
Hough, Jr., J.C. 143, 158
Houghton, C. 229, 230
Hubay, C.A. 73, 82
Hubbell, L.J. 75, 82
Hughes, E. 58, 65
Humblet, J.E. 76, 82
Humphry, D. 182, 193
Hunter, G.K. 180, 193
Huntington, S.P. 2, 13
Hurd, W.B. 96, 98
Husband, C. 179-181, 183-184, 186,
  188-190, 193
Hyman, H. 5, 13
Hymes, D. 75, 82, 120, 124, 126,
  137-138, 220, 222
Inglehart, R. 119, 138
Izzet, R. 148, 157
Jackson, J.D. 117, 138
Jahoda, G. 180, 194
Jakobson, R. 74, 82
Jansen, C.J. 82
Jaspars, J.M.F. 235, 240
Jefferson, T. 181-182, 187-188, 193
Jernudd, B.H. 119, 139
Johnson, N.B. 180, 194
Johnston, M. 87, 99
Johnston, R.J. 29, 44
Jones, E.E. 125, 138
Jordan, W.D. 180-181, 193
Joy, R.J. 71, 82
Kalbach, W.E. 73, 82
Kayiwada, G. 227, 230
Kelley, H.H. 125, 138
Kelly, L.G. 69, 82
Keller, G. 224, 230
Khleif, B.B. 160-162, 164, 168-169, 171
Kiernan, V.G. 180-181, 193
Kimble, Jr., J. 121, 138
Kjolseth, R. 228, 230
Kloss, H. 74, 82

Kochman, T. 152-153, 157
Kostash, M. 69, 83
Kovacs, M.C. 69, 83
Kralt, J. 94, 99
Krishnan, P. 95, 99
Kwan, K.M. 67, 73, 74, 76, 84
Kuo, E. 121, 138
Labov, W. 103, 115, 120, 138, 145, 154
  157
Lachapelle, R. 94, 99
Lambert, W.E. 23, 26, 75, 83, 126, 128,
  134, 135, 138-139, 234, 240
Lanigan, R.L. 154, 157
Lazarsfeld, P.Z. 166, 171
Lanphier, C.M. 75, 83
Leginski, W. 148, 157
Lemaine, J-M. 236, 240
Leopold, W.F. 76, 83
Le Page, R. 102-103, 115
LeVine, R.A. 143, 157
Lewis, M.M. 67, 83
Leyens, J-P. 126, 135, 147, 156
Lieberson, S. 74-75, 83, 87, 96, 99,
  144, 157
Lindenfeld, J. 145, 158
Loudon, D. 18, 26
Lubek, I. 238, 240
Lukens, J.G. 148, 150, 158
Lyons, C.H. 180-181, 193
Lysenko, V. 69, 77, 83
McConahay, J.B. 143, 158
McDavid, R.I. 144, 158
McKirnan, D.J. 237, 241
McRoberts, K. 7
Ma, R. 122, 139
Mackey, W.F. 74, 83
Mackinnon, K. 58, 65
Maclean, R.R. 69, 80
Maheu, R. 94, 99
Martin, G. 188, 190, 193
Marunchak, M.H. 69, 83
Massucco-Costa, A. 75, 83
Mazur, D.P. 87, 92, 99
Meinig, D.W. 44
Mercer, N. 24, 26
Meynard, R. 126, 140
Middleton, J. 2, 12
Midgett, D. 121, 139
Miles, R. 18, 26
Mills, C.W. 59, 65
Milner, A. 72, 83
Milosz, C. 161, 171
Mitchell-Kernan, C. 151, 158
Moore, R. 182-183, 194
Morris, R.N. 75, 83
Morrison, R. 58, 65
Moscovici, S. 128, 139, 183, 186, 194,
  233, 240
Mouton, J.S. 235, 240

Moynihan, D.P. 9, 12
Murdock, G. 181, 187, 193-194
Nahirny, V.C. 121, 136
Natale, M. 125, 139
Nemeth, C. 128, 139, 180, 194
Norris, M.J. 95, 99
Nouak, M. 166, 171
O'Barr, W.M. 121, 139
O'Connor, J.F. 87, 99
Olorunsola, V.A. 2, 13
Olsen, S.M. 29, 44
Osgood, C.E. 188, 194
Palmore, E.B. 143, 153, 158
Park, R.E. 67, 73, 83, 227, 230
Parker, M. 183-184, 188, 192
Parsons, T. 2, 13
Partridge, E. 172
Paulston, C.B. 228, 230
Peach, C. 186, 194
Peng, F. 128, 139, 143, 147-148, 158
Peterson, W. 74, 83
Philip, A.B. 28, 44
Plon, M. 238, 241
Plotnicov, L. 1, 13
Pohorecky, Z.S. 79, 84
Poll, S. 162, 165, 171
Pool, J. 131, 139
Posgate, D. 7
Powell, Jr., G.B. 2, 12
Powell, J.J. 218-219, 222
Powesland, P.F. 118, 120-121, 124-125,
    137, 234, 240
Potter, S. 67, 83
Pride, J.B. 120, 139
Priestley, T. 69, 84
Pupier, P. 121-122, 136
Pye, L.E. 2, 13
Radecki, H. 69, 84
Rawkins, P.M. 10, 13
Ray, P.S. 75, 84
Reddy, I. 95, 99
Reiger, D.W. 232, 241
Rex, J. 183, 194
Rhealt, E. 126, 140
Rich, A.L. 150, 158
Riggs, F.W. 2, 13
Riley, G.A. 144, 158
Rim, Y. 180, 194
Roberts, B. 181-182, 187-188, 193
Robinson, W.P. 120, 139
Rommetveit, R. 234, 241
Rock, P. 187, 194
Ros, M. 122, 139
Rose, E.J.B. 188, 194
Rosen, H. 152, 154, 158
Ross, J.A. 2, 9, 13
Ross, J-K. 159, 172
Rosten, L. `167, 172
Rothchild, D. 6, 13

Royal Commission on Bilingualism and
    Biculturalism. 58, 65, 69, 73, 84
Royick, A. 77, 84
Rubin, J. 58, 65, 119, 121, 130, 139,
    228, 230
Ruge, R.H. 181, 192
Runkel, P.J. 236, 241
Runnymede Trust. 183, 185, 194
Ryan, E.B. 19, 26, 121, 139, 152, 154,
    158, 238, 241
Ryder, N.B. 88-89, 99
Rydnyckyj, J.B. 75, 84
Salisbury, R.F. 123, 139
Sampson, E.E. 233, 241
Sanchez, T. 173-177
Sandlund, T. 232, 237, 241
Sankoff, G. 122, 139
Sautter, G. 75, 84
Sauard, J-G. 74-75, 84
Sawyer, J.B. 121, 139
Schemerhorn, R.A. 224, 230
Scherer, K.R. 233, 235, 240
Schrag, P. 166, 172
Scott-Blair, M. 225, 230
Scotton, C.M. 117, 123, 126, 139-140
Sealy, N. 71, 84
Sechrest, L. 121, 140
Segalowitz, N. 122, 126, 140
Seymour-Ure, C. 186, 188, 194
Sherbinin, M.A. 77, 84
Sherif, M. 180, 194
Shibutani, T. 67, 73-74, 76, 184
Shils, E.A. 2, 13, 159, 162, 172
Shryock, H. 88, 93, 99
Shuy, R. 126, 140
Siegel J.S. 88, 93, 99
Simard, L. 122, 125, 134, 140
Simon, W.B. 73-74, 76, 84
Sinclair, A. 126, 134, 136
Sivanandan, A. 182, 186, 188, 194
Smith, C.H. 77, 84
Smith, D.J. 183, 194
Smith, P.M. 75, 84, 231, 235, 241
Smithies, B. 186, 188, 194
Sondhi, R. 183-184, 188, 192
Sorenson, A.P. 123, 140
Sowell, T. 223, 225-226, 228, 230
St. Clair, R. 232, 241
Stabler, J.R. 145, 158
Steiner, I.D. 233, 241
Stewart, W.A. 74, 85
Sumner, W.G. 144, 158
Swadesh, M. 217, 222
Tabouret-Keller, A. 58, 65
Tajfel, H. 118, 126-127, 135, 140, 147,
    156, 179-180, 185-186, 194-195,
    233-234, 237-238, 240-241
Taylor, D. 101, 115

Taylor, D.M. 17, 19, 24-25, 59, 61,
  63-65, 67, 74-75, 81, 84, 117-119,
  122, 124-127, 129, 132, 134, 137,
  140, 145-147, 149, 152, 157, 233,
  235, 237, 240-241
Thomas, C.J. 28, 35, 44
Triandis, H.C. 125, 140, 236, 241
Trotsky, L. 153, 158
Trudgill, P. 25, 26, 67, 75, 85, 120,
  140
Tuchman, G. 187, 195
Tucker, G.R. 75, 84, 126, 128, 138-139
Tuden, A. 1, 13
Tunstall, J. 187, 195
Turner, J.C. 127, 140, 234, 237-238,
  241
Turner, J.E. 2, 13
Trench, R.C. 164, 172
Tzavaras, G. 25, 26
Ury, W. 117, 123, 126, 140
Valdman, A. 115
Vallée, F.G. 92, 96, 98, 99
van Amerigen, A. 121-122, 136
van de Berghe, P. 7, 12
Vanneste, A.M.S. 69, 85
Verba, S. 4, 12
Verdery, K. 6, 13

Verdoodt, A. 131, 140
Vigneault, R. 74-75, 84
von Raffler-Engel, W. 197, 211
Wallace, T. 182, 194
Waluin, J. 180, 195
Ward, M. 182, 193
Warner, W.C. 166, 172
Watson, A. 16, 26
Webb, K. 180, 195
Weinreich, V. 58, 65, 119, 140, 145,
  158
Wells, M. 229-230
Wentworth, H. 165, 172
Whiteley, W.H. 128, 140
Will, W.H. 77, 85
Williams, C.H. 28-29, 35-36, 44
Williams, G. 180, 195
Williams, G.A. 63, 65
Williams, J.E. 145, 158
Wilson, P. 122-123, 137
Wolfram, W. 103, 109, 115
Wodak-Leodolter, R. 69, 80
Woodward, M. 119, 138
Yashiro, K. 148, 158
Yinger, J.M. 67, 85
Young, C. 103, 116
Young, C.H. 69, 71, 77, 85